General M

Raleigh Schorling
William David Reeve

Alpha Editions

This Edition Published in 2020

ISBN: 9789354307294

Design and Setting By
Alpha Editions
www.alphaedis.com
Email – info@alphaedis.com

PREFACE

. The purpose of this book, as implied in the introduction, is as follows: to *obtain a vital, modern scholarly course in introductory mathematics that may serve to give such careful training in quantitative thinking and expression as well-informed citizens of a democracy should possess.* It is, of course, not asserted that this ideal has been attained. Our achievements are not the measure of our desires to improve the situation. There is still a very large "safety factor of dead wood" in this text. The material purposes to present such simple and significant principles of algebra, geometry, trigonometry, practical drawing, and statistics, along with a few elementary notions of other mathematical subjects, the whole involving numerous and rigorous applications of arithmetic, as the average man (more accurately the modal man) is likely to remember and to use. There is here an attempt to teach pupils things worth knowing and to discipline them rigorously in things worth doing.

The argument for a thorough reorganization need not be stated here in great detail. But it will be helpful to enumerate some of the major errors of secondary-mathematics instruction in current practice and to indicate briefly how this work attempts to improve the situation. The following serve to illustrate its purpose and program:

1. The conventional first-year algebra course is characterized by *excessive formalism*, and there is much drill work largely on nonessentials. The excessive formalism is

greatly reduced in this text and the emphasis placed on those topics concerning which there is general agreement, namely, *function, equation, graph,* and *formula.* The time thus gained permits more ample illustrations and applications of principles and the introduction of more significant material.

2. Instead of crowding the many difficulties of the traditional geometry course into one year, geometry instruction is spread over the years that precede the formal course, and the relations are taught inductively by experiment and by measurement. Many foreign schools and an increasing number of American schools proceed on this common-sense basis. This gives the pupil the vocabulary, the symbolism, and the fundamental ideas of geometry. If the pupil leaves school or drops mathematics, he nevertheless has an effective organization of geometric relations. On the other hand, if he later pursues a formal geometry course, he can work far more effectively because he can concentrate on the logical organization of space relations and the formal expression of these relations. The longer " time exposure " minimizes the difficulties met in beginning the traditional geometry courses and avoids the serious mistake of forcing deductive logic and philosophic criticism in these early years.

3. The traditional courses delay the consideration of much interesting and valuable material that the field of secondary mathematics has to offer, and which may well be used to give the pupil very early an idea of what mathematics means and something of the wonderful scope of its application. The material of the seventh, eighth, and ninth years is often indefensibly meaningless when compared with that of many foreign curricula. Trigonometry,

containing many easy real problems, furnishes a good example of this delay. Other examples are found in the use of logarithms, the slide rule, standardized graphical methods, the notion of function, the common construction of practical drawing, the motivation of precise measurement, a study of the importance of measurement in modern life, and the introductory ideas of the calculus. It appears that the mathematics student should be given an opportunity to use these important tools very early in his study. They lend to the subject a power and interest that drills on formal material cannot possibly give.

Particular emphasis is given to graphical representation of statistics. The growing complexity of our social life makes it necessary that the intelligent general reader possess elementary notions of statistical methods. The hundreds of articles in the current magazines so extensively read demand an elementary knowledge of these things in order that the pupil may not remain ignorant of the common, everyday things of life. Brief chapters on logarithms and the slide rule have been introduced in order that a greater number of students may use these practical labor-saving devices and in order that these devices may function in the student's subsequent work, whether in everyday life or in the classroom. Actual classroom experience with these chapters has proved them to be relatively simple and good material for eighth-grade and ninth-grade students.

4. Mathematics needs to be reorganized on the side of method. The information we now possess of individual differences and effective devices in supervised study should make the study of mathematics more nearly a laboratory course, in which more effective work can be done.

5. The teaching of algebra, geometry, and trigonometry in separate fields is an artificial arrangement that does not permit the easy solution of problems concerning projects that correlate with problems met in the physical and biological sciences or the manual and fine arts. To reject the formalism of algebra, to delay the demands of a logical unit in geometry, and to present the simple principles of the various branches of mathematics in the introductory course opens the door to a greater variety of problems that seem to be real applications. The pupil sees the usefulness of the various modes of treatment of the facts of quantity. Power is gained because the pupil is equipped with more tools, in that the method of attack is not limited to one field.

6. One of the most curious characteristics of American secondary-mathematics instruction is the obscurity in the teaching of the function notion. It is generally agreed that functional thinking (the dependence of one magnitude upon another) constitutes one of the most fundamental notions of mathematics. Because of the interrelations of the equation, the formula, the function, the graph, and the geometric relations inductively acquired, the material is easily correlated around the function idea as the *organizing and unifying principle.* The function concept (implicitly or explicitly) dominant throughout helps to lend concreteness and coherence to the subject. However, it would be false to assume that this material is presented to establish the principle of correlation. On the contrary, it happens that correlation around the function notion, though incidental, is a valuable instrument for accomplishing the larger aim, which is to obtain a composite introductory course in mathematics that all future citizens of our democracy should be required to take as a matter of general scholarship.

———

7. The traditional reticence of texts has made mathematics unnecessarily difficult for pupils in the early years. The style of this book, though less rigidly mathematical, is more nearly adapted to the pupils' mental age. The result is a misleading length of the book. The book can easily be taught in a school year of approximately one hundred and sixty recitations. In the typical high school it will be taught in the first year. (The Minnesota high schools taught it in this grade, five recitations per week.) In schools which control the seventh and eighth years the following are also possibilities which have been tested by the authors and coöperating teachers: (1) in the eighth year with daily recitations; (2) half of the book in the eighth year and the remainder in the ninth year, with three recitations per week (it was so used in the Lincoln School); (3) the course may be started in the seventh year provided the class has achieved good results in previous arithmetic work.

Specific references are given where material which is not of the common stock has been taken consciously, the purpose, however, being chiefly to stimulate pupils and teachers to become familiar with these books for reasons other than the obligations involved. Something of human interest is added by relating some of the well-known stories of great mathematicians. We are indebted to Professor David Eugene Smith on questions relating to historical material. In our thinking we are particularly indebted to Professors Nunn, Smith, Breslich, and Myers. We shall be obliged to all teachers who may think it worth while to point out such errors as still exist.

THE AUTHORS

CONTENTS

ix

INTRODUCTION

The movement to provide an introductory course in general mathematics is a part of an extensive movement toward making the materials of study in secondary education more concrete and serviceable. The trend of education expresses a determination that the seventh, eighth, and ninth school years should be enriched by the introduction of such significant experiences of science, civics, art, and other knowledge of human life as all enlightened citizens of a democracy should possess. The work of these grades cannot be liberalized by "shoving down" the conventional material a year or so. The reorganization must be more fundamental in order to revitalize and socialize the mathematics of these grades.

Competent authorities in mathematics have from time to time asserted, first, that American secondary-mathematics teaching has been characterized by a futile attempt to induce all pupils to become technical college mathematicians. Secondly, that instead of giving pupils an idea of the real meaning of mathematics and the wide range of its applications, they are forced to waste a great deal of time on abstract work in difficult problems in radicals, fractions, factoring, quadratics, and the like, which do not lead to anything important in mathematics. And, thirdly, that this meaningless juggling of symbolism fails to meet the needs of the great number of pupils who go rather early into their careers; it also wastes time and effort on the part of pupils with especial ability in the subject, who ought to get an early insight into the scope and power of the real science of mathematics.

Quantitative thinking and expression play so large a part in human experience that proper training in these matters will always be important. The growing complexity of social and industrial life is responsible for corresponding changes in the use of quantitative relationships. Old applications in many instances are disappearing, but new ones growing out of present-day relations are being introduced to take their places. These changes require a new kind of introductory text in mathematics. Action is forced by the demand that there shall be justification of the time and effort given to each subject and each item in the subject. New subjects which appear necessary in the proper training for citizenship are crowding the curriculum. Mathematics too must justify its place " in the sun " by a thorough reorganization that will meet modern needs. This is what is meant by revitalizing mathematics.

The practical administrator will be impressed by the fact that this program raises no administrative difficulties. The pupil may be expected to develop greater power in algebra, because the elimination of material which wastes time and effort has made possible the emphasizing of the topics concerning which there is general agreement. The supplementary material which is drawn from the other subjects constitutes a preparation for further study in these fields; for example, the text gives the pupil the vocabulary, the symbolism, and many of the ideas of plane geometry.

This type of introductory course should appeal to the progressive educator because of a number of other features. The " problem method" of teaching is followed throughout. Rationalized drills are provided in abundance. The course has been used in mimeographed form by experienced teachers. Scores of prospective teachers have found the treatment simple and easy to present. Inexperienced teachers have gone out into difficult situations and have taught the material with satisfaction. Pupils following this course have made better progress than pupils following the traditional course, and both pupils and teachers manifest a degree of interest seldom seen in the ordinary class in mathematics. The tests prepared by the authors will save time for teachers and enable them, if they desire, to diagnose their own situations and to compare their results with those obtained in other institutions using the same material. If the question is raised as to what students completing such a course will do when they get to college, it may be replied that enough of them have already entered college to convince the unbiased that they experience no handicap. The more important point, however, is that such a course enables one to understand and to deal with the quantitative world in which he lives.

This course in reorganized introductory mathematics, although but a part of a large movement in secondary education which looks toward more concrete teaching and more serviceable materials of study, has a further highly significant aspect. It is a potent and encouraging evidence that high-school teachers have become students of their own teaching, and as a result are preparing their own textbooks in the midst of real teaching situations, as the outcome of intelligent constructive experimentation.

Probably very few books have been subjected previous to publication to such thorough tests of teaching situations. The authors have been shaping this course for many years. During the last three years the manuscript as originally accepted by the publishers has been taught in mimeograph form to more than a thousand pupils distributed in a selection of typical schools, among these being the following : Minneapolis Central High School (large city high school), Bremer Junior High School, Seward Junior High School, University of Minnesota High School, Owatonna High School, Mabel High School (small town), and the Lincoln School of Teachers' College. Numerous consultations with the teachers in these schools resulted in many valuable suggestions which contributed directly toward making the text easily teachable.

Each of the authors has taught secondary mathematics for more than ten years in large public and private schools. They have supervised many teachers in training; they have taught teacher-training courses, and each during most of this time has had unusual opportunities for free experimentation. The text may be regarded by fellow teachers of mathematics as a report which shows in organization and subject matter the things that have seemed most useful.

LOTUS D. COFFMAN
OTIS W. CALDWELL

GENERAL MATHEMATICS

FIRST YEAR

CHAPTER I

THE EQUATION

1. A problem introducing the use of the equation. In order to find the weight of a bag of candy, it was placed on one pan of perfectly balanced scales (Fig. 1). The candy, together with a 4-ounce weight, balanced 10 oz. of weights on the other pan. How much did the bag of candy weigh?

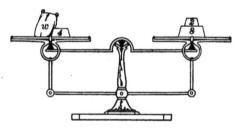

It is a familiar principle of balanced scales that if the same number of ounces be taken from each pan, the

FIG. 1. THE BALANCED SCALES ILLUSTRATE THE MEANING OF AN EQUATION

balance is not disturbed. Hence, if we suppose that a 4-ounce weight could be removed from each pan, the candy would be balanced by 6 oz.

This solves the problem, but let us analyze it a little further. The important fact in the situation above is that an unknown number of ounces of candy plus 4 oz. in one pan balances 10 oz. in the other pan. If we agree

1

to let the letter w represent the number of ounces of weight in the bag of candy and use the sign of equality $(=)$ to denote the perfect balance of the scales, the preceding mathematical fact may be conveniently translated into the following expression: $w + 4 = 10$, where $w + 4$ denotes the weight in the left pan and 10 the weight in the right pan. The abbreviated ("shorthand") statement, $w + 4 = 10$, expresses equality and is called an *equation*. The number to the left side of the equality sign is called the *left member* of the equation, the number to the right is the *right member*.

Just as the scales will balance if the same number of ounces are taken from each pan, so *we may subtract the same number from both sides of an equation and get another equation*. In the preceding problem the written work may be arranged thus:

Let $\qquad w = \begin{cases} \text{number of ounces of weight} \\ \text{ in the bag of candy.} \end{cases}$

Then $\qquad w + 4 = 10$

Subtracting 4 from each $\left.\right\}$ $\dfrac{4 = 4}{w = 6}$
 member of the equation,

Thus, the bag of candy weighs 6 oz.

The preceding problem illustrates the principle that *if the same number be subtracted from both members of an equation, the remainders are equal*; that is, another equation is obtained. [*Subtraction Law*]

EXERCISES

Find the value of the unknown numbers in the following equations, doing all you can orally:

1. $x + 2 = 6$.
2. $x + 6 = 10$.
3. $x + 7 = 13$.
4. $x + 11 = 18$.
5. $x + 13 = 23$.
6. $x + 9 = 26$.
7. $x + 10 = 27$.
8. $x + 14 = 21$.
9. $x + 33 = 44$.

2. The importance of the equation. The equation is a very important tool for solving problems in the mathematical sciences. The equation gives us a new method of attack on a problem, enabling us to solve many problems which would be very difficult, if not impossible, without its use.

3. Method of studying the nature of the equation. In making a study of the equation we shall continue by considering some very simple problems in order that we may clearly understand the laws which are involved. If these laws are mastered in connection with the simple cases, it will be easy to apply the equation as a tool for solving the more complicated and difficult problems. In the next article we shall continue to interpret the equation by considering a problem in weighing.

4. Division Law. Two equal but unknown weights, together with a 1-pound weight, just balance a 16-pound and a 1-pound weight together (Fig. 2). How heavy is each unknown weight?

.Let p equal the number of pounds in one of the unknown weights. Suppose that 1 lb. be removed from each pan, leaving $2\,p$ pounds in the left pan balancing the remaining 16 lb. in the right pan. Then, if $2\,p$ pounds balances 16 lb., p pounds (one half of the weight in the left pan) must balance 8 lb. (one half of the weight in

FIG. 2. THE BALANCED SCALES MAY BE USED TO ILLUSTRATE THE SUBTRACTION LAW AND THE DIVISION LAW

the right pan). By the use of the equation the discussion may be written in the following brief form:

$$2p + 1 = 17 \left\{ \begin{array}{l} \text{This is a translation of the first} \\ \text{sentence of the problem.} \end{array} \right.$$

Subtracting 1 from each member, $\left.\begin{array}{l} \\ \end{array}\right\} \dfrac{1 = 1}{2p = 16}$

Dividing each member of the equation by 2,

$$p = 8.$$

This problem illustrates the principle that *if both members of an equation are divided by the same number* (excluding division by zero, to be explained later), *the quotients are equal*; that is, another equation is obtained. [*Division Law*]

EXERCISES

Find the value of the unknown numbers, doing all you can orally:

1. $2x + 3 = 9.$
2. $3x + 4 = 16.$
3. $2a + 5 = 17.$
4. $3b + 7 = 28.$
5. $5r + 7 = 62.$
6. $9s + 21 = 93.$
7. $2y + 1 = 8.$
8. $5y + 3 = 15.$
9. $4x + 3.2 = 15.2.$
10. $6n + 4 = 49.$
11. $9e + 8 = 116.$

12. $5r + \frac{3}{5} = 13\frac{2}{5}.$
13. $14k + 7 = 79.$
14. $3e + 4\frac{1}{2} = 9.$
15. $15x + 0.5 = 26.$
16. $11m + \frac{1}{4} = \frac{7.8}{4}.$
17. $1.3y + 3 = 16.$
18. $11y = 33.$
19. $1.1x = 121.$
20. $2.3x + 4 = 50.$
21. $6.3z + 2.4 = 15.$
22. $5.3x + 0.34 = 2.99.$

5. Addition Law. In Fig. 3 the apparatus is so arranged that the 2-pound weight attached to the string which passes over the pulley pulls upward on the bar at *B*. This arrangement makes the problem different from the two which we have considered. If there were no pulley attachment, the weight pulling downward in the left pan would be $5x$ pounds. Since there is a lifting force of 2 lb. at B, the downward pulling force in the left pan is 2 lb. less than $5x$ pounds, or $5x-2$ pounds; this balances the 18 lb. in the right pan. Hence the equation which describes the

situation in Fig. 3 is $5x-2=18$. If the string be cut so as to remove the upward pull of 2 lb., then a 2-pound weight must be added to the right pan to keep the scales balanced, for removing the upward pull of 2 lb. gave us a down-

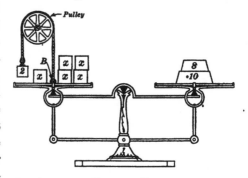

FIG. 3. IN THIS CASE THE SCALES ILLUSTRATE THE ADDITION LAW

ward pull in the left pan of $5x$ pounds. This is 2 lb. more than we had with the pulley attached, hence the necessity of adding 2 lb. to the right pan.

By the use of the equation the preceding discussion may take the following brief form:

$$5x-2=18 \left\{ \begin{array}{l} \text{This expresses the} \\ \text{original conditions.} \end{array} \right.$$

Adding 2 to both members, $\quad \dfrac{2=2}{5x \quad =20}$

Dividing both members by 5, $\quad x=4$.

This problem illustrates the principle that *if the same number is added to both members of an equation, the sums are equal*; that is, another equation is obtained. [**Addition Law**]

Find the value of the unknown number in each problem, doing all you can orally :

1. $x - 5 = 10$.

2. $2x - 15 = 13$.

3. $3x - 12 = 13$.

4. $3x - 8 = 17$.

5. $12y - 4 = 46$.

6. $4t - 16 = 16$.

7. $19r - 4\frac{1}{5} = 14\frac{4}{5}$.

8. $11y - 9 = 79$.

9. $5s - 0.1 = 0.9$.

10. $4y - \frac{3}{4} = 7\frac{1}{4}$.

11. $7t - 4 = 26$.

12. $12m - 35 = 41$.

13. $9c - 3.2 = 14.8$.

14. $7t - 2 = 5.7$.

15. $14k - 5 = 21$.

16. $2y - 3.1 = 3.2$.

17. $0.5x - 3 = 4.5$.

18. $2x - \frac{1}{3} = 6\frac{1}{3}$.

19. $3x - 9\frac{1}{2} = 17.5$.

20. $9x - 7.5 = 73.5$.

21. $1.5x - 3 = 1.5$.

22. $1.6x - 1.7 = 1.5$.

6. Solving an equation; check; root. The process of finding the value of the unknown number in an equation is called *solving the equation*. To illustrate :

Let $y + 3 = 8$ be the equation.

$$3 = 3$$

Then $y = 5$, and the equation is said to be solved.

To *test*, or *check*, the correctness of the result replace the unknown number in the original equation by 5, obtaining $5 + 3 = 8$. Since both members of the equation reduce to the same number, the result $y = 5$ is correct.

When a number is put in place of a literal number it is said to be *substituted* for the literal number.

When both sides of an equation reduce to the same number for certain values of the unknown number, the equation is said to be *satisfied*. Thus, 3 *satisfies* the equation $y + 2 = 5$.

A number that satisfies an equation is a *root* of the equation.

Thus, 5 is a *root* of the equation $z + 3 = 8$.

HISTORICAL NOTE. The word "root" first appears in the algebra of Mohammed ibn Musa Abu Jafar Al-Khwarizmi (about A.D. 830). The root of an equation (like the root of a plant) is hidden until found. See Ball's "A Short History of Mathematics," p. 163.

EXERCISES

Solve the following equations and check the results:

1. $5y + 3 = 18$.
2. $7x - 4 = 17$.
3. $2x - 1.3 = 2.7$.
4. $3a + 4.5 = 7.5$.
5. $2b + 2.7 - 1.3 = 11.4$.
6. $7x - 3x + 3.1 = 7.1$.
7. $5s + 14 - 9 = 15$.
8. $7m - 3\frac{2}{3} = 3\frac{1}{3}$.

7. Terms; monomial; order of terms. The parts of an expression separated by plus (+) and minus (−) signs are called the *terms* of a number. Thus, $2a$ and $3b$ are the terms of the number $2a + 3b$. A one-term number is called a *monomial*.

EXERCISES

1. $8 - 7 + 2 = ?$
2. $8 + 2 - 7 = ?$
3. $2 + 8 - 7 = ?$
4. $8x - 7x + 2x = ?$
5. $8x + 2x - 7x = ?$
6. $2x + 8x - 7x = ?$

These problems illustrate the principle (to be discussed more fully later) that the value of an expression is unchanged if the order of its terms is changed, provided each term carries with it the sign at its left. If no sign is expressed at the left of the first term of an expression, the plus sign is understood.

8. Similar and dissimilar terms. Terms which have a common literal factor, as $2x$, $3x$, and $5x$, are *similar* terms. Their sum is a one-term expression; namely, $10x$. When terms do not have a common literal factor, as $2x$ and $3y$, they are called *dissimilar* terms. Algebraic expressions are simplified by combining similar terms. Combining similar terms in either the right or the left member of an equation gives us the same equation in simpler form.

HISTORICAL NOTE. The word "algebra" first appears about A.D. 830 in an Arabian work called "Al-jebr wa'l-mukabala," written by Al-Khwarizmi. "Al-jebr," from which "algebra" is derived, may be translated by *the restoration* and refers to the fact that the same number may be added to or subtracted from both sides of the equation; "al-mukabala" means *the process of comparison,* and some writers say it was used in connection with the combination of similar terms into one term.

The mathematical interest of the Arabs ran high. In the seventh century religious enthusiasm had banded these nomadic tribes into a conquering, flourishing nation. Enormous fortunes demanded mathematical manipulation. Cantor cites a rumor of a merchant whose annual income was about seven million dollars and a Christian doctor of medicine whose annual income was about fifty thousand. These fortunes gave them the necessary leisure time for culture and learning. Among the many books translated was the Greek geometry, Euclid's "Elements." See Ball's "A Short History of Mathematics," p. 162, and Miller's "Historical Introduction to Mathematical Literature," p. 83.

EXERCISES

Solve the following equations and check the results:

1. $2x - 7 = x + 3$.

Subtract x from both members and proceed as usual.

2. $3x + 2 = x + 8$.
3. $5x - 3x + 2x - 2 = 2x + x + 12$.
4. $16y - 8y + 3y - 2 = 5y - 2y + 14$.
5. $20 - 4x = 38 - 10x$.
6. $5x + 3 - x = x + 18$.

7. $7r + 18 + 3r = 32 + 2r - 2.$

8. $18 + 6s + 30 + 6s = 4s + 8 + 12 + 3s + 3 + s + 29.$

9. $25y + 20 - 7y - 5 = 56 - 5y + 5.$

9. Multiplication Law. Solve for x: $\dfrac{x}{2} = 5.$

This problem offers a new principle. If we translate it into an English sentence, it reads as follows: One half of what unknown number equals 5? If one half of a number equals 5, all of the number, or twice as much, equals 2 times 5, or 10. The problem may be solved as follows:

$$\frac{x}{2} = 5.$$

Multiplying both members by 2,

$$2 \times \frac{x}{2} = 2 \times 5.$$

$$\frac{2x}{2} = 10.$$

$$x = 10.$$

The principle involved here may be further illustrated by the scales, for if an object in one pan of a scales will balance a 5-pound weight in the other, it will be readily seen that three objects of the same kind would need 15 lb. to balance them. This may be expressed in equation form as follows:

$$x = 5.$$

Multiplying both members by 3,

$$3x = 15.$$

From the preceding discussion it is evident that *if both members of an equation are multiplied by the same number, the products are equal*; that is, another equation is obtained. [*Multiplication Law*]

This multiplication principle is convenient when an equation contains fractions. It enables us to obtain a second equation containing no fraction but containing the same unknown number. To illustrate this:

Let $\frac{1}{3}x = 7.$

Multiplying both members by 3,

$$3 \times \tfrac{1}{3}x = 3 \times 7.$$

Reducing to simplest form, $x = 21.$

ORAL EXERCISES

Find the value of the unknown number in each of the following equations:

1. $\dfrac{a}{3} = 5.$ 4. $\dfrac{x}{5} = 3.$ 7. $\dfrac{3w}{7} = 3.$

2. $\dfrac{m}{7} = 8.$ 5. $\dfrac{b}{7} = 5.$ 8. $\dfrac{5x}{2} = 15.$

3. $\dfrac{r}{4} = 2.$ 6. $\dfrac{2w}{3} = 4.$ 9. $\dfrac{2x}{3} = \dfrac{4}{3}.$

The preceding list of problems shows that it is desirable to multiply both members of the equation by some number that will give us *a new equation without fractions*. The same principle holds when the equation contains two or more fractions whose denominators are different, as is illustrated by the following problem:

Find x if $\dfrac{x}{4} - \dfrac{x}{5} = 2.$

Solution. $\dfrac{x}{4} - \dfrac{x}{5} = 2.$

Multiplying by 20, $\dfrac{20x}{4} - \dfrac{20x}{5} = 40.$

Simplifying, $5x - 4x = 40;$

whence $x = 40.$

The fact that 4 and 5 will divide integrally (a whole number of times) into the numerators gives us a new equation without fractions. Obviously there are an unlimited number of numbers (for example, 40, 60, 80, etc.) which we could have used, but it was advantageous to use the smallest number in which 4 and 5 are contained integrally; namely, the least common multiple of 4 and 5, which is 20. The object of this multiplication is to obtain an equation in which the value of the unknown number is more easily found than in the preceding one. This discussion may be summarized by the following rule:

If the given equation contains fractions, multiply every term in both members by the least common multiple (L.C.M.) of the denominators in order to obtain a new equation which does not contain fractions.

EXERCISES

Find the value of the unknown number in each problem, and check:

1. $\dfrac{x}{3} - \dfrac{x}{6} = 10.$

2. $\dfrac{y}{5} + \dfrac{y}{4} = 9.$

3. $\dfrac{2r}{3} + \dfrac{3r}{4} = 17.$

4. $y + \frac{1}{2}y = 6.$

5. $y - \frac{1}{2}y = 7.$

6. $\dfrac{y}{2} - \dfrac{2}{3} = \dfrac{y}{6}.$

7. $\dfrac{y}{3} = \dfrac{y}{7} + 16.$

8. $\dfrac{2s}{5} + 3 = \dfrac{s}{3} + 4.$

9. $\dfrac{2x}{9} + \dfrac{x}{6} = \dfrac{x}{18} + \dfrac{1}{3}.$

10. $\dfrac{3y}{7} - \dfrac{1}{3} = \dfrac{y}{21} + 5.$

11. $\dfrac{5y}{6} + 2\frac{5}{12} = 3 + \dfrac{y}{4}.$

12. $\dfrac{x}{4} + 4x - \dfrac{5x}{3} = 26 + 1\frac{1}{2}x.$

13. $\dfrac{x}{2} + \dfrac{x}{3} + \dfrac{x}{4} + \dfrac{x}{10} = 71.$

10. Definition of the equation; properties of the equation.
The foregoing problems were used to show that *an equation is a statement that two numbers are equal.* It indicates that two expressions stand for the same number. It may be regarded as an expression of balance of values between the numbers on the two sides of the equality sign. Some unknown number which enters into the discussion of the problem is represented by a letter. An equation is written which enables one to find the value of that unknown number.

An equation is like a balance in that the balance of value is not disturbed so long as like changes are made on both sides. Thus, in equations we may *add* the same number to both sides, or *subtract* the same number from both sides, or we may *multiply* or *divide* both sides by the same number (except division by zero); the equality is maintained during all these changes.

On the other hand, the equality is destroyed if more is added to or subtracted from one side than the other or if one side is multiplied or divided by a larger number than is the other side.

11. Translation of an equation. The list of problems in the preceding exercises may appear abstract in the sense that the equations do not appear to be connected in any way either with a concrete situation of a verbal problem, or with our past experience. However, such a list need not be regarded as meaningless. Just as an English sentence which expresses a number relation may be written in the "shorthand" form of an equation, so, conversely, an equation may be translated into a problem; for example, the equation $3x + 5 = 2x + 20$ may be interpreted as follows: Find a number such that 3 times the number plus 5 equals 2 times the number plus 20. The equation $x - 3 = 5$ may be regarded as raising the question What number diminished by 3 equals 5? Or, again, $2\frac{1}{2}x + x + 2\frac{1}{2}x + x = 140$ may be considered as the translation of the following problem: What is the altitude of a rectangle whose base is $2\frac{1}{2}$ times as long as the altitude and whose perimeter is 140 ft.?

EXERCISES

State each of the following in the form of a question or a verbal problem:

1. $x - 6 = 3.$

2. $2x - 1 = 10.$

3. $9k - 10 = 87.$

4. $7y + 8 = 112.$

5. $7x - 3 = 81.$

6. $3x + 2 = 2x + 3.$

7. $7r - 2 = 6r + 8.$

8. $5.2x - 3 = 4.1x + 1.4.$

9. $3s = 12.$

10. $4s = 16.$

11. $2x + 3x + 4x = 18.$

12. $c = \frac{22}{7}d.$

12. Drill in the "shorthand" of algebra. The following exercises give practice in translating number expressions and relations from verbal into symbolical language:

1. ·*Consecutive numbers* are integral (whole) numbers which follow each other in counting; thus, 17 and 18, 45 and 46, are examples of consecutive numbers. Begin at $s + 5$ and count forward. Begin at $x + 3$ and count backward. Give four consecutive integers beginning with 18; ending with 18; beginning with x; ending with x. Give two consecutive even integers beginning with $2x$. Give two consecutive even integers ending with $2c$.

2. The present age, in years, of a person is denoted by x. Indicate in symbols the following: (a) the person's age fourteen years ago; (b) his age fourteen years hence; (c) his age when twice as old as now; (d) 60 decreased by his age; (e) his age decreased by 60; (f) his age increased by one half his age.

3. A boy has a marbles and buys b more. How many has he? What is the sum of a and b?

4. A boy having b marbles loses c marbles. How many has he?

5. (a) The home team made 8 points in a basket-ball game and the visiting team made 3 points. By how many points did the home team win? (b) If the home team scored h points to the visitors' n points, by how many points did the home team win? (c) Substitute numbers for h in the last question that will show the defeat of the home team. (d) If $h = 5$, what must be the value of n when the game is a tie?

6. What is the 5th part of n? $\frac{2}{3}$ of y? $\frac{5}{8}$ of t?

7. Two numbers differ by 7. The smaller is s. Express the larger number.

8. Divide 100 into two parts so that one part is a.

9. Divide a into two parts so that one part is 5.

10. The difference between two numbers is d and the larger one is l. Express the smaller one.

11. What number divided by 3 will give the quotient a?

12. A man's house, worth h dollars, was destroyed by fire. He received i dollars insurance. What was his total loss?

13. A is x years old and B lacks 5 yr. of being three times as old. Express B's age.

14. A has m ties and B has n ties. If A sells B 5 ties, how many will each then have?

15. A man has d dollars and spends c cents. How many cents does he have left?

16. A room is l feet long and w feet wide. How many feet of border does such a room require?

17. The length of a rectangle exceeds its width by c feet. It is w feet wide. (a) State the length of each side. (b) Find the distance around the rectangle.

18. What is the cost of 7 pencils at c cents each?

19. What is the cost of 1 sheet of paper if b sheets can be bought for 10¢?

20. It takes two boys 5 da. to make an automobile trip. What part can they do in 1 da.? If it takes them d days, what part of the trip do they travel in 1 da.?

21. If a man drives a car at the rate of 31 mi. per hour, how far can he drive in 3 hr.? in 5 hr.? in h hours?

22. If a man drives n miles in 3 hr., how many miles does he go per hour?

23. A tank is filled by a pipe in m minutes. How much of the tank is filled in 1 min.?

24. The numerator of a fraction exceeds the denominator by 3. (a) Write the numerator. (b) Write the fraction. (c) Read the fraction.

25. A pair of gloves costs d dollars. What is the cost if the price is raised 7¢? if lowered 7¢?

26. Write the sum of x and 17; of 17 and x. Write the difference of x and 17; of 17 and x.

27. A class president was elected by a majority of 7 votes. If the unsuccessful candidate received k votes, how many votes were cast?

13. Algebraic solution. Many problems may be solved by either arithmetic or the use of the equation. When the solution of a problem is obtained by the use of the equation, it is commonly called an *algebraic solution.*

The following problems illustrate the important steps in the algebraic solution of a problem. By way of contrast an arithmetic solution is given for the first problem.

1. Divide a pole 20 ft. long into two parts so that one part shall be four times as long as the other.

The shorter part is a certain length.
The longer part is four times this length.
The whole pole is then five times as long as the shorter part.
The pole is 20 ft. long.
The shorter part is $\frac{1}{5}$ of 20 ft., or 4 ft.
The longer part is 4 × 4 ft., or 16 ft.
Hence the parts are 4 ft. and 16 ft. long respectively.

ALGEBRAIC SOLUTION

Let n = number of feet in the shorter part.
Then $4\,n$ = number of feet in the longer part,
and $n + 4\,n$, or $5\,n$ = length of the pole.
Then $5\,n = 20.$
$$n = 4.$$
$$4\,n = 16.$$

Hence the parts are 4 ft. and 16 ft. long respectively.

2. A rectangular garden is three times as long as it is wide. It takes 80 yd. of fence to inclose it. Find the width and length.

ALGEBRAIC SOLUTION

Let x = number of feet in the width.
Then $3\,x$ = number of feet in the length,
and $x + 3\,x + x + 3\,x$ = distance around the garden.
Then $8\,x = 80.$
$$x = 10.$$
$$3\,x = 30.$$

Hence the width is 10 yd. and the length is 30 yd.

14. The important steps in the algebraic solution of verbal (or story) problems. Before proceeding to the solution of more difficult problems it is important that we organize the steps that are involved. The preceding list of problems illustrates the following method for solving a verbal problem:

(a) In every problem certain facts are given as known and one or more as unknown and to be determined. Read the problem so as to get these facts clearly in mind.

(b) In solving the problem denote one of the unknown numbers by some symbol, as y.

(c) Then express all the given facts in algebraic language, using the number y as if it, too, were known.

(d) Find two different expressions which denote the same number and equate them. (Join by the sign of equality $(=).$)

(e) Solve the equation for the value of the unknown number.

(f) Check the result by re-reading the problem, substituting the result in the conditions of the problem to see if these conditions are satisfied. Note that it is not sufficient to check the equation, for you may have written the wrong equation to represent the conditions of the problem.

EXERCISES

With the preceding outline of method in mind, solve the following problems, and check:

Problems involving Number Relations

1. If six times a number is decreased by 4, the result is 26. Find the number.

2. If four fifths of a number is decreased by 6, the result is 10. Find the number.

3. The sum of three numbers is 120. The second is five times the first, and the third is nine times the first. Find the numbers.

4. The sum of three numbers is 360. The second is fourteen times the first, and the third is the sum of the other two. Find the numbers.

5. Seven times a number increased by one third of itself equals 44. Find the number.

6. The following puzzle was proposed to a boy: "Think of a number, multiply it by 4, add 12, subtract 6, and divide by 2." The boy gave his final result as 13. What was his original number?

7. The sum of one half, one third, and one fourth of a number is 52. What is the number?

Consecutive-Number Problems

8. Find two consecutive numbers whose sum is 223.

9. Find three consecutive numbers whose sum is 180.

10. Find two consecutive odd numbers whose sum is 204.

11. Find three consecutive even numbers whose sum is 156.

12. It is required to divide a board 70 in. long into five parts such that the four longer parts shall be 1", 2", 3", and 4" longer respectively than the shortest part. Find the lengths of the different parts.

13. A boy in a manual-training school is making a bookcase. The distance from the top board to the bottom is 4 ft. 7 in., inside measure. He wishes to put in three shelves, each 1 in. thick, so that the four book spaces will diminish successively by 2 in. from the bottom to the top. Find the spaces.

Problems involving Geometric Relations

14. The length of a field is three times its width, and the distance around the field is 200 rd. If the field is rectangular, what are the dimensions?

15. A room is 15 ft. long, 14 ft. wide, and the walls contain 464 sq. ft. Find the height of the room.

16. The perimeter of (distance around) a square equals 64 ft. Find a side.

Note. Such geometric terms as "triangle," "rectangle," "square," etc., as occur in this list of problems (14–24), are familiar from arithmetic. However, they will later be defined more closely to meet other needs.

17. Find the sides of a triangle if the second side is 3 ft. longer than the first, the third side 5 ft. longer than the first, and the perimeter is 29 ft.

18. Find the side of an equilateral (all sides equal) triangle if the perimeter is $21\frac{3}{5}$ ft.

19. The perimeter of an equilateral pentagon (5-sided figure) is 145 in. Find a side.

20. The perimeter of an equilateral hexagon (6-sided figure) is 192 ft. Find a side.

21. Find the side of an equilateral decagon (10-sided figure) if its perimeter is 173 in.

22. What is the side of an equilateral dodecagon (12-sided figure) if its perimeter is 288 in.?

23. A line 60 in. long is divided into two parts. Twice the larger part exceeds five times the smaller part by 15 in. How many inches are in each part?

24. The perimeter of a quadrilateral $ABCD$ (4-sided figure) is 34 in. The side CD is twice as long as the side AB; the side AD is three times as long as CD; the side BC equals the sum of the sides AD and CD. Find the length of each side.

Miscellaneous Problems

25. Divide $48,000 among A, B, and C so that A's share may be three times that of B, and C may have one half of what A and B have together.

26. The perimeter of a rectangle is 132 in. The base is double the altitude. Find the dimensions of the rectangle.

27. A and B own a house worth $16,100, and A has invested twice as much capital as B. How much has each invested?

28. A regulation football field is $56\frac{2}{3}$ yd. longer than it is wide, and the sum of its length and width is $163\frac{1}{3}$ yd. Find its dimensions.

29. A man has four times as many chickens as his neighbor. After selling 14, he has $3\frac{1}{3}$ times as many. How many had each before the sale?

30. In electing a president of the athletic board a certain high school cast 1019 votes for three candidates. The first received 143 more than the third, and the second 49 more than the first. How many votes did each get?

31. A boy has $5.20 and his brother has $32.50. The first saves 20¢ each day and the second spends 10¢ each day. In how many days will they have the same amount?

32. One man has seven times as many acres as another. After the first sold 9 A. to the second, he had 36 A. more than the second then had. How many did each have before the sale?

33. To find the weight of a golf ball a man puts 20 golf balls into the left scale pan of a balance and a 2-pound weight into the right; he finds that too much, but the balance is restored if he puts 2 oz. into the left scale pan. What was the weight of a golf ball?

34. The number of representatives and senators together in the United States Congress is 531. The number of representatives is 51 more than four times the number of senators. Find the number of each.

35. A boy, an apprentice, and a master workman have the understanding that the apprentice shall receive twice as much as the boy, and the master workman four times as much as the boy. How much does each receive if the total amount received for a piece of work is $105?

36. A father leaves $13,000 to be divided among his three children, so that the eldest child receives $2000 more than the second, and twice as much as the third. What is the share of each?

37. A fence 5 ft. high is made out of 6-inch boards running lengthwise. The number of boards necessary to build the fence up to the required height is 5 and they are so placed as to leave open spaces between them. If each of these open spaces, counting from the bottom upwards, is half of the one next above it, what must be the distances between the boards; that is, what will be the width of each of the open spaces?

38. I paid $8 for an advertisement of 8 lines, as follows: 24¢ a line for the first insertion, 10¢ a line for each of the next five insertions, and 2¢ a line after that. Find the number of insertions.

39. The annual income of a family is divided as follows: One tenth is used for clothing, one third for groceries, and one fifth for rent. This leaves $660 for other expenses and for the savings account. How much is the income?

15. Axioms. Thus far we have used the four following laws in solving equations:

I. *If the same number be added to equal numbers, the sums are equal.* [**Addition Law**]

II. *If the same number be subtracted from equal numbers, the remainders are equal.* [**Subtraction Law**]

III. *If equal numbers be multiplied by the same number, the products are equal.* [**Multiplication Law**]

IV. *If equal numbers be divided by the same number (excluding division by zero), the quotients are equal.* [**Division Law**]

Statements like the four laws above, when assumed to be true, are called *axioms*. Usually axioms are statements so simple that they seem evident. A simple illustration is sufficient to make clear the validity of the axiom. For example, if two boys have the same number of marbles and 3 more are given to each, then our experience tells us that again one boy would have just as many as the other. This illustrates the validity of the addition axiom. Hereafter the preceding laws will be called **Axioms I, II, III,** and **IV** respectively.

16. Axiom V. In this chapter we have also made frequent use of another axiom. In solving a verbal problem we obtained the necessary equation by finding two expressions which denoted the same number and then we equated these two expressions. This step implies the following axiom:

If two numbers are equal to the same number (or to equal numbers), the numbers are equal. [**Equality Axiom**]

Illustrate the truth of Axiom V by some familiar experience.

The following exercises test and review the axioms.

Solve the following equations, and check. Be able to state at every step in the solution the axiom used.

1. $12\,t - 15 = 30$.

Solution.

$$12\,t - 15 = 30$$
$$\underline{15 = 15} \qquad \text{(Axiom I)}$$

Adding 15 to both members, $\quad 12\,t = 45$

Dividing both sides by 12, $\qquad t = \tfrac{45}{12}$, or $3\tfrac{3}{4}$. (Axiom IV)

2. $\dfrac{y}{2} + \dfrac{y}{4} = \dfrac{1}{3}$.

Solution. Multiplying both sides of the equation by the least common multiple of the denominators, that is, by 12,

$$\frac{12\,y}{2} + \frac{12\,y}{4} = \frac{12}{3}. \qquad \text{(Axiom III)}$$

Then $\qquad 6\,y + 3\,y = 4.$

By reducing the fractions of the first equation to lowest terms we obtain the second equation, which does not contain fractions.

Combining similar terms, $9y = 4$.

Dividing both sides of the equation by 9,

$$y = \tfrac{4}{9}.$$ (Axiom IV)

3. $12x + 13 = 73$.

4. $18r - 12r = 33$.

5. $21t + 15 = 120$.

6. $28k - 9 = 251$.

7. $20y + 2y - 18y = 22$.

8. $17s - 3s + 16s = 105$.

9. $17x + 3x - 9x = 88$.

10. $16m + 2m - 13m = 22\tfrac{1}{2}$.

11. $202y - 152y + 6y = 280$.

12. $3.4x - 1.2x + 4.8x = 70$.

13. $3.5y + 7.6y - 8.6y = 15$.

14. $5.8m - 3.9m + 12.6m = 58$.

15. $6r - 3.5r + 5.5r = 68$.

16. $3.41x + 0.59x - 1.77x = 22.3$.

17. $8y - 4.5y + 5.2y = 87$.

18. $2s + 7s - 3s - 6 = 24$.

19. $\tfrac{1}{3}x = 6$.

20. $\tfrac{1}{2}x = 2$.

21. $\tfrac{2}{3}x = 6$.

22. $\tfrac{5}{6}x = 25$.

23. $\dfrac{x}{3} + \dfrac{x}{2} = 10$.

24. $\dfrac{x}{2} + \dfrac{x}{4} = 3$.

25. $\dfrac{t}{5} + \dfrac{t}{3} = 8$.

26. $\dfrac{m}{4} - \dfrac{m}{7} = 6$.

27. $\dfrac{3x}{4} + \dfrac{x}{2} - \dfrac{x}{8} = 36$.

28. $15 = 3x - 3$.

Solution. Adding 3 to both members, $18 = 3x$.

Dividing both members by 3, $6 = x$.

Note that in the preceding problem the unknown appears in the right member.

29. $17 = 2x - 3$.

30. $x + 10 = 2x - 9$.

31. $2x - 2\tfrac{1}{4} = 5x - 17\tfrac{1}{4}$.

32. $\dfrac{16}{x} = 4.$

Solution. Multiplying both members by x,

$$16 = 4\,x.$$

Hence $\quad 4 = x.$

Note that in the preceding problem the unknown occurs in the denominator.

33. $\dfrac{15}{b} = 5.$

34. $\dfrac{16}{3\,x} = 8.$

Multiply both members by $3\,x$.

35. $\dfrac{3}{4\,z} = 1.$

36. $\dfrac{13}{2\,z} + 1 = 14.$

SUMMARY

17. This chapter has taught the meaning of the following words and phrases: equation, members of an equation, equation is satisfied, substituting, check, root of an equation, verbal problem, algebraic solution of a verbal problem, term, monomial, literal number, similar terms, dissimilar terms, order of terms, and axiom.

18. Axioms. In solving equations the following axioms are used:

I. *If the same number or equal numbers be added to equal numbers, the sums are equal.* [**Addition Axiom**]

II. *If the same number or equal numbers be subtracted from equal numbers, the remainders are equal.* [**Subtraction Axiom**]

III. *If equal numbers be divided by equal numbers (excluding division by zero), the quotients are equal.* [**Division Axiom**]

IV. *If equal numbers be multiplied by the same number or equal numbers, the products are equal.* [**Multiplication Axiom**]

V. *If two numbers are equal to the same number or to equal numbers, the numbers are equal.* [**Equality Axiom**]

19. If an equation contains fractions, a second equation involving the same unknown may be obtained by multiplying every term of the given equation by the L.C.M.

of the denominators and then reducing all fractions to integers. The solution of this equation is more readily obtained than that of the given equation.

20. The equation is a convenient tool for solving problems. In solving a verbal problem algebraically observe the following steps:

(a) Use a letter for the unknown number called for in the problem. Often the last sentence suggests the most convenient choice.

(b) Express the given facts in terms of the unknown (provided, of course, that these facts are not definite arithmetical numbers).

(c) Obtain two expressions for the same number and equate them. (This gives us the equation.)

(d) Solve the equation. Check the result by substituting in the conditions of the problem.

CHAPTER II

LINEAR MEASUREMENT. THE EQUATION APPLIED TO LENGTH[1]

21. Length, the important characteristic of lines. If in drawing an object we lay the ruler on a sheet of paper and pass a sharpened pencil as near the edge as possible, thus obtaining what is familiar to us as a *straight line*, we are at once concerned with the length of a part of the straight line drawn. In fact, length is the important characteristic of a line. In an exact sense a line has length only, not width nor thickness. Thus, the edge of a table has length only;

A |——————————————————————| B

FIG. 4. A LINE SEGMENT

the thickness and width of a crayon line are neglected; the wide chalk marks on a tennis court are not boundary lines, but are made wide to help us see the real boundary lines, which are the outside edges of the chalk marks.

The part of a line whose length we wish to determine is a *line segment* or, briefly, a *segment*, as *AB* in Fig. 4.

A line segment has a definite beginning point and a definite ending point. The word "point" is used to mean merely position, not length, breadth, nor thickness. The position of a point is shown by a short cross line; that is, *a point is determined by two intersecting lines.*

---

[1] The pupil should now provide himself with a ruler one edge of which is graduated to inches and fractional parts of an inch and the other to units of the metric scale. He should also obtain a pair of compasses and some squared paper ruled to the metric scale.

Give examples of line segments that can be seen in the classroom.

22. Measurement of length. In Fig. 5 the length of the line segment AB is to be determined. One edge of your ruler is graduated (divided) into inches and fractions of an inch as is shown in Fig. 5. Place the division marked zero on your ruler at A, with the edge of the ruler along

FIG. 5. HOW A LINE SEGMENT MAY BE MEASURED

the segment AB, and read the number of inches in the line segment AB; that is, find what reading on the ruler is opposite the point B.

In the preceding problem we compared the unknown length of the line segment AB with the well-established and well-known segment, the inch, and found the line segment to be $2\frac{1}{2}$ times as long as the inch. Hence the length of the line segment is $2\frac{1}{2}$ in. When we determine the length of a line segment we are *measuring* the line segment. The segment with which we compare the given line is called a *unit segment* or a *unit of measurement.* Hence to measure a line segment is to apply a standard unit segment to it to find out how many times the unit segment is contained in it.

1. Draw a line segment and express its length in inches.

2. Measure the length of your desk in inches.

3. Measure the width of your desk in inches.

23. Different units of length. The most familiar instruments for measuring are the foot rule, the yardstick, and several kinds of tape lines. The fractional parts of the unit are read by means of a graduated scale engraved or stamped on the standard unit used. In Fig. 6, below, is shown a part of a ruler. The upper edge is divided into inches and fractional parts of an inch. What is the length of the smallest line segment of the upper edge?

The lower edge of the ruler is divided into units of the *metric* (or French) scale. This system is based on the

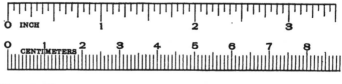

FIG. 6. PART OF A RULER, SHOWING DIFFERENT UNITS OF LENGTH

decimal system and is now very generally used in scientific work in all countries. The standard unit is called the meter (m.). It is divided into 1000 equal parts called millimeters (mm.). In the figure above, the smallest division is a millimeter. Ten millimeters make a centimeter (cm.). In the figure, *AB* is one centimeter in length, and you will note that this is about two fifths of an inch. Ten centimeters make a decimeter (dm.) (about 4 in.), and ten decimeters make a meter (39.37 in., or about 1.1 yd.). We may summarize these facts in the following reference table:

$$\left\{\begin{array}{l}1 \text{ millimeter} = 0.03937 \text{ inches}\\ 1 \text{ inch} \quad\;\, = 2.54 \text{ centimeters}\end{array}\right.$$

10 millimeters = 1 centimeter (0.3937 in., or nearly ⅖ in.)
10 centimeters = 1 decimeter (3.937 in., or nearly 4 in.)
10 decimeters = 1 meter (39.37 in., or nearly 3⅓ ft.)

24. Advantages of the metric system. One of the advantages of the system is that the value of the fractional part of the meter is more apparent than a corresponding decimal part of a yard. Thus, if we say a street is 12.886 yd. wide, the decimal 0.386 tells us nothing about the smaller divisions of a yardstick that enter into this number. At best we would probably say that it is something over one third of a yard. On the other hand, if we say that a road is 12.386 m. wide, we know at once that the road is 12 m. 3 dm. 8 cm. 6 mm. wide. This last statement is far more definite to one who has had a little practice with the metric system.

Obviously the advantages of the metric system lie in the fact that ten line segments of any unit are equal to one of the next larger. In contrast to this fact the multipliers of our system, though they may seem familiar, are awkward. Thus, there are 12 in. in a foot, 3 ft. in a yard, 5½ yd. in a rod, 1760 yd. in a mile, etc.

HISTORICAL NOTE. It is probable that most of the standard units of length were derived from the lengths of parts of the human body or other equally familiar objects used in measuring. Thus, we still say that a horse is so many hands high. The yard is supposed to have represented the length of the arm of King Henry I. Nearly all nations have used a linear unit the name of which was derived from their word for foot.

During the French Revolution the National Assembly appointed a commission to devise a system that would eliminate the inconvenience of existing weights and measures. The present metric system is the work of this commission.

This commission attempted to make the standard unit one ten-millionth part of the distance from the equator to the north pole measured on the meridian of Paris. Since later measurements have raised some doubt as to the exactness of the commission's determination of this distance, we now define the meter not as a fraction of the earth's quadrant, but *as the distance, at the freezing temperature, between two transverse parallel lines ruled on a bar of platinum-iridium which is kept at the International Bureau of Weights and Measures, at Sèvres, near Paris.*

25. Application of the metric scale. This article is intended to give practice in the use of the metric system.

EXERCISES

1. With a ruler whose edge is graduated into centimeters measure the segments AB and CD in Fig. 7.

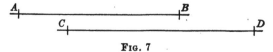

FIG. 7

2. Measure the length and width of your desk with a centimeter ruler. Check the results with those of Exs. 2 and 3, Art. 22.

3. Estimate the length of the room in meters and then measure the room with a meter stick. If a meter stick is not available, use a yardstick and translate into meters.

4. Turn to some standard text in physics (for example, Millikan and Gale, pp. 2 and 3) and report to the class on the metric system.

5. Refer to an encyclopedia and find out what you can about the "standard yard" kept at Washington.

26. Practical difficulty of precise measurement. In spite of the fact that measuring line segments is a familiar process and seems very simple, it is very difficult to measure a line with a high degree of accuracy. The following sources of error may enter into the result if we use a yardstick: (1) the yardstick may not be exactly straight; (2) it may be a little too long or too short; (3) it may slip a little so that the second position does not begin at the exact place where the first ended; (4) the edge of the yardstick may not always be along the line segment; (5) the graduated scale used for reading feet, inches, and fractional parts of inches may not be correct. Nor do we eliminate these errors by using other measuring devices. For example, a tape line tends to stretch, but contracts if wet, while a steel tape is affected by heat and cold.

From the preceding discussion it is apparent that a measurement is always an approximation. The error can be decreased but never wholly eliminated.

EXERCISES

1. Suppose you have measured a distance (say the edge of your desk) with great care and have found it to be equal to 2 ft. 7⅜ in. Is this the *exact* length of the desk? Justify your answer.

2. If you were to repeat the measurement with still greater care, making use of a finer-graduated scale, is it likely that you would find exactly the same result as before?

3. If you were asked to measure the length of your classroom, what would you use? Why?

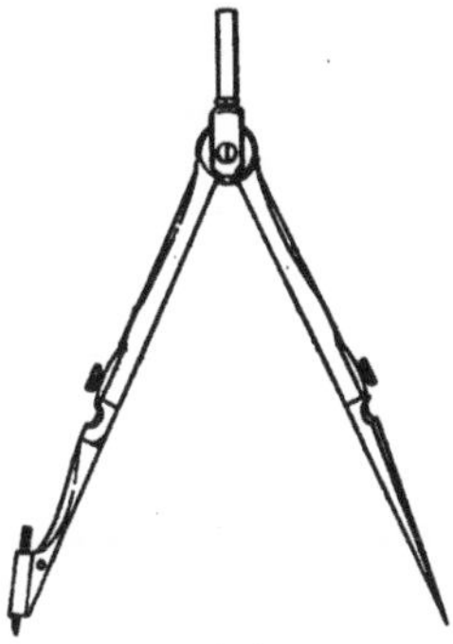

27. The compasses. A pair of compasses (Fig. 8) is an instrument that may be used in measuring line segments. Since the use of compasses greatly decreases some of the common errors in measuring that have been pointed out, and is consequently very useful in many forms of drawing which require a high degree of accuracy, it will be helpful if the student learns to use the compasses freely.

FIG. 8. A PAIR OF COMPASSES

28. Measuring a line segment with the compasses. To measure the line segment AB in Fig. 9 with the compasses, place the sharp points of the compasses on A and B. Turn

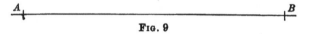

FIG. 9

the screw which clamps the legs of the compasses. Then place the points on the marks of the ruler and count the number of inches or centimeters between them.

EXERCISES

1. With the compasses measure AB in Fig. 9, in inches.

2. With the compasses measure AB in Fig 9, in centimeters.

3. Multiply the result of Ex. 1 by 2.54. What do you observe?

4. Estimate the number of centimeters in the length of this page. Measure the length of this page with the compasses and compare with your estimate.

29. Squared paper. Squared paper is another important device which is often useful in measuring line segments.

Squared paper is ruled either to inches and fractions of an inch (used by the engineer) or to the units of the metric scale. A sample part of a sheet is shown in Fig. 10. The method of measuring with squared paper is practically the same as measuring with the compasses and ruler. Thus, to measure the line segment AB in Fig. 10

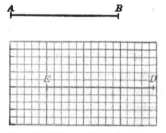

FIG. 10. HOW A LINE SEGMENT MAY BE MEASURED BY THE USE OF SQUARED PAPER

place the sharp points of the compasses on A and B. Clamp the compasses. Place the sharp points on one of the heavy lines, as at E and D. Each side of a large square being 1 cm., count the number of centimeters in ED and estimate the remainder to tenths of a centimeter. Thus, in Fig. 10 the segment ED equals 2.9 cm.

EXERCISES

1. Draw a line segment and measure its length in centimeters by the use of squared paper.

2. Why do you find it convenient to place one of the sharp points of the compasses where two heavy lines intersect?

3. What are the advantages of measuring with squared paper over measuring with a ruler?

30. Measuring a length approximately to two decimal places. By increasing the size of the unit of measurement we may express the result with approximate accuracy to two decimal places. In Fig. 11 let MN (equal to ten small units, or 2 cm., of the squared paper) be the unit. As before, lay off AB upon the squared paper with the compasses (CD in the new position). Now EF (a small unit) equals 0.1 of

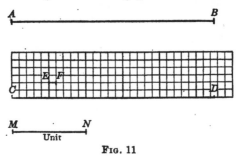

FIG. 11

a unit, and 0.1 of EF equals 0.01 of the unit MN. Reading the units in the line CD, we are sure the result is greater than 2.7, for the crossing line is beyond that. But it is not 2.8. Why? Now imagine a small unit, as EF, divided into tenths and estimate the number of tenths from the end of the twenty-seventh small unit to D. This appears to be 0.4, but this is 0.04 of a unit; hence *CD* equals 2.74 units. This means that *CD* is 2.74 times as long as the line *MN*. Of course the 4 is only an approximation, but it is reasonably close.

1. In Fig. 12 measure to two decimal places the segments *CD, DE,* and *EC.* Compare the results of your work with that of the other members of the class.

2. Is the result obtained by the method of Art. 30 more accurate than the result obtained by using 1 cm. as a unit and claiming accuracy to only one decimal place?

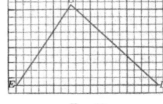

FIG. 12

31. Equal line segments. When the end points of one segment, as *a* in Fig. 13, coincide with (exactly fit upon) the ends of another segment, as *b*, the segments *a* and *b* are said to be equal. This fact may be expressed by the equation $a = b$.

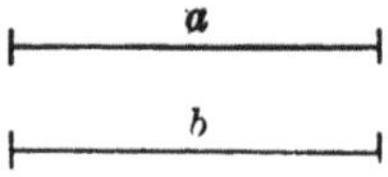

FIG. 13. EQUAL LINE SEGMENTS

32. Unequal segments; inequality. If the end points of two segments, as *a* and *b*, cannot possibly be made to coincide, the segments are said to be *unequal.* This is written $a \neq b$ (read "*a* is not equal to *b*"). The statement $a \neq b$ is called an *inequality.* In Fig. 14 segment *a* is less than segment *b* (written $a < b$), and segment *c* is greater than segment *b* (written $c > b$).

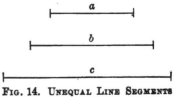

FIG. 14. UNEQUAL LINE SEGMENTS

In the preceding equation and inequalities we need to remember that the letters *a*, *b*, and *c* stand for the length of the segments. They represent *numbers* which can be determined by measuring the segments.

33. Ratio. This article will show that ratio is a fundamental notion in measurement.

INTRODUCTORY EXERCISES

(Exs. 1–4 refer to Fig. 15)

1. Measure the segment *a* accurately to two decimal places.

2. Measure the segment *b* accurately to two decimal places.

3. What part of *b* is *a* ?

4. Find the quotient of *b* divided by *a*.

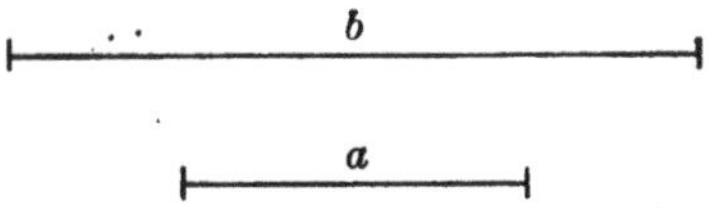

FIG. 15

The quotient of two numbers of the same kind is called their *ratio*. The ratio is commonly expressed as a fraction. Before forming the fraction the two quantities must be expressed in terms of the same unit; for example, the ratio of 2 ft. to 5 in. is the ratio of 24 in. to 5 in., that is, $\frac{24}{5}$. The unit of measure is 1 in. Obviously there is no ratio between quantities of different kinds; for example, there is no ratio between 7 gal. and 5 cm.

It should now be clear that every measurement is the determination of a ratio either exact or approximate. Thus, when we measure the length of the classroom and say it is 10 m. long, we mean that it is ten times as long as the standard unit, the meter; that is, the ratio is $\frac{10}{1}$.

1. The death rate in Chicago in a recent year was 16 to 1000 population. Express this ratio as a fraction.

2. An alloy consists of copper and tin in the ratio of 2 to 3. What part of the alloy is copper ? What part is tin ?

3. A solution consists of alcohol and water in the ratio of 3 to 6. What part of the solution is water ?

4. The ratio of weights of equal volumes of water and copper is given by the fraction $\frac{1}{8.9}$. How many times heavier is copper than water ?

5. Water consists of hydrogen and oxygen in the ratio of 1 to 7.84. Express this ratio as a decimal fraction.

34. Sum of two segments; geometric addition. It is possible to add two line segments by the use of compasses. Thus, in Fig. 16 if the segment a is laid off on the number scale of squared paper from point A to point B and if in turn b is laid off on the same line from B to C, then the

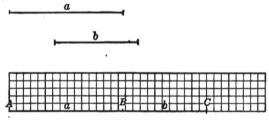

Fig. 16. Geometric Addition of Line Segments

sum of these lines can be read off at once. In Fig. 16 the sum is 5.4 cm. The segment AC is the sum of a and b. Very often in construction work we are not concerned about either the length of the segments or their sum. In that case lay off the segments as above on a working line and indicate the sum of a and b as $a + b$. Addition performed by means of the compasses is a *geometric addition*.

EXERCISES

1. In Fig. 17 find the sum of a, b, and c on a working line. Indicate the sum.

2. In Fig. 17 add the segments a, b, and c on the scale line of a sheet of squared paper. Express the value of $a + b + c$ in centimeters.

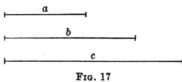

Fig. 17

3. On a working line draw one line to indicate the number of yards of fencing needed for the lot in Fig. 18.

Fig. 18

4. In Fig. 19 the whole segment is denoted by c. Show by measuring on squared paper that $c = a + b$.

5. In Fig. 19 what relation exists between c and either a or b? Why?

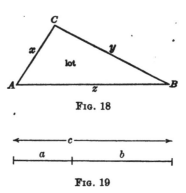

Fig. 19

35. Axioms. Exs. 4 and 5, above, illustrate the following two axioms:

VI. *The whole is equal to the sum of all its parts.*

VII. *The whole is greater than any one of its parts.*

EXERCISES

1. Draw the segments $a = 2.3$ cm.; $b = 3.2$ cm.; $c = 1.3$ cm. Draw the sum $a + b + c$.

2. Let a, b, and c denote three line segments. Draw a line segment to represent $2a + 3b + c$; to represent $4a + b + 2c$; to represent $a + 3b + 4c$.

3. In Fig. 20, if a, b, and c are three consecutive segments on a straight line, such that $a = c$, show by measuring that $a + b = b + c$.

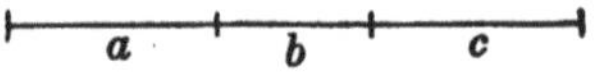

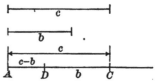

FIG. 20

4. Show without measuring that $a + b = b + c$. What axiom does this fact illustrate? Quote the axiom.

36. Order of terms in addition. The fact that we get the same sum when we lay off a segment a and then add b that we do when we lay off b first and then add a is a geometric illustration of the truth of the *commutative law*. This law asserts that *the value of a sum does not change when the order of the addends is changed.* In the first chapter we illustrated this principle by a familiar experience from arithmetic, as $2 + 5 + 4 = 2 + 4 + 5$.

EXERCISES

1. Illustrate the validity of the commutative law by a fact from your everyday experience.

2. Add in the most advantageous way, using the commutative law: $376 + 412 + 124$; $2187 + 469 + 213$; $36 + 142 + 164$.

37. Difference of two line segments. The difference of two line segments may also be found with the compasses. To find out how much greater the segment c is than the segment b we lay off the segment c on a working line (Fig. 21) from A to C, then lay the segment b backward from C toward A. Then the difference between

FIG. 21. GEOMETRIC SUBTRACTION OF LINE SEGMENTS

the segments b and c is expressed by the segment AD. In equation form this may be written $AD = c - b$. Illustrate this method by comparing the lengths of two pencils.

1. Transfer the line segments of Fig. 21 to squared paper and express the difference between c and b in centimeters.

2. Subtract a line segment 3.5 cm. long from one 6 cm. long.

3. In Fig. 22 the line segment AB equals the line segment MN. Show by measuring that $AB - MB = MN - MB$.

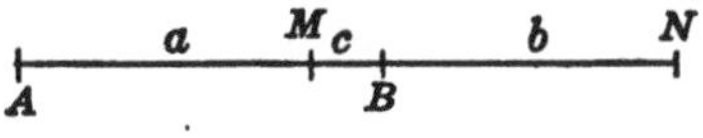

FIG. 22

4. Ex. 3 is simpler if we write the fact in algebraic form, using the small letters. Thus, $a + c = b + c$. How would you show that $a = b$?

5. What axiom of the first chapter is illustrated by Exs. 3 and 4? Quote the axiom.

6. If $a = 3$ cm., $b = 2$ cm., and $c = 1$ cm., construct a line segment representing $2a + 3b - c$; representing $5a - 2b + c$.

7. If a, b, and c represent the length of three respective segments, construct $3a + 2b - c$; $4a + 2b - 2c$; $5a - 2b + 3c$.

8. How long would each of the segments constructed in Ex. 7 be if $a = 5$, $b = 4$, and $c = 3$?

38. Coefficient. The arithmetical factor in the term $2x$ is called the *coefficient* of the literal factor x. When no coefficient is written, as in x, we understand the coefficient to be 1. Thus, x means $1x$. The coefficient of a literal number indicates how many times the literal number is to be used as an *addend*; thus, $5x$ means $x+x+x+x+x$

FIG. 23

and can be expressed by the equation $5x = x+x+x+x+x$. Written in this form we see that the use of a coefficient is a convenient method of abbreviating. Geometrically a coefficient may be interpreted as follows: Let x be the length of the segment in Fig. 23. Then the 5 in $5x$ indicates that the line segment x is to be laid off five times

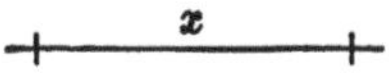

consecutively on a working line. $5x$ expresses the sum
obtained by this geometric addition. Find this sum. Usually the term "coefficient" means just the arithmetical factor
in a term, though in a more general sense the coefficient
of any factor, or number in a term, is the *product* of all the
other factors in that term. Thus, in $3\,aby$ the coefficient
of y is $3\,ab$, of by is $3\,a$, of aby is 3.

Give the coefficient in each of the following terms: $3\,b$;
$5\,ab$; x; $7\,x$; $8\,x$; $9\,x$.

39. Polynomials. An algebraic number consisting of two
or more terms (each called a *monomial*), as $5x + 3\,y - 2\,z$,
is a *polynomial.* The word "polynomial" is derived from
a phrase which means *many termed.* A polynomial of two
terms, as $5x + 3\,a$, is a *binomial.* A polynomial of three
terms, as $2\,a + 3\,b + 4\,c$, is a *trinomial.*

Classify the following expressions on the basis of the
number of terms:

(a) $2\,m + 3\,n - 5\,x + r.$ (c) $6\,x + 2\,y.$

(b) $6\,x.$ (d) $a + 2\,b + 3.$

40. Algebraic addition of similar terms. In simple problems we have frequently added similar terms. We shall
now review the process by means of the following example
in order to see clearly the law to be used in the more
complicated additions:

Add $4x + 3x + 2x.$

Solution. $4x$ can be considered as the sum of four segments each
x units long.

Therefore $4x = x + x + x + x.$

Similarly, $\qquad 3\,x = x + x + x,$

and $\qquad\qquad\qquad 2\,x = x + x.$

Adding,

$\qquad 4\,x + 3\,x + 2\,x = x + x + x + x + x + x + x + x + x,$ or $9\,x.$

Hence $\qquad\qquad 4\,x + 3\,x + 2\,x = 9\,x.$

The preceding example illustrates the law that *the sum of two or more similar monomials is a monomial whose coefficient is the sum of the coefficients of the given monomials and which has the same literal factor as the given monomials.*

The advantages of adding numbers according to this law may be seen by comparing the two solutions of the following problem:

The tickets for a school entertainment are sold at 25¢ each by a committee of five students, A, B, C, D, and E. A reports 38 sold; B, 42; C, 26; D, 39; and E, 57. At the door 173 tickets are sold. Find the total receipts.

Solution I.

A's receipts,	$38 \times \$0.25 =$	$\$9.50$
B's receipts,	$42 \times 0.25 =$	10.50
C's receipts,	$26 \times 0.25 =$	6.50
D's receipts,	$39 \times 0.25 =$	9.75
E's receipts,	$57 \times 0.25 =$	14.25
Door receipts,	$173 \times 0.25 =$	$\underline{43.25}$
Total receipts,		$\$93.75$

Since the common factor in the above multiplication is 25, a simpler solution is obtained if the numbers of tickets sold (coefficients) are first added and placed before the common factor; thus,

Solution II.

A's receipts,	$38 \times \$0.25$
B's receipts,	42×0.25
C's receipts,	26×0.25
D's receipts,	39×0.25
E's receipts,	57×0.25
Door receipts,	173×0.25
Total receipts,	$\overline{375} \times 0.25 = \$93.75$

1. Tickets were sold at c cents; A sells 12; B, 15; C, 36; and D, 14. There were 112 tickets sold at the gate. Find the total receipts.

2. Express as one term $3 \cdot 7 + 5 \cdot 7 + 4 \cdot 7$.

NOTE. A dot placed between two numbers and halfway up indicates multiplication and is read "times." Do not confuse with the decimal point.

3. Can you add $3 \cdot 7 + 14 \cdot 2 + 5 \cdot 4$ by the short cut above?

4. Indicate which of the following sums can be written in the form of monomials: $3x + 5x$; $4x + 7x + 3$; $13 + 5 + 3$; $3a + 2b + 4$.

5. Add as indicated: (a) $3x + 20x + 17x + 9x + 7x + 3x$; (b) $3y + y + 15y + 11y + 2y$; (c) $9s + 3s + 3s + 4s + 2s$; (d) $7.25d + 1.21d + 3d$; (e) $\dfrac{x}{2} + \dfrac{5x}{8} + \dfrac{x}{4}$.

6. The school's running track is f feet. While training, a boy runs around it five times on Monday, six on Tuesday, ten on Wednesday, seven on Thursday, six on Friday, and nine on Saturday morning. How many feet does he run during the week?

41. Subtraction of similar monomials. The law in subtraction is similar to the law in addition and may be illustrated as follows:

Subtract $2x$ from $5x$.

Solution. $\qquad 5x = x + x + x + x + x.$
$\qquad\qquad\qquad 2x = x + x.$

Subtracting equal numbers from equal numbers,
$\qquad\qquad 5x - 2x = x + x + x, \text{ or } 3x.$
Hence $\qquad\qquad 5x - 2x = 3x.$

The preceding example illustrates the law that *the difference of two similar monomials is a monomial having a coefficient equal to the difference of the coefficients of the given monomials and having the same literal factor.*

EXERCISES

1. Subtract $3\,b$ from $14\,b$.

2. Write the differences of the following pairs of numbers as monomials: $10\,x-3\,x$; $13\,x-5\,x$; $12\,z-3\,z$; $17\,k-5\,k$; $2.68\,r$ $-0.27\,r$; $1.03\,a-0.08\,a$; $\frac{2}{3}\,e-\frac{1}{4}\,e$; $\frac{3}{8}\,t-\frac{1}{4}\,t$.

3. The following exercises require both addition and subtraction. Write each result as a single term: $4\,x+6\,x-2\,x$; $13\,x-2\,x+3\,x$; $11.5\,c+2.3\,c-c$; $\frac{1}{3}\,a+\frac{5}{8}\,a-\frac{1}{4}\,a$.

42. Triangle; perimeter. If three points, as A, B, and C (Fig. 24), are connected by line segments, the figure formed is a *triangle*. The three points are called *vertices* (corners) of the triangle, and the three sides a, b, and c are the *sides* of the tri-

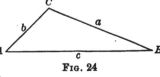

FIG. 24

angle. The sum of the three sides, as $a+b+c$ (the distance around), is the *perimeter* of the triangle.

EXERCISES

1. A yard has the form of an equal-sided (equilateral) triangle, each side being x rods long. How many rods of fence will be needed to inclose it?

2. What is the sum of the sides of a triangle (Fig. 25) whose sides are $2\,x$ feet, $2\,x$ feet, and $3\,x$ feet long? Express the sum as a certain number of times x.

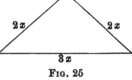

FIG. 25

3. What is the sum of the three sides $3\,b$, $4\,b$, and $6\,b$ of a triangle? Express the result as one term.

4. What is the perimeter of a triangle whose sides are $2\,x$, $8\,x$, and $9\,x$? Let p be the perimeter; then write your answer to the preceding question in the form of an equation.

43. Polygons. A figure, as $ABCDE$ (see Fig. 26), formed by connecting points, as A, B, C, D, and E, by line

segments, is a *polygon.*
The Greek phrase from
which the word "polygon"
is derived means *many cor-*
nered. Polygons having 3,
4, 5, 6, 8, 10, $\cdots$, n sides
are called *triangle, quadri-*
lateral, pentagon, hexagon,
octagon, decagon, $\cdots$, n-gon
respectively. The sum of

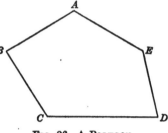

Fig. 26. A Polygon

the sides of a polygon is its perimeter. When all the sides of a polygon are equal it is said to be *equilateral.*

1. What is the perimeter of each of the polygons in Fig. 27? In each case express the result in the form of an equation; thus, for the first quadrilateral $p = 12\,x$.

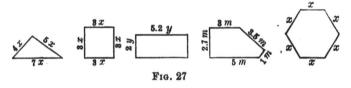

Fig. 27

2. Show by equations the perimeter p of the polygons in Fig. 28.

3. Show by equations the perimeter of an equilateral quadrilateral whose side is 11; 9; s; x; b; z; $2\,e$; $9+3$; $a+5$; $a+d$; $x+7$; $x+y$.

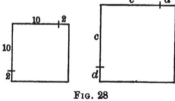

Fig. 28

4. Name the different figures whose perimeters might be expressed by the following equations:

$$p = 3s, \quad p = 5s, \quad p = 7s, \quad p = 9s, \quad p = 12s, \quad p = 20s,$$
$$p = 4s, \quad p = 6s, \quad p = 8s, \quad p = 10s, \quad p = 15s, \quad p = ns.$$

5. Assume that all the figures in Ex. 4 are equilateral. Find out how many of your classmates can give the name of each polygon.

6. Assume that at least six of the polygons in Ex. 4 are not equilateral. Sketch the figures of which the given equations may be the perimeters.

7. What is the perimeter of each figure of Ex. 4 if $s = 2$ in.? if $s = 3$ cm.? if $s = 4$ yd.? if $s = 5$ ft.?

8. Determine the value of s in the equations $p = 3s, p = 4s,$ $p = 5s, \ p = 6s, \ p = 10s,$ and $p = 15s$ if in each case the perimeter is 120 in.

9. What is the side of an equilateral hexagon made with a string 144 in. long? (Use all the string.)

10. Show by sketches polygons whose perimeters are expressed by $p = 8a + 6$; by $p = 4a + 12$; by $p = 6b + 6a$; by $p = 4a + 2b$; by $p = 3a + 2b$.

11. Find the value of the perimeters in Ex. 10 if $a = 3$ and $b = 2$; if $a = 5$ and $b = 3$; if $a = 1$ and $b = 5$.

12. If $x = 2$ and $y = 3$, find the value of the following expressions: $3x + y$; $3x - y$; $3x - 2y$; $2x - 3\frac{1}{2}$; $4x - 2\frac{1}{2}y$; $2.25x - y$; $2.27x - 1.12y$.

SUMMARY

44. This chapter has taught the meaning of the following words and phrases: line segment, point, measurement of length, unit segment, standard unit, ratio, metric system, coincide, intersect, equal segments, unequal segments, commutative law, coefficient, polynomial, binomial, trinomial, triangle, vertex of a polygon, vertices of a polygon, perimeter, sides of a triangle, polygon, quadrilateral, pentagon, hexagon, octagon, decagon, n-gon, equilateral.

45. Axioms. The following axioms were illustrated:

VI. *The whole is equal to the sum of all its parts.*

VII. *The whole is greater than any of its parts.*

46. The following instruments have been used in measuring line segments: the *ruler*, the *compasses*, and *squared paper*.

47. The following symbols were used: $\neq$ meaning *does not equal*; $<$ meaning *is less than*; $>$ meaning *is greater than*; and a dot, as in 3 · 5, meaning *times*, or *multiplied by*.

48. A point is determined by two intersecting lines.

49. The metric system has certain advantages over our English system.

50. The practical difficulty of precise measuring has been pointed out. Five possible errors were enumerated. Measurement implies the determination of a ratio.

51. The sum of two segments was found with the compasses. A law was discovered to serve as a short cut in algebraic addition.

52. The difference of two segments was found with the compasses and the law for algebraic subtraction was stated.

53. The Addition and Subtraction laws of Chapter I were illustrated geometrically.

54. The perimeter of a figure may be expressed by an equation.

55. The chapter has taught how to find the value of an algebraic number when the value of the unknowns are given for a particular case; for example, how to find the value of $3x + 2y$ when $x = 1$ and $y = 2$.

CHAPTER III

PROPERTIES OF ANGLES

56. Angle. If a straight line, as OX in either of the drawings of Fig. 29, rotates in a plane about a fixed point, as O, in the direction indicated by the arrowheads (counter-clockwise) until it reaches the position OT, it is said to

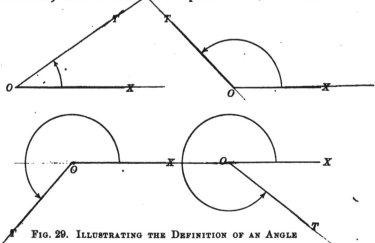

Fig. 29. Illustrating the Definition of an Angle

turn through the *angle XOT*. Thus, *an angle is the amount of turning made by a line rotating about a fixed point in a plane (flat surface)*. Note that as the rotation continues, the angle increases.

57. Vertex. The fixed point O (Fig. 29) is called the *vertex* of the angle. (The plural of "vertex" is "vertices.")

47

58. Initial side; terminal side. The line OX (Fig. 29) is called the *initial* side of the angle. The line OT is called the *terminal* side of the angle.

59. Symbols for "angle." The symbol for "angle" is $\angle$; for "angles," $\angle\!\!\angle$. Thus, "angle XOT" is written $\angle XOT$.

60. Size of angles. From the definition of an angle given in Art. 56 we see that it is possible for the line OX to stop rotating (Fig. 29) so that the angle may contain any given amount of rotation (turning).

EXERCISE

Draw freehand an angle made by a line OX which has rotated one fourth of a complete turn; one half of a complete turn; three fourths of a complete turn; one complete turn; one and one-fourth complete turns.

61. Right angle; straight angle; perigon.. If a line rotates about a fixed point in a plane so as to make one fourth of a complete turn, the angle formed is called a *right angle* (rt. $\angle$) (see Fig. 30, (a)).

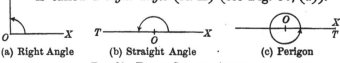

(a) Right Angle   (b) Straight Angle   (c) Perigon

Fig. 30. Three Special Angles

If the line makes one half of a complete turn, the angle formed is called a *straight angle* (st. $\angle$) (see Fig. 30, (b)); if the line makes a complete turn, the angle formed is called a *perigon* (see Fig. 30, (c)).

EXERCISES

1. Draw freehand an angle equal to 1 right angle; 2 right angles; 3 right angles; 4 right angles.

2. Draw freehand an angle equal to 1 straight angle; 2 straight angles; $1\frac{1}{2}$ straight angles; $2\frac{1}{2}$ straight angles.

3. How many right angles are there in a half turn of a rotating line? in a whole turn? in 5 turns? in $3\frac{1}{4}$ turns? in x turns? in $\frac{x}{2}$ turns? in $\frac{x}{4}$ turns?

4. How many straight angles are there in a half turn of a rotating line? in a whole turn? in $1\frac{1}{2}$ turns? in $1\frac{3}{4}$ turns? in x turns? in $2x$ turns? in $\frac{5x}{4}$ turns?

5. Through how many right angles does the minute hand of a watch turn in 3 hr.? in $3\frac{1}{2}$ hr.? in 4 hr.? in $2\frac{1}{2}$ hr.? in x hours? in 15 min.? in 30 min.? in 5 min.? in 10 min.?

6. How many straight angles are there in a perigon? in a right angle? in 10 right angles? in y right angles?

62. Acute angle; obtuse angle; reflex angle. Angles are further classified upon the basis of their relation to

FIG. 31. ACUTE ANGLE   FIG. 32. OBTUSE ANGLE

the right angle, the straight angle, and the perigon. An angle less than a right angle is called an *acute angle*, Fig. 31. An angle which is greater than a right angle and is less than a straight angle is called an *obtuse angle*, Fig. 32. An angle greater than a straight angle

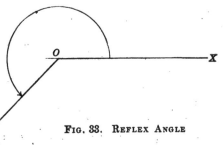

FIG. 33. REFLEX ANGLE

and less than a perigon is called a *reflex angle*, Fig. 33.

1. Draw an acute angle; an obtuse angle; a reflex angle.

2. Point out, in the classroom, examples of right angles; of obtuse angles.

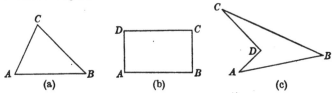

FIG. 34. ILLUSTRATING THE VARIOUS KINDS OF ANGLES

3. In the drawings of Fig. 34 determine the number of acute angles; of right angles; of obtuse angles; of reflex angles.

63. Notation for reading angles. There are three common methods by which one may denote angles: (1) Designate the angle formed by two lines OX and OT as the "angle XOT" or the "angle TOX" (Fig. 35). Here the first and last letters denote points on the lines forming the angle, and the middle letter denotes the point of intersection (the vertex). In reading "angle XOT" we regard OX as

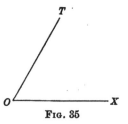

FIG. 35

the initial side and OT as the terminal side. (2) Denote the angle by a small letter placed as x in Fig. 36. In writing equations this method is the most convenient. (3) Denote the angle by the letter which is written at the point of intersection of the two sides of

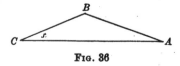

FIG. 36

the angle, as "angle A" (Fig. 36). This last method is used only when there is no doubt as to what angle is meant.

In the drawings of Fig. 37, below, select three angles and illustrate the three methods of notation described above.

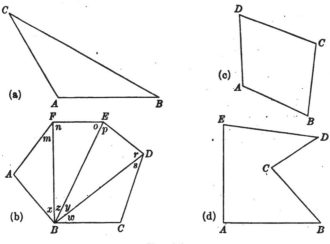

FIG. 37

64. Circle. If a line OX be taken as the initial side of an angle (see Fig. 38) and the line be rotated one complete turn (a perigon), any point, as P, on the line OX will trace a curved line which we call a *circle*. Thus, *a circle is a closed curve, all points of which lie in the same plane and are equally distant from a fixed point.*

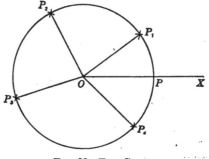

FIG. 38. THE CIRCLE

65. Center; circumference. The fixed point O is the *center* of the circle. The length of the curve (circle) is called the *circumference* (distance around) of the circle.

66. Radius; diameter. A line drawn from the center of a circle to any point on the circle is a *radius.* Thus, OP is a radius of the circle in Fig. 38. A line connecting two points on the circle and passing through the center of the circle is called a *diameter.*

From the definition of "radius" given above it is clear that in a given circle or in equal circles one radius has the same length as any other. Thus we obtain the following important geometric relation, *Radii of the same circle or of equal circles are equal.* ("Radii" is the plural of "radius.")

67. Arc; to intercept; central angle. An *arc* is a part of a circle. If two radii are drawn from the center of the circle to two different points on the circle, they cut off an arc on the circle. The symbol for "arc" is $\frown$. Thus, $\overset{\frown}{AB}$ is read "the arc AB." The angle formed at the center of the circle is said to *intercept* the arc. The angle at the center is called a *central angle.*

68. Quadrant; semicircle. An arc equal to one fourth of a circle is called a *quadrant.* An arc equal to one half of a circle is called a *semicircle.*

1. How does a diameter compare in length with a radius?

2. How many quadrants in a semicircle? in a circle? In what connection have we mentioned the idea expressed by the word "quadrant"?

69. Degrees of latitude and longitude. The use that is made of the circle in geography is no doubt familiar to all of us. The *prime meridian*, that passes through Greenwich, England (see Fig. 39), is the *zero* meridian. We speak of places lying to the west of Greenwich as being in west longitude and of those lying to the east of Greenwich as being in east longitude (see Fig. 39). Since it takes the earth twenty-four hours to make one complete rotation, the sun apparently passes over one twenty-fourth

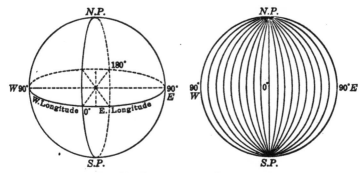

Fig. 39. Latitude and Longitude

of the entire distance around the earth every hour. Thus, points lying a distance of one twenty-fourth of a complete turn apart differ in time by an hour.

In order to carry the computations further the entire circle is divided into three hundred and sixty equal parts, each of which is called a degree (1°) of longitude. In order to express fractional parts of the unit each degree is divided into sixty minutes (60′) and each minute into sixty seconds (60″). With this agreement the longitude of a place is determined.

The position of a place north or south of the equator is indicated by the number of degrees of north or south latitude.

1. What is the greatest longitude a place can have? the greatest latitude?

2. How many seconds are there in a degree of longitude? in a degree of latitude?

3. What is the length of a degree arc on the earth's surface? of a minute arc? of a second arc? Try to find out how accurately the officers of a ship know the location of the ship out in mid-ocean.

4. How would you read 25° 14' west longitude? 33° 5' 17" north latitude?

5. Compare the method of locating by latitude and longitude to the method used in locating a house in a large city.

6. Find out in what longitude you live? in what latitude?

70. Amount of rotation determines the size of an angle. If we remember that an angle is formed by rotating a line in a plane about a fixed point, it will be clear that the

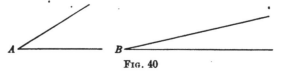

Fɪɢ. 40

size of the angle depends only on the amount of turning, not upon the length of the sides. Since the sides may be extended indefinitely, an angle may have short or long sides. In Fig. 40 the angle *A* is greater than angle *B*, but the sides of angle *B* are longer than the sides of angle *A*.

71. Measurement of angles; the protractor. In many instances the process of measuring angles is as important as that of measuring distances. An angle is measured when we find how many times it contains another angle selected as a unit of measure.

The *protractor* (Fig. 41) is an instrument devised for measuring and constructing angles. The protractor commonly consists of a semicircle divided into one hundred and eighty equal parts. Each of these equal parts is called a degree of arc (1°). In the geography work referred to in Art. 69, the unit for longitude and latitude was the degree of arc. In the measurement of angles we shall consider a unit corresponding to a unit of arc and called a *degree of angle.*

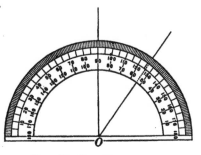

FIG. 41. THE PROTRACTOR

If straight lines are drawn from each of these points of division on the semicircle to the center *O*, one hundred and eighty equal angles are formed, each of which is a *degree of angle* (1°). Thus, the *unit* of angular measure is the *degree*. A degree is divided into sixty equal parts, each of which is called a *minute* (1').

Each minute is divided into sixty equal parts, each of which is called a *second* (1"). Of course the minute and the second graduations are not shown on the protractor. Why not?

EXERCISES

1. How many degrees in a right angle? in a straight angle? in a perigon?

2. A degree is what part of a right angle? of a straight angle? of a perigon?

3. What angle is formed by the hands of a clock at 3 o'clock? at 6 o'clock? at 9 o'clock? at 12 o'clock? at 4 o'clock? at 7 o'clock? at 11 o'clock?

4. Give a time of day when the hands of a clock form a right angle; a straight angle.

5. What is the correct way to read the following angles: 15° 17′ 2″? 5° 0′ 10″?

6. How many degrees are there in three right angles? in four straight angles? in one third of a right angle? in two thirds of a straight angle? in one fifth of a right angle? in x straight angles? in y right angles? in $2x$ right angles?

7. Ordinary scales for weighing small objects are sometimes made with a circular face like a clock face. The divisions of the scale indicate pounds. If the entire face represents 12 lb., what is the angle between two successive pound marks?

8. What is the angle between two successive ounce marks on the face of the scale in Ex. 7?

72. Measuring angles; drawing angles. The protractor may be used to measure a given angle. Thus, to measure a given angle x place the protractor so that the center of the protractor (point O in Fig. 42) falls upon the vertex and make the straight edge of the protractor coincide with (fall upon) the initial side of the given angle x. Now, observe where the terminal side of the given angle intersects (crosses) the rim of the protractor. Read the number of degrees in the angle from the scale on the protractor.

EXERCISES

1. Draw three different angles, one acute, one obtuse, and one reflex. Before measuring, estimate the number of degrees in each angle. Find the number of degrees in each angle by means of the protractor. Compare the results with the estimates.

2. Draw freehand an angle of 30°; of 45°; of 60°; of 90°; of 180°; of 204°. Test the accuracy of the first four angles by means of the protractor.

The protractor is also useful in constructing angles of a required size; for example, to construct an angle of 42° draw a straight line OX (Fig. 42) and place the straight edge of the pro- tractor on the line OX so that the center

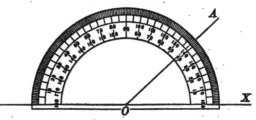

Fig. 42. Measuring Angles with a Protractor

rests at O. Count 42° from the point on OX where the curved edge touches OX and mark the point A. Connect A and O, and the angle thus formed will contain 42°.

EXERCISES

1. Construct an angle of 25°; of 37°; of 95°; of 68°; of 112°; of 170°. Continue this exercise until you are convinced that you can draw any required angle.

2. Construct an angle equal to a given angle ABC by means of the protractor.

HINT. Draw a working line MN. Measure the angle ABC. Choose a point P on the line MN as a vertex and construct an angle at P containing the same number of degrees as the given angle ABC. The angle is then constructed as required.

3. Draw a triangle. How many angles does it contain? Measure each with the protractor.

73. How to measure angles out of doors. It is possible to measure angles out of doors by means of a simple *field* (out-of-door) *protractor,* so that some simple problems in surveying can be solved. Such a field protractor may be made by a member of the class, as shown on the following page.

Secure as large a protractor as possible and fasten it on
an ordinary drawing board. Attach the board to a camera
tripod (if this is not to be had, a rough tripod can be
made). Make a slender pointer which may be attached at
the center of the circle with a pin so that it may swing freely
about the pin as a pivot. Place two inexpensive carpenter's
levels on the board, and the instrument is ready for use.

Thus, to measure an angle ABC (suppose it to be an
angle formed by the intersection of an avenue, BA, and a
street, BC), first put the board in a horizontal position
(make it stand level). Then place the center of the circle
over the vertex of
the angle to be meas-
ured and sight in
the direction of each
side of the angle,
noting carefully the
reading on the pro-
tractor. The number
of degrees through
which the pointer
is turned in passing
from the position of
BA to that of BC
is the measure of
angle ABC.

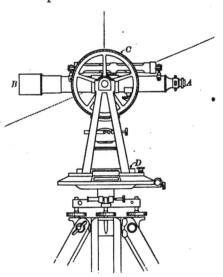

FIG. 43. THE TRANSIT

74. Transit. When
it is important to
secure a higher de-
gree of accuracy than is possible with the instrument
described in Art. 73, we use an instrument called a *transit*
(Fig. 43). This instrument is necessary in surveying.
Three essential parts of the transit are (1) a horizontal

graduated circle for measuring angles in the horizontal plane (see D in Fig. 43); (2) a graduated circle, C, for measuring angles in the vertical (up-and-down) plane; and (3) a telescope, AB, for sighting in the direction of the sides of the angle. For a fuller description of the transit see a textbook in trigonometry or surveying.

HISTORICAL NOTE. The division of the circle into three hundred and sixty degrees and each degree into sixty minutes and each minute into sixty seconds is due to the Babylonians. Cajori cites Cantor and others somewhat as follows: At first the Babylonians reckoned the year as three hundred and sixty days. This led them to divide the circle into three hundred and sixty degrees, each degree representing the daily part of the supposed yearly revolution of the sun around the earth. Probably they were familiar with the fact that the radius could be applied to the circle exactly six times and that as a result each arc cut off contained sixty degrees, and in this way the division into sixty equal parts may have been suggested. The division of the degree into sixty equal parts called minutes may have been the natural result of a necessity for greater precision. Thus the sexagesimal system may have originated. "The Babylonian sign ✳ is believed to be associated with the division of the circle into six equal parts," and that this division was known to the Babylonians seems certain " from the inspection of the six spokes in the wheel of a royal carriage represented in a drawing found in the remains of Nineveh."

Henry Briggs attempted to reform the system by dividing the degree into one hundred minutes instead of into sixty, and although the inventors of the metric system are said to have proposed the division of the right angle into one hundred equal parts and to subdivide decimally, instead of the division into ninety parts, we have actually clung to the old system. However, there is a tendency among writers to divide each minute decimally; for example, $52° 10.2'$ instead of $52° 10' 12''$. See Cajori, "History of Elementary Mathematics," 1917 Edition, pp. 10, 43, and 163.

75. Comparison of angles. In order to make a comparison between two angles, we place one over the other so that the vertex and the initial side of one coincide with the vertex and the initial side of the other. If the terminal sides coincide, the angles are *equal*; if the terminal sides do not coincide, the angles are unequal—assuming, of course, in both cases, that each of the two angles compared is less than 360°. In the exercises and articles that follow we consider no angle greater than 360°.

1. Compare angles x, y, and z, in Fig. 44, and arrange them in order as to size.

Hint. Make a tracing of each on thin paper and try to fit each on the other.

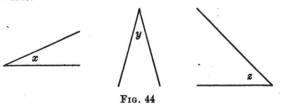

Fig. 44

2. Construct an angle equal to a given angle ABC. Lay a thin sheet of paper over the angle ABC and make a tracing of it. Cut out the tracing and paste it to another part of the paper. The angle thus shown is equal to the angle ABC.

3. Try to draw freehand two equal angles. Test your drawings by the method of Ex. 1.

4. Draw freehand one angle twice as large as another. Test your drawings with the protractor.

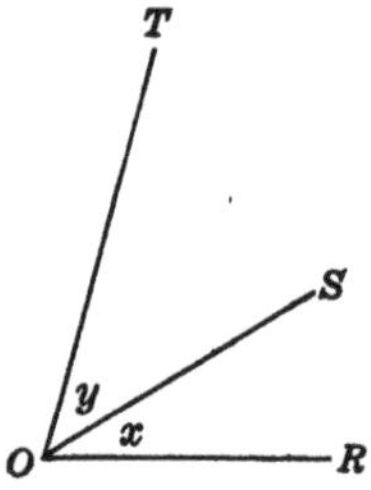

76. Adjacent angles; exterior sides. Angles x and y in Fig. 45 are two angles which have a common vertex and a common side between them. The angles x and y are said to be *adjacent angles*. Thus, *adjacent angles* are angles that have the same vertex and have a common side between them. The sides OT and OR are called the *exterior sides*.

Fig. 45

1. Indicate which angles in Fig. 46 are adjacent. Point out the common vertex and the common side in each pair of adjacent angles.

2. Draw an angle of 45° adjacent to an angle of 45°; an angle of 30° adjacent to an angle of 150°; an angle of 35° adjacent to an angle of 80°.

3. Do you notice anything particularly significant in any of the parts of Ex. 2?

4. Draw an angle of 30° adjacent to an angle of 60°. What seems to be the relation between their exterior sides? Does this relation need to exist in order that the angles shall be adjacent? What total amount of turning is represented?

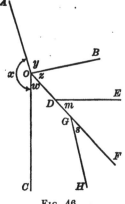

Fig. 46

77. Geometric addition and subtraction of angles. Exs. 2 and 4, above, suggest a method for adding any two given angles. Thus, to add a given angle y to a given angle x,

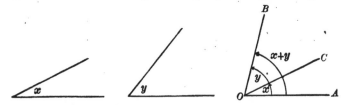

Fig. 47. Geometric Addition of Angles

Fig. 47, angle y is placed adjacent to angle x, and the resulting angle is called the sum of x and y. The angles may be transferred to the new position either by means of tracing paper or, more conveniently, by means of the protractor.

Add two angles by placing them adjacent to each other.

We may also find the difference between two angles. In Fig. 48 the two given angles are x and y. Place the smaller angle, y, on the larger, x, so that the vertices and

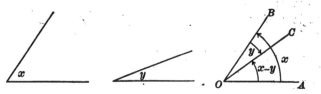

FIG. 48. GEOMETRIC SUBTRACTION OF ANGLES

one pair of sides coincide. The part remaining between the other two sides of x and y will be the difference between x and y. Thus, in Fig. 48 we obtain $\angle x - \angle y = \angle AOC$.

EXERCISES

1. Draw three unequal angles x, y, and z, so that $y > x$ and $x > z$. Draw an angle equal to $x + y + z$; equal to $y - x + z$; equal to $y + x - z$.

2. Draw an angle of 60° and draw another of 20° adjacent to it. What is their sum? Fold the 20-degree angle over the 60-degree angle (subtraction) and call the difference x. What is the equation which gives the value of x?

78. Construction problem. At a given point on a given line to construct by means of ruler and compasses an angle equal to a given angle. In this construction we make use of the following simple geometric relation between central angles and their intercepted arcs: *In the same circle or in equal circles equal central angles intercept* *equal arcs on the circle.* For example, if the central angle contains nineteen angle degrees, then the intercepted arc contains nineteen arc degrees.

The student may possibly see that this geometric relation is implied in our definitions of Art. 71. However, the two following paragraphs will assist him in understanding its application.

Make a tracing of the circle and the angle *ABC* in Fig. 49, (a), and place *B* upon *E* in Fig. 49, (b). The angles must coincide because they are given equal. Then the circle whose center is *B* (circle *B*) must coincide with the circle whose center is *E* (circle *E*), because the radii of equal circles are equal. Then *A* will fall on *D*, and *C* on *F*;

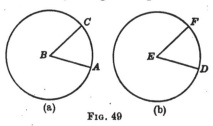

(a) Fig. 49 (b)

that is, the arc *CA* will fall on the arc *FD*, and the arcs are therefore equal.

It is easy to see that the following statement is also true: *In the same circle or in equal circles equal arcs on the circle are intercepted by equal central angles.* For circle *B* can be placed on circle *E* so that arc *CA* coincides with arc *FD*, since these arcs are given equal, and so that *B* falls on *E*. *A* will fall on *D*, and *C* on *F*. Then the angles must coincide and are therefore equal.

The two preceding geometric relations make clear why the protractor may be used to measure angles as we did in Art. 71. The method used there is based upon the idea that every central angle of one degree intercepts an arc of one degree on the rim of the protractor; that is, when we know the number of degrees in an angle at the center of a circle we know the number of degrees in the arc intercepted by its sides, and vice versa.

The idea can be expressed thus: *A central angle is measured by the arc intercepted by its sides* (when angular degrees and arc degrees are used as the respective units of measure).

How many degrees of an arc are intercepted by a central angle of 30°? of 40°? of 60.5°? of n°?

We are now ready to proceed with our problem: At a given point on a given line to construct by means of ruler and compasses an angle equal to a given angle.

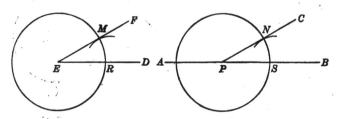

Fig. 50. Constructing an Angle Equal to a Given Angle

Construction. Let DEF in Fig. 50 be the given angle and let P be the given point on the given line AB.

With E as a center and ER as a radius draw a circle. With P as a center and with the same radius (ER) draw another circle. Place the sharp point of the compasses at R and cut an arc through M. With S as a center and the same radius cut an arc at N.

The $\angle BPC$ is the required angle. Why?

EXERCISES

1. Check the correctness of your construction for the preceding directions by measuring with a protractor.

2. How many ways have we for constructing an angle equal to a given angle?

3. Construct two angles, designating one of them as containing a degrees and the other as containing b degrees; using the angles a and b, construct an angle containing $a + b$ degrees; construct an angle containing $2a + b$ degrees.

4. Choose a and b in Ex. 3 so that $a > b$, then construct an angle equal to the difference of the two given angles.

5. Construct an angle equal to the sum of three given angles.

79. Perpendicular. We have seen in Art. 61 how right angles are formed by rotation. If two lines form right angles with each other, they are said to be perpendicular to each other. The symbol for "perpendicular" is ⊥.

80. Construction problem. At a given point on a given line to erect a perpendicular to that line by using ruler and compasses.

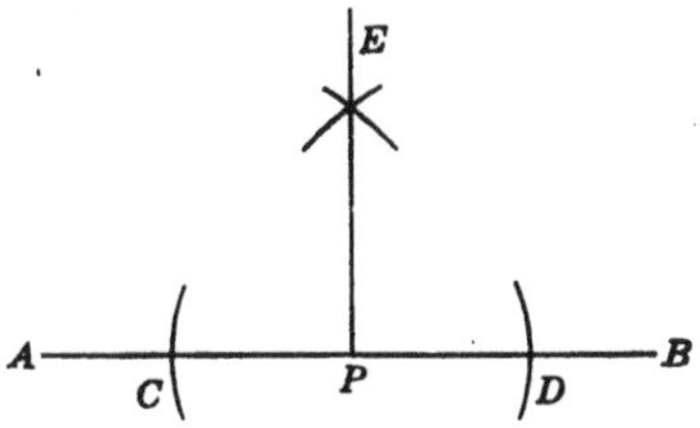

FIG. 51. HOW TO ERECT A PERPENDICULAR

Construction. Let AB be the given line and P the given point (Fig. 51). With P as a center and with a convenient radius draw arcs intersecting AB at C and D.

With C and D as centers and with a radius greater than $\frac{1}{2} CD$ draw arcs intersecting at E. Draw EP. Then EP is the required perpendicular.

EXERCISES

1. Test the accuracy of your construction in the problem of Art. 80 by using a protractor.

2. Why must the radius CE in Fig. 51 be greater than $\frac{1}{2} CD$?

3. In Fig. 52 how would you draw a perpendicular to the line AB at the point A? Do the construction work on paper.

FIG. 52

81. Construction problem. How to bisect a given line segment *AB.*

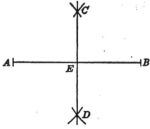

Construction. Let *AB* be the given line segment (Fig. 53). With *A* as a center and with a radius greater than $\frac{1}{2}$ *AB* describe arcs above and below *AB.* With *B* as a center and with the same radius as before describe arcs above and below and intersecting the first arcs at *C* and *D.* Draw *CD.* Then *E* is the point of bisection for *AB.*

Fig. 53. How to bisect a Line Segment

82. Perpendicular bisector. The line *CD* in Fig. 53 is called the *perpendicular bisector* of *AB.*

EXERCISES

1. How may a line be divided into four equal parts? into eight equal parts?

2. Draw a triangle all of whose angles are acute (acute-angled triangle). Construct the perpendicular bisectors of each of the three sides of the triangle.

3. Cut out a paper triangle and fold it so as to bisect each side.

4. Draw a triangle in which one angle is obtuse (obtuse-angled triangle) and draw the perpendicular bisectors of the three sides.

5. Draw a triangle in which one angle is a right angle and construct the perpendicular bisectors of the sides.

6. Draw a triangle *ABC.* Bisect each side and connect each point of bisection with the opposite vertex.

83. Median. A line joining the vertex of a triangle to the mid-point of the opposite side is called a *median.*

Draw a triangle; construct its medians.

84. Construction problem. From a given point outside a given line to drop a perpendicular to that line.

Construction. Let AB be the given line and P the given point (Fig. 54). With P as a center and with a radius greater than the distance from P to AB describe an arc cutting AB at M and R. With M and R as centers and with a radius greater than $\frac{1}{2} MR$ describe arcs either above or below (preferably below) the line AB. Connect the point of intersection E with P. Then the line PD is perpendicular to AB, as required. Test the accuracy of your work by measuring an angle at D.

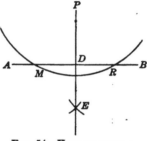

FIG. 54. HOW TO DROP A PERPENDICULAR

1. Why is it preferable to describe the arcs in Fig. 54 below the line AB?

2. Draw a triangle ABC all of whose angles are acute and draw perpendiculars from each vertex to the opposite sides.

85. Altitude. An *altitude* of a triangle is a line drawn from a vertex perpendicular to the opposite side.

1. Draw a triangle in which one angle is obtuse and draw the three altitudes.

2. Draw a triangle in which one angle is a right angle and draw the three altitudes.

3. When do the altitudes fall inside a triangle? outside?

86. To bisect a given angle. Suppose angle ABC to be the given angle (Fig. 55). With the vertex B as a center and with a convenient radius draw an arc cutting BA and BC at X and Y respectively. With X and Y as centers and with a radius greater than $\frac{1}{2}XY$ draw arcs meeting at D. Join B and D. Then BD is the *bisector* of $\angle ABC$.

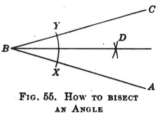

FIG. 55. HOW TO BISECT AN ANGLE

EXERCISES

1. Bisect an angle and check by folding the paper so that the crease will bisect the angle.

2. Bisect an angle of 30°; of 45°; of 60°; of 90°.

3. Divide a given angle into four equal parts.

4. Draw a triangle whose angles are all acute and bisect each of the angles.

5. Draw a triangle in which one angle is obtuse and bisect each of the angles; do the same for a triangle in which one angle is a right angle.

87. Parallel lines. AB and CD in Fig. 56 have had the same amount of angular rotation from the initial line EF. Thus, they have the same direction and are said to be *parallel*. The symbol for "parallel" is ∥. Thus, $AB \parallel CD$ is read "AB is parallel to CD."

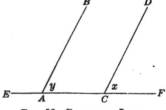

FIG. 56. PARALLEL LINES

88. Corresponding angles; transversal. Angles x and y in Fig. 56 are called *corresponding* angles. The line EF

is called a *transversal.* It is clear that the lines are parallel only when the corresponding angles are equal and that the corresponding angles are equal only when the lines are parallel.

EXERCISES

1. Draw figures to illustrate the importance of the last statement in Art. 88, above.

2. Point out the parallel lines you can find in the classroom.

89. Construction problem. How to draw a line parallel to a given line.

Construction. Choose a point *P* outside the given line *AB* in Fig. 57. Draw a line through *P* so as to form a convenient angle *x* with *AB*. Call the point of intersection *D*. At *P*, using *DP* as initial line, construct an angle *y* equal to angle *x* (as shown) by the method of Art. 78. Then *PR* and *AB* are parallel because they have had the same amount of rotation from the initial line *PD*.

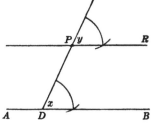

FIG. 57. HOW TO DRAW PARALLEL LINES

EXERCISES

1. Construct a line parallel to a given line through a given point outside the line.

2. A carpenter wants a straight-edge board to have parallel ends. He makes a mark across each end with his square. Why will the ends be parallel?

3. In Fig. 57 if angle *x* = 60°, what is the number of degrees in ∠*y*? Give a reason for your answer.

4. Two parallel lines are cut by a transversal so as to form two corresponding angles (*x* + 125°) and (3 *x* + 50°). Find *x* and the size of each angle. Make a drawing to illustrate your work.

5. In Fig. 58 if $AB \parallel CD$, what other angles besides x and y are equal corresponding angles?

6. In Fig. 58, $\angle x = \angle y$. Bisect $\angle x$ and $\angle y$ and show that these bisectors are parallel to each other.

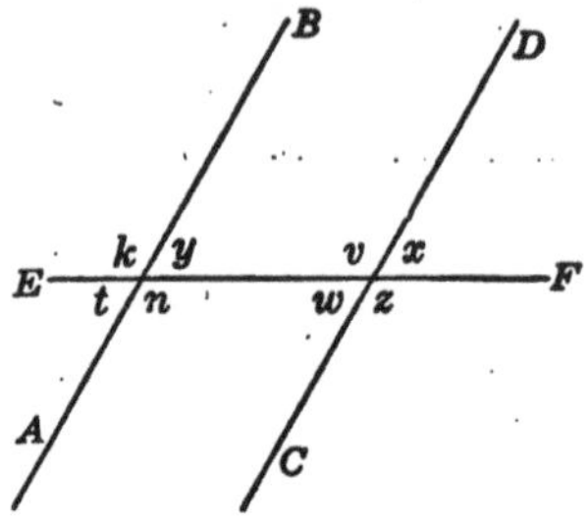

90. Parallelogram. If one pair of parallel lines cross (intersect) another pair, the four-sided figure thus formed is called a *parallelogram*; that is, *a parallelogram is a quadrilateral whose opposite sides are parallel.*

FIG. 58

91. How to construct a parallelogram. If we remember the method used in Art. 89 for constructing one line parallel to another, it will be easy to construct a parallelogram. Thus, draw a working line AB (Fig. 59). Draw AR making a convenient angle with AB. Through any point, as P, on AR draw a line PV parallel to AB. Through any point M on AB draw a line MT parallel to AR. The figure $AMSP$ is a parallelogram, for its opposite sides are parallel.

FIG. 59. HOW TO CONSTRUCT A PARALLELOGRAM

92. Rectangle. If one of the interior angles of a parallelogram is a right angle, the figure is a *rectangle* (Fig. 60). Thus, *a rectangle is a parallelogram in which one interior angle is a right angle.*

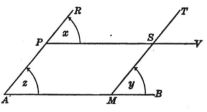

Rectangle

FIG. 60

Show that all the angles of a rectangle are right angles.

HINT. Extend the sides of the rectangle.

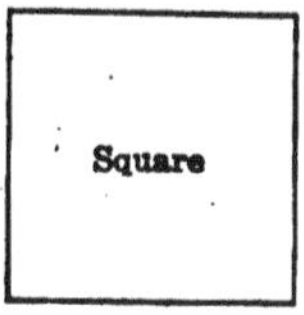

93. Square. If all the sides of a rec- tangle are equal, the figure is called a *square* (Fig. 61).

Square

FIG. 61

EXERCISES

1. Give examples of rectangles; of squares.

2. Construct a rectangle having two adjacent sides equal to 5 cm. and 8 cm. respectively (use compasses and straight-edge only).

3. Construct a rectangle hav-ing the two adjacent sides equal to the line segments *a* and *b* in Fig. 62.

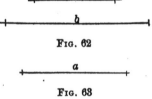

FIG. 62

4. Construct a square whose side is 7 cm. long.

FIG. 63

5. Construct a square a side of which is *a* units long (use line *a* in Fig. 63).

SUMMARY

94. This chapter has taught the meaning of the follow-ing words and phrases: angle, vertex, vertices, initial side of an angle, terminal side of an angle, right angle, straight angle, perigon, acute angle, obtuse angle, reflex angle, circle, center, circumference, radius, diameter, radii, arc, intercept, central angle, quadrant, semicircle, latitude, lon-gitude, degree of latitude, degree of longitude, minute, second, size of an angle, protractor, degree of arc, degree of angle, adjacent angles, exterior sides of an angle, field protractor, transit, perpendicular bisector, perpendicular to a line, altitude of a triangle, median of a triangle, bisector of an angle, parallel lines, corresponding angles, transversal, parallelogram, rectangle, and square.

95. The following symbols have been introduced: $\angle$ for *angle*; rt. $\angle$ for *right angle*; $\measuredangle$ for *angles*; $\frown$ for *arc*; $\perp$ for *is perpendicular to*; $\parallel$ for *is parallel to*; $°$ for *degree* or *degrees*; $'$ for *minute* or *minutes*; $''$ for *second* or *seconds*.

96. The following notations have been discussed: (1) notation for denoting and reading angles; (2) notation for denoting a circle by its center.

97. This chapter has presented the important methods of

1. Classifying angles.
2. Measuring angles.
3. Comparing angles.
4. Drawing angles containing any amount of turning or any number of degrees.
5. Adding and subtracting angles.
6. Measuring angles out of doors.

98. In this chapter the pupil has been taught the following fundamental constructions:

1. To draw a circle.
2. To draw an angle equal to a given angle.
3. To draw a line perpendicular to a given line at a given point.
4. To draw the perpendicular bisectors of the sides of a triangle.
5. To draw the medians of a triangle.
6. To draw a line perpendicular to a given line from a given point outside the line.
7. To draw the altitudes of a triangle.

8. To bisect a given angle.

9. To draw the bisectors of the angles of a triangle.

10. To draw a line through a given point parallel to a given line.

11. To construct a parallelogram.

12. To construct a rectangle.

13. To construct a square.

99. This chapter has taught the pupil to use the following instruments and devices: tracing paper, the protractor, and the field protractor.

IMPORTANT GEOMETRIC RELATIONS

100. *Radii of the same circle or of equal circles are equal.*

101. *In the same circle or in equal circles equal central angles intercept equal arcs on the circle.*

102. *In the same circle or in equal circles equal arcs on the circle are intercepted by equal central angles.*

103. *A central angle is measured by the arc intercepted by its sides.*

IMPORTANT DEFINITIONS

104. *An angle is the amount of turning made by a line rotating about a fixed point in a plane.*

105. *A circle is a closed curve all points of which lie in the same plane and are equidistant from a fixed point.*

106. (1) *A quadrilateral whose opposite sides are parallel is a parallelogram.* (2) *A rectangle is a parallelogram in which one interior angle is a right angle.* (3) *A square is a rectangle with all sides equal.*

CHAPTER IV .

THE EQUATION APPLIED TO AREA

107. Measuring areas. If we determine the amount of area inclosed within a polygon, as in the triangle ABC in Fig. 64, we are *measuring the area* of the triangle. As in measuring length, the process is one of comparison. We compare the area of the given polygon with some standardized (defined and accepted) unit of area and

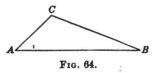

FIG. 64.

determine how many units are contained in the polygon; that is, we determine the ratio between the area of the given polygon and a standard unit of area.

108. Unit of area. The unit of area is a square each of whose sides is a standard unit of length. Such a unit involves length and width. Thus, we may measure area and express the result in square feet, square inches, square meters, square centimeters, etc.

FIG. 65. UNIT OF AREA IN THE METRIC SYSTEM

109. Practical method of estimating area. A practical way to estimate the area of a polygon is to transfer it to squared paper by means of tracing paper and then count the number of square units inclosed within the figure. If the bounding lines cut the squares, it becomes necessary to approximate. In such approximations we should be careful, but we should not go beyond reasonable limits of accuracy.

74

EXERCISES

1. The six figures in Fig. 66 were transferred by means of tracing paper. Estimate the areas of each of them by counting the squares. Express the areas either as square centimeters or as square millimeters.

HINT. One small square equals 4 sq. mm.

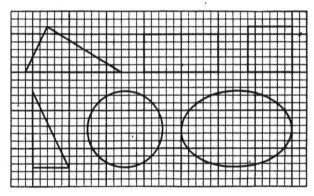

FIG. 66. ESTIMATING AREAS BY MEANS OF SQUARED PAPER

2. If the paper were ruled much finer, would you get a more accurate estimate? Give an argument for your answer.

3. Do you think that any of your results are accurate?

4. Write a paragraph in precise terms, supporting your answer to Ex. 3.

110. Area of a rectangle. CASE I. The sides of the rectangle that has been transferred to the squared paper of Fig. 67 are integral multiples of 1 cm. Using 1 sq. cm. as a unit, there are two rows of

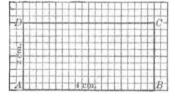

FIG. 67. HOW TO FIND THE AREA OF A RECTANGLE

units, and four units in a row. Counting, we see that the area equals 8, or 2 × 4. The law in this case is: *The area equals the base times the altitude.* In equation form this law may be written $A = b \times a$.

111. Area of a rectangle. CASE II. Let us suppose that we are given a square whose sides are *not integral* multiples of 1 cm.; for example, a rectangle whose base (length) is 2.3 cm. and whose altitude (width) is 1.3 cm. If we assume that the preceding law holds, then we ought to get $2.3 \times 1.3 = 2.99$ sq. cm. Instead of putting the rectangle on the kind of squared paper used in Case I, let us draw it again, by means of tracing paper, on squared paper that is ruled to a smaller unit, the millimeter, as in Fig. 68. Since there are 23 mm. in 2.3 cm. and

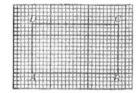

FIG. 68

13 mm. in 1.3 cm., if we temporarily adopt the square millimeter as a unit of area, then the sides of the rectangle are, as in Case I, integral multiples of the unit of length (in this case the millimeter). Hence there are 13 rows of units with 23 in a row, or 299 sq. mm. But there are 100 sq. mm. in 1 sq. cm.; hence, dividing 299 by 100, the result is 2.99 sq. cm., which is precisely the same number as that obtained by assuming the law of Case I.

112. Area of a rectangle. CASE III. This process of temporarily adopting a smaller square can be continued. If, for example, the base of a rectangle is 2.13 cm. and the altitude 1.46 cm., we may imagine the rectangle to be drawn upon squared paper still finer ruled, that is, ruled to 0.1 of a millimeter. From here the reasoning is the same as in Cases I and II.

1. Finish the reasoning of the foregoing paragraph.

2. The base of a rectangle is $3\frac{1}{4}$ cm. and its altitude is $5\frac{2}{5}$ cm. Show that the area may be found by counting squares.

3. The base of a rectangle is $5\frac{2}{5}$ cm. and its altitude is $2\frac{3}{8}$ cm. What unit would you temporarily adopt to find the area? Express the area in square centimeters.

The preceding exercises show that if the sides of a rectangle involve fractions which may be expressed as exact decimal parts of a unit, the problem is the same as in Case II.

113. Second method for finding area of a rectangle. It is possible to show that the transfer of a rectangle to the squared paper by means of tracing paper was unnecessary. Suppose we are given a rec-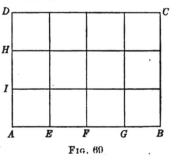tangle *ABCD* (see Fig. 69) whose base is 4 cm. and whose altitude is 3 cm. We wish to find the area. Draw a perpendicular line to the line *AB* at the end of each unit segment; that is, at the points *E*, *F*, and *G* (review the method of Art. 80).

FIG. 69

Also construct perpendiculars to the line *AD* at the points *H* and *I*. Then each small square is a unit of measure (by definition), and the figure is divided into three rows of units with four in a row. By counting, the area equals 12 (that is, *base times altitude*).

1. The base of a rectangle is 4.3 cm. long, and its altitude is 1.7 cm. Show how to find the area of this rectangle by counting, but without the use of squared paper.

2. Apply the law $A = b \times a$. What advantage has this law over the method of Ex. 1 ?

114. Formula. An equation which expresses some practical rule from arithmetic, the shop, the trades, the sciences, the business world, etc. is called a *formula.* Thus, $A = a \times b$ is a practical *formula* for finding the area of a rectangle. The plural of "formula" is "formulas" or "formulæ."

115. Formula for the area of a square. The square is a special case of a rectangle; that is, it is a rectangle in which $a = b$. The formula can be developed by the same method as for a rectangle. The only difference in the reasoning is that in every case there are as many rows of square units as there are square units in a row. (Why?) Hence the formula for the area of a square is $A = b \times b$. This formula may be written $A = b^2$, where b^2 means $b \times b$, and the formula is read "A equals b square."

1. By the method of counting squares find the area of a square whose side is $2\frac{1}{2}$ cm. long.

2. Apply the formula $A = b^2$ to the square in Ex. 1. Compare results.

3. Find the area of a square whose side is 5 ft.; a feet; x inches; y yards; m meters; 0.07 mm.; 2.41 m.

4. How many feet of wire fencing are needed to inclose a square lot whose area is 4900 sq. ft.? b^2 sq. ft.? $4x^2$ sq. yd.?

5. Express by an equation the area A of a rectangle that is 8 in. long and 5 in. wide; 8 in. long and 4 in. wide; 8 in. long and $3\frac{1}{2}$ in. wide; 8 in. long and $6\frac{1}{4}$ in. wide.

6. Express by an equation the area A of a rectangle 12 in. long and of the following widths: 6 in.; $8\frac{1}{4}$ in.; $9\frac{1}{8}$ in.; $10\frac{3}{4}$ in.; x inches; y inches.

7. A mantel is 54 in. high and 48 in. wide. The grate is 32 in. high and 28 in. wide. Find the area of the mantel and the number of square tiles contained in it if each tile is 3 in. on a side.

8. How many tiles 8 in. square are needed to make a walk 60 ft. long and 4 ft. wide?

9. Express by equations the areas of rectangles 1 in. long and of the following widths: 12 in.; 9 in.; h inches; n inches; x inches; a inches.

10. Express by equations the areas of rectangles of width w and of the following lengths: 8; 10; $12\frac{1}{2}$; x; a; l; b; z.

11. In each case write an equation for the other dimension of the rectangle, having given (a) altitude 8 in. and area 32 sq. in.; (b) altitude 5 ft. and area $7\frac{1}{2}$ sq. ft.; (c) base 9 ft. and area 30 sq. ft.; (d) base 6 in. and area 27 sq. in.; (e) base 3 in. and area A square inches; (f) base 5 in. and area A square inches; (g) altitude a inches and area A square inches; (h) base b inches and area A square inches.

116. Formula for the area of a parallelogram. Fig. 70 shows a parallelogram that has been transferred to that position by means of tracing paper. We wish to find its area. The line AB is produced (extended), and perpendiculars are dropped from D and C to the line AB (see Art. 84 for method of constructions), thus forming the triangles AED inside and BFC adjoining the given parallelogram.

(Exs. 1-7 refer to Fig. 70)

1. Estimate by count the number of square units in the triangle *AED*.

2. Estimate the number of square units in the triangle *BFC*.

3. Compare the results of Exs. 1 and 2.

4. If the area of the triangle *BFC* equals the area of the triangle *AED*, what is the relation between the area of the rectangle *CDEF* and the area of the parallelogram *ABCD*?

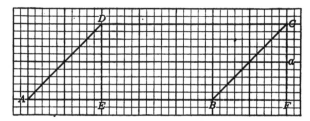

FIG. 70. HOW TO FIND THE AREA OF A PARALLELOGRAM BY
MEANS OF SQUARED PAPER

5. What is the formula for the area of the rectangle *CDEF*? Write the formula.

6. What seems to be the relation between the base of the parallelogram and the base of the rectangle? What evidence have you to support your answer?

7. What is the relation between the altitude of the parallelogram and the altitude of the rectangle? Give the evidence.

8. What seems to be the formula expressing the area of a parallelogram?

9. Without using squared paper construct a parallelogram (use ruler and compasses and follow the method of Art. 91). Divide the parallelogram into two parts — a triangle and a quadrilateral (as in Fig. 71). Now shift the triangle to the other side so as to form a rectangle. Show that the rectangle is equal to the parallelogram.

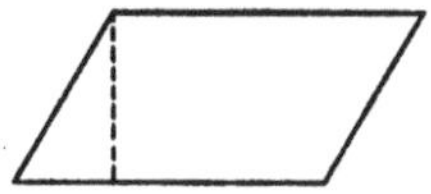

The preceding exercises furnish evidence to support the following law: *The area of a parallelogram equals the*

Fig. 71

product of its base and altitude. This law may be written in the form of the following well-known formula:

$$A = a \times b.$$

EXERCISE

Find the area of a parallelogram if $b = 17$ in. and $a = 5.3$ in.; if $b = 15.4$ in. and $a = 9.2$ in.

117. Area of a rhombus. The *rhombus* (Fig. 72) is a special case of the parallelogram, as *it is a parallelogram with all its sides equal.* Hence its area equals its base times its altitude.

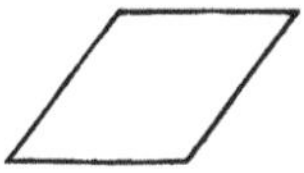

118. The area of a triangle. The exercises that follow will help the pupil

Fig. 72. Rhombus

to understand the formula for the area of a triangle.

EXERCISES

(Exs. 1–12 refer to Fig. 73)

1. Draw a triangle ABC as shown in Fig. 73.

2. Through C draw a line CD parallel to AB (review the method of Art. 89).

3. Through B draw a line parallel to AC, meeting CD at D.

4. What kind of a quadrilateral is the figure $ABDC$? Why?

5. By means of tracing paper transfer the parallelogram to squared paper.

6. Estimate the number of square units in triangle *ABC*.

7. Estimate the number of square units in triangle *CBD*.

8. Compare the results of Exs. 6 and 7. What relation does the triangle bear to the parallelogram?

9. What seems to be the relation between the base of the triangle and the base of the parallelogram? Why?

10. What is the relation between the altitude of the triangle and the altitude of the parallelogram? Explain why.

11. What is the formula then for the area of any parallelogram?

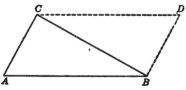

12. What appears to be the formula for the area of a triangle?

FIG. 73. How to find the Area
of a Triangle

13. Construct a parallelogram *ABCD*. Construct the diagonal *AC* (a line joining opposite vertices). With a sharp knife cut out the parallelogram and cut along the diagonal so as to form two triangles. Try to make one triangle coincide with the other.

14. What conclusion does the evidence of Ex. 13 support?

The preceding exercises furnish evidence to show that *the area of a triangle is equal to one half the product of its base and altitude.* This law may be written in the form of the following formula:

$$A = \frac{ab}{2}.$$

119. Area of a trapezoid. A quadrilateral having only two sides parallel is called a *trapezoid* (Fig. 74). The parallel sides are said to be its bases. In Fig. 74 the upper

base of the trapezoid is b, the lower base is a, and the
altitude is h. To find the area draw the diagonal BD.

The area of the triangle $ABD = \dfrac{a}{2} \cdot h$. Why?

The area of the triangle $BCD = \dfrac{b}{2} \cdot h$. Why?

Therefore the area of the trapezoid $= a\dfrac{h}{2} + b\dfrac{h}{2}$. Why?

Note that $a\dfrac{h}{2}$ and $b\dfrac{h}{2}$ are similar terms. Why? In the
first term a is the coefficient of $\dfrac{h}{2}$ and in the second term
b is the coefficient; hence, adding coefficients, as we may
always do in adding
similar terms, the area
of trapezoid is $(a+b)\dfrac{h}{2}$.

We can only indicate
the sum of the two
bases until we meet an

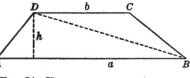

FIG. 74. HOW TO FIND THE AREA OF
A TRAPEZOID

actual problem. The *parenthesis* means that $a + b$ is to
be thought of as one number. The law is: *The area of
a trapezoid is equal to one half the product of its altitude by
the sum of its bases.* This law may be written in the form
of the following formula:

$$A = (a + b)\frac{h}{2}.$$

1. Find the area of the trapezoid whose altitude is 12.6 in.
and whose bases are 8 in. and 4.6 in. respectively.

2. The altitude of a parallelogram is $3x + 2$, and its base
is 4 in. Write an algebraic expression representing its area.
Find the value of x when the area is 28 sq. in.

3. The altitude of a triangle is 10 in., and the base is $3x + 2$ in. Write an algebraic number representing the area. Find the value of x when the area is 55 sq. in.

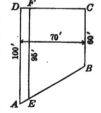

4. A man owns a city lot with the form and dimensions shown in Fig. 75. He wishes to sell his neighbor a strip $AEFD$ having a frontage DF equal to 10 ft. If the property is worth $5600, how much should he receive for the strip?

5. Of what kinds of polygons may the following equations express the areas?

FIG. 75

(a) $A = x^2$.

(b) $A = 3\,ax$.

(c) $A = 2(x + 1)$.

(d) $A = 5(x + 3)$.

(e) $A = x(a + 2)$.

(f) $A = a(x + 4)$.

(g) $A = x(y + 2)$.

(h) $A = y(x + 7)$.

(i) $A = \dfrac{3(x+1)}{2}$.

(j) $A = \dfrac{4(a+b)}{2}$.

(k) $A = a\left(\dfrac{b+c}{2}\right)$.

6. Find the value of A in Ex. 5 when $x = 3$, $y = 2$, $a = 4$, $b = 1$, and $c = 5$.

7. What quadrilaterals contain right angles?

8. In what respect does the square differ from the rectangle?

9. Having given a side, construct a square, using only ruler and compasses.

HINT. Review the method for constructing a perpendicular to a line segment (Art. 80).

10. How does a square differ from a rhombus?

11. Is a rhombus a parallelogram? Is a parallelogram a rhombus?

12. Construct a rhombus with ruler and compasses, given a side equal to 5 cm. and given the included angle between two adjacent sides as 41°.

HINT. Use the construction for parallel lines (Art. 89).

Geometric Interpretation of Products

120. A monomial product. The formulas for the area of the rectangle, the square, the triangle, the trapezoid, etc. show that the product of numbers may be represented geometrically; for example, the product of any two numbers may be represented by a rectangle whose dimensions are equal to the given numbers.

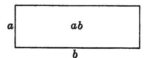

Fig. 76. Illustrating a Monomial Product

Thus the rectangle in Fig. 76 represents the product ab.

EXERCISES

1. Sketch a rectangle to represent the product $6x$.

2. Sketch an area to represent $4xy$.

3. Show from Fig. 77 that the area A is expressed by $4x^2$. What is the product of $2x \times 2x$?

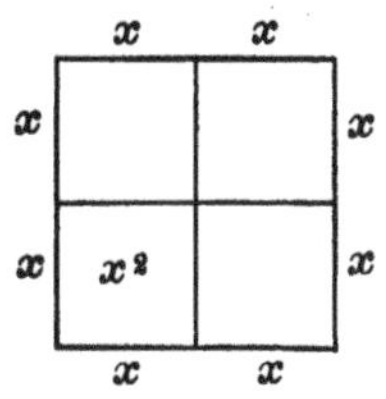

4. Show by means of a figure the area of a rectangle $3a$ by $5a$.

5. Draw a figure to represent the product of $5x$ and $4x$.

6. On squared paper draw an area representing the product ab. To the same scale draw the area ba. Compare the areas.

Fig. 77. Illustrating the Square of a Monomial

7. Show by a drawing on squared paper that $4 \cdot 5 = 5 \cdot 4$.

121. Law of order. The last two exercises illustrate that in algebra, as in arithmetic, *the factors of a product may be changed in order without changing the value of the product.* Thus, just as $2 \times 3 \times 5 = 5 \times 3 \times 2$, so $xyz = zyx$. This is called the Commutative Law of Multiplication.

Simplify the following: (a) $2x \cdot 3y \cdot 4z$; (b) $(2 \times y)(3 \times y)$; (c) $4 \times y \cdot 3 \times my$.

122. Product of a polynomial and a monomial. The formula for the trapezoid suggests the possibility of drawing areas to represent the product of a sum binomial by a monomial. The process is illustrated by the following exercises.

EXERCISES

1. Express by means of an equation the area of a rectangle of dimensions 5 and $x + 3$ (see Fig. 78). The area of the whole rectangle equals $5(x + 3)$. Why? If a perpendicular be erected at B (see Art. 80 for method), the rectangle is divided into two rectangles. The area of $DCBA$ equals $5x$. Why? The area of $ABEF$ equals 15. Why? It is now easy to find the entire area $DCEF$.

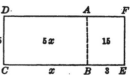

FIG. 78. ILLUSTRATING THE PRODUCT OF A POLYNOMIAL AND A MONOMIAL

Since $\qquad DCEF = DCBA + ABEF,$ $\qquad$ Why?

$\qquad\qquad 5(x + 3) = 5x + 15.$ $\qquad$ Why?

2. Show from Fig. 79 that $a(x + y) = ax + ay$.

3. Show by Fig. 80 that $a(x + y + z) = ax + ay + az$.

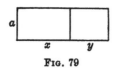

FIG. 79

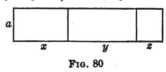

FIG. 80

4. Draw an area to represent $bm + bn + bc$.

5. Draw an area to represent $2ax + 2ay + 2az$.

6. Represent $2x + 4y + 6z$ by an area.

7. Sketch a rectangle whose area equals $2ax + 2ay + 6az$.

EUCLID

HISTORICAL NOTE. The word "geometry" comes from a Greek phrase which means to *measure the earth*. The early Egyptians had serious need for a reliable method of measuring the land after each overflow of the Nile. The early history of geometry appears to rest on this practical basis.

The oldest collection of geometry problems is a hieratic papyrus written by an Egyptian priest named Ahmes at a date considerably earlier than 1000 B.C., and this is believed to be itself a copy of some other collection a thousand years older.

Ahmes commences that part of his papyrus which deals with geometry by giving some numerical instances of the contents of barns. Since we do not know the shape of the barns, we cannot check the accuracy of his work. However, he gave problems on pyramids. The data and results given agree closely with the dimensions of the existing pyramids.

Geometry took definite form as a science when Euclid (about 300 B.C.) wrote his "Elements of Geometry." The proofs of his text were so excellent that the book replaced all other texts of the time and has held an influential position to this day. The form of Euclid is practically the same as most American geometry texts, and in England boys still say they are studying Euclid (meaning geometry).

We know little of Euclid's early life. He may have studied in the schools founded by the great philosophers Plato and Aristotle at Athens, in Greece. He became head of the mathematics school at Alexandria, Egypt, and proceeded to collect and organize into a set form the known geometric principles. He is said to have insisted on the knowledge of geometry for its own sake. Thus, we read of his telling the youthful Prince Ptolemy, "There is no royal road to geometry." At another time, so the story goes, when a lad who had just begun geometry asked, "What do I gain by learning all this stuff?" Euclid made his slave give the boy some coppers, "since," said he, "he must make a profit out of what he learns."

Euclid organized his text so as to form a chain of reasoning, beginning with obvious assumptions and proceeding step by step to results of considerable difficulty. The student should read about his work in Ball's "A Short History of Mathematics." Cajori's "History of Elementary Mathematics" and Miller's "Historical Introduction to Mathematical Literature" are further sources of information about Euclid.

123. Partial products. The products ax, ay, and az in the polynomial $ax + ay + az$ are called *partial products.* Each term of such an expression may be used to represent the area of some part of a rectangle. For example, Fig. 80 shows a rectangle divided into the parts ax, ay, and az respectively. Here the polynomial $ax + ay + az$ may be said to represent the area of the whole rectangle.

124. Algebraic multiplication. The list of exercises in Art. 122 also shows that *the product of a polynomial and a monomial is found by multiplying each term of the polynomial by the monomial and then adding the partial products.*

EXERCISES

1. Perform the following indicated multiplications :

(a) $3(2x + 3y)$.   (c) $3c(2a + 3b)$.

(b) $(5x + 2z)4a$.   (d) $3e(2c + 3)$.

2. Letting $x = 3$, $y = 1$, and $z = 2$, find the value of the following numbers : $(x + y)z$; $2(x + y) - z$; $3x + 2(y + z)$; $7x + (3y + 2z)$; $2z + 5(x + y)$.

125. Geometric product of two polynomials. The product of $a + c$ and $x + y$ may be indicated as $(a + c)(x + y)$. This product may be represented geometrically (Fig. 81) by a rectangle whose base is $x + y$ and whose altitude is $a + c$.

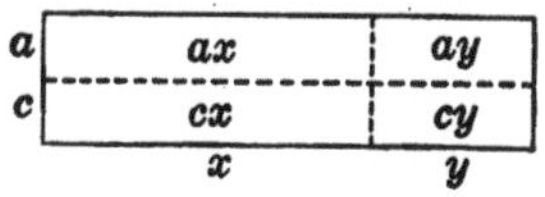

The rectangle is composed of four rectangles: ax, ay, cx, and cy.

FIG. 81. ILLUSTRATING THE PRODUCT OF TWO POLYNOMIALS

By the axiom that the whole is equal to the sum of its parts, the whole rectangle, $(a + c)(x + y)$, equals $ax + ay + cx + cy$, the sum of the parts.

1. Sketch a rectangle whose area will be the product of $(a + b)(c + d)$.

2. Find the geometric product of $(c + t)(m + n)$.

3. Perform the multiplication $(2 + x)(m + n)$ by means of a geometric figure.

4. Find the product $(3x + 2y)(a + b)$. Sketch the area represented by this product.

5. Find the product $(a + b)(x + y + z)$, using a geometric figure.

126. Algebraic product of two polynomials. The figures drawn in the preceding exercises indicate a short cut in the multiplication of two polynomials. Thus, *a polynomial is multiplied by a polynomial by multiplying each term of one polynomial by every term of the other and adding the partial products.*

1. Using the principle of Art. 126, express the following indicated products as polynomials:

(a) $(m + n)(a + b)$.

(b) $(r + s)(e + t)$.

(c) $(r + t)(2 + x)$.

(d) $(2x + 3)(3a + 4b + 2c)$.

(e) $(2a + 3)(a + 5)$.

(f) $5(4 + 7 + 3)$.

(g) $3(2a^2 + a + 5)$.

(h) $\left(\dfrac{8a}{3} + 2\right)(b + 1)$.

(i) $(a + 2)\left(\dfrac{3b}{7} + 4\right)$.

(j) $(3x + 7)(2y + \frac{4}{3})$.

(k) $(5b + 2c + 3d)(2x + 3y + 4z)$.

(l) $(2m + 3n + 4p)(3a + 7b + 5c)$.

2. One side of a rectangle is 4 yd. and the other is 6 yd. How much wider must it be made so as to be $1\frac{1}{3}$ times as large as before?

3. Multiply the following as indicated and check the result:
$$2\,x(x + 2\,y + y^2).$$

Solution. $2\,x(x + 2\,y + y^2) = 2\,x^2 + 4\,xy + 2\,xy^2.$

Check. Let $x = 2$ and $y = 3$.

$$2\,x(x + 2\,y + y^2) = 4\,(2 + 6 + 9) = 68.$$
$$2\,x^2 + 4\,xy + 2\,xy^2 = 8 + 24 + 36 = 68.$$

NOTE. Avoid letting $x = 1$, for in this case $2\,x$, $2\,x^2$, $2\,x^3$, etc. are each equal to 2. Why?

4. Multiply the following as indicated and check the results:

(a) $4\,x(x + 2\,y + 1).$

(b) $(x + y)(2\,x + 3\,y).$

(c) $(m + n + a)(m + n + a).$

(d) $(m + n + 2\,a)(m + n + 2\,a).$

(e) $(0.4\,x + 0.3\,y + 0.6\,z)(10\,x + 20\,y + 30\,z).$

127. Geometric square of a binomial. The product of $(x + y)(x + y)$, or $(x + y)^2$, is an interesting special case of the preceding laws. The product may be represented by a square each of whose sides is $x + y$ (see Fig. 82). The square is composed of four parts, of which two parts are equal. Since these two parts are represented by similar algebraic terms, they may be added; thus, $xy + xy = 2\,xy$. Hence the area of a square whose side is $x + y$ is $x^2 + 2\,xy + y^2$. The same product is obtained by applying the law for the product of two polynomials; thus,

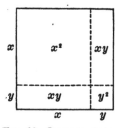

FIG. 82. ILLUSTRATING THE SQUARE OF A BINOMIAL

$$
\begin{array}{l}
x + y \\
\underline{x + y} \\
x^2 + xy \\
 \underline{xy + y^2} \\
x^2 + 2\,xy + y^2
\end{array}
$$

. In algebraic terms we may say that *the square of the sum of two numbers equals the square of the first, plus twice the product of the two numbers, plus the square of the second.*

Use Fig. 82 to show what this law means.

1. By means of figures express the following squares as polynomials:

(a) $(x + a)^2$. (d) $(e + d)^2$. (g) $(3 + x)^2$.
(b) $(m + n)^2$. (e) $(x + 2)^2$. (h) $(2x + y)^2$.
(c) $(c + d)^2$. (f) $(m + 3)^2$. (i) $(2x + 3y)^2$.

2. Sketch squares that are suggested by the following trinomials:

(a) $a^2 + 2ab + b^2$. (e) $m^2 + 8m + 16$.
(b) $x^2 + 2ax + a^2$. (f) $x^2 + 10x + 25$.
(c) $k^2 + 2kr + r^2$. (g) $49 + 14x + x^2$.
(d) $x^2 + 4x + 4$. (h) $c^2 + c + \frac{1}{4}$.

3. Indicate what number has been multiplied by itself to produce

(a) $x^2 + 2xy + y^2$. (c) $x^2 + 6x + 9$.
(b) $r^2 + 4r + 4$. (d) $b^2 + 10b + 25$.

4. What are the factors in the trinomials of Ex. 3?

5. The following list of equations review the fundamental axioms as taught in Chapter I. Solve each equation and check by the methods of Chapter I.

(a) $3(z + 4) = 22 + z$.

(b) $9(a + 35) = 5(2a + 45)$.

(c) $3(x + 15) + 5 = 2(2x + 9) + 4(x + 3)$.

(d) $\dfrac{2(z + 2)}{3} = 8$. (f) $\dfrac{z}{7} - \dfrac{z}{8} = 1$. (h) $\dfrac{m}{3} - \dfrac{m}{5} = 3$.

(e) $\dfrac{s + 7}{7} = \dfrac{s + 11}{14} + 2$. (g) $\dfrac{n}{2} + \dfrac{n}{5} = 2$. (i) $\dfrac{2(x + 2)}{3} = 8$.

128. Evaluation. The area of each of the geometrical figures considered in this chapter has been found to depend upon the dimensions of the figure. This dependence has been expressed by means of formulas, as $A = ab$ in the case of the rectangle. Whenever definite numbers are substituted in the expression ab in order to find the area, A, for a particular rectangle, the expression ab is said to be *evaluated*. This process implies getting practical control of the formulas.

EXERCISES

1. Find the value of A in the formula $A = ab$ when $a = 22.41$ ft. and $b = 23.42$ ft.

2. Find the value of A in the formula $A = \dfrac{ab}{2}$ when $a = 12.41$ ft. and $b = 2.144$ ft.

3. Find the value of A in the formula $A = (a + b)\dfrac{h}{2}$ when $a = 12.42$ ft., $b = 6.43$ ft., and $h = 20.12$ ft.

129. The accuracy of the result. In finding the area in Ex. 1 above we get $A = (22.41)(23.42) = 524.8422$ sq. ft. This is a number with four decimal places. As it stands it claims accuracy to the ten-thousandth of a square foot. The question arises whether this result tells the truth.

Suppose the numbers above represent the length and width respectively of your classroom. Does the product 524.8422 sq. ft. indicate that we actually know the area of the floor accurate to one ten-thousandth of a square foot? Shall we discard some of the decimal places? If so, how many are meaningless? How much of the multiplication was a waste of time and energy? These questions are all involved in the fundamental question. *How many decimal places shall we regard as significant in the process of multiplication?*

It is important that we have a clear understanding of the question. For if we carry along in the process meaningless decimals we are wasting time and energy, and, what is more serious, we are dishonestly claiming for the result an accuracy which it does not have. On the other hand, we are not doing scientific work when we carelessly reject figures that convey information.

The following facts are among those which bear on our problem:

(a) In Art. 26 we pointed out that any number obtained by measurement is an approximation. The application of the area formulas involves the measurement of line segments. Hence an area is an approximation. This fact alone is sufficient to make us exceedingly critical of the result 524.8422 sq. ft. as an absolutely accurate measure of the area of the classroom floor.

(b) If we measure the length of a room with a reliable tape measure and record the result as 23.42 ft., this does not mean that we regard the result as absolutely accurate. If the scale is graduated to hundredths of a foot, it means that 23.42 ft. is the result nearest to the true value. The eye tells us that 23.425 ft. is too high and 23.415 ft. is too low, but that the result may be anywhere between these. Thus, the length of the room lies anywhere between 23.415 ft. and 23.425 ft. Similarly, the width may be anywhere between 22.405 ft. and 22.415 ft. The student should practice measuring objects with a yardstick or a meter stick till the point of this paragraph is clear to him. Test question: How does 2.4 ft. differ from 2.40 ft.?

Multiplying the smallest possible length (23.415 ft.) of the classroom by the smallest width (22.405 ft.) we get a possible area of 524.613075 sq. ft. By multiplying the greatest length (23.425 ft.) by the greatest width (22.415 ft.) we get 525.071375 sq. ft. Subtracting the smallest possible area from the largest possible area gives us a range of over 0.45 of a square foot. In short, the result might be wrong by practically one half of a square foot. We are not actually sure of the third figure from the left. It may be a 4 or a 5. We shall be reasonably near the truth if we record the result simply as 524.8 sq. ft., a number chosen roughly halfway between the largest and smallest possible areas.

It can thus be shown that the product of two approximate four-place numbers is not to be regarded accurate to more than four places.

*130. Abbreviated multiplication. It is apparent in the preceding discussion that it is a waste of time to work out all the partial products in multiplication. It is easier (when the habit is once established) to work out only the partial products which go to make up the significant part of the answer.

Thus, 47.56 × 34.23 may take the following forms:

ABBREVIATED FORM	USUAL METHOD
47.56	By multiplication we get
34.23	47.56
1427	34.23
190	1 | 4268
10	9 | 512
1	190 | 24
1628.	1426 | 8
	1627 | 9788

The difference is accidentally only a little more than 0.02 sq. ft. It can be shown by the method used in the classroom problem (Art. 129) that 1628 is easily in the range of probable areas; that is, we are not actually sure about the fourth figure from the left.

* Hereafter all articles and exercises marked with an asterisk may be omitted without destroying the sequence of the work.

The abbreviated method consists of writing only the significant parts of the usual method (see numbers to left of the line). Add 1 unit when the number to the right is the figure 5 or larger. The method will appear awkward until sufficiently practiced.

A similar discussion concerning accuracy could be given for division. In addition or subtraction it is easy to see that the sum or difference of two numbers cannot be regarded as more accurate than the less accurate of the two numbers. Illustrate the truth of the last statement.

While the discussion of this very important topic has been by no means complete, perhaps enough has been said to fulfill our purpose, which is to make the student exceedingly critical of results involving the significance of decimal places.

EXERCISES

*1. Assuming that the dimensions of a hall are measured with a reliable steel tape and that the dimensions are recorded as 47.56 ft. and 34.23 ft. respectively, show by the method used in Art. 129 that the difference between the smallest and the largest possible area of the hall is actually over four fifths of a square foot.

*2. By means of the abbreviated multiplication method write the product of 46.54 and 32.78; of 23.465 and 34.273.

*3. Multiply by the usual method and compare the short-cut result with this result.

*4. Which result is the more accurate?

SUMMARY

131. This chapter has taught the meaning of the following words and phrases: area, measuring area, unit of area, rhombus, trapezoid, Commutative Law of Multiplication, partial products, parenthesis, formula, formulas.

132. The following formulas have been taught:

(a) $A = ba$. (For the area of a rectangle.)

(b) $A = b^2$. (For the area of a square.)

(c) $A = bh$. (For the area of a parallelogram.)

(d) $A = \dfrac{bh}{2}$. (For the area of a triangle.)

(e) $A = (a + b)\dfrac{h}{2}$. (For the area of a trapezoid.)

(f) $(x + y)^2 = x^2 + 2xy + y^2$. (For the area of a square whose side is $x + y$.)

133. The product of two numbers may be represented geometrically as an area.

134. The algebraic product of a monomial and a polynomial is found by multiplying each term of the polynomial by the monomial and then adding the partial products.

135. The product of two polynomials is the sum of all the partial products obtained by multiplying each term of one polynomial by every term of the other.

*136. We need to be very critical of the number of decimal places that we submit in a result. The product of two approximate four-digit numbers is only approximately correct for four digits.

CHAPTER V

THE EQUATION APPLIED TO VOLUME

137. Solids. The drawings in Fig. 83 represent geometric solids. A solid is commonly thought of as an object that occupies a portion of space. It is separated from

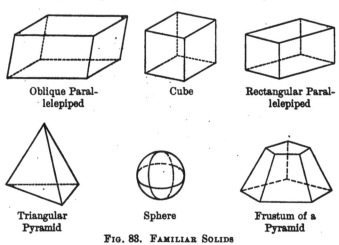

Oblique Paral-
lelepiped   Cube   Rectangular Parallelepiped

Triangular
Pyramid   Sphere   Frustum of a
Pyramid

Fig. 83. Familiar Solids

the surrounding space by its surface. In geometry we study only the form of the solid and its size. We are not interested in color, weight, etc. A solid differs from the figures we have been studying in that it does not lie altogether in a plane, but involves a third dimension. What figures in two dimensions are suggested by the solids in Fig. 83 ? For example, the square is suggested by the cube.

138. Cube. The cube has six faces all of which are squares. Two faces intersect in an *edge*. How many *edges* has a cube? How many *corners*? How is a corner formed?

139. Oblique parallelepiped. The faces of an oblique parallelepiped are all parallelograms. How many faces has it? How many vertices? How many edges?

140. Rectangular parallelepiped. The faces of a rectangular parallelepiped are rectangles.

141. Measurement of volume; unit of volume. When we determine the amount of space inclosed within the surface of a solid we are measuring the *volume* of the solid. To measure the volume of a solid we compare the solid with a cube each of whose edges equals a unit of length. The volume is expressed numerically by the number of times the unit cube goes into the solid. The unit cube is called the *unit of volume.*

142. Formula for the volume of a rectangular parallelepiped. In Fig. 84 a rectangular parallelepiped is shown which is 5 cm. long, 3 cm. wide, and 4 cm. high. The unit cube is represented by K. Since the base of the solid (the face on which it stands) is 5 cm. long and 3 cm. wide, a layer of 3×5 unit cubes could be placed upon it. Since the solid is 4 cm. high, it contains 4 layers of unit cubes; that is, $4 \times 3 \times 5$, or 60, unit cubes. Thus the volume of a rectangular parallelepiped

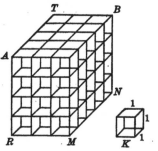

FIG. 84. How to find the Volume of a Rectangular Parallelepiped

is obtained by multiplying the length by the width by the height. This law may be expressed by the formula $V = lwh.$

1. Find the volume of a rectangular parallelepiped if its dimensions are $l = 63$ in., $h = 42$ in., and $w = 56$ in.

*2. If in the preceding discussion the edges of the rectangular parallelepiped had not been given as integral multiples of the unit cube, it would have been necessary temporarily to adopt a smaller unit cube. Show that the formula $V = lwh$ holds when $l = 2.3$ cm., $h = 3.4$ cm., and $w = 1.7$ cm.

HINT. Follow the method suggested in Art. 111.

*3. Show by means of a general discussion that the formula would be true if $l = 3\frac{1}{4}$, $h = 2\frac{1}{8}$, $w = 3\frac{3}{5}$.

HINT. See Ex. 3, Art. 112.

*143. Volume of an oblique parallelepiped. Fig. 85 shows in a general way the method used in a more advanced mathematics course to show that the formula $V = lwh$ holds

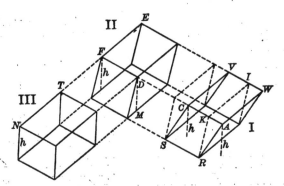

FIG. 85. MODEL ILLUSTRATING HOW TO FIND THE VOLUME OF AN OBLIQUE PARALLELEPIPED

even for an oblique parallelepiped. Parallelepiped III is a rectangular parallelepiped, and we know the formula holds for it. Parallelepiped II is a right parallelepiped (it has four rectangular faces, and two are parallelograms) and by advanced methods is shown equal to parallelepiped III. Parallelepiped I is oblique and is shown equal to parallelepiped II. Since parallelepiped I equals parallelepiped II, and parallelepiped II in turn equals parallelepiped III, the formula holds for parallelepiped I. The student should not be concerned if he cannot fully understand this discussion. He should be ready to apply the formula for an oblique parallelepiped when the need for it arises in shop or factory just as he does many principles of arithmetic.

EXERCISES

*1. It will be easy for some student to make models of the preceding figures in the shop. Thus, to show parallelepiped II equal to parallelepiped III construct parallelepiped II and drop a perpendicular from D to the base. Then saw along the edges MD and DF. Place the slab obtained on the right side, and parallelepiped II will look exactly like parallelepiped III. This will be helpful to your classmates, and you will find the exercise easy and interesting.

*2. A much more difficult and interesting exercise is to make parallelepiped I look like parallelepiped III.

HINT. Construct $RK \perp$ to AC and $KI \perp$ to AC. Saw along the edges RK and KI and place the slab obtained on the left side. Now the figure will be transformed to parallelepiped II. Continue as in Ex. 1 to make parallelepiped I look like parallelepiped III.

3. A rectangular reservoir 120 ft. long and 20 ft. wide contains water to a depth of 10.5 ft. A second reservoir 125 ft. long and 18 ft. wide contains water to a depth of 36.5 ft. How much more water is there in the second reservoir than in the first?

4. A rectangular tank 6 ft. long, 4 ft. wide, and 5 ft. deep is to be lined with zinc $\frac{1}{8}$ in. thick. How many cubic feet of zinc will be required if 4 sq. ft. are allowed for overlapping?

5. If 1 cu. in. of pure gold beaten into gold leaf will cover 30,000 sq. ft. of surface, what is the thickness of the gold leaf?

6. An open tank is made of iron $\frac{1}{4}$ in. thick. The outer dimensions are as follows: length, 3 ft.; width, 1 ft. 9 in.; height, 2 ft. If 1 cu. ft. of iron weighs 460 lb., find the weight of the tank.

7. In a rainfall of 1 in. how many tons of water fall upon an acre of ground if 1 cu. ft. of water weighs 62.5 lb.?

144. Formula for the volume of a cube. The volume of a cube is computed in the same way as that of a parallelepiped. The cube is a special case in the sense that the length, width, and height are all equal. Hence, if s equals an edge of a cube, the volume may be expressed by the formula $V = s \times s \times s$. The formula $V = s \times s \times s$ may be written more briefly $V = s^3$ (read "V equals s cube"); s^3 being an abbreviated form of $s \times s \times s$. The formula may be translated into the following law: *The volume of a cube equals the cube of an edge.*

EXERCISES

1. Find the volume of a cube whose edge is $\frac{1}{8}$ in.; $\frac{1}{4}$ in.; $\frac{1}{2}$ in.

2. Find the volume of a cube whose edge is $1\frac{1}{4}$ in.; 2.2 cm.; 3 in.; 1 m.; 0.01 m.

145. Equal factors; exponents; base; power. The products of two equal dimensions and three equal dimensions have been represented by the area of a square and the volume of a cube respectively. Hence the notation "a square" and "s cube." The product of four equal factors cannot be represented geometrically, though you may already have heard people talk vaguely about the fourth dimension. However, the product of four equal algebraic factors, say $s \times s \times s \times s$, is as definite as $2 \times 2 \times 2 \times 2$

in arithmetic. Thus, we extend the process indefinitely in algebra and write $s \times s \times s \times s = s^4$ (read "s fourth") or $b \times b \times b \times b \times b = b^5$ (read "b fifth"), etc.

The term b^5 is obviously much more convenient than $b \times b \times b \times b \times b$. The 5 in b^5 is called an *exponent*. It is *a small number written to the right and a little above another number to show how many times that number is to be used as a factor*. In 5^3 (meaning $5 \times 5 \times 5$) the 3 is the *exponent*, the number 5 is the *base*, and the product of $5 \times 5 \times 5$ is the *power*. Thus, 125, or 5^3, is the third power of 5. When no exponent is written, as in x, the exponent is understood to be 1. Thus, in $2\,xy$ both x and y are each to be used only once as a factor. The meaning is the same as if the term were written $2\,x^1y^1$.

1. State clearly the difference between a coefficient and an exponent. Illustrate with arithmetical numbers.

2. Letting $a = 5$, give the meaning and the value of each of the following numbers:

(a) $3\,a$. (c) $2\,a$. (e) $4\,a$. (g) $5\,a$. (i) $2\,a^2$. (k) $4\,a^2$.

(b) a^3. (d) a^2. (f) a^4. (h) a^5. (j) $3\,a^2$. (l) $2\,a^4$.

3. Write the following products in briefest form:

$$y \cdot y \cdot y \cdot y \cdot y; \quad \frac{1}{5} \cdot \frac{1}{5} \cdot \frac{1}{5} \cdot \frac{1}{5}; \quad \frac{3}{5} \cdot \frac{3}{5} \cdot \frac{3}{5} x \cdot x; \quad \frac{a}{b} \cdot \frac{a}{b} \cdot \frac{a}{b};$$

$2\frac{1}{3} \cdot 2\frac{1}{3} \cdot 2\frac{1}{3}; \quad 5 \cdot 4 \cdot 4 \cdot 5 \cdot 3 \cdot 3 \cdot 3 \cdot x \cdot x \cdot y \cdot y \cdot y$.

4. Find the value of 2^8; 6^3; $(\frac{1}{2})^4$; 3^5; $(1.3)^2$; 9^3; $(0.03)^3$; $(1.1)^3$.

5. Letting $m = 2$ and $n = 3$, find the value of the following polynomials: $m^2 + 2\,mn + n^2$; $m^3 + 3\,m^2n + 3\,mn^2 + n^3$; $5(m^2 + 2\,mn + n^2)$; $5(m + n)$; $6(2\,m^3 + 3\,m^2 + 4\,mn + n + 3)$.

6. Find the value of the following numbers, where $z = 3$:

(a) $2z$; (b) z^2; (c) $(2z)^2$; (d) $2z^2$; (e) $3z^2$; (f) $(3z)^2$; (g) $(3z)^2$.

7. Letting $x = 1$, $y = 2$, $z = 3$, and $u = 4$, find the value of the following:

$$\frac{xy + xz + yu + zu}{x + y + z + u} ; \quad \frac{x^4 + 4x^3y + 6x^2y^2 + 4xy^3 + y^4}{xy}.$$

146. Exponents important. Since the subject of exponents is fundamental to a clear understanding of two very important labor-saving devices, namely the slide rule and logarithms, which we shall presently study, it is necessary to study the laws of exponents very carefully.

147. Product of powers having the same exponents. The law to be used in this type may be illustrated by the problem, "Multiply a^2 by a^3." The expression a^2 means $a \cdot a$, or aa, and the expression a^3 means $a \cdot a \cdot a$, or aaa. Hence $a^2 \cdot a^3$ means $aa \cdot aaa$, or, in short, a^5.

EXERCISE

In each case give orally the product in briefest form:

(a) $3^2 \cdot 3^3$.   (i) $x^3 \cdot x^6$.   (q) $x^2 \cdot m$.
(b) $6 \cdot 6^3$.   (j) $ax \cdot x$.   (r) $5 \cdot 5 \cdot x \cdot x^3$.
(c) $5^2 \cdot 5^4$.   (k) $b \cdot c \cdot b$.   (s) $4 b^2 c \cdot 5 b^3 c^3$.
(d) $10 \cdot 10^3$.   (l) $b \cdot b$.   (t) $xyz \cdot x^2yz^2 \cdot 2 xy^2z^3$.
(e) $x \cdot x^2$.   (m) $e \cdot e \cdot 2 \cdot 2$.   (u) $(2 xy)^2$.
(f) $12^2 \cdot 12^5$.   (n) $c \cdot c^3$.   (v) $(2 x^3y^2)^3$.
(g) $x^2 \cdot x^3$.   (o) $x \cdot x^5$.   (w) $(3 x^2y)^2$.
(h) $x \cdot x^4$.   (p) $m \cdot x^2$.   (x) $3 \cdot 5 \cdot 2 \cdot 5 \cdot 2 \cdot 3^3$.

The exercise above shows that the *product of two or more factors having the same base is a number whose base is the same as that of the factors and whose exponent is the sum of the exponents of the factors*; thus, $b^2 \cdot b^3 \cdot b^5 = b^{10}$.

148. Quotient of powers having the same base. *The quotient of two factors* having the same base may be simplified by the method used in the following problem:

Divide b^5 by b^2.

HINT. Since a fraction indicates a division, this quotient may be indicated in the form $\dfrac{b^5}{b^2}$.

Solution.
$$\frac{b^5}{b^2} = \frac{b \cdot b \cdot b \cdot b \cdot b}{b \; b}.$$

Hence, dividing numerator and denominator by $b \cdot b$, or b^2,

$$\frac{b^5}{b^2} = b \cdot b \cdot b = b^3.$$

EXERCISE

In each case give orally the quotient in briefest form:

(a) $\dfrac{2^{10}}{2^6}$.

(b) $\dfrac{5^6}{5^2}$.

(c) $b^7 \div b^2$.

(d) $b^6 \div b^2$.

(e) $b^{15} \div b^3$.

(f) $b^{15} \div b^{12}$.

(g) $x^6 \div x^2$.

(h) $x^6 \div x^3$.

(i) $x^8 \div x^7$.

(j) $x^{21} \div x^{17}$.

The preceding exercise shows that the *quotient obtained by dividing a power by another power having the same base is a number whose base is the common base of the given powers and whose exponent is obtained by subtracting the exponent of the divisor from the exponent of the dividend.*

Thus, $x^{10} \div x^3 = x^7$. Here x^7 has the same base as the dividend x^{10} and the divisor x^3; and its exponent, 7, is obtained by subtracting 3 from 10.

149. Review list of problems involving application of algebraic principles to geometric figures. The following exercises are intended to help the student to see how to apply algebraic principles to geometric figures.

EXERCISES

1. Find an algebraic number which will express the sum of the edges of the solid in Fig. 86.

2. If the sum of the edges of the solid in Fig. 86 is 172, what are the actual dimensions of the solid?

3. Find an algebraic expression for the total surface of the solid in Fig. 86. Also for the volume.

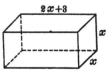

FIG. 86

4. What is the total surface and volume of the solid in Fig. 86 if x equals 10?

5. Express algebraically the sum of the edges of the cube in Fig. 87.

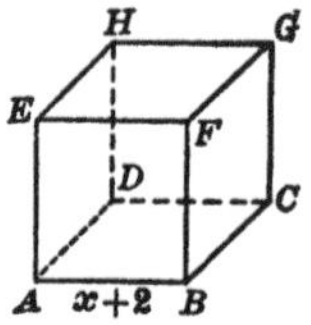

6. If the sum of the edges of the cube in Fig. 87 is 112, what is the length of one edge?

7. Express algebraically the total surface and volume of the cube in Fig. 87.

FIG. 87

8. What is the total surface of the cube in Fig. 87 if $x = 2$?

9. The edge of a tetrahedron (Fig. 88) is denoted by $2x + \frac{3}{4}$. Express algebraically the sum of all the edges of the tetrahedron.

NOTE. A tetrahedron is a figure all of whose edges are equal and whose faces are equal equilateral triangles.

FIG. 88

10. Find the length of an edge of the tetrahedron in Fig. 88 if the sum of the edges is 40.5 cm.

11. Fig. 89 shows a frustum of a *pyramid*. The upper and lower bases are equilateral pentagons; the sides are trapezoids with the edges denoted as in the figure. Find the sum of all the edges. If e equals 2, what is the sum of the edges?

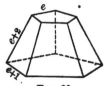

FIG. 89

RENÉ DESCARTES

HISTORICAL NOTE. The idea of using exponents to mark the power to which a quantity was raised was due to René Descartes, the French philosopher (1596–1650). It is interesting to read of the struggle for centuries on the part of mathematicians to obtain some simple method of writing a power of a number. Thus, we read of the Hindu mathematician Bhaskara (1114–   ) using the initials of the Hindu words " square " and " solid " as denoting the second and third power of the unknown numbers in problems, which he gave a practical setting with many references to fair damsels and gallant warriors. In the following centuries a great variety of symbols for powers are used; for example, arcs, circles, etc., until we come to a French lawyer, François Vieta (1540–1603), who wrote on mathematics as a pastime. Vieta did much to standardize the notation of algebra. Thus, in the matter of exponents he employed " A quadratus," " A cubus," to represent x^2 and x^3, instead of introducing a new letter for each power. From this point it is only a step to Descartes's method.

The biographies of the three mathematicians Bhaskara, Vieta, and Descartes are exceedingly interesting. Thus, you may enjoy reading of Bhaskara's syncopated algebra in verse, in which many of the problems are addressed to "lovely and dear Lilavati" (his daughter) by way of consolation when he forbade her marriage.

You may read of Vieta's being summoned to the court of Henry IV of France to solve a problem which involved the 45th power of x. The problem had been sent as a challenge to all mathematicians in the empire. Vieta appeared in a few moments and gave the king two correct solutions. Next King Henry asked Vieta to decipher the Spanish military code, containing over six hundred unknown characters, which was periodically changed. King Henry gave the cipher to Vieta, who succeeded in finding the solution to the system, which the French held greatly to their profit during the war.

Or you may read of Descartes, a member of the nobility, who found the years of his army life exceedingly irksome, for he craved leisure for mathematical studies. He resigned his commission in 1621 and gave his time to travel and study. In 1637 he wrote a book, " Discourse on Methods." In this text he made considerable advance toward the system of exponents now used. The text shows that he realized the close relation existing between geometry and algebra. He is often called " the father of modern algebra."

12. A tetrahedron may be constructed from a figure like Fig. 90. Draw the figure on cardboard, using a larger scale. Cut out the figure along the heavy lines; then fold along the dotted lines. Join the edges by means of gummed paper.

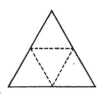

FIG. 90. HOW TO CONSTRUCT A TETRAHEDRON

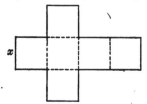

FIG. 91. HOW TO CONSTRUCT A CUBE

13. The cube may be constructed from a figure like Fig. 91. Draw the figure on cardboard, using a larger scale; for example, let $x = 3$ cm. Cut out the figure along the heavy lines, then fold along the dotted lines. Join the edges by means of gummed paper. This will form a model of a cube.

14. Measure the edge of the cube constructed for Ex. 13 and compute the area of the whole surface. Find the volume also.

15. A rectangular parallelepiped may be constructed from

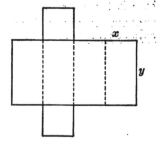

FIG. 92. HOW TO CONSTRUCT A RECTANGULAR PARALLELEPIPED

a figure like Fig. 92. Compute the volume of the solid and the area of the surface.

SUMMARY

150. This chapter has taught the meaning of the following words and phrases: a solid, surface of a solid, volume of a solid, unit of volume, cube, parallelepiped, rectangular parallelepiped, right parallelepiped, oblique parallelepiped, triangular pyramid, exponent, base, power, tetrahedron.

151. The volume of a solid is determined by applying the unit cube to see how many times it is contained in the solid. The process is essentially comparison. The unit cube is a cube each of whose edges is one unit long.

152. The following formulas have been used:

$$v = lwh,$$
$$v = s^3.$$

153. The product of factors having a common base equals a number whose base is the same as the factors and whose exponent is the sum of the exponents of the factors.

154. The quotient obtained by dividing a power by another power having the same base is a number whose base is the common base of the given powers and whose exponent is obtained by subtracting the exponent of the divisor from the exponent of the dividend.

CHAPTER VI

THE EQUATION APPLIED TO FUNDAMENTAL ANGLE RELATIONS

155. Fundamental angle relations. In Chapter III we discussed the different kinds of angles and the methods of constructing them. In this chapter we shall study some of the fundamental relations between angles and see how the equation is applied to them.

156. Relation of exterior sides of supplementary adjacent angles. Draw two adjacent angles of 64° and 116°, of 75° and 105°, of 157° and 23°. What is the sum of each pair? What is the relation of the exterior sides of each pair?

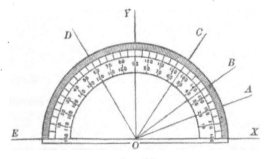

FIG. 93

157. Important geometric relation. The preceding article illustrates the following geometric relation: *If the sum of two adjacent angles is a straight angle, their exterior sides form a straight line.*

111

1. Show that the geometric relation stated in Art. 157 agrees with the definition of a straight angle (Art. 61).

2. In Fig. 93 read the number of degrees in angles XOA, XOB, XOC, XOY, XOD, XOE.

3. What is the sum of $\angle XOA$ and $\angle AOB$?

4. Express $\angle XOD$ as the sum of two angles.

5. Express $\angle AOB$ as the difference of two angles.

6. Express $\angle XOE$ as the sum of three angles.

158. Sum of all the angles about a point on one side of a straight line. Draw a line AB and choose a point
P on it. Draw lines PR,
PS, and PT as shown in
Fig. 94 and find the sum
of the four angles formed.
Estimate first and then
measure with the pro-
tractor. What seems to
be the correct sum? Ex-

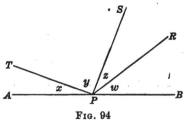

Fig. 94

press the sum of the angles x, y, z, and w by means of
an equation. Give a word statement for the equation.

159. Important geometric relation. Art. 158 illustrates
the truth of the geometric relation that *the sum of all the
angles about a point on one side of a straight line is a straight
angle (180°).*

1. Find the value of x and the size of each angle in Fig. 95.

2. In the following examples each expression represents one
of the angles into which all the angular space about a point
on one side of a straight line has been divided. Write an
equation expressing the sum of all the angles, solve for x,

and find the size of each angle in degrees. Draw figures to illustrate your results in the first three examples.

(a) x, $3x$, $5x + 9$.
(b) $3x$, $4x - 10$, $33 - 2x$, $10x + 7$.
(c) $2x + 18\frac{1}{3}$, $5x + 9\frac{1}{6}$, $8\frac{1}{2} + x$.
(d) $2(x + 5)$, $3x + 24$, $2(35 + x)$.
(e) $5.83x$, $3.94x$, $1.27x + 11.55$, $138.45 - 8.04x$.

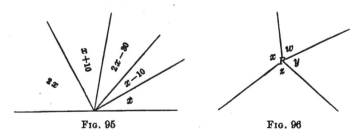

FIG. 95   FIG. 96

160. Sum of all the angles about a point in a plane. If we choose a point in a plane, as P in Fig. 96, and from this point draw four lines so as to make four angles, we can measure these angles and thus determine the sum of all the angles in a plane about a point.

EXERCISES

1. Measure the angles in Fig. 96 and write an equation expressing their sum.

2. What is another way to show that the sum of the angles that exactly fill a plane about a point is two straight angles (360°)? See the definition of a perigon (Art. 61).

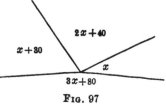

FIG. 97

3. Find the value of x and the size of each angle in Fig. 97.

4. The expressions in the following examples represent the angles into which the angular space about a point in a plane has been divided. Find the size of each angle.

(a) $3x$, x, $2x + 35$, $125 - x$.

(b) $2x$, $72 + 3x$, $4x - 10$, 118.

(c) $10x + 20\frac{1}{2}$, $35\frac{1}{2} - x$, $8x + 49$.

(d) $5x$, $3x + 27\frac{2}{3}$, $7x - 20$, $9x + 112\frac{1}{8}$.

(e) $x + 1$, $7(x + 1)$, $3(35 + x)$, $2x + 169$.

(f) $3x$, $117 + 15x$, $9x - 27$.

(g) $14x + 48$, $28x + 106\frac{3}{4}$, $133\frac{1}{4} - 6x$.

The first two exercises in this article show that *the sum of all the angles about a point in a plane is 360°.*

161. Left side of an angle; right side of an angle. If in Fig. 98 we imagine ourselves standing at the vertex of $\angle ABC$ and looking off over the angular space, say in the direction BD, then the side BC is called the *left side* of the angle (because it lies on our left), and the side BA is called the *right side* of the angle.

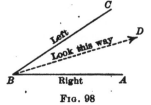

Fig. 98

162. Notation. In lettering angles and figures it is often desirable to denote angles or lines that have certain characteristic likenesses by the same letter so as to identify them more easily. It is clear that to use l for the left side of one angle and the same l for the left side of another angle in the same discussion might be misleading. In order to be clear, therefore, we let l_1 stand for the left side of one angle, l_2 stand for the left side of a second angle, and l_3 stand for the left side of a third angle, etc. Then the three sides would be read "l sub-one," "l sub-two," "l sub-three," etc.

163. Important geometric relation. Two angles, x_1 and x_2, in Fig. 99, are drawn so that their sides are parallel left to left and right to . right. How do they seem to compare in size ? Check your estimate by measuring with a protractor. Give an argument showing that $x_1 = x_2$.

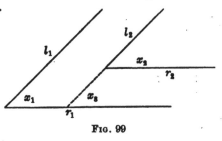

FIG. 99

This article shows that *if two angles have their sides parallel left to left and right to right, the angles are equal.*

Draw freehand two obtuse angles so that their sides will look parallel left to left and right to right. (The angles should be approximately equal. Are they ?)

HINT. Take two points for vertices and in each case imagine yourself standing at the point. Draw the left sides to your left and the right sides to your right. Assume the drawing correct and prove the angles equal.

164. Important geometric relation. Two angles, x and y, in Fig. 100, have been drawn so that their sides are parallel left to right and right to left. What relation seems to exist between them ? Measure each with a protractor. Give an argument showing that $x + y = 180°$.

This article shows that *if two angles have their sides parallel left to right and right to left, their sum is a straight angle.*

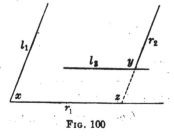

FIG. 100

Practice drawing freehand a pair of angles whose sides are parallel according to the conditions in the theorem of Art. 164. Is the sum approximately 180° ?

165. Supplementary angles; supplement. Two angles whose sum is equal to a straight angle (180°) are said to be *supplementary angles.* Each angle is called the *supplement* of the other.

Fɪɢ. 101

166. Supplementary adjacent angles. Place two supplementary angles adjacent to each other as in Fig. 101. Angles so placed are called *supplementary adjacent* angles.

EXERCISES

1. In Fig. 101 what is the angle whose supplement is $\angle x$?

2. In Fig. 102 are several angles, some pairs of which are supplementary. Make tracings of these angles on paper and by placing them adjacent decide which pairs are supplementary.

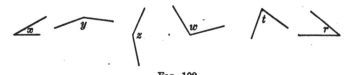

Fɪɢ. 102

3. State whether the following pairs of angles are supplementary: 40° and 140°; 30° and 150°; 35° and 135°; 55° and 135°.

4. How many degrees are there in the supplement of an angle of 30°? of 90°? of 150°? of x°?

5. What is the supplement of y°? of z°? of $3 w$°? of $\dfrac{2 s°}{3}$?

6. Write the equation which expresses the fact that $y°$ and $130°$ are supplementary and solve for the value of y.

7. Write equations that will show that each of the following pairs of angles are supplementary:

    (a) $y°$ and $80°$.   (d) $30°$ and $y° + 40°$.

    (b) $90°$ and $z°$.   (e) $3y° + 5°$ and $12y° - 4°$.

    (c) $x°$ and $y°$.   (f) $\frac{2}{3}x°$ and $1\frac{4}{5}x° + 75\frac{1}{3}°$.

8. Two supplementary angles have the values $2x° + 25°$ and $x° + 4°$. Find x and the size of each angle.

.9. What is the size of each of two supplementary angles if one is $76°$ larger than the other?

10. One of two supplementary angles is $33°$ smaller than the other. Find the number of degrees in each.

11. What is the number of degrees in each of two supplementary angles whose difference is $95°$?

12. Find the value of x and the angles in the following supplementary pairs:

    (a) $x°$ and $6x°$.

    (b) $2x°$ and $3x° + 2°$.

    (c) $4\frac{1}{2}x°$ and $6x°$.

    (d) $2x° + 5°$ and $7x° - 8°$.

13. Write the following expressions in algebraic language:

    (a) Twice an angle y.

    (b) Four times an angle, plus $17°$.

    (c) $23°$ added to double an angle.

    (d) Seven times an angle, minus $14°$.

    (e) $45°$ less than an angle.

    (f) $52°$ subtracted from four times an angle.

    (g) Twice the sum of an angle and $10°$.

    (h) One half the difference of $22°$ and $x°$.

14. If an angle is added to one half its supplement, the sum is $100°$. Find the supplementary angles.

15. If an angle is increased by 5° and if one fourth of its supplement is increased by 25°, the sum of the angles thus obtained is 90°. Find the supplementary angles.

16. Construct the supplement of a given angle.

17. Find the size of each of the following adjacent pairs of supplementary angles :

(a) $\frac{2}{3}x$, $112 + \frac{1}{3}x$.

(d) $\frac{3x}{2} - 60$, $130 - \frac{2}{5}x$.

(b) $\frac{5}{6}x + 32$, $88 - \frac{1}{6}x$.

(e) $2(x + 10)$, $\frac{3x + 68}{2}$.

(c) $\frac{x}{2} + 150$, $\frac{x}{3} - 10$.

(f) $65 + \frac{2x}{3}$, $92 + \frac{3x}{7}$.

167. Construction problem. To construct the supplements of two equal angles.

Construction. Let x and y be the given angles. Construct $\angle z$, the supplement of $\angle x$, adjacent to it (Fig. 103). In the same manner construct $\angle w$, the supplement of $\angle y$.

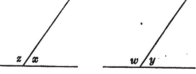

FIG. 103. How to construct the Supplements of Two Given Angles

Compare the supplements of $\angle x$ and $\angle y$ and show that $\angle z = \angle w$.

This article shows that the *supplements of equal angles are equal.*

EXERCISES

1. Prove the preceding fact by an algebraic method.

HINT. In Fig. 103 prove that if $\angle x + \angle z = 180°$ and $\angle y + \angle w = 180°$, then $\angle z = \angle w$.

2. Are supplements of the same angle equal? Why?

3. Show that the bisectors of two supplementary adjacent angles are perpendicular to each other; for example, in Fig. 104 show that $\angle x + \angle y = 90°$.

4. In Fig. 104, if $\angle BOD = 60°$ and $\angle AOD = 120°$, find the size of $\angle x$ and $\angle y$.

*5. The following examples furnish a review. In each case solve for the value of the unknown, and check.

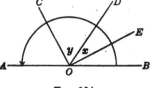

Fig. 104

(a) $\dfrac{2x}{3} + 75 + \dfrac{x}{3} = 150.$

(e) $2(x + 4) + \dfrac{x + 2}{3} = 9.$

(b) $\dfrac{4}{5}y + 15 - \dfrac{2}{3}y = 17.$

(f) $3(y + 3) + y - 4 = 11.$

(c) $\dfrac{z}{2} + 15 + \dfrac{z}{3} - 12 = 8.$

(g) $\dfrac{x + 9}{2} + 7 = 12.$

(d) $\dfrac{3}{5}t - 16 + \dfrac{2}{3}t = 3.$

(h) $\dfrac{5x - 2}{7} - 2 = \dfrac{9}{7}.$

168. Complementary angles. If the sum of two angles is a right angle, the two angles are called *complementary angles*. Each angle is called the *complement* of the other. Thus, in Fig. 105 $\angle x$ is the complement of $\angle y$.

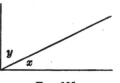

Fig. 105

EXERCISES

1. What is the complement of 30°? of 60°?

2. Are 23° and 57° complementary? 32° and 58°?

3. Draw two complementary angles of 40° and 50° and place them adjacent. Check the construction.

4. What is the relation existing between the exterior sides of two adjacent complementary angles?

5. In Fig. 106 decide by means of tracing paper which pairs of angles seem to be complementary.

6. What are the complements of the following angles: $20°$? $50°$? $12\frac{1}{2}°$? $48\frac{2}{3}°$? $x°$? $3y°$? $\dfrac{3z°}{4}$?

7. $40°$ is the complement of $y°$. How many degrees does y represent?

8. Write the equation which says in algebraic language that $x°$ and $50°$ are complementary and solve for the value of x.

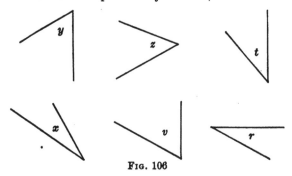

FIG. 106

9. In the equation $x° + y° = 90°$ is there more than one possible pair of values of x and y? Explain.

10. Write equations that will express the fact that the following pairs of angles are complementary:

(a) $x°$ and $40°$. (c) $x° + 25°$ and $x° - 30°$.

(b) $35°$ and $y°$. (d) $2x° - 3°$ and $3x° + 8°$.

11. Write the following expressions in algebraic language:

(a) The sum of angle x and angle y.

(b) Four times an angle, increased by $15°$.

(c) $85°$ diminished by two times an angle.

(d) Five times the sum of an angle and $13°$.

(e) Three times the difference between an angle and $12°$.

(f) Four times an angle, minus $6°$.

12. Find two complementary angles such that one is 32° larger than the other.

13. Find two complementary angles such that one is 41° smaller than the other.

14. Find the number of degrees in the angle x if it is the complement of $3x°$; of $5x°$; of $8\frac{1}{2}x°$.

15. Find the number of degrees in the angle x if it is the complement of twice itself; of five times itself; of one third itself.

16. Construct the complement of a given acute angle.

169. Construction problem. To construct the complements of two equal acute angles.

Construction. Let $\angle x$ and $\angle y$ be the given angles. Draw the complement of $\angle x$ adjacent to it (Fig. 107). Do the same for $\angle y$.

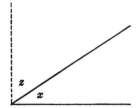 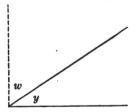

FIG. 107. HOW TO CONSTRUCT THE COMPLEMENTS OF TWO GIVEN ANGLES

Compare the complements of $\angle x$ and y and show that $\angle z = \angle w$.

This construction problem shows that *complements of equal angles are equal.*

EXERCISES

1. Prove the preceding relation by an algebraic method.

2. Does it follow that complements of the same angle are equal? Why?

170. Vertical angles. Draw two intersecting straight lines AB and CD as in Fig. 108. The angles x and z are called *vertical*, or *opposite*, angles. Note that vertical angles have a common vertex and that their sides lie in the same straight line but in opposite directions. Thus, *vertical angles* are angles which have a common vertex and their sides lying in the same straight line but in opposite directions. Are w and y in Fig. 109 vertical angles?

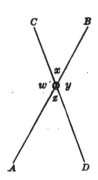

Fig. 108. Vertical Angles

EXERCISES

(Exs. 1–6 refer to Fig. 108)

1. Make a tracing of $\angle x$ and $\angle z$ and compare them as to size.

2. Check your estimate in Ex. 1 by measuring the two angles with a protractor.

3. What is the sum of $\angle x$ and $\angle y$? of $\angle z$ and $\angle y$?

4. Show that $x + y = z + y$.

5. How does Ex. 4 help in obtaining the relation between x and z? What is this relation?

6. Show that $y + x = x + w$ and from this that $y = w$.

The six exercises above show that *if two lines intersect, the vertical angles are equal.*

171. Value of mathematical thinking. The preceding relation between vertical angles is of course so easily seen that in most cases the truth would be granted even without measuring the angles involved. However, the discussion in Exs. 3–6 above is another simple illustration of the power of mathematical thinking which makes the discovery of new truths rest finally on nonmeasurement, that is to say, on an intellectual basis. This type of thinking will be used to an increasing extent in subsequent work.

1. Upon what does the proof (Exs. 3–6, Art. 170) of the geometric relation concerning vertical angles rest?

2. Find x and the size of each angle in Fig. 109.

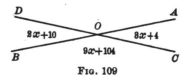

FIG. 109

First method. Since vertical angles are equal,

$$\angle AOC = \angle DOB.$$

Then $\qquad 3x + 4 = 2x + 10.$

Subtracting 4 from each member,

$$3x = 2x + 6.$$

Subtracting $2x$ from each member,

$$x = 6.$$

Substituting 6 for x, $\quad 3x + 4 = 3 \cdot 6 + 4 = 22,$

$$2x + 10 = 2 \cdot 6 + 10 = 22,$$

$$9x + 104 = 9 \cdot 6 + 104 = 158 \text{ (for } \angle BOC),$$

and since vertical angles are equal,

$$\angle AOD = 158.$$

Check. $22 + 22 + 158 + 158 = 360°.$

Second method. By definition of supplementary angles,

$$3x + 4 + 9x + 104 = 180.$$

Solving, $\qquad x = 6.$

The remainder of the work is the same as that of the first method.

3. Find the values of the unknowns and each of the following vertical angles made by two intersecting straight lines :

(a) $3x + 15$ and $5x - 5$.

(b) $x + 105$ and $3x + 15$.

(c) $x - 10$ and $2x - 160$.

(d) $\dfrac{3y}{5} + 18\frac{1}{2}$ and $\dfrac{2y}{5} + 21\frac{1}{2}$.

(e) $\dfrac{3}{4}z - 8$ and $\dfrac{z}{4} + 12$.

(f) $\frac{1}{2}x + \frac{7}{2}x$ and $\frac{3}{2}x + 55$.

(g) $3x + \dfrac{5x}{4}$ and $\dfrac{5x}{2} + 14$.

(h) $\dfrac{y}{3} + \dfrac{y}{6}$ and $\dfrac{y}{4} + 18$.

(i) $\dfrac{8x}{3} - \dfrac{3x}{4}$ and $\dfrac{2x}{3} + 11\frac{1}{4}$.

172. Alternate-interior angles. In Fig. 110 the angles x and y, formed by the lines AB, CD, and the transversal EF, are called *alternate-interior angles* (on alternate sides of EF and interior with respect to AB and CD).

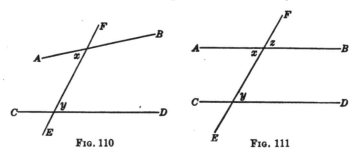

FIG. 110   FIG. 111

EXERCISES

(Exs. 1-4 refer to Fig. 111)

1. Measure and compare $\angle x$ and $\angle y$.

2. The lines AB and CD and FE are drawn so that $\angle x = \angle y$. What seems to be the relation between the lines AB and CD?

3. Show that if $\angle x = \angle y$, then $\angle y = \angle z$.

4. Show that AB is parallel to CD (see the definition for parallel lines, Art. 87).

Exercises 1–4 show that *if the alternate-interior angles formed by two lines and a transversal are equal, the lines are parallel.*

The proof may take the following brief form:

Proof. In Fig. 111, $\angle x = \angle y$ (given). $\angle x = \angle z$ (vertical angles are equal). Then $\angle y = \angle z$ (things equal to the same thing are equal to each other). Therefore $AB \parallel CD$ (by definition of $\parallel$ lines, Art. 87).

EXERCISE

In Fig. 112 construct a line through P parallel to the line AB by making an alternate-interior angle equal to $\angle x$. Show why the lines are parallel.

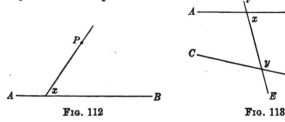

FIG. 112   FIG. 113

173. Interior angles on the same side of the transversal. In Fig. 113 angles x and y are called *interior angles on the same side of the transversal.*

EXERCISES

1. Measure angles x and y in Fig. 113 and find their sum.

2. In Fig. 114 the lines are drawn so that $\angle x + \angle y = 180°$. What seems to be the relation between AB and CD?

3. Prove that, *if the interior angles on the same side of a transversal between two parallel lines are supplementary, the lines are parallel.*

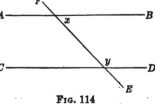

FIG. 114

4. In Fig. 115 select all the pairs of corresponding angles, alternate-interior angles, and interior angles on the same side of the transversal.

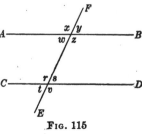

FIG. 115

174. Important theorems relating to parallel lines. The following exercises include theorems which supplement the work of Arts. 172 and 173.

EXERCISES

1. Show by reference to the definition of parallel lines in Art. 87 that if two parallel lines are cut by a transversal, the corresponding angles are equal.

2. Show that if two parallel lines are cut by a transversal, the alternate-interior angles are equal.

3. Show that if two parallel lines are cut by a transversal, the interior angles on the same side of the transversal are supplementary.

4. Two parallel lines are cut by a transversal so as to form angles as shown in Fig. 116. Find x and the size of all the eight angles in the figure.

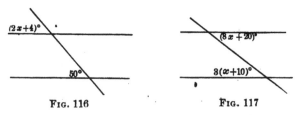

FIG. 116   FIG. 117

5. Find x and all the eight angles in Fig. 117.

6. Draw two parallel lines and a transversal. Select all the equal pairs of angles; all the supplementary pairs.

175. Outline of angle pairs formed by two lines cut by a transversal. When two lines are cut by a transversal, as in Fig. 118,

the angles of the
angle pairs
$\begin{cases} a \text{ and } e \\ b \text{ and } f \\ d \text{ and } h \\ c \text{ and } g \end{cases}$ are called *corresponding* angles;

angles *c, d, e, f* are called *interior* angles;
angles *a, b, g, h* are called *exterior* angles;

the angles of the
angle pairs
$\begin{cases} d \text{ and } e \\ c \text{ and } f \end{cases}$ are called *interior* angles on the *same side* of the transversal;

the angles of the
angle pairs
$\begin{cases} d \text{ and } f \\ c \text{ and } e \end{cases}$ on *opposite* sides of the transversal are called *alternate-interior* angles;

the angles of the
angle pairs
$\begin{cases} b \text{ and } h \\ a \text{ and } g \end{cases}$ on *opposite* sides of the transversal are called *alternate-exterior* angles.

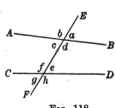

Fɪɢ. 118

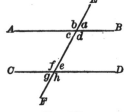

Fɪɢ. 119

The student should remember

(a) that corresponding angles are equal,
(b) that alternate-interior angles are equal,
(c) that alternate-exterior angles are equal,
(d) that interior angles on the same side of
the transversal are supplementary,

only when the lines cut by the transversal are parallel (Fig. 119).

SUMMARY

176. This chapter has taught the meaning of the following words and phrases: left side of an angle, right side of an angle, parallel right to right and left to left, parallel right to left and left to right, supplementary angles, supplement, supplementary-adjacent angles, complementary angles, complement, vertical angles, alternate-interior angles, interior angles on the same side of the transversal.

177. The following fundamental constructions have been presented:

1. How to construct the supplement of a given angle.

2. How to construct the supplements of two equal given angles.

3. How to construct the complement of a given angle.

4. How to construct the complements of two equal angles.

5. A new method of drawing parallel lines.

6. How to form vertical angles.

178. This chapter has discussed the following fundamental geometric relations:

1. If the sum of two adjacent angles is a straight angle, their exterior sides form a straight line.

2. The sum of all the angles about a point on one side of a straight line is a straight angle (180°).

3. The sum of all the angles in a plane about a point is two straight angles (360°).

4. If two angles have their sides parallel left to left and right to right, the angles are equal.

5. If two angles have their sides parallel left to right and right to left, the angles are supplementary.

6. Supplements of the same angle or of equal angles are equal.

7. Complements of the same angle or of equal angles are equal.

8. If two lines intersect, the vertical angles formed are equal.

9. Two lines cut by a transversal are parallel

(a) if the corresponding angles are equal;

(b) if the alternate-interior angles are equal;

(c) if the interior angles on the same side of the transversal are supplementary.

10. If two parallel lines are cut by a transversal, then

(a) the corresponding angles are equal;

(b) the alternate-interior angles are equal;

(c) the interior angles on the same side of the transversal are supplementary.

CHAPTER VII

THE EQUATION APPLIED TO THE TRIANGLE

179. Notation for triangles. It is customary to denote the three points of intersection of the sides of a triangle by capital letters and the three sides which lie opposite these respective sides with the corresponding small letters.

Thus, in Fig. 120 we denote the points of intersection of the sides (the vertices) by A, B, and C, and the sides opposite by a, b, and c.

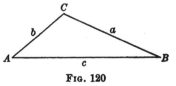

Fig. 120

The sides may also be read BC, AC, and AB. The symbol for "triangle" is a small triangle ($\triangle$). The expression $\triangle ABC$ is read "triangle ABC." The three angles shown in Fig. 120 are called *interior* angles.

180. Measuring the interior angles of a triangle. We shall now consider some of the methods of measuring the interior angles of a triangle.

EXERCISES

ANGLE	TRIANGLE *ABC* No. OF DEGREES		TRIANGLE *DEF* No. OF DEGREES		TRIANGLE *GHI* No. OF DEGREES	
	Estimated	Measured	Estimated	Measured	Estimated	Measured
x						
y						
z						
Sum						

1. Fill in the table on the preceding page with reference to the triangles *ABC*, *DEF*, and *GHI* (Fig. 121).

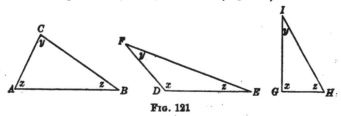

FIG. 121

2. Draw a triangle on paper (Fig. 122). Cut it out and tear off the corners as shown in Fig. 123. Then place the three angles adjacent as shown. What seems to be the sum of the three angles of the triangle? Test your answer with a straightedge.

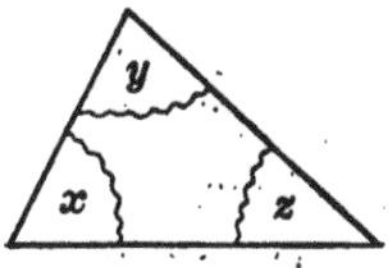

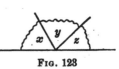

FIG. 122

181. Theorem. The results of Exs. 1 and 2, above, illustrate the geometric relation that *the sum of the interior angles of a triangle is a straight angle* (180°). The statement "The sum of the interior angles of a triangle is a straight angle" can be proved by more advanced geometric methods. Such a statement of a geometric relation to be proved is called a *theorem.*

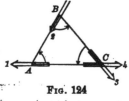

FIG. 123

182. More advanced methods of proof for the preceding theorem. The truth of the theorem that the sum of the interior angles of a triangle is 180° may be illustrated as follows: Draw a triangle as in Fig. 124. Place a pencil at *A* as indicated in the figure, noting the direction in which it points. Rotate the pencil through angle *A* as

FIG. 124

shown by the arrowhead. Then slide it along *AB* to the
position indicated in the figure. Rotate the pencil next
through angle *B* as indicated and slide it along *BC* to
the position shown. Then rotate the pencil through angle
C to the last position shown. This rotation through
angles *A*, *B*, and *C* leaves the point of the pencil in what
position in respect to its original position? What part of
a complete turn has it made? Through how many right

angles has it turned? Through
how many straight angles?
Through how many degrees?

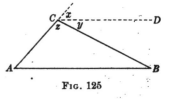

Fig. 125

The theorem that " the sum
of the interior angles of a triangle is 180° " may be proved
as follows:

Given triangle *ABC* (Fig. 125), to prove that $\angle A + \angle B + \angle C = 180°$.

Proof

STATEMENTS	REASONS
Draw $CD \parallel AB$.	
Then $\angle x = \angle A$.	Because corresponding angles formed by two parallel lines cut by a transversal are equal.
And $\angle y = \angle B$.	Because alternate-interior angles formed by two parallel lines cut by a transversal are equal.
But $\angle x + \angle y + \angle z = 180°$.	Because the sum of all the angles about a point in a plane on one side of a straight line is 180°.
$\therefore \angle A + \angle B + \angle C = 180°$.	By substituting $\angle A$ for $\angle x$, $\angle B$ for $\angle y$, and $\angle C$ for $\angle z$.

This is a more formal proof of the theorem, inasmuch as it
is independent of measurement. Write an equation which will
express the number of degrees in the sum of the angles of
a triangle.

This equation is a very useful one, as it enables us to find one angle of a triangle when the other two are known. Thus, if we know that two angles of a triangle are 50° and 70°, we know that 60° is the third angle. This is of great practical value to the surveyor, who is thus enabled to know the size of all three angles of a triangle by measuring only two directly.

HISTORICAL NOTE. Thales (640 B.C. – about 550 B.C.), the founder of the earliest Greek school of mathematics, is supposed to have known that the sum of the angles of a triangle is two right triangles. Someone has suggested that this knowledge concerning the sum of the angles of a triangle may have been experimentally demonstrated by the shape of the tiles used in paving floors in Thales' day. What has been regarded as the most remarkable geometrical advancement of Thales was the proof of a theorem which depended upon the knowledge that the sum of the angles of a triangle is two right angles. It is related that when Thales had succeeded in proving the theorem, he sacrificed an ox to the immortal gods. The large number of stories told about Thales indicates that he must have been a man of remarkable influence and shrewdness both in science and in business. Thus, we read that at one time he cornered the olive market and that at another time he was employed as engineer to direct a river so that a ford might be constructed. The following story is told illustrative of his shrewdness:

It is said that once when transporting some salt which was loaded on mules one of the animals, slipping in a stream, got its load wet and so caused some of the salt to be dissolved. Finding its burden thus lightened, it rolled over at the next ford to which it came ; to break it of this trick, Thales loaded it with rags and sponges, which, by absorbing the water, made the load heavier and soon effectually cured it of its troublesome habit.[1]

183. Problems involving the theorem "The sum of the interior angles of a triangle is a straight angle." In the problems that follow the pupil will need to apply the theorem proved in the preceding article.

[1] Ball, "A Short Account of the History of Mathematics," p. 14.

In the following problems

(a) Draw freehand the triangle.

(b) Denote the angles properly as given.

(c) Using the theorem of Art. 182, write down the equation representing the conditions of the problem.

(d) Solve the equation and find the value of each angle.

(e) Check your solution by the conditions of the problem.

1. The angles of a triangle are x, $2x$, and $3x$. Find x and the number of degrees in each angle.

2. The first angle of a triangle is twice the second, and the third is three times the first. Find the number of degrees in each angle.

3. If the three angles of a triangle are equal, what is the size of each?

4. If two angles of a triangle are each equal to 30°, what is the value of the third angle?

5. One angle of a triangle is 25°. The second angle is 55° larger than the third. How large is each angle?

6. The first angle of a triangle is four times the second, and the third is one half the first. Find each angle.

7. Find the angles of a triangle if the first is one half of the second, and the third is one third of the first.

8. The first angle of a triangle is two fifths as large as another. The third is four times as large as the first. How large is each angle?

9. Find the angles of a triangle if the first angle is 16° more than the second, and the third is 14° more than the second.

10. Find the angles of a triangle if the difference between two angles is 15°, and the third angle is 43°.

11. The first angle of a triangle is 30° more than the second, and the third is two times the first. Find the angles.

12. Find the angles of a triangle if the first angle is twice the second, and the third is 15° less than two times the first.

13. The angles of a triangle are to each other as 1, 2, 3. What is the size of each?

· HINT. Let x = the first, $2x$ the second, and $3x$ the third.

14. Find the angles of a triangle if the first is $2\frac{1}{2}$ times the second increased by 10°, and the third is one fourth of the second.

15. In a triangle one angle is a right angle; the other two angles are represented by x and $\frac{x}{4}$ respectively. Find each angle.

16. How many right angles may a triangle have? How many obtuse angles? How many acute angles at most? How many acute angles at least?

17. Two angles x and y of one triangle are equal respectively to two angles m and n of another triangle. Show that the third angle of the first triangle equals the third angle of the second triangle.

184. Theorem. By solving Ex. 17 we obtain the theorem *If two angles of one triangle are equal respectively to two angles of another triangle, the third angle of the first is equal to the third angle of the second.*

185. Right triangle. If one angle of a triangle is a right angle, the triangle is called a right triangle. The symbol for " right triangle " is rt. $\triangle$.

EXERCISES

1. Show that the sum of the acute angles of a right triangle is equal to a right angle.

2. Find the values of the acute angles of a right triangle if one angle is two times the other; if one is 5° more than three times the other.

3. The acute angles of a right triangle are $\frac{x}{2}$ and $\frac{x}{3}$. Find x and the number of degrees in each angle.

4. Draw a right triangle on cardboard so that the two acute angles of the triangle will contain 30° and 60° respectively. Use the protractor.

HINT. First draw a right angle. Then at any convenient point in one side of the right angle construct an angle of 60° and produce its side till a triangle is formed. Why does the third angle equal 30°?

*5. Cut out the cardboard triangle made in Ex. 4 and tell what angles may be constructed by its use without a protractor or tracing paper.

6. Draw on cardboard a right triangle whose acute angles are each equal to 45°, cut it out, and show how it may be used to draw angles of 45° and 90° respectively.

186. Wooden triangles. A wooden triangle is a triangle (usually a right one) made for convenience in drawing triangles on paper or on the blackboard (see Fig. 126)..
The acute angles are usually 60° and 30° or 45° and 45°. These wooden right triangles furnish a practical method of drawing a perpendicular to a line at a given point on that line. If no triangles of this kind can be had, a cardboard with two perpendicular edges or a cardboard right triangle will serve the purpose just as well.

FIG. 126. WOODEN TRIANGLE

FIG. 127. SET SQUARE

187. Set square. A set square is made up of a wooden triangle fastened to a straightedge so that it will slide along the straightedge (see Fig. 127).

1. Construct a right triangle, using the method of Art. 80.

2. The set square (Fig. 127) is a mechanical device for drawing parallel lines. Show how it may be used to draw parallel lines.

3. Show that two lines perpendicular to the same line are parallel (see the definition of parallel lines, Art. 87).

4. Show how a wooden triangle may be used to draw parallel lines.

5. What are three ways of drawing parallel lines?

188. Problems concerning the acute angles of a right triangle. The following problems will help the student to understand the relations concerning the acute angles of a right triangle.

1. Draw a right triangle as in Fig. 128 and show that angles A and B are complementary; that is, show that $\angle A + \angle B = 90°$.

Note. In lettering a right triangle ABC the letter C is usually put at the vertex of the right angle.

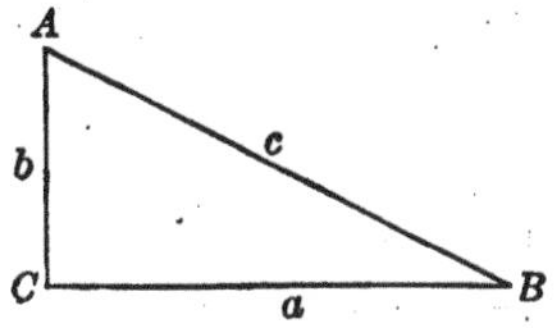

Fig. 128

2. State a theorem concerning the acute angles of a right-angled triangle.

3. If $\angle A = \angle B$ (Fig. 128), what is the size of each? How do the sides about the right angle compare in length?

4. If $\angle A$ is twice as large as $\angle B$ (Fig. 128), what is the size of each?

*5. Using the method of Ex. 4, Art. 185, draw a right triangle whose acute angles are 30° and 60° respectively. Measure the side opposite the 30-degree angle. Measure the side opposite the 90-degree angle. (This side is called the *hypotenuse*.) Compare the two results obtained.

6. To measure the distance AB across a swamp (Fig. 129), a man walks in the direction AD, so that $\angle BAD = 60°$, to a point C, where $\angle BCA = 90°$. If $AC = 300$ yd., what is the length of AB?

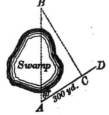

7. Find the number of degrees in each acute angle of a right triangle if one angle is

    (a) four times the other;

    (b) three fourths of the other;

    (c) two and a half times the other;

    (d) 5° more than three times the other;

    (e) 5° less than four times the other.

Fig. 129

*8. Practice drawing angles of 30°, 45°, 60°, and 90° by using wooden or cardboard triangles.

Ex. 5 illustrates the truth of the theorem *In a right triangle whose acute angles are 30° and 60° the side opposite the 30° angle is one half the hypotenuse.* This theorem will be proved formally later. It is very important because of its many practical applications in construction work and elsewhere.

189. Isosceles triangle; base angles. A triangle which has two equal sides is called an *isosceles* triangle. The angles opposite the equal sides are called the *base angles* of the isosceles triangle.

EXERCISES

1. Two equal acute angles of a right triangle are represented by $2x + 5$ and $3x - 15$. Find the size of each angle.

2. Draw a right triangle ABC (Fig. 130). Draw a line from $C \perp AB$; call the foot of the perpendicular P. Show that the perpendicular (CP) divides the $\triangle ABC$ into two right triangles.

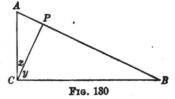

Fig. 130

3. In Ex. 2 the angle x is the complement of what two angles? What is the relation between these two angles?

4. In Ex. 2, $\angle y$ is the complement of two angles. Indicate them. Show that $\angle y = \angle A$.

5. Draw freehand three isosceles triangles.

190. Scalene triangle. A scalene triangle is a triangle no two of whose sides are equal.

EXERCISES

1. Draw freehand a scalene triangle.

2. Do you think that a right triangle whose acute angles are 30° and 60° is a scalene triangle? Support your answer.

3. Draw an obtuse-angled scalene triangle.

191. Exterior angles of a triangle. If the three sides of a triangle are extended, one at each vertex, as in Fig. 131, the angles thus formed (x, y, and z) are called *exterior* angles of the triangle ABC.

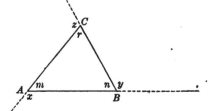

FIG. 131. ILLUSTRATING THE EXTERIOR ANGLES OF A TRIANGLE

EXERCISES

1. How many exterior angles can be drawn at each vertex of a triangle?

2. How many interior angles has a triangle? How many exterior angles?

3. Draw a triangle and extend the sides as in Fig. 131. Measure the three exterior angles with a protractor. What is their sum?

4. Draw another triangle and extend the sides as in Fig. 131. Cut out the exterior angles (taking one at each vertex) with a pair of scissors and place them next to each other with their vertices together. What does their sum seem to be?

5. Find the sum of the three exterior angles x, y, and z in Fig. 132 by rotating a pencil as indicated by the arrowheads.

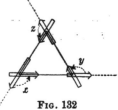

Fig. 132

6. Show that *the sum of the exterior angles of a triangle* (taking one at each vertex) *is 360°* (two straight angles).

HINT. How many degrees are in the sum $x + m$? $y + n$? $z + r$? (See Fig. 131.)

Show that the sum

$$(x + m) + (y + n) + (z + r) = 3 \times 180° = 540°.$$

Then this fact may be expressed as follows:

$$(x + y + z) + (m + n + r) = 540°.$$

But $\qquad\qquad (x + y + z) = 180°.$ $\qquad$ Why?

Therefore $\qquad (m + n + r) = 360°.$ $\qquad$ Why?

7. The three interior angles of a triangle are equal. Find the size of each interior and each exterior angle.

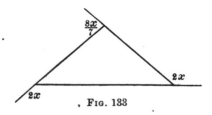

, Fig. 133

8. Find the value of the interior and exterior angles in the triangle of Fig. 133.

9. Show that the exterior angle x of the triangle ABC in Fig. 134 is equal to the sum of the two nonadjacent interior angles A and C.

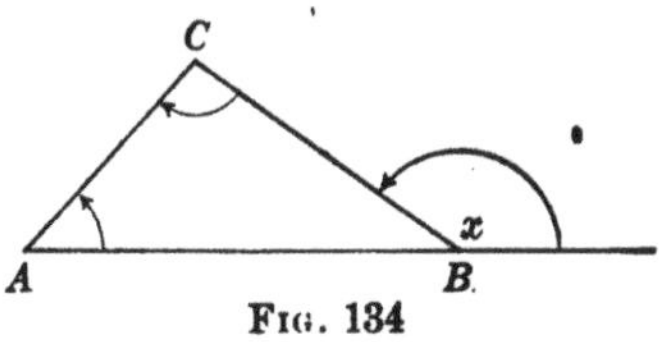

10. Using Fig. 135, in which $BD \parallel AC$, prove that *an exterior angle of a triangle is equal to the sum of the two nonadjacent interior angles.*

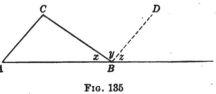

Fig. 134

Note that two different methods are suggested by this figure.

11. Prove Ex. 10 by drawing a line through C parallel to AB.

HINT. Extend line AC.

12. Draw a quadrilateral. Tear off the corners and place the interior angles next to each other by the method of Ex. 2, Art. 180. What does the sum of the interior angles seem to be?

Fig. 135

13. Draw a quadrilateral as in Fig. 136. Draw the diagonal AC. This divides the quadrilateral into two triangles. What is the sum of the interior angles in each triangle? What, then, is the sum of the interior angles of a quadrilateral?

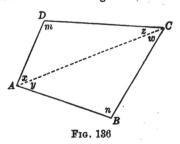

14. Draw a quadrilateral as in Fig. 136. Produce each side (one at each vertex). What do you think is the sum of the exterior angles of the quadrilateral? Check your estimate by measuring the angles.

Fig. 136

15. Find the angles of a quadrilateral in which each angle is 25° smaller than the consecutive angle.

16. Prove that *the consecutive angles of a parallelogram are supplementary*; that is, prove $x + y = 180°$, in Fig. 137.

17. Prove that the opposite angles of a parallelogram are equal.

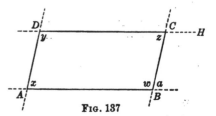

FIG. 137

HINT. In Fig. 137 show that $\angle x = \angle a = \angle z$.

18. If one angle of a parallelogram is twice as large as a consecutive angle, what is the size of each angle in the parallelogram?

19. The difference between two consecutive angles of a parallelogram is 30°. Find the size of all four angles in the parallelogram.

20. Show that *the sum of the interior angles of a trapezoid is two straight angles* (180°).

21. Prove that *two pairs of consecutive angles of a trapezoid are supplementary.* (Use Fig. 138.)

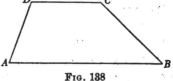

FIG. 138

22. In Fig. 138, $\angle D$ is 40° more than $\angle A$, and $\angle B$ is 96° less than $\angle C$. Find the number of degrees in each angle.

192. The construction of triangles. We shall now proceed to study three constructions which require the putting together of angles and line segments into some required combination. With a little practice the student will see that the processes are even simpler than the thinking involved in certain games for children which require the various combinations of geometric forms.

These constructions are very important in all kinds of construction work; for example, in shop work, mechanical drawing, engineering, and surveying. The student should therefore master them.

193. Construction problem. To construct a triangle when the three sides are given.

Construction. Let the given sides be a, b, and c, as shown in Fig. 139. Draw a working line XY, and lay off side c, lettering it AB. With A as a center and with a radius equal to b construct an arc as shown.

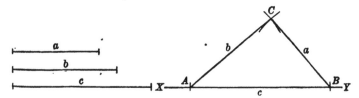

FIG. 139. HOW TO CONSTRUCT A TRIANGLE WHEN THREE SIDES ARE GIVEN

With B as a center and with a radius equal to a construct an arc intersecting the first. Call the point of intersection C. Then the triangle is constructed as required.

EXERCISES

1. Construct triangles with the following sides :

        (a) $a = 5$ cm., $b = 5$ cm., $c = 8$ cm.
        (b) $a = 7$ cm., $b = 8$ cm., $c = 4$ cm.
        (c) $a = 7$ cm., $b = 9$ cm., $c = 3$ cm.

2. Is it always possible to construct a triangle when three sides are given ?

3. Construct a triangle, using the sides given in Fig. 140.

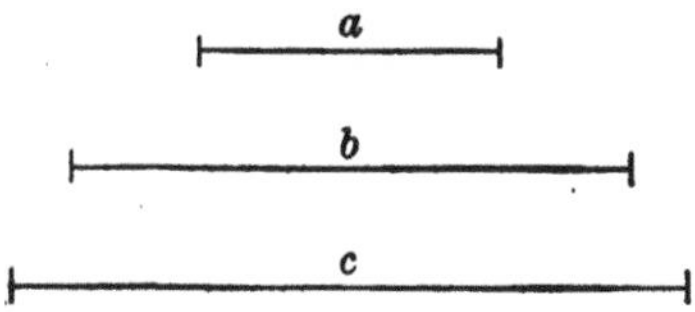

4. Compare as to size and shape the triangle drawn by

FIG. 140

you for Ex. 3 with those drawn by other pupils. (See if the triangles will fold over each other.)

5. Make a wooden triangle by nailing three sticks together. Is it possible to change the shape of the triangle without breaking a stick or removing the corner nails ?

6. A great deal of practical use is made of the fact that a triangle is a rigid figure; for example, a rectangular wooden gate is usually divided into two triangles by means of a wooden diagonal so as to make the gate more stable (less apt to sag). Try to give other examples of the practical use that is made of the stability of the triangular figure.

7. Construct an isosceles triangle having given the base and one of the two equal sides.

HINT. Use c in Fig. 140 as the base and use b twice; that is, in this case take $a = b$.

8. Measure the base angles of the isosceles triangle drawn for Ex. 7. What appears to be the relation between the base angles of an isosceles triangle ?

9. Make tracings of the base angles drawn for Ex. 7 and attempt to fold one angle over the other. Do the two angles appear to represent the same amount of rotation ?

10. Compare your results with those obtained by your classmates.

NOTE. Results obtained from Exs. 7–10 support the following theorem : *The base angles of an isosceles triangle are equal.*

11. Construct an equilateral triangle having given a side.

12. Study the angles of an equilateral triangle by pairs in the manner suggested by Exs. 8–9. State the theorem discovered.

13. To measure the distance AB (Fig. 141) we walk from B toward M so that $\angle B = 50°$, until we reach C, a point at which $\angle ACB = 50°$. What line must we measure to obtain AB ? Why ?

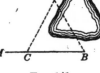

FIG. 141

14. At a point C (Fig. 142), 70 ft. from the foot of a pole AB, the angle ACB was found to be 45°. How high is the pole?

*15. Walking along the bank of a river from A to C (Fig. 143), a surveyor measures at B the angle ABD, and walking 500 ft. further to C, he finds angle BCD to be one half of angle ABD. What is the distance BD?

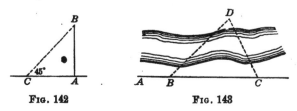

FIG. 142 FIG. 143

194. Construction problem. To construct a triangle, having given two sides and the angle included between the sides.

Construction. Let the given sides be a and b and the given angle be $\angle C$, as shown in Fig. 144.

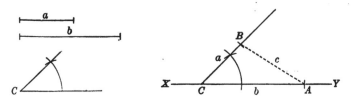

FIG. 144. HOW TO CONSTRUCT A TRIANGLE WHEN TWO SIDES AND THE INCLUDED ANGLE ARE GIVEN

Draw a working line XY, and lay off CA equal to b. At C draw an angle equal to angle C by the method of § 78. With C as a center and a radius equal to a lay off CB equal to a. Join B and A, and the triangle is constructed as required.

EXERCISES

1. Is the construction given in Art. 194 always possible?

2. Draw triangles with the following parts given:

      (a) $a = 3$ cm., $b = 4$ cm., $\angle C = 47°$.

      (b) $c = 1$ in., $b = 2$ in., $\angle A = 112°$.

      (c) $b = 1\frac{1}{2}$ in., $c = 1\frac{3}{4}$ in., $\angle A = 87°$.

3. Construct a triangle with the parts given in Fig. 145.

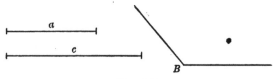

Fig. 145

4. Compare as to size and shape the triangle drawn for Ex. 3 with those drawn by other students in your class. (Place one triangle over the other and see if they fit.)

195. Construction problem. To construct a triangle when two angles and the side included between them are given.

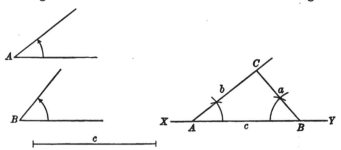

Fig. 146. How to construct a Triangle when Two Angles and the Side included between them are given

Construction. Let $\angle A$ and $\angle B$ be the given angles and line c be the given included side (Fig. 146).

Lay down a working line XY and lay off AB equal to line c on it. At A construct an angle equal to the given angle A; at B construct an angle equal to the given angle B and produce the sides of those angles till they meet at C, as shown. Then the $\triangle ABC$ is the required triangle.

EXERCISES

1. Draw triangles with the following parts given:

    (a) $\angle A = 30°$, $\angle B = 80°$, $c = 4$ cm.
    (b) $\angle C = 110°$, $\angle B = 20°$, $a = 2$ in.

2. Draw a triangle with the parts as given in Fig. 147.

3. Is the construction of Ex. 2 always possible?

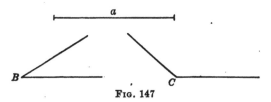

Fig. 147

4. Compare as to size and shape the triangle drawn for Ex. 2 with those drawn by other members of your class. (Fold them over each other and see if they fit.)

SUMMARY

196. This chapter has taught the meaning of the following words and phrases: right triangle, cardboard triangle, wooden triangle, set square, isosceles triangle, scalene triangle, interior angles of a triangle, exterior angles of a triangle, base angles.

The following notations have been given: notation for the angles and sides of triangles, notation for right triangle (rt. $\triangle$).

197. This chapter has presented methods of

1. Finding the sum of the interior angles of a triangle.

2. Finding the sum of the exterior angles of a triangle.

3. Drawing right triangles by means of wooden or cardboard triangles.

4. Drawing parallel lines by means of the wooden triangle or the set square.

198. This chapter has taught the pupil the following constructions:

1. *Given three sides of a triangle, to construct the triangle.*

2. *Given two sides and the included angle of a triangle, to construct the triangle.*

3. *Given two angles and the included side of a triangle, to construct the triangle.*

199. The following theorems have been presented in this chapter:

1. The sum of the interior angles of a triangle is a straight angle (180°).

2. The sum of the exterior angles of a triangle is two straight angles (360°).

3. If two angles of one triangle are equal respectively to two angles of another triangle, the third angle of the first triangle is equal to the third angle of the second.

4. The acute angles of a right triangle are complementary.

5. In a right triangle whose acute angles are 30° and 60° the side opposite the 30-degree angle is one half the hypotenuse.

6. An exterior angle of a triangle is equal to the sum of the two nonadjacent interior angles.

7. The sum of the interior angles of a quadrilateral is four right angles (360°).

8. The sum of the exterior angles of a quadrilateral is four right angles (360°).

9. The opposite angles of a parallelogram are equal.

10. The consecutive angles of a parallelogram are supplementary.

11. Two pairs of consecutive angles of a trapezoid are . supplementary.

12. The base angles of an isosceles triangle are equal.

13. An equilateral triangle is equiangular (all angles equal).

CHAPTER VIII

POSITIVE AND NEGATIVE NUMBERS. ADDITION AND SUBTRACTION

200. Clock game. Mary and Edith were playing with a toy clock. Each took her turn at spinning the hand. The object of the game was to guess the number on which the hand of the clock stopped. A correct guess counted five points. If a player missed a guess by more than three, she lost three points. If she came within three she either won or lost the number of points missed, according to whether she had guessed under or over the correct number. After five guesses they had the following scores:

<table>
<tr><td colspan="2">MARY</td></tr>
<tr><td>Won</td><td>2</td></tr>
<tr><td>Lost</td><td>1</td></tr>
<tr><td>Lost</td><td>3</td></tr>
<tr><td>Won</td><td>2</td></tr>
<tr><td>Won</td><td>1</td></tr>
<tr><td colspan="2">EDITH</td></tr>
<tr><td>Lost</td><td>1</td></tr>
<tr><td>Lost</td><td>2</td></tr>
<tr><td>Won</td><td>5</td></tr>
<tr><td>Won</td><td>2</td></tr>
<tr><td>Lost</td><td>2</td></tr>
</table>

Who won the game?

Solution. The score as kept by the players (the words are inserted) appeared as follows:

MARY		EDITH	
First score	2	First score	①
Lost	1	Lost	2
Second score	1	Second score	③
Lost	3	Won	5
Third score	②	Third score	$\bar{2}$
Won	2	Won	2
Fourth score	0	Fourth score	$\bar{4}$
Won	1	Lost	2
Final score	$\bar{1}$	Final score	$\bar{2}$

Edith won the game, 2 to 1.

150

201. Positive and negative numbers. Algebraic numbers.
The adding of scores in many familiar games like the one
cited above illustrates an extension of our idea of counting that will be found very useful in our further study of
mathematics. It is important to notice that the players
began at zero and counted their scores in *both directions*.
Thus, Mary began with zero and won two points, and the
2 she wrote meant to her that her score was two above
zero. On the other hand, Edith had zero and lost one.
In order to remember that she was "one in the hole"
she wrote 1 within a circle. On the next turn she lost
two more, and she continued to count away from zero
by writing 3 within a circle. The same idea is shown in
Mary's score. Her second score was 1. On the next turn
she lost three. She subtracted 3 from 1. In doing so she
counted backward over the zero point to two *less than zero*.
In writing the scores it was necessary to indicate whether
the number was *above or below zero*.

We shall presently have numerous problems which
involve pairs of numbers which possess *opposite qualities*,
like those above. It is generally agreed to call numbers greater than zero *positive* and those less than zero
negative. Such numbers are called *algebraic numbers*.

The opposite qualities involved are designated by the
words "positive" and "negative." In the preceding game,
numbers above zero are positive, whereas numbers below
zero are negative.

202. Use of signs. To designate whether a number is
positive or negative we use the plus or the minus sign.
Thus, $+4$ means a positive 4 and -4 means a negative 4.
The positive sign is not always written. When no sign precedes a number the number is understood to be a positive
number. Thus, 3 means $+3$.

The following stock quotations from the *Chicago Daily Tribune* (March 24, 1917) illustrate a use of the plus and minus signs:

CHICAGO STOCK EXCHANGE

	SALES	HIGH	LOW	CLOSE	NET CHANGE
American Radiator . . .	20	$295\frac{7}{8}$	295	295	-2
Commonwealth Edison . .	79	$136\frac{1}{2}$	$136\frac{1}{2}$	$136\frac{1}{2}$	$-\frac{1}{2}$
Diamond Match	40	81	81	81	. . . .
Swift & Co.	515	$114\frac{1}{2}$	$142\frac{3}{4}$	$144\frac{1}{2}$	$+2\frac{3}{8}$
Peoples Gas	397	95	$90\frac{1}{2}$	91	-5
Prest-o-Lite	40	$129\frac{3}{4}$	129	129	-3
Sears Roebuck	325	192	$190\frac{3}{4}$	$191\frac{1}{2}$	$-\frac{1}{2}$
Booth Fisheries	20	79	79	79	$+\frac{1}{2}$

The last column shows the net gain or loss during the day; for example, American Radiator stock closed two points lower than on the preceding day, Swift & Co. gained $2\frac{3}{8}$, Peoples Gas lost 5, etc. The man familiar with stock markets glances at the first column to see the extent of the sales and at the last column to see the specific gain or loss. To check the last column one would need the quotations for the preceding day.

In order that we may see something of the importance of the extension of our number system by the preceding definitions, familiar examples of positive and negative numbers will be discussed.

203. Geometric representation of positive numbers. Origin. We have learned in measuring a line segment that when a unit (say $\overset{M}{\mid}\!\!\overset{N}{\mid}$) is contained five times in another segment, the latter is five units long. (In general, if it is contained a times, the measured segment is a units long.) We may also say that the two segments represent the numbers 1 and 5 respectively. This suggests the following representation of positive integers: On any line OX (Fig. 148) beginning at O (called the *origin* of the scale) but unlimited in the direction toward X, we lay off line segments OA, AB, BC, CD, DE, etc., each one unit in length. We thus obtain a series of points on the line, each of which corresponds to some positive integer, and vice versa. We also

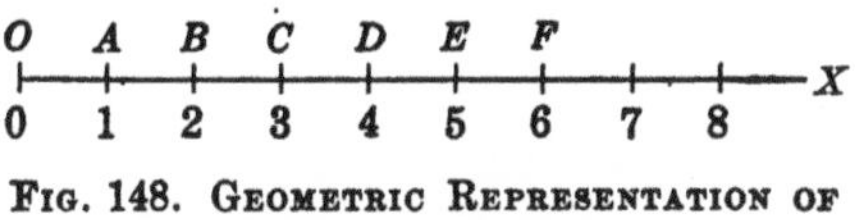

FIG. 148. GEOMETRIC REPRESENTATION OF POSITIVE NUMBERS

note that the line segment which connects the origin with some point (say E) is the corresponding number of units in length. (Thus, $OE = 5$.) Hence the positive integers $+1$, $+2$, $+3$, $+4$, $+5$, etc. are represented by OA, OB, OC, OD, OE, etc.

204. Geometric representation of negative numbers. Number scale. If we prolong OX to the left from O in the direction OX' (Fig. 149), we may lay off line segments in either of two opposite directions. Segments OC and OD' differ not only in length but also in direction. This difference in direction is indicated by the use of the

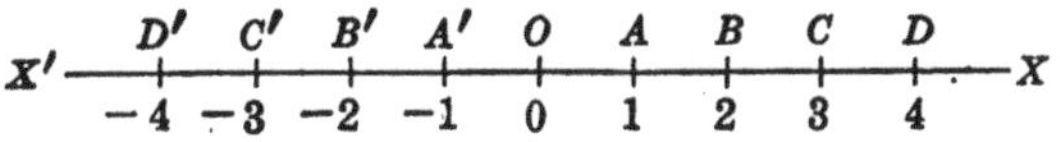

FIG. 149. GEOMETRIC REPRESENTATION OF NEGATIVE NUMBERS

signs $+$ and $-$. Thus, OC represents $+3$, whereas OD' represents -4. The integers of algebra may now be arranged in a series on this line called the *number scale*, beginning at 0 and extending both to the right and to the left. In order to locate the points of the number scale (Fig. 149) we need not only an integer of arithmetic to determine how far the given point is from zero but also a *sign* of *quality* to indicate on which side of 0 it is found.

1. Locate the following points on the number scale: $+3$, -3, -7, $+12$, -8, $+6$.

2. If we imagine that each of the players in the clock game (Art. 200) has a string or tape measure graduated to the number scale, with a ring on it, they could add their scores from time to time by sliding the ring back and forth.

Indicate on the number scale how the sum of the following consecutive scores could be found: Began at 0, lost 1, lost 2, won 5, won 2, lost 1.

3. Starting from the middle of the field in a certain football game, the ball shifted its position in yards during the first fifteen minutes of play as follows: $+45$, -15, $+11$, -10, -2, $+23$. Where was the ball at the end of the last play?

205. Addition and further use of positive and negative numbers. The preceding exercises show that positive and negative numbers may be added by counting, the direction (forward or backward) in which we count being determined by the sign ($+$ or $-$) of the numbers which we are adding. Thus,

To add $+4$ to $+5$ on the number scale of Fig. 149, begin at $+5$ and count 4 to the *right*.

To add -4 to $+5$ begin at $+5$ and count 4 to the *left*.

To add -4 to -5 begin at -5 and count 4 to the *left*.

To add $+4$ to -5 begin at -5 and count 4 to the *right*.

The results are as follows:

$+5 + (+4) = +9$; $+5 + (-4) = +1$; $-5 + (-4) = -9$; $-5 + (+4) = -1$.

$+5 + (-4) = +1$ is read "*positive 5 plus negative 4 equals positive 1.*"

$-5 + (-4) = -9$ is read "*negative 5 plus negative 4 equals negative 9.*"

1. Give the sum in each of the following. Be prepared to interpret the result on the number scale.

(a) $3 + (+2)$.   (g) $6 + (-1)$.   (m) $-2 + (-5)$.

(b) $4 + (-3)$.   (h) $6 + (-3)$.   (n) $-4 + 6$.

(c) $5 + (+2)$.   (i) $7 + (-7)$.   (o) $-5 + 5$.

(d) $4 + (-4)$.   (j) $8 + (-5)$.   (p) $-7 + 9$.

(e) $5 + (-6)$.   (k) $-2 + (-2)$.   (q) $-7 + 5$.

(f) $5 + (-7)$.   (l) $-2 + (-4)$.   (r) $-6 + 3$.

2. On a horizontal straight line, as $X'OX$ in Fig. 150, consider the part OX as positive, and the part OX' as negative. Construct line segments corresponding to the following numbers: -2, $+6$, -3, -5, 0.

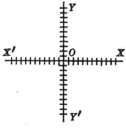

FIG. 150

3. Consider OY as positive and OY' as negative and construct segments on the line YOY' corresponding to -4, -2, $+3$, $+4$, -3, 0.

4. A bicyclist starts from a certain point and rides 18 mi. due northward ($+18$ mi.), then 12 mi. due southward (-12 mi.). How far is he from the starting point?

5. How far and in what direction from the starting point is a traveler after going eastward ($+$) or westward ($-$) as shown by these pairs of numbers: $+16$ mi., then -3 mi.? -2 mi., then $+27$ mi.? -16 mi., then $+16$ mi.? $+100$ mi., then $+52$ mi.?

6. Denoting latitude north of the equator by the plus sign and latitude south by the minus sign, give the meaning of the following latitudes: $+28°$, $+12°$, $-18°$, $+22°$, $-11°$.

7. Would it be definite to say that longitude east of Greenwich is positive and west is negative? What is the meaning of the following longitudes: $+42°$? $+142°$? $-75°$? $-3°$?

8. A vessel starting in latitude $+ 20°$ sails $+ 17°$, then $- 63°$, then $+ 42°$, then $- 16°$. What is its latitude after all the sailings ?

9. What is the latitude of a ship starting in latitude $- 53°$ after the following changes of latitude : $+ 12°$, $- 15°$, $+ 28°$, $- 7°$, $+ 18°$, $- 22°$, $+ 61°$?

206. Double meaning of plus and minus signs. Absolute value. The many illustrations of negative number show that there is a real need in the actual conditions of life for the extension of our number scale so as to include this kind of number. It must be clearly understood that a minus sign may now mean two entirely different things : (1) It may mean the *process of subtraction*, or (2) it may mean that the number is a negative number. In the latter case it denotes quality. Show that a similar statement is true for the plus sign.

This double meaning does not often confuse us, since it is usually possible to decide from the context of the sentence which of these two meanings is intended. Sometimes a parenthesis is used to help make the meaning clear, thus $4° + (- 3°)$ means add a negative $3°$ to a positive $4°$.

Sometimes we wish to focus attention merely on the number of units in a member regardless of sign. In that case we speak of the *absolute value*, or *numerical value*. Thus, the absolute value of either $+ 4$ or $- 4$ is 4.

207. Forces. In mechanics we speak of forces acting in opposite directions as positive and negative. Thus, a force acting upward is positive, one acting downward is negative.

EXERCISES

1. Three boys are pulling a load on a sled, one with a force of 27 lb., another with a force of 56 lb., and the third with a force of 90 lb. With what force is the load being pulled?

2. Two small boys are pulling a small wagon along; one pulls with a force of 23 lb., and the other pulls with a force of 36 lb. A boy comes up behind and pulls with a force of 47 lb. in the opposite direction from the others. What is the result?

3. An aëroplane that can fly 48.3 mi. an hour in still air is flying against a wind that retards it 19.6 mi. an hour. At what rate does the aëroplane fly?

FIG. 151

4. A balloon which exerts an upward pull of 512 lb. has a 453-pound weight attached to it. What is the net upward or downward pull?

5. A toy balloon (Fig. 151) tends to pull upward with a force of 8 oz. What happens if we tie a 5-ounce weight to it? an 8-ounce?

6. A boy can row a boat at the rate of 4 mi. per hour. How fast can he go up a river flowing at the rate of $2\frac{1}{4}$ mi. per hour? How fast can he ride down the river? How fast could he go up a stream flowing 5 mi. per hour?

208. The thermometer. The thermometer (Fig. 152) illustrates the idea of positive and negative numbers in two

FIG. 152. THE THER-MOMETER ILLUSTRATES THE IDEA OF POSI-TIVE AND NEGATIVE NUMBERS

ways. In the first place, the number scale is actually produced through the zero, and degrees of temperature are read as positive (above zero) or negative (below zero). In the second place, the thermometer illustrates positive and negative motion discussed in the preceding article. Thus, when the mercury column rises, its change may be considered as positive, + 5 indicating in this case not a reading on the thermometer, as before, but a change (rise) in the reading; similarly, − 3° in this sense indicates a drop of 3° in the temperature from the previous reading.

EXERCISES

1. What is the lowest temperature you have ever seen recorded ?

2. The top of the mercury column of a thermometer stands at 0° at the beginning of an hour. The next hour it rises 5°, and the next 3°; what does the thermometer then read ?

3. If the mercury stands at 0°, rises 8°, and then falls 5°, what does the thermometer read ?

4. Give the final reading in each case :

A first reading of 10° followed by a rise of 2°.

A first reading of 10° followed by a fall of 12°.

A first reading of 20° followed by a fall of 18°.

A first reading of $x°$ followed by a rise of $y°$.

A first reading of $x°$ followed by a fall of $y°$.

A first reading of $a°$ followed by a rise of $a°$.

A first reading of $a°$ followed by a fall of $a°$.

A first reading of $− a°$ followed by a fall of $− a°$.

5. The reading at 6 P.M. was 7°. What was the final reading if the following numbers express the hourly rise or fall : $+ 2°, + 1°, 0°, − 3°, − 3°, − 2°, − 2°, − 1°, − 1°, − 3°, − 1°, + 2°$?

6. Add the following changes to find the final reading, the first reading being 0°: $+3°$, $+2°$, $-4°$, $-3°$, $-2°$, $+3°$.

7. The differences in readings of a thermometer that was read hourly from 5 A.M. until 5 P.M. were as follows: 3°, 4°, 7°, 10°, 12°, 9°, 8°, 5°, 0°, $-22°$, $-17°$, $-12°$. How did the temperature at 5 P.M. compare with that at 5 A.M.? If the temperature at 5 A.M. was $+20°$, make a table showing the temperature at each hour of the day.

209. Positive and negative angles. By rotating line AB in a plane around A until it takes the position AC the angle BAC is formed (Fig. 153). By rotating AB in the *opposite direction* angle BAC_1 is formed. To distinguish between these directions one angle may be denoted by the *plus* sign, and the other by the *minus* sign. We agree to consider an angle positive when it is formed by rotating a line counterclockwise and negative when it is formed by clockwise rotation. This is simply another illustration of motion in opposite directions.

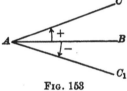

Fig. 153

EXERCISES

1. In this exercise the sign indicates the *direction* of rotation. Construct the following angles with ruler and protractor, starting with the initial line in the horizontal position: $+30°$, $+45°$, $+90°$, $+43°$, $+212°$, $-30°$, $-45°$, $-90°$, $-53°$, $-182°$, $-36°$.

2. Find the final position of a line which, starting at OX (horizontal), swings successively through the following rotations: $+72°$, $-38°$, $+112°$, $-213°$, $+336°$, $-318°$, $-20°$, $+228°$.

3. Do you see a short cut in finding the final position of the line in Ex. 2?

210. Business relations. Finally, the idea of positive and negative numbers may be further illustrated by the gain or loss in a transaction; by income and expenditure; by a debit and a credit account; by money deposited and money checked out; and by the assets and liabilities of a business corporation. Thus, a bankrupt company is one which has not been able to prevent the negative side of the ledger from running up beyond the limit of the confidence of its supporters.

EXERCISES

1. The assets of a company are $26,460, and its liabilities are $39,290. What is its financial condition?

2. A newsboy having $25 in the bank deposits $10.25 on Monday, checks out $16.43 on Tuesday, checks out $7.12 on Wednesday, deposits $5 on Thursday, deposits $7.25 on Friday, and checks out $11.29 on Saturday. What is his balance for the week?

3. If a man's personal property is worth $1100 and his real estate $12,460, and if his debts amount to $2765, what is his financial standing?

4. A boy buys a bicycle for $10.25 and sells it for $6. Does he gain or lose and how much?

211. Addition of three or more monomials. The following exercises will help us to see how the addition of monomials may be extended.

EXERCISES

1. Add the following monomials:

(a) $2 + 3 + (-4) + (5)$.   (c) $(-4) + 2 + 3 + (-5)$.

(b) $3 + 2 + (-4) + (-5)$.   (d) $(-5) + (-4) + 3 + 2$.

2. In what form has the commutative law of addition been stated? (Art. 36.) Does it seem to hold when some of the addends are negative?

3. Show by a geometric construction on. squared paper that the commutative law holds when some of the addends are negative.

HINT. First take a line segment $-a$ units long (Fig. 154) and add a segment $+b$ units long (Fig. 154); then take the segment that is $+b$ units long and add the segment that is $-a$ units long. The results should be the same.

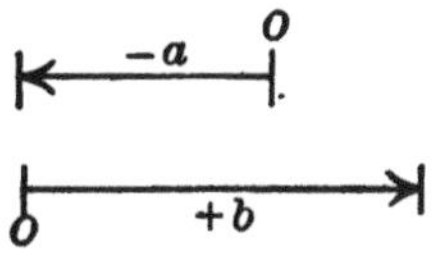

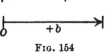

4. Does a bookkeeper balance the account every time an entry is made or does he keep the debits and credits on separate pages and balance the two sums at the end of the month?

FIG. 154

The process of adding several positive and negative numbers can be explained in detail by the following problem:

Add $-10, +50, -27, +18, -22, -31, +12$.

Arrange the numbers as follows:
$$
\begin{aligned}
&-10 \\
&+50 \\
&-27 \\
&+18 \\
&-22 \\
&-31 \\
&+12 \\
\end{aligned}
$$

There are three positive terms, 50, 18, and 12, whose sum is 80. There are four negative terms, $-10, -27, -22,$ and -31, whose sum is -90. Adding $+80$ to -90 gives -10.

The process consists of the following three steps:

1. *Add all the positive terms.*
2. *Add all the negative terms.*
3. *Add these two sums by the following process:* (a) *Determine how much larger the absolute value of one number is than the absolute value of the other.* (b) *Write this number and prefix the sign of the greater addend.*

212. Algebraic addition. The results of the preceding
exercises show that positive and negative numbers may
be added according to the following laws:

1. *To add two algebraic numbers having like signs find
the sum of their absolute values and prefix to this sum their
common sign.*

2. *To add two algebraic numbers having unlike signs find
the difference of their absolute values and prefix to it the sign
of the number having the greater absolute value.*

EXERCISES

1. Show that the sum of two numbers with like signs is the
sum of their absolute values with the common sign prefixed.
Illustrate with a concrete experience.

2. Show that the sum of two numbers having unlike signs
but the same absolute value is zero. Illustrate with some fact
from actual experience.

3. Find the following sums, performing all you can orally:

(a) -5	(d) -7	(g) $-\frac{5}{8}$	(j) $-17\frac{2}{3}x$
$+7$	-5	$+\frac{3}{4}$	$+26\frac{5}{8}x$
(b) $+5$	(e) $-8a$	(h) $-\frac{2}{3}ab$	(k) $+62\frac{1}{2}x^2$
-7	$+4a$	$+\frac{5}{6}ab$	$-28\frac{2}{3}x^2$
(c) $+7$	(f) $-12m$	(i) $3.16x$	(l) $-2.3xm^2$
$+5$	$-16m$	$-5.28x$	$+6.5xm^2$

Find the following sums:

4. $-\ 6$	5. $+\ 3$	6. $+51$	7. -242
$+10$	$+10$	$+23$	$+726$
$-\ 8$	$-\ 7$	-18	$-\ 58$
$-\ 4$	$-\ 4$	$-\ 7$	$+\ 24$

8. $+ 7.5$
$+ 12.5$
$- 9.5$
$+ 2.5$

12. $+ \frac{3}{4}$
$+ \frac{5}{8}$
$- \frac{1}{2}$

16. $+ 7\frac{3}{5}$
$- 7\frac{4}{5}$
$- 12\frac{1}{4}$
$- 2\frac{1}{2}$

20. $0.5\,x^2$
$0.23\,x^2$
$0.12\,x^2$
$0.07\,x^2$

9. $- 8x$
$+ 4x$
$+ 17x$
$- 9x$

13. $- \frac{7}{8}$
$+ \frac{6}{8}$
$- \frac{3}{4}$
$+ \frac{1}{2}$

17. $- 12.18$
$- 11.88$
$+ 13.16$
$- 14.08$

21. $+ 27\,x^2$
$- 15\,x^2$
$+ 17\,x^2$
$- 12\,x^2$

10. $+ 7x$
$- 10x$
$- 12x$
$+ 16x$

14. $+ 3\frac{1}{2}$
$- 2\frac{1}{3}$
$- 5\frac{1}{4}$
$- 2\frac{3}{8}$

18. $+ 10.05$
$+ 4.85$
$- 3.25$
$- 12.35$

22. $+ 23\,xm$
$- 14\,xm$
$- 17\,xm$
$+ 20\,xm$

11. $+ 24a$
$- 6a$
$- 7a$
$- 3a$

15. $+ 4\frac{3}{4}$
$- 6\frac{1}{8}$
$- 6\frac{2}{3}$
$+ 8\frac{5}{6}$

19. $- 3.1s$
$- 5.4s$
$+ 7.2s$
$- 3.1s$

23. $- 18.25\,x^2m$
$+ 17.34\,x^2m$
$- 19.64\,x^2m$
$+ 21.17\,x^2m$

213. Drill exercises. The following exercises constitute
a drill in determining the common factor of similar monomials and applying the law for the addition of similar
monomials (Art. 40). We need to recall that *the sum of
two or more similar monomials is a number whose coefficient
is the sum of the coefficients of the addends and whose literal
factor is the same as the similar addends.* The exercises
are the same as a preceding set (Art. 40) except that in
this case the step in which the coefficients of the addends
are added involves the addition of positive and negative
numbers.

In each case (1) point out with respect to what factor the following terms are similar; (2) express as a monomial by adding like terms:

1. $3y, -6y, 20y, -35y$.

Solution. The common factor is y.

The sum of the coefficients is $3 + (-6) + 20 + (-35) = -18$.

Whence the required sum is $-18y$.

2. $5x, -7x, -9x, +12x, -3x$.

3. $7b, -12b, -9b, +11b, -13b$.

4. $9ab, -17ab, -11ab, +13ab$.

5. $-8mnx^2, +12mnx^2, -15mnx^2, -13mnx^2$.

6. $5a^2b, -7a^2b, +9a^2b, -5a^2b$.

7. $3ax, 4ax, -8ax, -7ax$.

8. $-5pq^2, 7pq^2, -8\frac{1}{2}pq^2, -6pq^2$.

9. $az, -14z, -bz, +12z$.

Solution. The common factor is z.

The sum of the coefficients is $a + (-14) + (-b) + 12$.

Since a and $-b$ are still undetermined, we can only indicate that sum thus: $a - 14 - b + 12$.

Whence the sum written as a monomial is $(a - b - 2)z$.

10. $mx, +5x, -7x, +cx$.

11. $my^2, -ny^2, +5y^2, -12y^2, +cy^2$.

12. $2\frac{1}{2}ab, +4\frac{1}{3}ab, -5\frac{1}{2}ab, -6\frac{2}{3}ab$.

214. Addition of polynomials. We have had numerous examples of the addition of polynomials in dealing with perimeters. In applying the principles involved to polynomials having positive and negative terms we need to recall that in addition the terms may be arranged or grouped in any order. Thus,

$$2 + 3 + 4 = 3 + 2 + 4 \text{ (Commutative Law)}$$
$$5 + (-3) + 4 = -3 + (5 + 4) \text{ (Associative Law)}$$

In adding polynomials it is convenient to group similar terms in the same column, much as we do in adding denominate numbers in arithmetic.

1. Add the following polynomials and reduce the sum to its simplest form: 3 yd. + 1 ft. + 6 in., 5 yd. + 1 ft. + 2 in., and 12 yd. + 3 in.

Solution. Writing the similar terms in separate columns we have

3 yd.	1 ft.	6 in.
5 yd.	1 ft.	2 in.
12 yd.		3 in.
20 yd.	2 ft.	11 in.

Note that the common mathematical factors are not *yards*, *feet*, *inches*, but the unit common to all of them, or *inches*. The problem may be written as follows:

$$3 \times 36 + 1 \times 12 + 6$$
$$5 \times 36 + 1 \times 12 + 2$$
$$12 \times 36 \qquad\qquad + 3$$
$$20 \times 36 + 2 \times 12 + 11$$

2. Add $9y + 3x + 2i$, $5y + 2x + 6i$, and $3y + 2x + 8i$.

$$9y + 3x + 2i$$
$$5y + 2x + 6i$$
$$3y + 2x + 8i$$
$$17y + 7x + 16i$$

3. Add $27x^3 - 13xy + 16y^2$, $-14x^3 + 25xy + 4y^2$, and $-11x^3 - 18xy - 12y^2$.

Solution. Writing similar terms in separate columns and adding, we have

$$27x^3 - 13xy + 16y^2$$
$$-14x^3 + 25xy + 4y^2$$
$$-11x^3 - 18xy - 12y^2$$
$$2x^3 - 6xy + 8y^2$$

In the following exercises add the polynomials:

4.
$$6a + 2b + 7c$$
$$3a - 9b - 2c$$
$$4a + 3b - 5c$$
$$-5a + 2b - 3c$$

7.
$$-6x + 15y - 16z - 8w$$
$$-8x + 22y + 16z - 12w$$
$$3x + 4y - 5z + 6w$$
$$9x - 8y + 7z - 6w$$

5.
$$2x + 3y + 4z$$
$$5x - 6y - 7z$$
$$4x + 5y + 8z$$
$$-2x - 5y - 2z$$

8.
$$6r - 2s + 3t$$
$$5r \qquad - 3t$$
$$2r + 6s - 5t$$
$$3s + t$$

6.
$$2a + 5b + 7c$$
$$-3a - 8b - 5c$$
$$4a + 5b - 6c$$
$$3a - 2b + 8c$$

9.
$$2x - 3y + 4z$$
$$x + y - 3z$$
$$-3x - 4y + 2z$$

10. $-2x - 6b + 13c, -11x + 19b - 30c,$ and $5x + 4c.$

11. $12k - 10l + 9m, -2k + 2l - 4m,$ and $-5l + 3k - 2m.$

12. $14e - 3y + 7z, 5e + 5y - 3z,$ and $6e + 4y + 2z.$

13. $(24x - 6y + 12z) + (-12x + 8y + 2z) + (9x - 5y - 4z).$

NOTE. Here certain terms are inclosed in grouping symbols ( ) called *parenthesis*. These indicate that the terms within are to be treated as one number or one quantity. Other grouping symbols will be given when needed (see pp. 175, 177).

14. $(5a - 12b + 4c) + (8a - 2b - 24c) + (-6a - 4b - 8c).$

15. $(3m + 12n + 2e) + (-14m - 6n - 5e) + (-5n + 2e).$

215. Degree of a number. The degree of a number is indicated by the exponent of the number. Thus, x^2 is of the second degree; x^3, of the third degree; y^4, of the fourth degree; etc. The monomial $3xy^2r^3$ is of the first degree with respect to x, of the second degree with respect to y, and of the third degree with respect to r.

216. Degree of a monomial. The degree of a monomial is determined by the sum of the exponents of the literal factors. Another way of saying this is: The number of literal factors in a term is called the degree of the term. Thus, x^2 is of the second degree; xy^2, of the third degree; and $4\,xy^2z^2$, of the fifth degree.

EXERCISES

Determine the degree of the following monomials:

1. $2\,x^2y^2$.　　3. $3\,b^4$.　　5. $24\,mxy$.　　7. $\dfrac{xy}{2}$.　　9. r^2s^3.

2. $2\,ab^3$.　　4. $5\,xy^2z^5$.　　6. $\dfrac{x^3}{2}$.　　8. rs^4.　　10. $m^3x^2y^2z^2$.

217. Degree of a polynomial. The degree of a polynomial is determined by the degree of the term having the highest degree. Thus, $x^2y^2 + x + 3\,y + 5$ is of the fourth degree, and $5\,x^2 - x^3 + 7$ is a third-degree expression.

EXERCISES

Indicate the degree of the following polynomials:

1. $x^4 + 2\,x^3 - x^4 + 2\,x^2 + y + 7$.　　4. $x - 2\,xy^2 + y^3$.

2. $x + 2\,xy + y^2$.　　5. $x^4 + 4$.

3. $x^2 - 2\,xy + y^2$.　　6. $x^5 + x^3 + x^2 + 1$.

218. Arrangement. A polynomial is said to be arranged according to the *descending powers* of x when the term of the highest degree in x is placed first, the term of next lower degree next, etc., and the term not containing x last. Thus, $2 + x + x^3 + 3\,x^2$ when arranged according to the *descending powers* of x takes the form $x^3 + 3\,x^2 + x + 2$. When arranged in the order $2 + x + 3\,x^2 + x^3$, the polynomial is said to be arranged according to the *ascending powers* of x.

Find the sum of $-3a^2 + 2a^3 - 4a$, $-a^2 + 7$; $5a^3 - 4a + 3$, and $-2a^3 - 7 - 2a^2$.

Arranging according to descending powers and adding, we have

$$
\begin{array}{l}
2a^3 - 3a^2 - 4a \\
\quad\ \ - a^2 \qquad\ \ +7 \\
5a^3 \qquad\quad - 4a + 3 \\
\underline{-2a^3 - 2a^2 \qquad\quad -7} \\
5a^3 - 6a^2 - 8a + 3
\end{array}
$$

Check. One way to check is to add carefully in reverse order, as in arithmetic.

A second method for checking is shown by the following:

Let $a = 2$. Then we have

$$
\begin{array}{lr}
2a^3 - 3a^2 - 4a \qquad\quad = - & 4 \\
\quad\ \ - a^2 \qquad\ \ +7 = & 3 \\
5a^3 \qquad\quad - 4a + 3 = & 35 \\
\underline{-2a^3 - 2a^2 \qquad\quad -7 = - 31} \\
5a^3 - 6a^2 - 8a + 3 = & 3
\end{array}
$$

The example checks, for we obtained 3 by substituting 2 for a in the sum and also by adding the numbers obtained by substituting 2 for a separately in the addends.

EXERCISES

In the following list arrange the polynomials in columns either according to the ascending or the descending order of some one literal factor. Add and check as in the preceding problem.

1. $x^2 + y^2 + xy$, $x^2 - xy + y^2$, $-14xy + 3x^2 - 2y^2$.

2. $26xy$, $-5y^2 + 12x^2$, $-10xy - 18xy + 16y^2$.

3. $5.3x^2 - 13.6xy - 2.3y^2$, $-0.02y^2 + 5xy + 3.2x^2$.

4. $4x^3 - 8x^2 - 5x - 12$, $3x^2 + 3x - 5x^3 + 8$.

5. $8a^3 - 2a^2 + 3a - 6$, $-3a^3 + 2a^2 + a + 7$.

6. $3r^2 + 2r^3 + 3r - 5$, $-r^2 - 2r + r^3 + 1$, $r^2 - 2$.

7. $\frac{3}{8}s^2 - \frac{1}{3}rs - \frac{3}{4}r^2$, $-s^2 - \frac{2}{3}rs + r^2$, $\frac{3}{5}s^2 - 5r^2$.

8. $- 21\,x^2y + 40\,x^2z + 55\,x^2y - 14\,y^2z,$
$+ 2\,cx^2z + 58\,xz^2 - 23\,y^2z,$
$- 20\,x^2z + 18\,y^2z - 15\,z^2x.$

9. $4\,(m + n) - 6\,(m^2 + n^2) + 7\,(m^3 + n^3) - 8\,(m^4 + n^4),$
$9\,(m^4 + n^4) - 3\,(m^3 + n^3) + 4\,(m^2 + n^2) - 3\,(m + n).$

10. $3\,(a + b) - 5\,(a^2 + b) + 7\,(a - b^2) - 5\,(a^2 + ab + b^2),$
$5\,(a + b) - 3\,(a - b^2) + 4\,(a^2 + b) + 2\,(a^2 + ab + b^2).$

219. Subtraction. The following exercises will help to make clear the process of subtraction.

EXERCISES

1. If the thermometer registers $+ 24°$ in the morning and $+ 29°$ in the evening, how much warmer is it in the evening than in the morning? How do you find the result?

2. A thermometer registers $+ 10°$ one hour and $+ 14°$ the next hour. What is the difference between these readings?

3. If the thermometer registers $- 2°$ one hour and $+ 3°$ the following hour, how much greater is the second reading than the first? The question might be stated: What is the difference between $- 2°$ and $+ 3°$? In what other form could you state this question?

4. If you were born in 1903, how old were you in 1915? State the rule you use in finding your age.

5. The year of Christ's birth has been chosen as zero of the time scale in Christian countries. Thus, we record a historic event as 60 B.C. or A.D. 14. Instead of using B.C. and A.D. we may write these numbers with the minus and plus signs prefixed. How old was Cæsar when he died if he was born in $- 60$ and died in $+ 14$?

6. A boy was born in $- 2$. How old is he in $+ 5$? Apply your rule for subtraction in this case.

7. Subtract $- 3$ from $+ 5$; $- 4$ from $+ 5$; $- 5$ from $+ 5$; $- 50$ from $+ 25$.

8. A newsboy has 41 ¢. How much must he earn during the day so as to have 85 ¢ in the evening? State the rule which you use to solve problems of this kind.

9. A newsboy owes three other newsboys a total of 65 ¢. How much must he earn to pay his debts and have 20 ¢ left? Apply your rule for solving Ex. 8 to this problem.

10. John is $25 in debt, Henry has $40 in cash. How much better off is Henry than John? Apply the rule stated for Ex. 8.

11. What is the difference between 12 and 20? 5 and 45? 0 and 20? — 1 and 20? — 5 and 25? — 12 and 18?

12. Interpret each of the parts of Ex. 11 as a verbal problem.

13. Through how many degrees must the line OR_1 turn (Fig. 155) to reach the position OR_2?

14. Archimedes, a great mathematician, was born about the year — 287 and was slain by a Roman soldier in — 212 while studying a geometrical figure that he had drawn in the sand. How old was he?

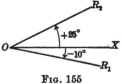

Fig. 155

15. Livy, a famous Roman historian, was born in — 59 and lived to be 76 yr. old. In what year did he die?

16. Herodotus, the Greek historian, sometimes called the Father of History, was born in — 484 and died in — 424. At what age did he die?

220. Subtraction illustrated by the number scale. In subtracting 4 from 6 we find what number must be added

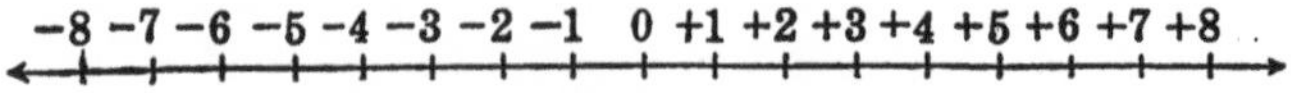

$$-8 \;-7\; -6\; -5\; -4\; -3\; -2\; -1 \quad 0 \;+1\; +2\; +3\; +4\; +5\; +6\; +7\; +8$$

Fig. 156. The Number Scale

to the 4 (the subtrahend) to get the 6 (the minuend). On the number scale (Fig. 156) how many spaces (beginning at 4) must we count until we arrive at 6?

1. Subtract − 2 from 3.

Solution. Beginning at − 2 we need to count 5 spaces to the right (*positive*) to arrive at 3. Hence, subtracting − 2 from 3 equals 5. Note that we might have obtained the result by adding + 2 to 3.

2. Subtract + 5 from − 2.

Solution. Beginning at 5 on the number scale we need to count 7 to the left (*negative*) to arrive at − 2. Hence, subtracting + 5 from − 2 equals − 7. Note that we could have obtained the same result by adding − 5 to − 2.

This exercise may be stated as a temperature problem; namely, What is the difference between 5 above zero and 2 below zero?

3. Subtract − 8 from − 2. Interpret as a verbal problem.

Solution. Beginning at − 8 on the number scale we need to count 6 to the right (*positive*). Hence, subtracting − 8 from − 2 equals + 6. Notice that the same result is obtained if + 8 is added to − 2.

These examples show that *since subtraction is the reverse of addition, we can subtract a number by adding its opposite.* Thus, adding $100 to the unnecessary expenses of a firm is precisely the same as subtracting $100 gain, or, on the other hand, eliminating (subtracting) $1000 of lost motion in an industrial enterprise is adding $1000 to the net gain.

It is convenient for us to make use of this relation, for by its use there will be no new rules to learn, but merely an *automatic change of sign* when we come to a subtraction problem, and a continuation of the process of addition.

221. Algebraic subtraction. The preceding discussion shows that subtraction of algebraic numbers may be changed into algebraic addition by the following law: *To subtract one number from another change the sign of the subtrahend and add the result to the minuend.*

Thus, the subtraction example

$$+ \ 7\,a$$
$$- \ 3\,a$$
$$+ 10\,a$$

may be changed to the addition example

$$+ \ 7\,a$$
$$+ \ 3\,a$$
$$+ 10\,a$$

EXERCISES

Subtract the lower number from the upper number in the following. Illustrate Exs. 1–11 with verbal problems.

1. $\quad 29$
   $\quad -10$

2. -55
   $\quad -15$

3. -65
   $\quad +15$

4. $+18$
   $\quad +24$

5. $\frac{7}{12}$
   $\frac{5}{12}$

6. $-\frac{3}{8}$
   $-\frac{1}{4}$

7. $\quad 3$
   $\quad 14$

8. $\quad 14$
   $\quad -3$

9. -14
   $\quad -3$

10. $+14$
    $\quad +3$

11. $-\frac{9}{10}$
    $\quad +\frac{2}{3}$

12. $-5\,x^2$
    $\quad +\ x^2$

13. $-12\,b^3$
    $\quad\ 7\,b^3$

14. $-\ 9\,r$
    $\quad -14\,r$

15. $+\ 7\,a^2$
    $\quad -14\,a^2$

16. $-7\,m^3$
    $\quad +3\,m^3$

17. $+x$
    $\quad +x$

18. $-x$
    $\quad +x$

19. $+x$
    $\quad -x$

20. $+5.74\,x^3$
    $\quad -6.26\,x^3$

21. $-3.15\,a^2$
    $\quad -\ .34\,a^2$

22. $+6(a+b)$
    $\quad -8(a+b)$

23. $-5(a-b)$
    $\quad\ 3(a-b)$

24. $-4.36\,t$
    $\quad\ 8.64\,t$

25. $+0.81\,x^2$
    $\quad -2.62\,x^2$

26. $-.66\,¢$
    $\quad -.84\,¢$

27. $+0.82\,r$
    $\quad +2.41\,r$

28. $-3.34\,a$
    $\quad +5.37\,a$

29. $+2.04\,y$
    $\quad -4.23\,y$

30. $+8.92\,x$
    $\quad +9.17\,x$

31. $-7.42\,z$
    $\quad -3.71\,z$

32. $-2.41\,y$
    $\quad +8.62\,y$

33. Translate each of the following subtraction exercises into a verbal problem, using the suggestion given:

(a) As assets and liabilities : $\begin{array}{r} + 8246 \\ - 5216 \\ \hline \end{array}$

(b) As gain or loss : $\begin{array}{r} + 5 \\ - 7 \\ \hline \end{array}$

(c) As debit or credit : $\begin{array}{r} + 15 \\ - 27 \\ \hline \end{array}$

(d) As an angle problem : $\begin{array}{r} - 48° \\ - 14° \\ \hline \end{array}$

(e) As an age problem (time): $\begin{array}{r} + 22 \\ - 48 \\ \hline \end{array}$

(f) As line segments on the number scale : $\begin{array}{r} - 11 \\ - 5 \\ \hline \end{array}$

(g) As a bank account : $\begin{array}{r} - 246 \\ - 112 \\ \hline \end{array}$

(h) As a latitude problem : $\begin{array}{r} - 40 \\ + 25 \\ \hline \end{array}$

(i) As a longitude problem : $\begin{array}{r} + 50 \\ + 75 \\ \hline \end{array}$

(j) As a problem involving forces : $\begin{array}{r} + 52 \\ - 46 \\ \hline \end{array}$

222. Subtraction of polynomials. When the subtrahend consists of more than one term the subtraction may be performed by subtracting each term of the subtrahend from the corresponding term of the minuend.

For example, when we wish to subtract 5 dollars, 3 quarters, and 18 dimes from 12 dollars, 7 quarters, and 31 dimes, we subtract 5 dollars from 12 dollars, leaving 7 dollars; 3 quarters from 7 quarters, leaving 4 quarters; and 18 dimes from 31 dimes, leaving 23 dimes.

The subtraction of algebraic polynomials is, then, not different from the subtraction of monomials and may therefore be reduced to addition, as in the following two examples, which are exactly equivalent:

SUBTRACTION	ADDITION
$7\,a^2 - 14\,ab - 11\,b^2$	$7\,a^2 - 14\,ab - 11\,b^2$
$+\,5\,a^2 + \ 3\,ab + \ 3\,b^2$	$-\,5\,a^2 - \ 3\,ab - \ 3\,b^2$
$2\,a^2 - 17\,ab - 14\,b^2$	$2\,a^2 - 17\,ab - 14\,b^2$

The student should change the signs of the subtrahend in the written form until there is no doubt whatever as to his ability to change them mentally. The example will appear as follows:

$$a^2 + 2\,ab + b^2$$
$$-\ \ \ +\ \ \ -$$
$$+\ a^2 - 2\,ab + b^2$$
$$4\,ab$$

NOTE. The lower signs are the actual signs of the subtrahend. They are neglected in the adding process.

Numerous verbal problems have been given with the hope of giving a reasonable basis for the law of subtraction. The student should now apply the law *automatically* in the following exercises.

EXERCISES

Subtract the lower from the upper polynomial:

1. $4\,a^2 - 3\,ab + 6\,b^2$
   $4\,a^2 - 5\,ab - 4\,b^2$

2. $\ \ \ \ x^2 - 5\,xy + \ \ y^2$
   $-\,3\,x^2 - 4\,xy - 3\,y^2$

3. $x^3 + 3\,x^2y + 3\,xy^2 + y^3$
   $\ \ \ \ -\,7\,x^2y + 3\,xy^2 + y^3$

4. $\ \ 2\,mn^2 + 5\,m^3n + \ \ 6$
   $-\,7\,mn^2 - 4\,m^3n + 18$

5. From $10\,xy - 5\,xz + 6\,yz$ subtract $-\,4\,xy - 3\,xz + 3\,yz$.

6. From $16\,x^3 - 5\,mx^2 + 4\,m^3$ subtract $7\,x^3 - 4\,mx^2 + 12\,m^3$.

7. From $2\,a^3 - 2\,a^2b + ab^2 - 2\,b^3$ subtract $a^3 - 3\,a^2b + ab^2 - b^3$.

Subtract as indicated, doing as much of the work as possible mentally.

8. $(4r^3 - 5r^2s + 10s^3 - 6rs^2) - (2r^3 + 6r^2s + 4s^3 + 3rs^2).$

9. $(-8m^2pq - 4m^3p - 10m^2q^2) - (-6m^3p - 8m^2pq - 15m^2q^2).$

10. $(15x^3 - 12x^2y + 7y^3) - (-11x^3 + 8x^2y - 5y^3).$

11. $(\frac{1}{2}a^3 - 3\frac{1}{2}ab^2 - 3a^2b) - (-\frac{3}{4}ab^2 + 5\frac{1}{2}a^2b - 3a^3).$

12. $(5\frac{2}{3}rst - 7\frac{1}{2}r^2s - 8\frac{2}{5}s^2t - 6\frac{1}{3}t^2r) - (4\frac{1}{3}s^2t + 3\frac{1}{5}rst + 7\frac{1}{3}r^2s).$

13. $(2.3a^2b^4 - 4.6a^4b^3 + 8.7a^6b^2) - (-1.1a^4b^3 - 2.1a^6b^2 - 3a^2b^4).$

14. $(3x^2 - 4x + 5) + (2x^2 + 5x - 3) - (-2x^2 + 3x + 6).$

15. $(5.2x^2y - 41xy + 2y^2) - (31x^2y + 3.2xy + 5y^2).$

16. $(2.42a^2b^2 + 5ab + 6) - (3.12a^2b^2 - 2ab - 9).$

17. $(3ab^3 - 3abc^3) - (-2ab^3 + 3a^3 - 4abc^3) - (-4a^3 - 2b^3).$

18. $(5x^2 + 2xy + 3y^2) + (2x^2 - 5xy - y^2) - (9x^2 - 5xy + 2y^2).$

19. Compare the signs of the terms of the subtrahend in the foregoing exercises before and after the parenthesis are removed.

20. State a rule as to the effect of the minus sign preceding a polynomial in parenthesis.

21. What is the rule when the plus sign precedes a polynomial in parenthesis?

223. Symbols of aggregation. It has been found very convenient to use the *parenthesis* for grouping numbers. Such a symbol indicates definitely where a polynomial begins and ends. Other symbols used with exactly the same meaning and purpose are [ ] (brackets); { } (braces); and $\overline{}$ (vinculum). Thus, to indicate that $a + b$ is to be subtracted from $x + y$ we may use any one of the following ways: $(x + y) - (a + b)$, $[x + y] - [a + b]$. $\{x + y\} - \{a + b\}$, or $\overline{x + y} - \overline{a + b}$. The vinculum is like the familiar line separating numerator and denominator of a fraction, as in $\frac{2}{3}$ or $\frac{a + b}{a - b}$.

Sometimes the symbols are inclosed one pair within another; thus, $19 - \{16 - (9 - 2)\}$.

In an example like the preceding the common agreement is to remove first the innermost parenthesis. First, 2 is to be subtracted from 9, then the result, 7, is to be subtracted from 16. This result, 9, is in turn to be subtracted from 19; whence the final result is 10.

EXERCISES

1. Give the meaning of the following:

    (a) $15 - \{4 + (6 - 8)\}$.

    (b) $-5 - [7 - \{-3 + 6\}]$.

    (c) $-5x - [-7x - \{-2x + 4x\}]$.

    (d) $3(x + y) - 5\{x - \overline{.2x - 3y}\}$.

    (e) $5(x + y) - 7\{2x - \overline{-3x + 2y}\}$.

2. Keep definitely in mind the rules governing the effect of a minus or a plus sign before a grouping symbol. Perform the following indicated operations and simplify the results:

    (a) $12 - \{5 - (-2x - 5)\}$.

    (b) $17 - \{-12x - \overline{3x - 4}\}$.

    (c) $4a^2 - \{a^2 - 3a^3 + \overline{3a^2 - a^3}\}$.

    (d) $2e - [6e - \overline{3b - 4e} - (2e - 4b)]$.

    (e) $7a - \{5b - (4a + 3c) - (7b - 4c)\}$.

    (f) $15x^2 - \{-3x^2 - (3x^2 + 5)\} - (20x^2 + 5)$.

SUMMARY

224. This chapter has taught the meaning of the following words and phrases: positive number, negative number, algebraic numbers, absolute value of a number (or numerical value), degree of a number, degree of a monomial, degree of a polynomial, descending power, ascending power.

225. The following symbols were used: + (plus sign) and − (minus sign) for positive and negative number respectively, ( ) (parenthesis), [ ] (brackets), { } (braces), and ‾‾‾ (vinculum).

226. Positive and negative numbers have been illustrated by game scores, directed line segments, latitude, longitude, time, the number scale, forces, the thermometer, angles, profit and · loss, debit and credit, assets and liabilities, deposits and checks.

227. The sum of two algebraic numbers with like signs is the sum of their absolute values with their common sign prefixed.

The sum of two algebraic numbers with unlike signs equals the difference of their absolute values with the sign of the number having the greater absolute value prefixed.

The sum of three or more monomials is found most easily by the following method: (1) add all positive terms, (2) add all negative terms, (3) add the two sums obtained.

228. To add polynomials add the similar terms (write similar terms in the same column).

229. To find the difference of two numbers change the sign of the subtrahend and add.

230. A parenthesis is used for grouping. If preceded by a plus sign, it may be removed without making any other changes; if preceded by a minus sign, it may be removed if the sign of every term within the parenthesis is changed.

CHAPTER IX

POSITIVE AND NEGATIVE NUMBERS. MULTIPLICATION AND DIVISION. FACTORING

231. Multiplication. The laws of multiplication of numbers having plus or minus signs are easily applied to a considerable number of interesting problems. These laws are illustrated in the following examples:

ILLUSTRATIVE EXAMPLES

1. Find the product of $(+4)$ and $(+2)$.

Solution. Geometrically we interpret this as follows: Take a segment $+4$ units long and lay it off two times to the *right* of zero on the number scale; that is, in its *own* direction (Fig. 157). Thus, $(+2)(+4) = +8$.

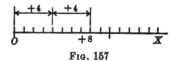

FIG. 157

2. Find the product of (-4) and $(+2)$.

Solution. Geometrically this means: Take a segment -4 units long and lay it off two times to the *left* of zero on the number scale; that is, in its *own* direction (Fig. 158). Thus, $(+2)(-4) = -8$.

FIG. 158

3. Find the product of $(+4)$ and (-2).

Solution. Geometrically we interpret this as follows: Take a

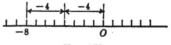

FIG. 159

segment $+4$ units long and lay it off two times to the *left* of zero; that is, *opposite* its *own* direction (Fig. 159). Thus, $(-2)(+4) = -8$.

178

4. Find the product of (-4) and (-2).

Solution. If the first factor were a positive 2, then we should interpret this geometrically by laying off -4 twice, obtaining a line segment -8 units long (see OR_1, in Fig. 160) just as we did in Ex. 2. But since it is a negative 2, we lay it off not in the direction of OR_1 but in the opposite direction; namely, OR (see Fig. 161). Thus, $(-2)(-4) = +8$.

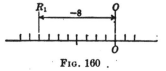

Fig. 160

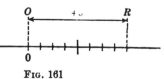

Fig. 161

Note that in this last case, as in Ex. 1, the signs of the multiplicand and the multiplier are alike, and the product is positive; while in Exs. 2 and 3 the signs of the multiplicand and multiplier are unlike, and the product is negative.

1. Find geometrically the products of $(+2)(+5)$; $(-2)(+5)$; $(+2)(-5)$; $(-2)(-5)$.

2. State the law of signs for the product of two algebraic numbers as suggested by the preceding work.

232. The law of signs for multiplication. The law of signs for multiplication is as follows:

The product of two factors having like signs is positive.
The product of two factors having unlike signs is negative.

Find the value of the following products, using the law of signs. Illustrate the first ten geometrically.

1. $(+3)(+5)$.	**3.** $(-3)(+5)$.	**5.** $(-2)(+3)$.
2. $(-3)(-5)$.	**4.** $(+3)(-5)$.	**6.** $(-2)(-3)$.

7. $(-2)(+7)$.   **11.** $(2)(-x)$.   **15.** $(-3)(-5x)$.

8. $(+2)(+7)$.   **12.** $(-1)(-1)$.   **16.** $(-\frac{2}{3})(-12b^5)$.

9. $(9)(-3)$.   **13.** $(-2x)(-3)$.   **17.** $(-\frac{2}{3})(-\frac{3}{4}r)$.

10. $(-4)(-x)$.   **14.** $(2ab)(-3)$.   **18.** $(-2xy)(-\frac{3}{8})$.

233[1]. Law of multiplication illustrated by the balance.
The law of signs may be illustrated with a balanced bar
(Fig. 162). A light bar is balanced at M. The points r_1, r_2,
etc. represent pegs or small
nails driven at equal distances.
We shall speak of r_1, r_2, etc.
as "first right peg," "second
right peg," etc. and of l_1, l_2,
etc. as "first left peg," "second left peg," etc. with the bar
in a position facing the class as
in Fig. 162. The weights, w,
are all equal; hence we shall

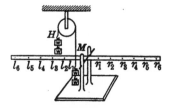

FIG. 162. THE LAW OF MULTI-
PLICATION ILLUSTRATED BY THE
BALANCED BEAM

merely speak of them as "two weights," "three weights,"
etc. instead of mentioning the number of ounces or grams
contained. In Experiments 1–3 the string over the pulley
is fastened on the first left peg.

EXPERIMENTS

1. Hang two weights on l_1. This tends to turn the bar. How
many must be attached to the hook H to keep the bar level? Hang
three weights on l_1. What do you notice about the turning tendency
as compared with the first case? Answer the same question for four
weights on l_3.

---

[1] The entire article may be omitted at the teacher's discretion. The
device has, however, proved useful in the hands of many teachers. The
apparatus may be bought at several of the large book companies or,
better still, made in the shop by a member of the class, using a part of
a yardstick for the lever and small nails for pegs.

2. Hang one weight on l_1. How many must be placed on the hook to keep the bar level? Hang one weight on l_2; remove it and hang one weight on l_3; on l_4; and so on. What do you notice about the turning tendency in each case? What two things does the turning tendency seem to depend on?

3. With the string passing over the pulley fastened to l_1 how many weights must be put on the hook to balance two weights on l_3? three weights on l_3? one weight on l_4? two weights on l_4? three weights on l_4?

4. Repeat Experiments 1–3 for the pegs on the right side, with the pulley string fastened to r_1. What seems to be the only difference?

Results of experiments. The experiments show that

1. *The turning tendency (force) varies as the number of weights hung on a peg on the bar. Thus, the more weights hung on any peg, the stronger the force.*

2. *The turning tendency also varies as the distance of the peg from the turning point.*

3. *The turning tendency is equal to the product of the weights multiplied by the distance of the peg on which the weight hangs from the turning point.*

4. *When a weight is hung on a right peg, the bar turns in the same direction as the hands of a clock; when a weight is hung on a left peg, the bar rotates in a direction opposite to the hands of a clock.*

234. Signs of turning tendency; weight; lever arm. It is conventionally agreed that when the bar turns *counterclockwise* (as you face it), the turning tendency is positive; while if the bar rotates *clockwise*, the turning tendency is *negative*.

Weights attached to the pegs are downward-pulling weights and are designated by the minus sign. Weights attached at H pull upward on the bar and are designated by the plus sign.

The distance from the turning point to the peg where the weight, or force, acts will be called the *lever arm*, or arm of the force. Lever arms measured from the turning point toward the right will be marked +; those toward the left, −. For example, if the distance from M to peg r_1 is represented by + 1, then the distance from M to r_3 will be + 3; the distance from M to l_2 will be − 2; and so on.

235. Multiplication of positive and negative numbers. By means of the apparatus (Fig. 162) the product of positive and negative numbers is now to be found.

ILLUSTRATIVE EXAMPLES

1. Find the product of $(+ 2)(- 4)$.

Solution. We may interpret this exercise as meaning, Hang four downward-pulling, or negative, weights on the second peg to the right (positive). The bar turns clockwise. The force is negative; hence the product of $(2)(- 4)$ is − 8.

2. Find the product of $(- 2)(- 4)$.

Solution. Hang two downward-pulling, or negative, weights on the fourth peg to the left (negative). The bar turns counterclockwise. The force is positive; hence the product of $(- 2)(- 4)$ is + 8.

3. Show that $(+ 3)(+ 4) = + 12$.

HINT. Fasten the string over the pulley to the fourth peg to the right and hang three weights on the hook.

4. Show that $(- 3)(+ 2) = - 6$; that $(+ 2)(- 3) = - 6$. How does the beam illustrate the law of order in multiplication?

5. Compare the results of Exs. 1–4 with the law of signs in multiplication (Art. 232).

It is hoped that the law of signs is made reasonably clear by means of these illustrations. The student should now proceed to apply the law automatically.

EXERCISES

State the products of the following, doing mentally as much of the work as possible:

1. $(+4)(-6)$.
2. $(-4)(+6)$.
3. $(+4)(+6)$.
4. $(-4)(-6)$.
5. $(+2)(+5)$.
6. $(+3)(-4)$.
7. $(-5)(-2)$.
8. $(-3)(-7)$.
9. $(-5)(+6)$.
10. $(-12)(-13)$.

11. $(-3.1)(-5)$.
12. $(-\frac{2}{3})(\frac{5}{6})$.
13. $(\frac{3}{5})(\frac{5}{9})$.
14. $(-\frac{5}{8})(-\frac{2}{15})$.
15. $(-\frac{5}{8})(+\frac{2}{15})$.
16. $(-6\frac{1}{4})(-6\frac{1}{4})$.
17. $(+6\frac{1}{4})(+6\frac{1}{4})$.
18. $(+6\frac{1}{4})(-6\frac{1}{4})$.
19. $(-6\frac{1}{4})(+6\frac{1}{4})$.
20. $(+5)(+x)$.

21. $(+5)(-x)$.
22. $(-5)(-x)$.
23. $(-8)(-xy)$.
24. $(-c)(-ab)$.
25. $(-2\frac{1}{3})(-xy)$.
26. $(-3\frac{1}{3})(+ab)$.
27. $(5\frac{1}{3})(-gl^2)$.
28. $(-9)(+x^2m)$.
29. $(-1)^3$.
30. $(-2)^3$.

236. Multiplication by zero. The product of 3×0 means $0 + 0 + 0 = 0$.

EXERCISES

1. Show geometrically that $a \times 0 = 0$.

2. Show by the beam (Fig.162) that $a \times 0 = 0$; that $0 \times a = 0$.

3. State a verbal problem in which one of the factors is zero. In general both $a \times 0$ and $0 \times a$ equal zero. Hence the value of the product is zero when one of the factors is zero.

4. What is the area of the rectangle in Fig.163? How would the area change if you were to make the base smaller and smaller? What connection has this with the principle $a \times 0 = 0$?

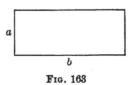

FIG. 163

5. How would the area of the rectangle in Fig. 163 change if b were not changed but a were made smaller and smaller? What does this illustrate?

237. Product of several factors. The product of several factors is obtained by multiplying the first factor by the second, the result by the third, and so on. By the law of order in multiplication the factors may first be rearranged if this makes the exercise easier. This is often the case in a problem which involves fractions.

1. Find the value of the following products:

(a) $(+2)(-3)(-5)(-4)$.

(b) $(-\frac{5}{7})(+\frac{3}{4})(-\frac{14}{15})(+\frac{8}{3})$.

(c) $(-\frac{11}{13})(-\frac{4}{6})(-\frac{10}{22})(1\frac{3}{2})$.

2. Find the value of $(-1)^2$; $(-1)^3$; $(-1)^4$; $(-2)^2(-2)^3$ $(-2)^4$; $(-2)^5$; $(-3)^2(-3)^3(-3)^4$; $(-4)^2(-4)^3$.

3. Find the value of $3x^4 - 5x^3 + x^2 - 12x - 5$ when $x = -2$.

4. Find the value of $x^3 - 3x^2y + 3xy^2 + y^2$ when $x = 3$ and $y = -2$.

5. Find the value of $x^3 + 3x^2 + 3x + 1$ when $x = 10$.

6. Compare $(-2)^3$ and -2^3; -3^3 and $(-3)^3$; $(-2)^4$ and -2^4; $(-a)^3$ and $-a^3$; $(-a)^4$ and $-a^4$.

7. What is the sign of the product of five factors of which three are negative and two are positive? of six factors of which three are negative and three are positive?

8. What powers of -1 are positive? of -2? of $-x$? State the rule.

238. Multiplication of monomials. Find the product of $(2x^2)(-3xy^2)(-5xy)$.

The sign of the product is determined as in Art. 232 and is found to be $+$.

By the law of order in multiplication the factors may be arranged as follows: $$2(-3)(-5)xxxxyyy,$$ which is equal to $30x^4y^3$.

Hence, to find the product of two or more monomials

1. *Determine the sign of the product.*

2. *Find the product of the absolute values of the arithmetical factors.*

3. *Find the product of the literal factors.*

4. *Indicate the product of the two products just found.*

Simplify the following indicated products, doing mentally as much of the work as possible:

1. $(13)(-8)(-5)$.

2. $(-2x)(-3x)(4x)$.

3. $(5x^2yz^2)(-3x^2y^2z)(2x^2y^2z^2)(-7xy^2z^2)$.

4. $(-2a^2bcd)(5ab^2cd)(-7abc^2d)(-2abcd^2)$.

5. $(-3mnx)(-5\frac{1}{3}m^2nx)(-2x)$.

6. $(\frac{3}{5}x^2y)(-\frac{10}{9}xy^2z)(-\frac{2}{15}xyz^2)$.

7. $(-3\frac{1}{2}ab)(-5\frac{1}{2}a^2b^2)(+8ab)$.

8. $(5\frac{1}{4}q^2r^3)(\frac{1}{7}r^2p^5)(-2\frac{1}{8}p^2q^5)$.

9. $(\frac{3}{5}b^2z)(\frac{6}{5}b^2cz^2w)(-\frac{10}{4}bz^2w)$.

10. $(\frac{3}{5}b^2z)(\frac{6}{5}m^2nr^2y)(-6mn)(\frac{1}{4}ny)(\frac{1}{6}my)$.

11. $(1.3x^{11}y^2z)(-2x^2y^{11}z^{12})(-0.3x^2y^2z^2)$.

12. $(1.1xy^2)(1.1mxy^2)(10m^2x^2)$.

13. $(-2)^2(-3)^2(-4)(2)^2$.

14. $(-3)^2(-2)^2(-1)^3$.

15. $(5)(-4)(3)^2(0)(2)^2$.

16. $(-a)^2(-a)^3(-a^2)(-a^5)$.

17. $(x+y)(x+y)^3(x+y)^5$.

18. $3(x+y)^3(x-y)^2(x+y)^5(x-y)^3$.

19. Find the value of $1+(-5)(-3)-(-2)(4)-(-3)(3)$ $-(-3)^2+12(-1)^2$.

20. What is a short method of determining the sign of the product containing a large number of factors ?

NOTE. It is agreed that when an arithmetical expression contains plus or minus signs in connection with multiplication or division signs, the multiplication and division shall be performed first. This amounts to the same thing as *finding the value of each term and then adding or subtracting as indicated.*

239. Multiplication of a polynomial by a monomial. We shall now see how the process of algebraic multiplication is extended.

INTRODUCTORY EXERCISES

1. Review the process of finding the product of $a(x + y + z)$ in Art. 122.

2. Illustrate by a geometric drawing the meaning of the product obtained in Ex. 1.

3. How many parts does the whole figure contain ?

4. What is the area of each part ?

The preceding exercises serve to recall the law that *a polynomial may be multiplied by a monomial by multiplying every term of the polynomial by the monomial and adding the resulting products.*

DRILL EXERCISES

Find the products as indicated and check by substituting arithmetical values for the literal numbers :

1. $3a(a^2 - 2ab + 3b^2)$.

Solution.
$$a^2 - 2ab + 3b^2 = 19$$
$$3a = 6$$
$$\overline{3a^3 - 6a^2b + 9ab^2 = 114}$$

Check. Let $a = 2$ and $b = 3$. Then the same result is obtained by substituting in the product as by substituting in the factors and then multiplying the numbers. Note that the check is not reliable if we let a literal number in a product containing a power of that literal number (as x in a product $x^5 - 4\,x$) equal 1, for if $x = 1$, then $x^5 - 4\,x$ also equals $x^3 - 4\,x$, $x^2 - 4\,x$, $x^9 - 4\,x$, etc. Explain.

2. $5\,x(2\,x^2 - 3\,x - 7)$.

3. $3\frac{1}{5}\,x(10\,x - 15\,x^2 - 25\,x^3)$.

4. $2\,x(3\,x - 4\,y) + 5\,y(3\,x - 5\,y)$.

5. $-5.1\,a^4(\frac{2}{17}\,a^2 m - 1\frac{3}{17}\,a m^2 - 3\frac{1}{17}\,a m)$.

6. $(5\,x^2 y + 4\,xy + 2\,y^2 - 1)\,xy^2$.

7. $(m^3 n^4 - 3\,m^4 n^5 + 4\,m^2 n^7 - 9\,m^5 n^4)\,3.5\,m^2 n^3$.

8. $2(3\,x - 2\,y) - 4(x + 3\,y) + 3(2\,x - y)$.

9. $2\,x + y(x - 2\,y) + (3\,x - 7)\,3 + y$.

10. $(x^2 - 3\,x + 4)\,3\,x - (x + 2)\,2\,x^2 - (x^3 - 7\,x^2 + 4\,x)$.

11. $3\,c^2(3\,e - 2\,d) - 2\,ed(3\,e - 2\,d) + (3\,e - 2\,d)\,4\,d$.

240. Product of two polynomials. In Art. 126 we found the *product of two polynomials to be the sum of all the partial products obtained by multiplying every term of one polynomial by each term of the other.* After reviewing briefly the case for positive terms we shall proceed to interpret the above law geometrically even when negative terms are involved.

ILLUSTRATIVE EXAMPLES

1. Find the product of $(c + d)(a + b)$.

Solution. The area of the whole rectangle in Fig. 164 is expressed by $(a + b)\,(c + d)$. The dotted line suggests a method for expressing the area as the sum of two rectangles; namely, $a(c + d) + b(c + d)$. If we use the line MN, the area may be expressed as the sum of four rectangles; namely, $ac + ad + bc + bd$. Each expression equals the area of one of the rectangles; hence

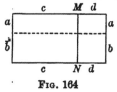

Fig. 164

$$(a + b)\,(c + d) = a(c + d) + b(c + d) = ac + ad + bc + bd.$$

2. Illustrate, by means of Fig. 165, the law for the multiplication of two polynomials.

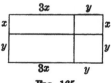

Fig. 165

3. Find the product of $(a-b)(c+d)$.

Solution. In this case one of the factors involves a negative term.

The product $(a-b)(c+d)$ is represented by a rectangle having the dimensions $(a-b)$ and $(c+d)$ (Fig. 166). The rectangle $ABEF = ac + ad$. Subtracting from this the rectangles bc and bd, we obtain the rectangle $ABCD$.

Therefore $(a-b)(c+d) = ac + ad - bc - bd$, each side of the equation representing the area of rectangle $ABCD$.

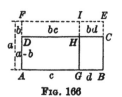

Fig. 166

*4. Find the product of $(a-b)(a-b)$.

Solution. Let $ABCD$ (Fig. 167), represent a square whose side is $(a-b)$ feet. Show that the area of $ABCD$ equals $EFGC + GHIB - FKDE - KHIA$.

Then

$$(a-b)(a-b) = (a-b)^2 \qquad \text{Why?}$$
$$= a^2 + b^2 - ab - ab$$
$$= a^2 - 2ab + b^2.$$

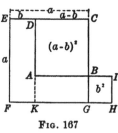

Fig. 167

*5. Sketch a rectangle whose area is $(m+n)(r-s)$; whose area is $24\,b^2 - 6\,bc$.

DRILL EXERCISES

Apply the law of multiplication to two polynomials in the following exercises. Check only the first five.

1. $(x^2 + 2\,xy + y^2)(x+y)$.

Solution.
$$x^2 + 2\,xy + y^2$$
$$\underline{x + y}$$
$$x^3 + 2\,x^2y + xy^2$$
$$\underline{x^2y + 2\,xy^2 + y^3}$$
$$x^3 + 3\,x^2y + 3\,xy^2 + y^3$$

Check by letting $x = 2$ and $y = 3$.

2. $(rs + tm)(rs - tm)$.

3. $(x^3 + ax^2 + a^2)(a + x)$.

4. $(x^2 + 4x + 3)(x - 2)$.

5. $(x^2 - 3x + 5)(2x + 3)$.

6. $(k^2 + 3k + 1)(k - 2)$.

7. $(2a + 3b)(2a - 3b)$.

8. $(\frac{1}{3}ab - \frac{1}{2}bc)(\frac{3}{4}ab + \frac{4}{3}bc)$.

9. $(a + b - c)^2$.

10. $(a - b + c - d)^2$.

11. $(-2a + 3b - 4c)^2$.

12. Comment on the interesting form of the results in Exs. 9–11.

13. $(0.3a + 0.4b - 0.5c)(10a - 30b + 40c)$.

14. $(2y^2 - 12xy + 5x^2)(2y^2 - 5x^2)$.

15. $(x^2 + xy + y^2)(x - y)(x + y)$.

16. $(9x^2 + 6xy + y)(3x + y)(3x - y)$.

17. $(x + y)^3$; $(x - y)^3$; $(2x - y)^3$; $(x + 2y)^3$.

18. Comment on the form of the results in Ex. 17.

19. $(r^2 + rs - s^2)(r^2 + rs + s^2)$.

20. $(3r^2 + 5r + 6)(3r^2 + 3x - 6)$.

21. $(3x + 2y)^3 - (3x - 2y)^3$.

22. $(3x^2 + y^2)^2 - (3x^2 - y^2)^2 - 4x^2(x - 2y)^2$.

23. $(2a - 3b)^2 - (2a + 3b)^2 + (2a - 3b)(2a + 3b)$.

24. $(0.3a - 0.4b)^2 - (0.5a + 0.6b)^2$
$- (0.3a - 0.4b)(0.3a + 0.4b)$.

25. $\left(\frac{x}{2} - 3\right)^2 - \left(\frac{x}{2} + 3\right)^2 - \left(\frac{x}{2} - 3\right)\left(\frac{x}{2} + 3\right)^2$.

26. $(5 + 3)^2 - (5 - 3)^2 - (5 + 3)(5 - 3)$.

27. Why may 3527 be written $3 \cdot 10^3 + 5 \cdot 10^2 + 2 \cdot 10 + 7$?

28. Multiply 352 by 243.

HINT. Write in the form $3 \cdot 10^2 + 5 \cdot 10 + 2$
$2 \cdot 10^2 + 4 \cdot 10 + 3$

29. Write 56,872 as a polynomial arranged according to the descending powers of 10.

30. Find the product of 5 and 3427 by the method suggested in Ex. 28.

241. Product of two binomials. We shall now see how the algebraic product of two binomials may be obtained automatically. The following exercises will help the student to discover and understand the method.

Find by actual multiplication the following products:

1. $(2x + 3)(4x + 5)$.

Solution. $2x + 3$
$4x + 5$
$\overline{8x^2 + 12x}$
$+ 10x + 15$
$\overline{8x^2 + 22x + 15}$

2. $(3a + 5)(2a - 8)$.

Solution. $3a + 5$
$2a - 8$
$\overline{6a^2 + 10a}$
$- 24a - 40$
$\overline{6a^2 - 14a - 40}$

3. $(5y + 4)(5y - 4)$.

Solution. $5y + 4$
$5y - 4$
$\overline{25y^2 + 20y}$
$- 20y - 16$
$\overline{25y^2 - 16}$

4. $(4x + 5)(4x + 5)$.

5. $(3x - 2)(3x - 2)$.

6. $(x + 2)(x + 9)$.

7. $(2x + 1)(x + 6)$.

8. $(b + 3)(b + 5)$.

9. $(a - 7)(a - 3)$.

10. $(3x + 8)(x + 2)$.

11. $(3x + 4)(2x - 3)$.

12. $(x - 3)(x - 10)$.

13. $(x^2 - 9)(x^2 + 9)$.

14. $(x^2 - 5)(x^2 + 10)$.

15. $(3x - 5)(4x - 2)$.

16. $(2y - 3)(5y - 8)$.

17. $(m^3 - 11)(m^3 + 9)$.

18. $(x - 2y)(x + 8y)$.

19. $(c - 5d)(c + 12d)$.

20. $(3x + 4y)(3x - 4y)$.

21. $(4a + 2b)(7a - 5b)$.

22. 53×57.

Solution. $53 \times 57 = (50 + 3)(50 + 7)$
$ = 50^2 + (7 + 3)50 + 21$.

23. 61×69.   **24.** 52×56.   **25.** 37×33.

26. Can you see any way of formulating a rule for finding the products of two binomials?

If we agree to use the binomials $ax + b$ and $cx + d$ to represent any two binomials where a, b, c, and d are known numbers like those in the products above, then we may discover a short cut in multiplying $ax + b$ by $cx + d$.

ILLUSTRATIVE EXAMPLE

Find the product of $(ax + b)$ and $(cx + d)$.

Solution.

$$ax + b$$

$$cx + d$$

$$\overline{acx^2 + bcx}$$
$$\qquad + adx + bd$$
$$\overline{acx^2 + (bc + ad)x + bd}$$

The arrows show the cross-multiplications or cross-products whose sum is equal to the middle term. It is seen that *the first term of the product is the product of the first terms of the binomials, that the last term is the product of the last terms of the binomials, and that the middle term is the sum of the two cross-products.*

EXERCISES

Using the rule stated above, give the products of the following binomials:

1. $(2a + 3)(3a + 5)$.

Solution. The product of the first terms of the two binomials is $6a^2$, the product of the last terms is 15, and the sum of the cross-products is $19a$. Therefore the product is $6a^2 + 19a + 15$.

2. $(4x + 3)(2x + 1)$.

3. $(2x - 7)(3x + 2)$.

4. $(3x + 4)(3x + 4)$.

5. $(7x - 2)(7x + 2)$.

6. $(3a - 2b)(3a - 2b)$.

7. $(x - 7)(4x + 9)$.

8. $(x + 7)(x - 4)$.

9. $(x + 5)(x + 8)$.

10. $(3x - 2)(7x - 2)$.

11. $(4x + 3)(3x - 4)$.

12. $(x + 9b)(x + 7b)$.

13. $(2x + 4y)(3x - 5y)$.

14. $(5a + 4)(4a - 2)$.

15. $(7 a + 2 b)(7 a - 2 b)$.   **18.** $(3 a - 7 b)(3 a - 7 b)$.

16. $(5 a + 4 b)(5 a + 4 b)$.   **19.** $(6 xy + 2)(3 xy - 5)$.

17. $(3 x + 2)(12 x - 20)$.   **20.** $(7 ab + 5 c)(6 ab - 8 c)$.

21. Do you notice anything especially significant about the product of two binomials that are exactly alike? Explain by using the product of $x + y$ and $x + y$, $a - b$ and $a - b$ (compare with Ex. 1, Art. 127).

22. Do you notice anything especially significant about the product of two binomials that are the same except for the signs between the two terms? Explain by using the product of $m + n$ and $m - n$.

23. Try to formulate a rule for obtaining automatically the products referred to in Exs. 21 and 22.

242. Special products. We have seen in Art. 241 how the multiplication of two binomials may be performed automatically. Such products are called *special products*. The student should observe that Exs. 21 and 22, Art. 241, furnish examples of such products. For example, the product of $x + y$ and $x + y$ is equal to $x^2 + 2 xy + y^2$, and is called *the square of the sum* of x and y; while the product of $a - b$ and $a - b$ is equal to $a^2 - 2 ab + b^2$, and is called *the square of the difference* of a and b. Further, the product of $m + n$ and $m - n$ is equal to $m^2 - n^2$, and is called *the product of the sum and difference* of m and n.

EXERCISES

1. Find automatically the following special products and classify each:

(a) $(x + 3)(x + 3)$.   (c) $(2 x + 4)(2 x + 4)$.

(b) $(y - 2)(y - 2)$.   (d) $(3 x - 5)(3 x - 5)$.

(e) $(2 x + 4)^2$.   (g) $(2 x + 4 y)^2$.   (i) $(2 a + 4 b)^2$.

(f) $(4 x - 2)^2$.   (h) $(5 x - 2 y)^2$.   (j) $(3 a - 2 b)^2$.

2. State a rule for finding automatically the square of the sum of two numbers.

3. State a rule for finding automatically the square of the difference of two numbers.

The preceding exercises should establish the following short cuts for finding the square of the sum and the square of the difference of two numbers:

1. *The square of the sum of two numbers is equal to the square of the first number increased by two times the product of the first number and the second number plus the square of the second number.* Thus, $(a+b)^2 = a^2 + 2\,ab + b^2$.

2. *The square of the difference of two numbers is equal to the square of the first number decreased by two times the product of the first number and the second number plus the square of the second number.* Thus, $(a-b)^2 = a^2 - 2\,ab + b^2$.

EXERCISES

1. Find automatically the following products:

(a) $(x+5)(x-5)$.

(b) $(a+4)(a-4)$.

(c) $(y-3)(y+3)$.

(d) $(c+7)(c-7)$.

(e) $(y-11)(y+11)$.

(f) $(r+8)(r-8)$.

2. Study the form of the results in Ex. 1. Give the products in the following list at sight:

(a) $(y-10)(y+10)$.

(b) $(2x+5)(2x-5)$.

(c) $(3d-4)(3d+4)$.

(d) $(5-x)(5+x)$.

(e) $(y-\frac{1}{2})(y+\frac{1}{2})$.

(f) $(5x-y)(5x+y)$.

3. Write the sum of x and y; the difference; find the product of the sum and the difference. Check by multiplication.

4. State the rule for finding the product of the sum and the difference of two numbers.

The preceding exercises should establish the following short cut for finding the product of the sum and the difference of two numbers:

1. *Square each of the numbers.*
2. *Subtract the second square from the first.*

Thus, $(2x-3y)(2x+3y)=(2x)^2-(3y)^2=4x^2-9y^2$.

DRILL EXERCISES

Find the following products mentally:

1. $(x+2)(x+2)$.
2. $(y+3)(y-3)$.
3. $(z-4)(z-4)$.
4. $(2w-5)(2w+5)$.
5. $(z-2b)(z+2b)$.
6. $(3z+2a)(3z+2a)$.
7. $(3r-4s)(3r+4s)$.
8. $(\frac{1}{2}a+\frac{1}{3}b)(\frac{1}{2}a-\frac{1}{3}b)$.
9. $(\frac{2}{5}xy-z)(\frac{2}{5}xy+z)$.
10. $(x-1)(x+1)$.

11. $(x-1)(x+1)(x^2+1)$.
12. $(w-c)(w+c)(w^2-c^2)$.
13. $(10x+9)(10x+9)$.
14. $(x^2y^2-0.5)(x^2y^2+0.5)$.
15. $(11+fgh^2)(11+fgh^2)$.
16. $(a^5+b^5)(a^5-b^5)$.
17. $(20+2)(20-2)$.
18. $(30+1)(30-1)$.
19. $(18)(22)$.
20. $(31)(29)$.

243. Division. The law for algebraic division is easily learned because of the relation between division and multiplication. We recall from arithmetic that *division* is the process of finding one of two numbers when their product and the other number are given and also we remember that *quotient* × *divisor* = *dividend*.

These facts suggest the law of division. Thus we know that $+12 \div +2 = +6$ because $(+2)(+6) = +12$.

1. Since $(2)(-6) = -12$, what is $-12 \div 2$?

2. Since $(-2)(+6) = -12$, what is $-12 \div -2$?

3. Since $(-2)(-6) = +12$, what is $+12 \div -2$?

4. Since $(+a)(+b) = +ab$, what is $(+ab) \div a$?

5. If the signs of dividend and divisor are alike, what is the sign of the quotient?

6. If the signs of dividend and divisor are unlike, what is the sign of the quotient?

244. Law of signs in division. The work of the preceding article may be summed up in the following law: *If the dividend and divisor have like signs, the quotient is positive; if the dividend and divisor have unlike signs, the quotient is negative.*

245. Dividing a monomial by a monomial. We shall now have an opportunity to apply the law learned in the preceding article.

Find the quotient in the following, doing mentally as much of the work as possible:

1. $(+15) \div (-3) = ?$

2. $(-15) \div (-3) = ?$

3. $(-15) \div (+3) = ?$

4. $(+15) \div (+3) = ?$

5. $(-18) \div (-3) = ?$

6. $(-12) \div (-12) = ?$

7. $(+5) \div (+5) = ?$

8. $(+x) \div (+x) = ?$

9. $(-2x) \div (x) = ?$

10. $(-10x) \div (-2x) = ?$

11. $(-ab) \div (-a) = ?$

12. $(-ab) \div (+b) = ?$

13. $(\frac{4}{3}x) \div (-\frac{2}{15}) = ?$

14. $(-0.5x) \div (-\frac{1}{3}x) = ?$

15. $(-1.21x^2) \div (-1.1x) = ?$

16. $(-\frac{7}{8}) \div (-\frac{3}{14}) = ?$

17. $(\frac{5}{7}) \div (\frac{2}{7}) = ?$

18. $(-\frac{5}{6}) \div (-\frac{2}{3}) = ?$

19. $(\frac{5}{7}) \div (-\frac{3}{8}) = ?$ **31.** $(-x^4) \div (x^3) = ?$

20. $(\frac{5}{8}) \div (-\frac{7}{8}) = ?$ **32.** $(-x^2) \div (x^2) = ?$

21. $(\frac{5}{6}) \div (\frac{3}{7}) = ?$ **33.** $(-9 a^3) \div (3 a) = ?$

22. $(\frac{2}{7}) \div (-\frac{5}{6}) = ?$ **34.** $(-3 ab) \div (-b) = ?$

23. $(-2) \div (+\frac{1}{2}) = ?$ **35.** $(6\frac{2}{3} e) \div (-2\frac{1}{3} e) = ?$

24. $(-3 x) \div \left(-\frac{x}{3}\right) = ?$ **36.** $(+ ae^3) \div (- a) = ?$

     37. $(- ae^3) \div e^2 = ?$

25. $(+12 x) \div (- x) = ?$ **38.** $(-xyz) \div (-\frac{1}{2}) = ?$

26. $(+ x) \div (-\frac{1}{2} x) = ?$ **39.** $(- mnt) \div (- t) = ?$

27. $(- x) \div (-\frac{1}{4} x) = ?$ **40.** $(- abc^2) \div (- ab) = ?$

28. $(- x^3) \div (- x) = ?$ **41.** $(7\frac{1}{3} ax) \div (- 22) = ?$

29. $(x^2) \div (- x) = ?$ **42.** $(5\frac{1}{3} rs) \div (- 3\frac{1}{5} r) = ?$

30. $(- x^4) \div (- x) = ?$ **43.** $24 xy \div 3 x = ?$

NOTE. The algebraic solution of the more difficult problems of this type are best interpreted as fractions, since a fraction is an indicated quotient. Thus, $24 xy \div 3 x$ may be written $\dfrac{24 xy}{3 x}$. The problem now is one of reducing to lower terms. Thus, in $\dfrac{24 xy}{3 x}$ both numerator and denominator may be divided by $3 x$. The result is $\dfrac{8 y}{1}$, or $8 y$ units.

In algebra, as in arithmetic, the quotient is not altered if dividend and divisor are both divided by the same factor. Dividing dividend and divisor by the highest common factor reduces the quotient (or fraction) to the simplest form (or to lowest terms).

44. $\dfrac{48 x^5 y^3 m^2}{- 8 x^2 y^3 m^3}.$

Solution. The sign of the quotient is negative. Why?

The numerical factors can be divided by 8; x^5 and x^2 are divisible by x^2; y^3 and y^3 are divisible by y^3; m^2 and m^3 are divisible by m^2.

Hence $\dfrac{48 x^5 y^3 m^2}{- 8 x^2 y^3 m^3} = \dfrac{6 x^3}{- m} = - \dfrac{6 x^3}{m}.$

45. $\dfrac{2\,xy}{-xz}$.

46. $\dfrac{-27\,a^3}{-9\,a}$.

47. $\dfrac{-8\,x^5b}{-2\,xb^2}$.

48. $\dfrac{-15\,x^5b^2z^5}{5\,b^2x^2z^3}$.

49. $\dfrac{343}{49\,x}$.

50. $\dfrac{12\,d^2m^3z^3}{3\,ab^2}$.

246. Dividing a polynomial by a monomial. The division process will now be extended.

1. Divide $6\,x^2 + 4\,xy + 8\,xz$ by $2\,x$.

As in dividing monomials, this quotient may be stated as a rectangle problem. Find the length of the base of a rectangle whose area is $6\,x^2 + 4\,xy + 8\,xz$ and whose altitude is $2\,x$. Indicating this quotient in the form of a fraction, we have

$$\frac{6\,x^2 + 4\,xy + 8\,xz}{2\,x}.$$

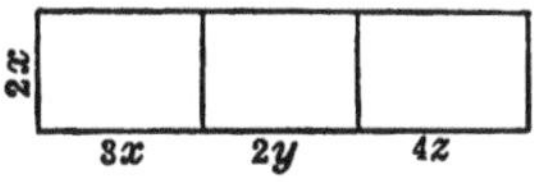

Fig. 168

Dividing numerator and denominator by $2\,x$, the result is $3\,x + 2\,y + 4\,z$. Show that the problem may now be interpreted by a rectangle formed by three adjacent rectangles (Fig. 168).

2. Show that the total area of three adjacent flower beds (Fig. 169) may be expressed in either of the following forms:

$$5 \cdot 3 + 5 \cdot 5 + 5 \cdot 4$$

or
$$5(3 + 5 + 4).$$

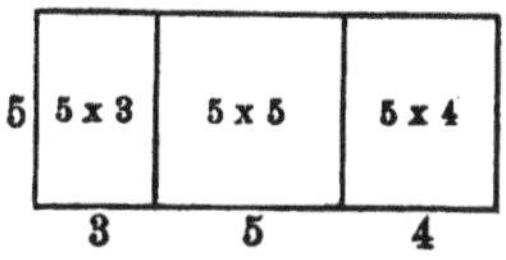

Fig. 169

Which form is the better? . Why ?

3. Find the following quotients, obtaining as many as you can mentally:

(a) $\dfrac{9\,a^2 - 6\,a^5}{3\,a^2}$.

(b) $\dfrac{a^3 + a^2 + a}{a}$.

(g) $\dfrac{4\,a^2b + 6\,ab^3 + 8\,a^2b^2}{4\,a^2b^2}$.

(c) $\dfrac{27\,ab + 6\,a^2}{3\,a}$.

(d) $\dfrac{12\,x^4e^2 + 8\,x^3e^3}{-4\,x^3e^2}$.

(e) $\dfrac{14\,m^2n^4 - 2\,m^5n^6r^2}{-7\,m^2n^3}$.

(f) $\dfrac{x^4 + x^3y - x^2y^2}{x^2y}$.

(h) $\dfrac{9\,x^5y^3 + 6\,x^4y^2 + 3\,xy}{3\,xy^2}$.

247. Factoring; prime numbers. *To factor a number* is to find two or more numbers which when multiplied together will produce the number. Thus, one may see by inspection that 2, 2, and 3 are the factors of 12. In like manner, $x + y$ and a are the factors of $ax + ay$.

A number which has no other factors except itself and unity is said to be a *prime number*; as, 5, x, and $a + b$.

A monomial is expressed in terms of its prime factors, thus:

$$15\,ax^2y^3 = 3 \cdot 5 \cdot a \cdot x \cdot x \cdot y \cdot y \cdot y.$$

The following is an example of the method of expressing a factored polynomial:

$$a^2x^2 + b^2x^2 = x^2(a^2 + b^2).$$

In algebra, as in arithmetic, certain forms of number expression occur very frequently either as multiplications or as divisions — so much so, that it is of considerable advantage to memorize the characteristics of these numbers that we may factor them by inspection and thus be able to perform the multiplications and divisions automatically. In this text we shall study two general types of factoring.

248. Factoring Type I. Taking out a common monomial factor. *Type form* $ax + bx + cx = x(a + b + c)$.

A number of this type we shall call *a number containing a common monomial factor*. The products obtained in the exercises of Art. 239 are numbers of this type. Although this type of factoring is not difficult, nevertheless it is important and should be kept in mind. We shall learn that many verbal problems lead to equations which can readily be solved by a method which depends upon factoring. Factoring also enables us to transform formulas into their most convenient form.

The method of factoring this type consists of the following steps:

1. *Inspect the terms and discover the factor which is common to all the terms.*

2. *Divide by the common monomial factor. The result obtained is the other factor.*

3. *In order to find out whether he has factored correctly the student should multiply the two factors together.*

NOTE. In all factoring problems the student should first look to see if the number contains a common monomial factor.

EXERCISES

Factor the following by inspection and check your work by multiplication:

1. $bx - 5b - bc$.

Solution. Each term has the factor b. Divide the expression by b. The quotient is $x - 5 - c$.

Check. $b(x - 5 - c) = bx - 5b - bc$.

Therefore the factors of $bx - 5b - bc$ are b and $x - 5 - c$.

2. $5a - 5b$.   **8.** $x^4 - x^3$.

3. $4x + 4y$.   **9.** $25x^2 - 5x^3$.

4. $5xa - 10xb$.   **10.** $2x^2 + 4xy + 2y^2$.

5. $5ax^2 - 10axy^2$.   **11.** $a^2b + ab^2 + a^3$.

6. $2rx^3 - 8ry^3$.   **12.** $4x^2 - 8xy + 4y^2$.

7. $3x^2 - 6x$.   **13.** $a^2x^2 - 2a^2x^2y^2 + 4ax^2y^2$.

14. $3a^2 - 15a + 18$.

249. Factoring Type II. The "cut and try" method of factoring. *Type form* $acx^2 + (bc + ad)x + bd = (ax + b)(cx + d)$.

The products obtained in the exercises of Art. 241 can all be factored easily by inspection. The method of factoring such products is known as the "cut and try" or "trial and error" method. The method consists simply of guessing the correct pair of factors from all of the possible ones and then verifying the result by multiplying the factors together. The method is illustrated by the following example:

Factor $2x^2 + 9x + 10$.

Solution. There are four possible pairs of factors, as shown below :

$$
\begin{array}{cccc}
2x + 10 & 2x + 10 & x + 5 & 2x + 5 \\
\underline{x + 1} & \underline{2x + 1} & \underline{2x + 2} & \underline{x + 2}
\end{array}
$$

It is clear that the last pair is the correct one, since the sum of the cross-products is $9x$. Of course the correct pair of factors may be found at any stage of the "cut and try" method, and while the process may seem slow at first, practice soon develops such skill that the factors can easily be found.

It is very important for the student always to be sure that the factors he has obtained are prime numbers. Such factors are called *prime factors*. Incidentally it is important to remember that there are some numbers that are not factorable, because they are already prime numbers. For example, $x^2 + 16$ and $x^2 + 2x + 12$ are not factorable. See if you can explain why they are not factorable.

From what has been said the student will see that in all factoring problems it is important to hold in mind three things; namely:

1. Try to discover a common monomial factor.
2. Find the prime factors by the "cut and try" method.
3. Check by multiplying the factors together.

Find the prime factors of the following expressions:

1. $6x^2 - x - 2$.

Solution. Since the x and the 2 are both negative, the last terms of the factors are opposite in sign. The possible combinations of pairs of factors (regardless of signs) are shown below:

$6x$	2		$6x$	1		$3x$	2		$3x$	1
x	1		x	2		$2x$	1		$2x$	2

The third pair is seen to be correct, provided we write them $3x - 2$ and $2x + 1$. Therefore $6x^2 - x - 2 = (3x - 2)(2x + 1)$.

2. $2a^2 + 9a + 9$.

3. $x^2 + 2xy + y^2$.

4. $a^2 - 16$.

5. $x^2 + 2x - 3$.

6. $x^2 - 2x - 3$.

7. $4x^2 + 16x + 16$.

8. $7x^2 + 9x + 2$.

9. $9x^2 - 30x + 25$.

10. $y^4 - z^2$.

11. $x^2 - 5x + 4$.

12. $5x^2 - 80$.

13. $6x^2 - 19x + 15$.

14. $y^2 - 5y - 6$.

15. $x^2 - 1$.

16. $1 - m^4$ (3 factors).

17. $3x^2 - 17x + 10$.

18. $a^2 - 9b^2$.

19. $49 - x^2$.

20. $3x^2 - 4x + 1$.

21. $m^2 + m - 12$.

22. $5x^2 - 17x - 12$.

23. $2x^2 - x - 28$.

24. $5x^2 - 33x + 18$.

25. $16x^6 - 25y^4$.

26. $18x^2 + 21x - 15$.

27. $6a^2 - a - 2$.

28. $16 - 36x^6$.

29. $a^2 - 4a - 45$.

30. $2x^2y + 11xy + 12y$.

31. $2 - 2x^2$.

32. $24c^3d + 138cd - 36d$.

33. $a^2 - 6ab - 55b^2$.

34. $a^2b^2 - 5ab + 6$.

35. $100x^4z^2 - 49$.

36. $20x^2 - x - 99$.

37. $15 - 4x - 4x^2$.

38. $18 - 33x + 5x^2$.

39. $289a^2b^2c^2 - 81d^2$.

40. $8a^2 - 2$.

41. $3x^2 + 4x + 2$.

42. $19x + 22x^2 - 31$.

43. $x^2 + 20x + 84$.

250. Factoring perfect trinomial squares. *Type form* $a^2 \pm 2\,ab + b^2 = (a \pm b)^2$. Numbers like $4\,x^2 + 16\,x + 16$ or $x^2 - 2\,xy + y^2$, which are obtained by multiplying a binomial by itself, are called *perfect trinomial squares*. They are special cases of the second type of factoring discussed in Art. 249. We have already seen perfect trinomial squares where all the terms are positive in the problems of Ex. 2, Art. 127. See if you can formulate a short method of factoring perfect trinomial squares.

. Factor the following perfect trinomial squares by a short method :

1. $a^2 + 2\,ab + b^2$.
2. $m^2 - 2\,mn + n^2$.
3. $9\,x^2 + 12\,xy + 4\,y^2$.
4. $16\,a^2 - 40\,ab + 25\,b^2$.

5. $9\,x^2 + 42\,xy + 49\,y^2$.
6. $64\,a^2 - 32\,ab + 4\,b^2$.
7. $4\,x^2y^2 - 12\,xyz + 9\,z^2$.
8. $9\,x^4y^4 + 30\,x^2y^2z^2 + 25\,z^4$.

251. Factoring the difference of two squares. *Type form* $a^2 - b^2 = (a + b)(a - b)$. Numbers of the form $a^2 - b^2$ are called the *difference of two squares*. The products obtained in the exercises on page 194 are numbers of this type. This is a special case of the type discussed in Art. 249.

ORAL EXERCISES

1. What is the product of $(x + 3)(x - 3)$? What then are the factors of $x^2 - 9$?

2. State the factors of the following :

(a) $x^2 - 4$.
(b) $c^2 - 25$.

(c) $r^2 - 4\,s^2$.
(d) $25 - x^2$.

3. Show by means of Fig. 170 on the following page that
$$a^2 - b^2 = (a + b)(a - b).$$

The equation $a^2 - b^2 = (a - b)(a + b)$ asserts that a binomial which is the difference of two squares may be readily factored as follows :

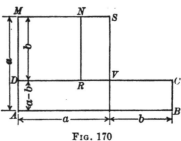

One factor is the sum of the square roots of the terms of the binomial, and the other the difference of the square roots of the terms of the binomial.

Thus, to factor $49 - a^2b^2$ first find the square root of

FIG. 170

each term; that is, 7 and ab. Then, according to the rule, one factor is $7 + ab$ and the other $7 - ab$. Obviously, the factors may be given in reverse order. Why ?

EXERCISES

Factor the following binomials. Check by multiplication when you are not absolutely certain the result is correct.

1. $x^2 - 16$.

2. $x^4 - a^2$.

3. $y^2 - 1$.

4. $1 - x^4$.

5. $x^2 - 9y^2$

6. $9 - y^2$.

7. $16 a^2 - 25 b^2$.

8. $81 a^2 - 16 z^2$.

9. $25 x^6 - 36 z^4$.

10. $49 - 36 x^6$.

11. $1 - 25 x^2y^2$.

12. $\frac{1}{4} - x^2$.

13. $100 z^4x^2 - 36$.

14. $289 m^2 - 81 n^2$.

15. $169 a^2b^2c^2 - 9 d^2$.

16. $121 r^2s^2 - 16 t^2$.

17. $196 - 100 b^2c^2$.

18. $361 r^2k^2 - 196$.

19. $225 a^6 - m^4n^6h^{12}$.

20. $x^4 - y^4$.

21. $25 n^4r^4 - 81 m^4$.

22. $x^8 - y^8$.

23. $625 a^2b^4 - 256 a^4$.

24. $64 x^6 - 9$.

25. $(a + b)^2 - 9$.

26. $9(a + x)^2 - 16$.

27. $(x^3 - y)^2 - x^6$.

28. $\dfrac{x^2y^2}{9} - 4 y^2$.

29. $0.25 a^2 - 0.64 b^2$.

30. $0.25 a^2 - \dfrac{b^2}{16}$.

Knowledge of the special products considered above enables · us to multiply certain arithmetic numbers with great rapidity. Thus the product of 32 by 28 may be written $(30 + 2)(30 - 2) = (30)^2 - (2)^2 = 896$.

EXERCISES

1. Give mentally the following products :

(a) $18 \cdot 22.$	(e) $32 \cdot 27.$	(i) $67 \cdot 73.$	(m) $75 \cdot 85.$
(b) $17 \cdot 23.$	(f) $37 \cdot 43.$	(j) $66 \cdot 74.$	(n) $79 \cdot 81.$
(c) $26 \cdot 34.$	(g) $38 \cdot 42.$	(k) $68 \cdot 72.$	(o) $42 \cdot 38.$
(d) $29 \cdot 31.$	(h) $47 \cdot 53.$	(l) $75 \cdot 65.$	(p) $95 \cdot 75.$

2. Find the value of the following :

(a) $71^2 - 19^2.$	(c) $146^2 - 54^2.$	(e) $1215^2 - 15^2.$
(b) $146^2 - 46^2.$	(d) $312^2 - 288^2.$	(f) $2146^2 - 10^2.$

252. Different ways of carrying out the same calculations. The preceding problems show that the formula $a^2 - b^2 = (a - b)(a + b)$ provides us with a method of making calculations easier. In fact, the expressions which are linked by the equality sign in $a^2 - b^2 = (a - b)(a + b)$ simply represent two different ways of carrying out the same calculations, of which the one on the right is by far the easier.

253. Distinction between identity and equation. An equality such as $a^2 - b^2 = (a - b)(a + b)$ is called an *identity*. It represents two ways of making the same calculation. The statement is true for all values of a and b. The pupil should not confuse the meaning of an identity with that of an equation. Thus $x^2 - 4 = (x - 2)(x + 2)$ is true for all values of x, but $x^2 - 4 = 32$ is a statement that is true only when $x = 6$ or $x = -6$; that is, it is a statement of equality in some special situation; it may be the translation of an area problem, a motion problem, an alloy problem, etc., but it always represents some concrete situation, whereas $x^2 - 4 = (x - 2)(x + 2)$ is an abstract formula for calculation and is true for all values of x.

EXERCISES

1. Tell which of the following are equations and which are identities:

(a) $4x^2 - 16 = 20.$

(b) $9x^2 - 49 = (3x - 7)(3x + 7).$

(c) $9x^2 + 12x + 4 = (3x + 2)^2.$

(d) $4x^2 + 12xy + 9y^2 = (2x + 3y)^2.$

(e) $\dfrac{a^2 - b^2}{a - b} = a + b.$

(f) $\dfrac{x^2 - 9}{x + 3} = 4.$

2. Solve, by factoring, the following equations:

(a) $ax + bx = ac + bc.$

(b) $c + d = \dfrac{ca}{y} + \dfrac{da}{y}.$

(c) $5a^2x - 4b^2x = 10a^2c - 8b^2c.$

(d) $\dfrac{20}{2x + 1} - \dfrac{6}{4x + 2} = 2.$

(e) $\dfrac{1}{2x - 2} + \dfrac{2}{3x - 3} + \dfrac{3}{4x - 4} = 4.$

*254. Calculating areas. The following exercises furnish applications of the preceding work of this chapter.

EXERCISES

1. Show that the shaded area A in Fig. 171 may be expressed as follows: $A = (S - s)(S + s)$, where S is a side of the large square and s a side of the small square.

2. A carpet 20 ft. square is placed in a room 25 ft. square. The uncovered border strip is to be painted. Find the area of the strip. Find the cost of painting this area at 80 cents per square yard. Write a formula to be used in calculating the cost of painting similar strips at c cents per yard, the carpet to be x feet square and the room r feet square.

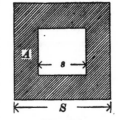

FIG. 171

3. A metal plate is cut as shown in Fig. 172. If $a = 10$ and $b = 2$, what is the area of the plate? In what two ways may the calculating be done? What is the volume of metal if the piece is $\frac{1}{4}$ in. thick? What is the weight if a cubic inch of the metal weighs 20 grams? Write a general formula for a plate cut in the form of the figure, t inches thick and weighing g grams per square inch. Write the result in a form which is easily calculated.

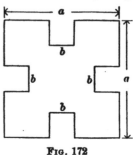

FIG. 172

4. A design pattern is cut in the form shown in Fig. 173. Calculate the area. Make a verbal problem illustrating this formula.

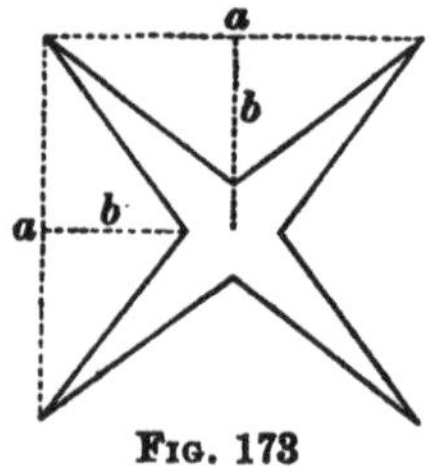

5. We can make an application of our knowledge of factoring in problems related to circles, as will be seen by solving the following:

(a) The area of a circle whose radius is r is πr^2. What is the area of a circle whose radius is R?

FIG. 173

(b) How can you find the area of the ring shaded in Fig. 174? Indicate the area.

(c) Simplify the result of (b) by removing the monomial factor.

(d) What is the area of a running track in which $R = 100$ and $r = 90$?

(e) Calculate the area of the shaded ring in Fig. 174 if $R = 5.5$ in. and $r = 5$; if $R = 3.75$ and $r = 0.25$.

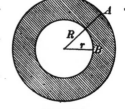

FIG. 174

6. Allowing 500 lb. to a cubic foot, find the weight of a steel pipe 20 ft. long if $R = 12$ in. and $r = 11$ in.

HINT. Find a rule or formula for the volume of a cylinder.

7. Find the weight of an iron rod 6 ft. long cast in the form shown in Fig. 175 if $a = 2$ in., $b = \frac{1}{4}$ in., and $c = \frac{1}{8}$ in.

HINT. Allow 500 lb. per cubic foot.

255. Division of polynomials illustrated by arithmetical numbers. The process of dividing one polynomial by another may be clearly illustrated by a long-division problem in arithmetic;

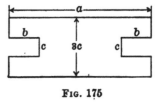

FIG. 175

for example, we shall consider $67,942 \div 322$. Ordinarily we divide in automatic fashion, adopting many desirable short cuts which, though they make our work more efficient, nevertheless obscure the meaning.

In multiplication it was pointed out that because of our decimal system the 9 in 67,942 does not stand for 9 units, but for 900 units or $9 \cdot 10^2$ units. Similarly, the 7 means 7000, or $7 \cdot 10^3$, etc.

If we arrange dividend and divisor in the form of polynomials, the division may appear in either of the following forms:

$$
\begin{array}{r|l}
60000 + 7000 + 900 + 40 + 2 & 300 + 20 + 2 \\
60000 + 4000 + 400 & \overline{200 + 10 + 1} \\
\hline
3000 + 500 + 40 & \\
3000 + 200 + 20 & \\
\hline
300 + 20 + 2 & \\
300 + 20 + 2 & \\
\end{array}
$$

$$
\begin{array}{r|l}
6 \cdot 10^4 + 7 \cdot 10^3 + 9 \cdot 10^2 + 4 \cdot 10 + 2 & 3 \cdot 10^2 + 2 \cdot 10 + 2 \\
6 \cdot 10^4 + 4 \cdot 10^3 + 4 \cdot 10^2 & \overline{2 \cdot 10^2 + 10 + 1} \\
\hline
3 \cdot 10^3 + 5 \cdot 10^2 + 4 \cdot 10 & \\
3 \cdot 10^3 + 2 \cdot 10^2 + 2 \cdot 10 & \\
\hline
3 \cdot 10^2 + 2 \cdot 10 + 2 & \\
3 \cdot 10^2 + 2 \cdot 10 + 2 & \\
\end{array}
$$

The student should study the two preceding examples carefully in order to be better able to understand the similarity of these with the division of algebraic polynomials which we shall now discuss.

256. Division of algebraic polynomials. The division of algebraic polynomials arranged according to either the ascending or the descending power of some letter is similar to the preceding division of arithmetical numbers; thus:

$$
\begin{array}{r|l}
8\,y^4 + 6\,y^3 + 9\,y^2 + 3\,y + 2 & 4\,y^2 + y + 2 \\
\underline{8\,y^4 + 2\,y^3 + 4\,y^2} & \overline{2\,y^2 + y + 1} \\
 4\,y^3 + 5\,y^2 + 3\,y & \\
 \underline{4\,y^3 + y^2 + 2\,y} & \\
 4\,y^2 + y + 2 & \\
 \underline{4\,y^2 + y + 2} &
\end{array}
$$

or

$$
\begin{array}{r|l}
a^3 + b^3 & a + b \\
\underline{a^3 + a^2 b} & \overline{a^2 - ab + b^2} \\
-\,a^2 b + b^3 & \\
\underline{-\,a^2 b - ab^2} & \\
 + ab^2 + b^3 & \\
 \underline{+ ab^2 + b^3} &
\end{array}
$$

257. Process in division. From a study of the preceding exercises we see that in dividing one polynomial by another we proceed as follows:

1. *Arrange both dividend and divisor according to ascending or descending powers of some common letter.*

2. *Divide the first term of the dividend by the first term of the divisor and write the result for the first term of the quotient.*

3. *Multiply the entire divisor by the first term of the quotient and subtract the result from the dividend.*

4. *If there is a remainder, consider it as a new dividend and proceed as before.*

The student should observe that the process in division furnishes an excellent review of the other fundamental processes, inasmuch as they are necessary in almost every division problem. They should therefore be mastered as soon as possible.

258. Checking a division. We shall now illustrate the method of checking a division:

Divide $x^3 - 3x^2y + 3xy^2 - y^3$ by $x - y$.

$$
\begin{array}{l}
x^3 - 3x^2y + 3xy^2 - y^3 \,\lfloor\, x - y \\
\underline{x^3 - x^2y} \qquad\quad \lfloor\, x^2 - 2xy + y^2 \\
\quad -2x^2y + 3xy^2 \\
\quad \underline{-2x^2y + 2xy^2} \\
\qquad\qquad\quad xy^2 - y^3 \\
\qquad\qquad\quad \underline{xy^2 - y^3}
\end{array}
$$

First method of checking. Since the division is exact (that is, there is no remainder), multiply the divisor by the quotient. If the product equals the dividend, the problem checks. This may be expressed in cases where there is no remainder by the formula $q \times d = D$, or $q = \dfrac{D}{d}$.

How would you check if there were a remainder? If the answer is not obvious, try to check similar problems in long division in arithmetic.

Second method of checking. Assume values for x and y. Let $x = 5$ and $y = 2$.

Substituting in the example,
$$q = 9,$$
$$D = 27,$$
and
$$d = 3.$$

Substituting, the formula $q = \dfrac{D}{d}$ becomes $\dfrac{27}{3} = 9$, or $9 = 9$.

Since $\qquad 9 \text{ (or } q) = 9\left(\text{or } \dfrac{D}{d}\right)$, the problem checks.

259. Importance of a thorough drill in division. In the process of division practically all the principles of the last two chapters are involved. Hence the following exercises are important as a means of reviewing the fundamental laws of addition, subtraction, multiplication, and division.

Divide, and check by either method:

1. $(x^2 - 11x + 30) \div (x - 5)$.

2. $(y^3 - y^2 - 4y + 4) \div (y^2 - 3y + 2)$.

3. $(a^3 + 7a^2 + 18a + 40) \div (a^2 + 2a + 8)$.

4. $(9 - 9x + 8x^2 - 4x^3) \div (3 - 2x)$.

5. $(4 + 2x - 8x^2 + 29x^3 - 15x^4) \div (2 - 3x + 5x^2)$.

6. $(27x^3 - 54x^2y + 36xy^2 - 8y^3) \div (3x - 2y)$.

7. $(27x^3 + 54x^2y + 36xy^2 + 8y^3) \div (3x + 2y)$.

8. $(x^3 - y^3) \div (x - y)$.

9. $(8x^3 - 125y^3) \div (2x - 5y)$.

10. $(8x^3 + 125y^3) \div (2x + 5y)$.

11. $(15 + 8m - 32m^2 + 32m^3 - 15m^4) \div (3 + 4m - 5m^2)$.

12. $(x^2 + 2xy + xz + yz + y^2) \div (x + y + z)$.

13. $(14x + 2x^4 + 11x^2 + 5x^3 - 24) \div (2x^2 + 3x - 4)$.

14. $(r^3 + 65r - 15r^2 - 63) \div (r - 7)$.

15. $(25a - 20a^2 + 6a^3 - 12) \div (-4a + 2a^2 + 3)$.

16. $(8x - 4 + 6x^4 + 8x^3 - 11x^2) \div (4x^2 + 2x^3 - x + 2)$.

17. $(9x^2y^2 - 6x^3y + x^4 - 4y^4) \div (x^2 - 3xy + 2y^2)$.

18. $(25x^4 - 60x^2y^2 + 36y^4) \div (5x^2 - 6y^2)$.

19. $(4x^4 + 12x^2y^2 + 9y^4) \div (2x^2 + 3y^2)$.

20. $(a^5 - 1) \div (a - 1)$; $(a^2 - 1) \div (a - 1)$.

21. $(a^5 - y^5) \div (a - y)$; $(a^4 - y^4) \div (a - y)$.

22. $(25m^4 - 49n^4) \div (5m^2 + 7n^2)$.

23. $(25m^4 - 49n^4) \div (5m^2 - 7n^2)$.

24. $(0.027a^3b^3 + c^3) \div (0.2ab + c)$.

25. $(8a^3 - b^3) \div (4a^2 + 2ab + b^2)$.

260. Division by zero. The quotients $\frac{1}{0}$, $\frac{2}{0}$, $\frac{-3}{0}$, $\frac{x}{0}$, $\cdots$, etc. have no meaning, for a number multiplied by 0 cannot give $1, 2, -3, x$, etc. (see the definition of division in Art. 243). The quotient $\frac{0}{0}$ is undetermined, as every number multiplied by 0 equals 0. Therefore we shall assume that in all quotients hereafter the divisor is not zero nor equal to zero.

EXERCISES

1. The following solution is one of several that are sometimes given to show that $1 = 2$. Find the fallacy.

Two numbers are given equal, as $x = y$.

Then	$x - y = 0$,	Why?
and	$2(x - y) = 0$.	Why?
Then	$x - y = 2(x - y)$.	Why?
Dividing both sides by $x - y$,	$1 = 2$.	

2. Give a similar argument which seems to show that 2 equals 5.

SUMMARY

261. This chapter has taught the meaning of the following words and phrases: turning tendency, force, lever arm, multiplication, division, factoring, factors, prime number, number containing a monomial factor.

262. The law of signs in multiplication was illustrated (1) geometrically with line segments and (2) by means of the balanced beam.

263. The following agreements were used:

1. A weight pulling downward is negative; one pulling upward is positive.

2. A force tending to rotate a bar clockwise is negative; counterclockwise, positive.

3. *A lever arm to the right of the point where the bar is balanced is positive; to the left, negative.*

The turning tendency (or force) acting upon a balanced bar is equal to the product of the weight times the lever arm.

264. Law of signs in multiplication: *The product of two numbers having like signs is positive; the product of two numbers having unlike signs is negative.*

265. The chapter has taught and geometrically illustrated the following processes of multiplication:

1. The multiplication of several monomials.
2. The multiplication of a monomial by a polynomial.
3. The multiplication of polynomials by polynomials.

The order of factors may be changed without changing the product.

The value of a product is zero if one of the factors is zero.

266. Law of division: *The quotient of two numbers having like signs is positive; the quotient of two numbers having unlike signs is negative.*

Arithmetical numbers may be arranged in the form of polynomials according to powers of 10.

The process of dividing one polynomial by another is essentially the same as the process of dividing arithmetical numbers.

In all problems of the text the divisor is not zero.

267. The chapter has taught the following forms of division:

1. The division of a monomial by a monomial.
2. The division of a polynomial by a monomial.
3. The reduction of a fraction to lowest terms.
4. The division of a polynomial by a polynomial.

268. Division has been illustrated geometrically. Two methods for checking division were taught.

269. The following types of factoring were taught:

Type I. Taking out a common monomial factor,

$$ax + bx + cx = x(a + b + c).$$

Type II. The "cut and try" method,

$$acx^2 + (bc + ad)x + bd = (ax + b)(cx + d).$$

CHAPTER X

270. Facts presented in the form of a table. The following table of facts shows in part the recreational interests
of the boys and girls of certain Cleveland (Ohio) high
schools. Thus, of 4528 boys, 4075 play baseball; of 3727
girls, 2608 play baseball; 7402 children out of a total of
8255 attend the movies regularly; and so on.

TABLE OF RECREATIONAL INTERESTS

	BOYS	GIRLS	TOTAL
Number of students	4528	3727	8255
Number who play baseball	4075	2608	6683
Number who play basketball	3018	1390	4408
Number who play tennis	1811	1864	3675
Number who belong to Camp Fire Girls .		621	621
Number who wrestle	1358		1358
Number who attend movies	4010	3392	7402
Number who attend movies daily	754	485	1239

EXERCISE

Study the preceding table until you understand the meaning of the columns of figures.

271. Pictograms; graphs. Tables made up of columns of
figures are common in newspapers, magazines, and books,
but a table like the preceding is not the best device for

214

expressing the meaning of an array of facts. The ordinary mind cannot see the relations if the list is at all extended; hence it often happens that the real meaning of a series of facts is lost in a complicated table. Newspapers, magazines, trade journals, and books, realizing this fact, are beginning to add to tables of statistics pictures which show their meaning and their relationships more clearly than can be done by columns of figures.

The significance of the facts of the preceding table is far more vividly expressed by the pictures of Fig. 176. Thus the pictures show that of the high-school girls one out of every two (50 per cent) plays tennis; two out of every dozen (16⅔ per cent) are Camp Fire Girls; of the high-school boys six out of every twenty (30 per cent) wrestle; 85 per cent of all the elementary-school and high-school boys attend the movies regularly; and so on.

The pictures constitute a more powerful method of teaching numerical relations, because they teach through the eye. For this reason they are called *graphic pictures*, *pictograms*, or simply *graphs*.

EXERCISES

By means of the pictograms in Fig. 176 answer the following questions:

1. What per cent of the Cleveland boys play tennis? of the Cleveland girls? With which group is tennis the more popular?

2. Assuming that every sound-bodied boy should learn to wrestle, does your class make a better or a worse showing in per cents than the Cleveland boys?

3. Are a larger per cent of the girls of your class Camp Fire Girls than is the case in the Cleveland high schools?

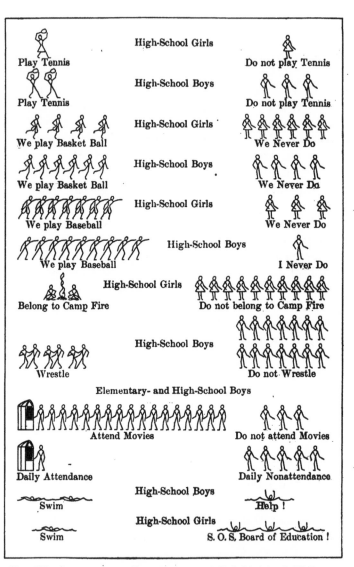

FIG. 176. SHOWING HOW PICTOGRAMS ARE USED TO EXPRESS FACTS
(Adapted from Johnson's "Education through Recreation")

216

4. Compare your class's swimming record with the Cleveland record.

5. Continue the discussion with your classmates until it is clear to you just how the figures of the pictograms represent the facts of the table.

272. The circle pictogram. The circle is frequently used to show quantitative relations. It shows two things: (1) the relation of each magnitude to each of the others; (2) the relation of each magnitude to the sum of all.

The graph in Fig. 177 shows that in a certain year Portland (Oregon) spent 30.7¢ out of every dollar on its school system. This is practically $\frac{3}{10}$ of all the money spent by the city and about $1\frac{1}{2}$ times as much as the next highest item. Compare the part spent for education with each of the other parts shown in the figure.

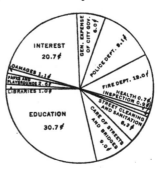

FIG. 177. THE CIRCLE
PICTOGRAM

(From Cubberly's "Portland Survey")

The scale used in making circle pictograms is based on the degree. The angular space around the center of the circle (360°) is divided into parts so as to express the numerical relations; for example, since almost $\frac{3}{10}$ of the money is spent for education, an angle of $\frac{3}{10}$ of 360°, or 108°, is constructed with the protractor at the center of the circle and the sides of the angle extended until they intersect the circle. The *sector* (the part of a circle bounded by two radii and an arc) formed shows the part of the city's money that goes toward education.

EXERCISES

1. In Fig. 177 how does the amount paid as interest compare with the amount paid for police and fire protection?

2. Do you think it would have been more profitable in the long run for Portland to pay cash for all public improvements?

HINT. A definite answer to this problem may be obtained if several members of the class will solve Ex. 3 and report to the class.

*3. What will it cost a city to build a $100,000 high-school building if $20,000 of its cost is paid in cash and the remainder paid by issuing 4 per cent bonds of which $4000 worth are to be retired (paid) annually? (All interest due to be paid annually.)

NOTE. The problem must not be interpreted as an argument showing that bonding (borrowing) is never justifiable.

*4. The discussion of the method of paying the expenses of the United States for the first year of our participation in the European War was sharply divided between two groups. One group favored a large amount of borrowing by the issuance of bonds, while the other advocated a pay-as-you-go policy, that is, raising the money by taxation. Debate the merits of the two plans.

5. Show the following facts by means of a circle divided into sectors:

TABLE SHOWING DISPOSITION OF THE GROSS REVENUE OF THE BELL TELEPHONE SYSTEM FOR THE YEAR 1917

ITEMS	PER CENT
Salaries, wages, and incidentals	50
Taxes	7
Surplus	4
Materials, rent, and traveling expenses	20
Interest	7
Dividends	12

Though widely used, the circle divided into sectors is not a quite satisfactory method of showing the ratio of numbers. In fact, the objections are so serious that the method of construction was given to protect the student against false conclusions. The method is not inaccurate when the parts which constitute a unit are shown by the use of one circle. It frequently happens, however, that the comparison is made by circles differing in size. In such a case, since the eye tends to make the comparison on an area basis, the ratio of the two numbers should be expressed by the ratio of the areas of the two circles, and statistical authorities so recommend.

FIG. 178. CIRCLES DRAWN ON AN AREA BASIS SHOWING THE NUMBER OF BANK DEPOSITORS

In Fig.178 the circles are drawn on an area basis, but the right-hand circle appears less prominent than the figures justify, thus causing the reader to underestimate the ratio. In Fig. 179 the circles are drawn on a diameter basis. The right-hand circle appears more prominent than the figures justify, thus causing the reader to overestimate the ratio. This feature

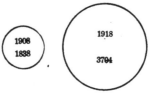

FIG. 179. CIRCLES DRAWN ON A DIAMETER BASIS

is frequently utilized by those who make dishonest use of circle diagrams. The conclusion is that a comparison between circles differing in size should be avoided altogether. Better graphic methods will be taught. Space is given here to circle pictograms because of their extensive use in many fields.

EXERCISE

Test the accuracy of circle pictograms which you may find in magazine articles and advertisements. Discuss their value with your classmates.

273. Area pictograms. The picture of the two traveling men given here is intended to show the increase in the passenger traffic of the railroads. The two men are compared on the basis of height. The 1911 man, on account of his far greater area, looks more than $2\frac{1}{4}$ times as large as the 1899 man. The men should be compared on the basis of area.[1] This type too should be avoided because it tends to deceive the ordinary reader.

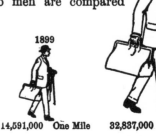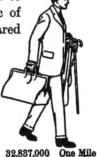

1899

1911

14,591,000 One Mile   32,837,000 One Mile

FIG. 180. A POPULAR TYPE OF PICTOGRAM, TO BE AVOIDED

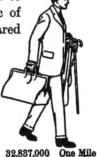

1911 32,837,000 ONE MILE

1899 14,591,000 ONE MILE

FIG. 181. A MORE ACCURATE METHOD OF PORTRAYING FACTS

EXERCISES

1. Why would it be difficult to make a drawing on the basis of area?

2. Do you know any method which could be used to check a drawing made on the basis of area? (See Art. 109.)

274. Volume or block pictograms. Cubes, parallelepipeds, and spheres are frequently used in comparing relative volumes; for example, pictures of bales of hay or cotton

---

[1] Brinton, in his excellent text, "Graphic Methods for Presenting Facts," presents à chart (Fig. 181) drawn from the same facts as that in Fig. 180. Note that the facts are portrayed much more clearly and accurately.

are used to show the output of the states producing these articles. The comparison should be made on a basis of volume, but often there is no way for the reader to tell on what basis the drawing was constructed, whether by height, area, or volume. Certainly it would be difficult to check the statement made in such a case.

275. Limitations of area and volume pictograms. The student will need to remember that in a correctly constructed area graph the quantities represented should vary directly as the number of square units within the outlines of the figures. Thus, in the comparison of passenger service relative size should not be determined by the relative heights of the men but by the number of square units within the outlines. Hence a rough method of checking is to transfer the pictures of the traveling men to squared paper by means of tracing paper and compare the number of square millimeters in the area of each with the corresponding facts of the table. Similarly, in accurate volume or block graphs the quantities should vary as the number of cubic units.

Many who use this form of statistical interpretation carelessly fail to observe these principles, and the difficulty of a check makes this form of graph a convenient device for those who would dishonestly misrepresent the facts. The general public is not always able to interpret the graphs correctly even if they have been properly drawn. Because of these limitations it is somewhat unfortunate that this type of graph is so extensively used in bulletins and current magazines.

EXERCISE

Try to obtain and present to the class an advertisement illustrating the misuse of an area or volume pictogram.

276. Practice in interpreting the bar diagram. Fig. 182 shows one of the suggestions of the Joint Committee on Standards for Graphic Presentation. The diagram, Fig. 182, (a), based on linear measurement, is called a *bar diagram.* We shall study this topic further in the next article. Review

FIG. 182. BAR DIAGRAMS SHOW FACTS BETTER THAN AREA AND VOLUME PICTOGRAMS

the objections to the other two diagrams (the squares and blocks shown in Fig. 182, (b)). Where it is possible the student should represent quantities by linear magnitudes, as representation by areas or volumes is more likely to be misinterpreted.

EXERCISES

1. Study Fig. 183 and determine to what extent the two horizontal bars are helpful in expressing the ratio of the two numbers given.

2. Would the bars in Fig. 183 be sufficient without the illustrations at the left of the numbers?

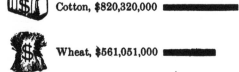

FIG. 183. A FAIR DIAGRAM. (AFTER BRINTON)

3. With the aid of compasses check the accuracy of Fig. 184. Note that the figures are written to the left of the bars. In many

FIG. 184.[1] DIAGRAM SHOWING AMERICAN EXPORTS OF AUTOMOBILES. (AFTER BRINTON)

bar diagrams the figures are written to the right of the bars. Can you think of a serious objection to that method?

[1] See paragraph 7 under Art. 277

4. Why is there a space left between the bars for 1906 and 1911 in Fig. 184 ? Do you see any other way to improve the diagram ? (See Art. 277.)

5. Draw on the blackboard a figure similar to Fig. 184, adding a bar for the year 1917. (The sum for this year is about 900,000,000.)

6. Explain Fig. 185.

7. Show that the bars of Fig. 186 reveal

FIG. 185. DIAGRAM SHOWING DEATH RATE FROM TYPHOID IN 1912 PER HUNDRED THOUSAND POPULATION

more clearly than the following table the rank of the United States in respect to wealth. These are the 1914 estimates.

United States $150,000,000,000
Great Britain and Ireland   . . .   85,000,000,000
Germany   80,000,000,000
France   50,000,000,000
Russia   40,000,000,000
Austria-Hungary   25,000,000,000
Italy   20,000,000,000

8. Show that it would have been as accurate and more convenient to draw the preceding diagrams on squared paper.

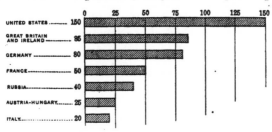

FIG. 186. COMPARATIVE WEALTH OF NATIONS IN 1914

9. The table for the wealth of nations contains estimates prepared at the beginning of the European War (1914–1918).

These estimates are now far from facts. The student should attempt to get the latest estimates from the "World Almanac" and construct a bar diagram which will present the situation to date and will enable him to make an interesting comparison.

10. Discuss bar diagrams similar to those given on pages 222–223 which you may find in *Popular Mechanics Magazine, Motor, Popular Science Monthly,* and *Industrial Management.* For the time being limit yourself to the simpler diagrams.

277. How to construct a bar diagram. An understanding of how to construct bar diagrams and how to interpret those he may find in newspapers and magazines should be a part of the education of every general reader, just as it is of every engineer, physician, statistician, and biologist.[1] As civilization advances there is being brought to the attention of the reading public a constantly increasing amount of comparative figures of a scientific, technical, and statistical nature. A picture or a diagram which presents such data in a way to save time and also to gain clearness is a graph. The bar diagram is a widely used method of conveying statistical information *graphically.* The solution of the introductory exercises along with the discussion of such supplementary graphs as may have seemed profitable for the class to discuss will help the pupil to understand the following outline of the method of constructing a bar diagram:

1. The bars should be constructed to scale. To obtain a convenient unit first inspect the size of the smallest and the largest number and then choose a line segment to

[1] Neither pupils nor teachers should be misled by the apparent simplicity of this work. The details are of the greatest importance. It will be helpful to obtain the reports of the Joint Committee on Standards for Graphic Presentation. This is a competent committee of seventeen, which has expended considerable effort on these elementary phases. The preliminary report may be had from the American Society of Mechanical Engineers, 29 W. 39th St., New York; price, 10 cents.

represent a number such that it will be possible to draw an accurate bar for the smallest number and a bar not too long for the largest number. The lines in Fig. 186 on page 223 are so constructed that the relation between the lengths of any two is the same as the relative size of the quantities represented. A line segment 1 mm. long represents $2,500,000,000 of wealth. In the table on page 223 the United States is estimated as possessing three times as much wealth as France, and so the line segments representing the wealth of the United States and France are respectively 60 mm. and 20 mm. long.

2. The scale and sufficient data should appear on the diagram.

3. Each bar should be designated.

4. The bars should be uniform in width.

5. The diagram should have a title or legend.

6. Accuracy is the important characteristic.

7. The space between the bars should be the same as the width of the bars, except in a case like Fig. 184, where a larger space indicates that the three bars do not represent consecutive years.

8. In general the zero of the scale should be shown. However, there are exceptions ; for example, in graphing the temperature of a patient we are particularly concerned with how much above or below the *normal* the patient's temperature is. Hence, in a case like this we should emphasize the *normal* temperature line.

EXERCISES

1. Present the facts of the table given on page 226 by means of a bar diagram, using the scale 1 mm. = $2,000,000. The table is arranged to show the twenty heaviest buyers of American goods, as indicated by the value of exports from the United States during the fiscal year 1914.

AMERICA'S TWENTY BEST CUSTOMERS

(From the report of the Bureau of Foreign and Domestic Commerce)

	VALUE OF PURCHASES		VALUE OF PURCHASES
1. England . .	$548,641,399	11. Argentina . .	$45,179,089
2. Germany . .	344,794,276	12. Mexico . . .	38,748,793
3. Canada . . .	344,716,981	13. Scotland . . .	33,950,947
4. France . . .	159,818,924	14. Spain	30,387,569
5. Netherlands .	112,215,673	15. Russia	30,088,643
6. Oceania . .	83,568,417	16. Brazil	29,963,914
7. Italy . . .	74,235,012	17. China	24,698,734
8. Cuba	68,884,428	18. Austria-Hungary	22,718,258
9. Belgium . .	61,219,894	19. Panama . . .	22,678,234
10. Japan . . .	51,205,520	20. Chile	17,432,392

*2. If possible, ascertain the facts to date (see "World Almanac"), graph results as in Ex. 1, and compare the two diagrams. Account for unusual changes. Are new customers appearing among the "twenty best"? Have old ones dropped out?

3. Present the statistics of the following table by means of a bar diagram showing the comparative length of rivers. (Use the scale 1 cm. = 400 mi.; the lengths given in the table are in miles.)

	LENGTH		LENGTH
Missouri-Mississippi . .	4200	Volga	2400
Amazon	3800	Mackenzie	2300
Nile	3766	Plata	2300
Yangtze	3400	St. Lawrence . . .	2150
Yenisei	3300	Danube	1725
Kongo	3000	Euphrates	1700
Lena	3000	Indus	1700
Niger	3000	Brahmaputra . . .	1680
Ob	2700	Ganges	1500
Hoangho	2600	Mekong	1500
Amur	2500	Rio Theodoro . . .	950

4. Represent the statistics of the following table by bar diagrams. The estimates of the leading crops in the United States for the year 1917 are here compared with the revised figures for the crops of the preceding nine years. The pupil should note that each column is a separate problem.

REPORT OF THE UNITED STATES DEPARTMENT OF
AGRICULTURE FOR 1917

YEAR	CORN	WHEAT	OATS	BARLEY	RYE	COTTON
	Bushels	Bushels	Bushels	Bushels	Bushels	Bales
1917	3,159,494,000	650,828,000	1,587,286,000	208,975,000	60,145,000	10,949,000
1916	2,583,241,000	639,886,000	1,251,992,000	180,927,000	47,383,000	12,900,000
1915	2,994,793,000	1,025,801,000	1,549,030,000	228,851,000	54,000,050	12,862,000
1914	2,672,804,000	891,017,000	1,141,060,000	194,953,000	42,778,000	15,136,000
1913	2,446,988,000	763,380,000	1,121,768,000	178,189,000	41,381,000	14,552,000
1912	3,124,746,000	730,267,000	1,418,377,000	223,824,000	35,664,000	14,104,000
1911	2,531,488,000	621,338,000	922,298,000	160,240,000	33,119,000	16,101,000
1910	2,886,260,000	635,121,000	1,186,341,000	173,832,000	34,897,000	12,075,000
1909	2,552,190,000	683,350,000	1,007,129,000	173,321,000	29,520,000	10,513,000
1908	2,668,651,000	664,602,000	807,156,000	166,756,000	31,851,000	13,817,000

278. Bar diagrams used to show several factors. We shall now see how bar diagrams may be used to show several factors.

INTRODUCTORY EXERCISES

1. Fig. 187, on page 228, differs from those in Art. 277 in that it presents two factors. What is the scale of the diagram? Note that the bars representing new buildings extend from the top to the bottom of the black bar. Try to account for the heavy losses by fire in 1904 and 1906. Why is the bar so short for new buildings in 1908? (The values are given in millions of dollars.) Criticize this diagram according to the principles of Art. 277.

2. Give the facts of Fig. 187 for the twelfth year; the eighteenth year.

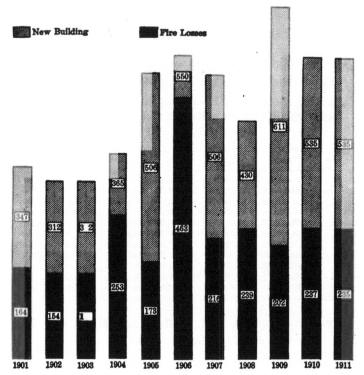

FIG. 187. DIAGRAM OF YEARLY VALUES OF NEW BUILDINGS, AND OF ALL
BUILDINGS LOST BY FIRE IN THE UNITED STATES, 1901–1911, INCLUSIVE

(Courtesy of W. C. Brinton)

3. Fig. 188 shows the business relations involved when a city
bonds itself to buy some present need or luxury. The parts
of a single bar (say the tenth) show the following: (a) the
interest paid to date (the black portion); (b) the amount
of the $75,000 still outstanding (the plain portion); (c) the
part of the debt that has been paid (the crosshatched portion).

Show that a public bond issue is not only a debt but that
it "comes dangerously near to a perpetual tax."

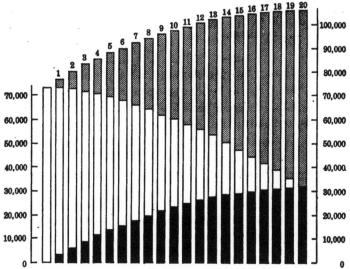

FIG. 188. BAR DIAGRAM USED TO SHOW MONEY TRANSACTIONS
INVOLVED IN PAYING FOR A $75,000 SCHOOL BUILDING
(Adapted from Ayres's "Springfield Survey")

The preceding exercises show how a bar diagram may
be used to compare several factors of some problem
which are more or less related. If the pupil is especially
interested in this side of the subject, he may do the
following exercises. The topic is not particularly important, however, because another method which we shall
presently study is much more efficient.

EXERCISES

*1. Go to the township, county, or city-hall authorities and
find out how one or more of your public improvements is
being paid for; that is, find out (a) if bonds were issued;
(b) how many dollars' worth are retired (paid for) each year;
(c) how much interest must be paid each year. Construct a

bar diagram similar to the one reprinted from the Ayres report, showing what it will ultimately cost your community to pay for the project.

*2. A certain county in Indiana built 20 mi. of macadamized road by issuing $40,000 worth of 4 per cent nontaxable bonds. Twenty $100 bonds were to be retired each year. By means of a bar diagram show how much it ultimately cost this township to build its turnpike.

*3. Ten years after the turnpike referred to in Ex. 2 was built it was practically worn out. Did this township lend to posterity or borrow from it? Give reasons for your answer.

279. Cartograms. Statistical maps which show quantities that vary with different geographic regions are sometimes called cartograms. The student will doubtless find examples in his geography. He should also examine the " Statistical Atlas of the United States," published by the Census Bureau. Various colors and shades are used to help express the meaning.

When the cost of color printing is prohibitive the same ends may be attained by crosshatch work. The student should examine rainfall maps containing cartograms and which are often printed in newspapers.

A special form of cartogram is the dotted map. If we wish to show the density of population of a city, we may take a map of the city and place a dot within a square for every fifty people living in the square. The scale should be so chosen that the dots will be fairly close together in the sections whose population is of greatest density. Space is not given here to illustrating this type, but the pupil will have no difficulty with the exercises that follow.

EXERCISES

1. Obtain at least five different forms of pictograms and cartograms from newspapers, magazines, trade journals, or government bulletins. Explain very briefly what each intends to show.

2. Discuss the merits or defects of the graphs of Ex. 1.

280. Interpreting (or reading) graphic curves. The introductory exercises given below will furnish the student with some practice in the interpretation of graphic curves.

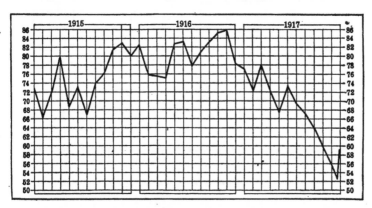

FIG. 189. SHOWING RAILWAY-STOCK FLUCTUATIONS, BY MONTHS, IN THE AVERAGE PRICE OF TWENTY-FIVE OF THE LEADING STOCKS ON THE NEW YORK STOCK EXCHANGE

(Adapted from the *New York Times*)

INTRODUCTORY EXERCISES

1. Explain the curve in Fig. 189, noting the highest price, the lowest price, the cause of the upward trend in 1915, the cause of the downward movement in 1917, and the cause of the sharp break upward in the closing days of 1917.

2. Explain the curve in Fig. 190. Check the graph for the early years. Give a reason for such results as you may find.

3. Fig. 191 is a temperature chart of a case of typhoid fever. (a) Explain the rise and fall of the curve. (b) What is the meaning of the dots? Do these points mark the tops of bars? (c) What assumption does the physician make when he connects these points by a curve? (d) Note that this diagram does not have a zero scale; why was it omitted? The chart would be improved if it had an empha-

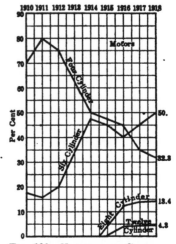

FIG. 190. NUMBER OF CARS OF DIFFERENT TYPES

(Adapted from *Motor*)

sized line representing normal temperature (98.4°). Why? Construct a line in color in your text for the normal-temperature line.

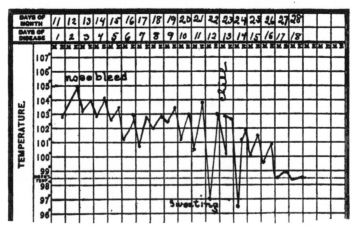

FIG. 191. A TEMPERATURE CHART OF A CASE OF TYPHOID FEVER

4. Explain the heavy line (temperature) of Fig. 192.

5. Explain the light line (wind) of Fig. 192.

6. If your study of science has familiarized you with the term "relative humidity," explain the dotted line of Fig. 192.

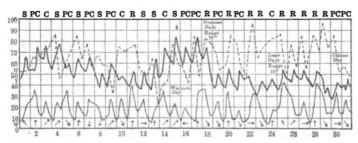

FIG. 192. WEATHER RECORD IN ST. LOUIS FOR OCTOBER, 1917

The heavy lines indicate temperature in degrees F. The light lines indicate wind in miles per hour. The broken lines indicate relative humidity in percentage from readings taken at 8 A.M. and 8 P.M. The arrows fly with the prevailing direction of the wind. S, clear; PC, partly cloudy; C, cloudy; R, rain.

(From the *Heating and Ventilating Magazine*, December, 1917)

The curves of the preceding exercises are called *graphic curves*. The graphic curve is particularly useful in comparing the relation that exists between two quantities; for example, the relation between the price of wheat and the annual yield; the relation between the price of beef and the amount produced or exported; the relation between office expenses and the size of the corporation; the tariff necessary in order that an article may be manufactured in this country; and so on.

281. How the graphic curve is drawn. The graphic curve in Fig. 193 represents the growth of the population in the United States from 1790 to 1910, as shown by the table on page 234.

(1) The horizontal line *OM* represents the time line. 1 mm. represents 2½ yr.; that is, 10 yr. is represented by

Year	Population	Year	Population
1790	3,929,214	1860	31,443,321
1800	5,308,483	1870	38,558,371
1810	7,239,881	1880	50,155,783
1820	9,638,453	1890	62,947,714
1830	12,860,702	1900	75,994,575
1840	17,063,363	1910	91,972,266
1850	23,191,876		

two small spaces. (2) The vertical scale represents the population in millions. Two small spaces represent ten million. Therefore a bar about 1.6 mm. long is placed on the 1790 line, and a second bar a little over 2 mm. long is placed on the 1800 line. Similarly, bars were placed on the other lines. (3) The upper end points of the vertical segments (bars) are joined by a curve. In so far as the bars are concerned the figure does not differ from an

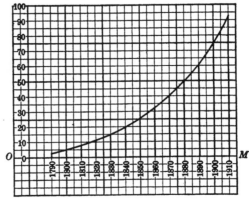

FIG. 198. THE GRAPHIC CURVE

ordinary bar diagram. We may assume, however, that *increase in population between any two periods was gradual*; for example, we may estimate that in 1795 the population was reasonably near some number halfway between 3,900,000 and 5,300,000; that is, about 4,600,000. Similarly, we may estimate the population in the year 1798.

This assumption leads us to draw the smooth curve which enables us to estimate the change in population without knowing the exact length of the bars. By means of the curve predict what the population will be in 1920. In what way will the accuracy of your prediction be affected by the European War?

EXERCISES

1. The following table shows the total monthly sales of a bookstore through a period of two years.

	1917	1918		1917	1918
January	$2125	$2329	July	$2271	$2380
February	2237	2416	August	2231	2350
March	2460	2479	September	2542	2620
April	2521	2590	October	2725	2831
May	2486	2580	November	2345	2540
June	2393	2482	December	2825	3120

Draw a graphic curve for each year on the same sheet of graphic paper. Draw the two curves with different-colored ink or else use a dotted line for one and an unbroken line for the other. Explain the curves.

2. On a winter day the thermometer was read at 9 A. M. and every hour afterward until 9 P. M. The hourly readings were $-5°$, $0°$, $-2°$, $-8°$, $-10°$, $-10°$, $-5°$, $0°$, $-5°$, $-4°$, $-2°$, $-3°$, $-7°$. Draw the temperature graph.

3. Using a convenient scale and calling the vertical lines age lines, graph these average heights of boys and girls:

AGE	BOYS	GIRLS	AGE	BOYS	GIRLS
2 yr.	1.6 ft.	1.6 ft.	12 yr.	4.8 ft.	4.5 ft.
4 .	2.6	2.6	14	5.2	4.8
6	3.0	3.0	16	5.5	5.2
8	3.5	3.5	18	5.6	5.3
10	4.0	3.9 .	20	5.7	5.4

At what age do boys grow most rapidly? At what age do girls grow most rapidly? Is it reasonable to assume that the average height of a boy nineteen years old is 5.65 ft.?

4. The standings of the champion batters from 1900–1907, inclusive, are here given for the National and American leagues.

The National League:

0.384 0.382 0.367 0.355 0.349 0.377 0.339 0.350

The American League:

0.387 0.422 0.376 0.355 0.381 0.329 0.358 0.350

Graph the data for each league to a convenient scale, both on the same sheet. Tell what the lines show.

5. Draw a temperature chart of a patient, the data for which are given below (see Fig. 191).

Hour . . .	6 P.M.	7	8	9	10	11	12	1 A.M.	2	3	4	5
Temperature	100.5°	101°	101.5°	103.2°	102.5°	101.4°	101.3°	101.3°	101.2°	101.2°	101°	100.7°

6. If possible, get a copy of a temperature curve such as is commonly kept in hospitals and explain the graph to the class. The class will profit more by your discussion if the curve presents the data for a long period.

7. Be on the lookout for graphic curves which convey information of general interest to your class. In nearly every newspaper you will find tables of statistics which may be plotted to advantage. Glance occasionally through the "Statistical Abstract of the United States" or the "Statistical Atlas of the United States" (published by the Bureau of Foreign and Domestic Commerce), *Popular Mechanics Magazine, Popular Science Monthly, Scientific American,* and so on, with the purpose of finding interesting graphs. If a lack of time prevents class discussion, post these graphs on bulletin boards.

282. Continuous and discrete series. We may represent a continuous change in wealth, in population, in the growth of boys and girls, etc. by a smooth curve. Thus, if we read four reports of deposits made in a country bank as $20,000 on January 1, $25,000 on April 1, $18,000 on June 1, and $19,000 on September 1, we assume that there was a gradual increase of deposits from January 1 to April 1, a rather rigorous withdrawal from April 1 to June 1, and a slow rally from June 1 to September 1. This is precisely the way a physician treats the temperature of a patient, even though he may take the temperature but twice per day. However, the data of every table cannot be considered as continuous between the limits. This fact is clearly illustrated by the following table of Fourth of July accidents:

YEAR	KILLED	INJURED	TOTAL
1909	215	5092	5307
1910	131	2792	2923
1911	57	1546	1603
1912	41	945	986
1913	32	1163	1195
1914	40	1506	1546

If we were to draw a continuous curve, it would not state the facts. Though a few Fourth of July accidents may occur on the third or on the fifth of July, we are certain that a continuous curve would not represent the facts for the rest of the year. Such a collection of items is said to be a *discrete*, or broken, series. A record of wages paid in a factory is likely to be a discrete series, for the wages are usually (except in piecework) a certain number of dollars per week, the fractional parts being seldom less than 10¢. We should find very few men getting odd sums, say, $18.02 per week. Hence there would be many gaps in the series.

283. Statistics as a science defined. We have now progressed far enough for the student to understand that the term "statistics" refers to a large mass of facts, or data, which bear upon some human problem. One of the chief uses of statistics as a science is to render the meaning of masses of figures clear and comprehensible at a glance. Statistics gives us a bird's-eye view of a situation involving a complex array of numerous instances in such a way that we get a picture which centers our attention on a few significant relations. Such a view shows how one factor in a complicated social or economic problem influences another; in short, it enables us to understand the relation between variable (changing) quantities.

284. The uses of statistics. Statistical studies do not exist merely to satisfy idle curiosity. They are necessary in the solution of the most weighty social, governmental, and economic problems. Do certain social conditions make for increase in crime and poverty? The sociologist determines statistically the relations bearing on the question. Are certain criminal acts due to heredity? The biologist presents statistical data. Is tuberculosis increasing or decreasing? Under what conditions does it increase? Reliable statistics presented by the medical world guide our public hygienic policies. Further possibilities of statistical studies in the medical world are suggested by the recent work of Dr. Alexis Carrel. The work of Dr. Carrel has been widely discussed. Though authorities disagree concerning some of the details, all will probably agree that the mathematical attack on the problem of war surgery is a distinct scientific advance.

What insurance rates ought we to pay? Statistical investigations have determined laws for the expectation of life under given conditions which for practical purposes are as accurate as the formula for the area of a square.

The business world at times trembles under the threat of gigantic strikes that would paralyze all business. Are the demands of the men unreasonable? Are the corporations earning undue dividends? The public does not know and will not know until a scientific group of citizens present reliable statistics of earnings and expenditures.

There is now in existence in Washington a nonpartisan tariff commission which consists of five members appointed by the president, which collects statistics and makes recommendations to Congress from time to time. It is now thought that this commission may tend to do away with the old haphazard methods of handling tariff questions.

How rapidly and with what degree of accuracy should a fourth-grade pupil be able to add a certain column of figures? The educator is able to present an answer based on tests of more than 100,000 fourth-grade children for that particular problem.

Because of the numerous trained enumerators which they employed to cover the world's output, the large speculators on the Chicago Board of Trade knew with absolute certainty for days in advance of the record-breaking jump in the price of wheat in August, 1916.

We might continue indefinitely to present evidence showing that the intelligent reader in any field will profit by a knowledge of the elementary principles of statistical methods.

285. Frequency table; class limits; class interval. In the investigation of a problem it is necessary that the data be tabulated in some systematic fashion that will enable us to grasp the problem. Suppose we measured the length of 220 ears of corn. Let us say the smallest ear measures between 5 in. and 6 in., the longest between

12 in. and 13 in. We could then group the ears by inches, throwing them into eight groups, and tabulate the results somewhat as follows:

FREQUENCY TABLE SHOWING LENGTH OF EARS OF CORN

Length in Inches	Number of Ears	Length in Inches	Number of Ears
5-5.99	2	9- 9.99	74
6-6.99	4	10-10.99	47
7-7.99	20	11-11.99	21
8-8.99	48	12-12.99	4

Such an arrangement of data is called a *frequency table.* The ears of corn have been divided into classes. The table should be read as follows: " There are two ears measuring somewhere between 5 in. and 6 in., four between 6 in. and 7 in.," etc. The boundary lines are known as *class limits,* and the distance between the two limits of any class is designated as a *class interval.* The class interval in the preceding case is 1 in. Class intervals should always be equal.

The facts of the table are shown by the graph in Fig. 194. This graph is the same as the bar diagram (Fig. 186) which we have drawn, with the exception that in this case *the bars cover the scale intervals.*

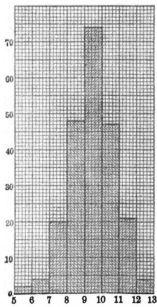

Fig. 194. Distribution of Frequency Polygon of 220 Ears of Corn

1. What is your guess as to the shape of the graph if the corn were classified into half-inch groups? into fourth-inch groups?

2. Are there many very long ears of corn? many very short ears? How do you tell?

3. Into what class interval does the largest group fall?

4. The following table of frequency shows the lengths of 113 leaves picked from a tree purely at random. (See King's "Elements of Statistical Method," p. 102.)

LENGTH OF LEAF IN CENTIMETERS	NUMBER OF LEAVES IN EACH GROUP	LENGTH OF LEAF IN CENTIMETERS	NUMBER OF LEAVES IN EACH GROUP
3–3.99	4	8–8.99	6
4–4.99	5	9–9.99	4
5–5.99	13	10–10.99 . . .	3
6–6.99	56	11–11.99 . . .	2
7–7.99	19	12–12.99 . . .	1

The table should be read as follows: "There are four leaves between 3 cm. and 4 cm. long, five between 4 cm. and 5 cm.," etc. Graph as in Fig. 194 the data of this table.

5. The frequency table on page 242 shows the weights of 1000 twelve-year-old boys, 1000 thirteen-year-old boys, and 1000 fourteen-year-old boys. (The weights are taken from Roberts's "Manual of Anthropometry" and include 9 lb. of clothing in each case. Figures are reduced to the thousand basis.)

6. Study each of the groups for Exs. 4 and 5 as to

(a) Where the smallest classes are found.

(b) Where the largest class is located.

(c) The gradual rise and fall of the figures.

FREQUENCY TABLE OF WEIGHTS SHOWING 1000 TWELVE-
YEAR-OLD BOYS, 1000 THIRTEEN-YEAR-OLD BOYS, AND 1000
FOURTEEN-YEAR-OLD BOYS

WEIGHTS IN POUNDS	NUMBER OF 12-YEAR-OLD BOYS	NUMBER OF 13-YEAR-OLD BOYS	NUMBER OF 14-YEAR-OLD BOYS
49–56	4	0	0
56–63	24	6	0
63–70	118	38	3
70–77	233	100	38
77–84	273	225	41
84–91	221	256	130
91–98	79	187	228
98–105	36	112	247
105–112	12	43	118
112–119	0	17	82
119–126	0	16	29
126–133	0	0	12
133–140	0	0	18

NOTE. The fact that the third column in the table lacks 54 boys of totaling 1000 is because 54 boys in this group weighed over 140 pounds. The 49–56 means from 49 up to but not including 56. Wherever the last number of a class is the same as the first number of the next class, the first class includes up to that point, but does not include that point.

Construct the graph (similar to Fig. 194) for each of the groups of the table above.

7. The following test on the ability to use the four fundamental laws in solving simple equations was given to 115 first-year high-school students, the time given for the test being fifteen minutes.

DIRECTIONS TO PUPIL

Find the value of the unknown numbers in each of the following equations. Do not check your results. Work the problems in order if possible. If you find one too difficult, do not waste too much time on it, but pass on to the next. Be sure that it is too difficult, however, before you pass on. Do not omit any problem which you can solve.

The Test

1. $x + 3 = 7.$

2. $2y = 4.$

3. $2k + 7 = 17.$

4. $z - 2 = 3.$

5. $2x - 4 = 6.$

6. $\dfrac{x}{3} = 5.$

7. $\dfrac{5y}{2} = \dfrac{15}{2}.$

8. $\dfrac{48}{4x} = 6.$

9. $\dfrac{x}{2} + \dfrac{x}{3} = 15.$

10. $\dfrac{y}{3} - \dfrac{y}{6} = 5.$

11. $\dfrac{m}{4} + 1 = 6.$

12. $\dfrac{y}{2} - 4 = 10.$

13. $16y + 2y - 18y + 2y = 22.$

14. $7x + 2 = 3x + 10.$

15. $\dfrac{x}{4} + 4x - \dfrac{5x}{3} = 26 - 1\tfrac{1}{2}x.$

16. $3x + 4\tfrac{1}{2} = 9.$

17. $5.3y + 0.34 = 2.99.$

18. $0.5x - 3 = 4.5.$

19. $3x - 9\tfrac{1}{2} = 17.5$

20. $7y + 20 - 3y = 60 + 4y + 40 - 8y.$

21. $\dfrac{2x}{6} + \dfrac{x}{6} = \dfrac{x}{18} + \dfrac{1}{3}.$

22. $\dfrac{5x}{6} + 2\tfrac{5}{12} = 3 + \dfrac{x}{4}.$

23. $\dfrac{5m}{2} - 1 = \dfrac{17m}{3} - \dfrac{5}{3} - 2\tfrac{1}{2}m.$

24. $\dfrac{15x}{4} - \dfrac{3}{2} = 34x - 2.5 - \dfrac{25x}{4}.$

The results of the test are given by the following table of frequency. The student should study it carefully.

Number of Examples	Number of Students Attempting	Number of Students Successful	Number of Examples	Number of Students Attempting	Number of Students Successful
0	0	0	13	1	11
1	0	1	14	4	15
2	0	1	15	4	8
3	0	0	16	10	10
4	0	0	17	13	3
5	0	0	18	13	7
6	0	3	19	8	1
7	0	4	20	22	2
8	1	5	21	13	0
9	0	9	22	18	0
10	0	14	23	6	1
11	0	13	24	1	0
12	1	7			

Explanation. The table consists of two parts, of which the first part is the first, second, fourth, and fifth columns, which should be read, "Of the one hundred and fifteen students taking the test one tried but 8 examples, one attempted 12, one attempted 13, four attempted 14," etc. The second part consists of the first, third, fourth, and sixth columns and should be read, "Of the one hundred and fifteen students taking the test one solved only 1 problem correctly, one solved only 2 correctly, three solved 6 correctly, four solved 7 correctly," etc.

8. Construct a graph showing the facts of the table given on page 243 for the number of students attempting.

9. Under the directions of your instructor take the test in Ex. 7.

10. Ask your instructor to give you a frequency table showing the number of attempts and successes in the test taken by your class and determine how the work done by your class compares in speed and accuracy with that done by the one hundred and fifteen students in the test described in Ex. 7.

286. Measure of central tendencies; the arithmetic average. A frequency table and a frequency graph help us to understand a mass of facts because they show us the distribution of the items, so that we see where the largest groups and the smallest groups fall. The graph shows us the general trend of the facts. The large groups assume importance. We need terms to describe the central tendency. Often the word "average" is used to meet this need. Such a term is helpful in making a mass of facts clear. Thus, a group of farmers could not possibly learn much about a field of corn if we read a list to them showing the length of every ear in a field. But they would get some idea of what yield to expect if told that the average length of an ear is $9\frac{1}{2}$ in. They could certainly give a fair estimate of the yield if in addition we told them that on the average a row in a square 40-acre field grew 620 stalks. We shall presently learn that the word " average," as commonly used, is not correct. The phrase " arithmetic average " means *the quotient obtained by dividing the sum of all the items by the number of items.* Thus, to find the average mark obtained by your class on a test we need to add the marks of all the students and divide by the number of students in the class. If two or more students obtain the same mark (say 70), we can shorten the first step of the process by multiplying the mark by the number of times it occurs instead of adding 70 five times. This means that in a frequency table a student must remember to *multiply each item by its frequency before adding.* When the size of the item is only approximately known, the mid-point of the class interval is taken to represent the size of each item therein. To illustrate, suppose that we should try to find the average number of problems attempted in the simple-equation test. We shall suppose that three students report that they attempted 6 problems. This does not really mean that all three exactly completed 6 problems when time was called. In all probability one had made a slight start on number 7, the second was about in the middle of number 7, and the third had almost completed 7. Of course the number of students is too small to make this certain, but if we should take a larger number of students (say thirteen), in all probability there would be as many who were more than half through with the seventh problem as there would be students less than half through. Hence, to find the average we say that the thirteen students attempted $6\frac{1}{2}$ and not 6, as they reported. To illustrate :

Find the average number of equations attempted by a class on the simple-equation test if two students report 5 problems

attempted, four report 6, five report 7, three report 8, and two
report 9.

Solution.

$$2 \times 5\tfrac{1}{2} = 11$$
$$4 \times 6\tfrac{1}{2} = 26$$
$$5 \times 7\tfrac{1}{2} = 37.5$$
$$3 \times 8\tfrac{1}{2} = 25.5$$
$$\underline{2 \times 9\tfrac{1}{2} = 19}$$
$$16 \qquad 119$$

$$119 \div 16 = 7.4.$$

Therefore the average number of problems attempted by the
class is 7.4.

The point is that the series of facts in the table is not
a discrete series, as one would at first be inclined to think,
but a continuous series.

EXERCISES

*1. Calculate the average number of equations attempted by
your class in the simple-equation test (Art. 285).

2. Using the table of Ex. 5, Art. 285, find the average
weight of the twelve-year-old boys; of the thirteen-year-old
boys; of the fourteen-year-old boys.

3. Find the average length of the 113 leaves in Ex. 4,
Art. 285.

4. Find the average length of the 220 ears of corn of the
first table in Art. 285.

5. Find the average number of Fourth of July accidents
for the six years of the table of Art. 282.

6. Compare the averages of the champion batters for the
last eight years (Ex. 4, Art. 281).

7. At Minneapolis the 7 A.M. temperature readings for
the ten days beginning February 1 were as follows : $- 5, - 3,$
$- 5, - 3, - 7, - 9, - 8, - 2, 0, - 6.$ Find the average 7 A.M.
temperature reading for the period.

8. Find the average of the following temperatures: 8 A.M., − 6°; 9 A.M., − 5°; 10 A.M., − 2°; 11 A.M., −1°; 12 M., − 2°; 1 P.M., − 4°; 2 P.M., − 6°; 3 P.M., − 7°; 4 P.M., − 7°; 5 P.M., − 5°; 6 P.M., − 2°; 7 P.M., − 1°.

9. Find the average church contributions according to the following frequency table.

TABLE OF CHURCH CONTRIBUTIONS

INDIVIDUAL CONTRIBUTIONS	NUMBER OF CONTRIBUTORS	INDIVIDUAL CONTRIBUTIONS	NUMBER OF CONTRIBUTORS
No contribution .	2	10 cents . . .	13
1 cent	23	25 cents . . .	9
5 cents	42	$50	1

287. Disadvantages of the arithmetic average. Some of the preceding exercises suggest that there are certain objections to the arithmetic average. For example, it means little to say that the average church contribution in Ex. 9, Art. 286, is 62 cents. People ordinarily use the word "average" thinking it means the most usual occurrence; that is, *the common thing*. As a matter of fact nobody gave 62 cents, and only one person gave as much as that. The objection to the arithmetic average is that it gives too much emphasis to the extreme items. To illustrate more fully: A boy who has just finished an elementary surveying course learns that the average weekly wage of a railway-surveying group is $23. This is very encouraging until an analysis shows him that the chief engineer gets $55 a week; his assistant, $30; and all others but $15. To say that the average weekly earning of ten men working in an insurance office is $80 a week may be misleading, for one man may be a $5000-a-year man, in which case the usual salary is much lower than $30 per week. Other objections

to the arithmetic average are the following: (a) it cannot
be located either in a frequency table or in a frequency
graph; (b) it cannot be accurately determined when the
extreme items are missing; (c) it is likely to fall where
no item exists (for example, a sociologist may discover
that the average-size family in a given community has 4.39
members, though such a number is evidently impossible).

For these reasons it is desirable to have some other
measure of the central tendency of a group.

288. Central tendency; the mode. One of the most useful measures is the *mode*. It may be defined as the scale
interval that has the most frequent item, or we may say it
is the place where the longest bar of a bar diagram is
drawn. The term describes the most usual occurrence, or
the common thing. The popular use of the term "average"
approximates the meaning of the word. When we hear of
the average high-school boy he is supposed to represent
a type — one who receives exactly the most common mark
of his classes, is of the most common athletic ability,
spends the most common amount of time in study, shows
the most common amount of school spirit, wastes the most
common amount of time, is of the most common age, etc.
It is obvious that no such high-school boy can be found.
Though a boy may possess some of these attributes he is
certain to differ from the common type in others.

The word "average" is thus incorrectly used for "mode,"
which means the common type. Thus the mode in the
church-contribution table (Ex. 9, Art. 286) is five cents.
More people in this church gave a nickel than any other
coin. The mode in the frequency table for the simple-
equation test for attempts (Ex. 7, Art. 285) is twenty
examples. In the test more students were at this point
when time was called than at any other point.

1. Find the mode for your class in the frequency table for successes in the simple-equation test of Ex. 7, Art. 285.

2. From the table of Ex. 5, Art. 285, find the mode for the weight of the twelve-year-old boys; of the thirteen-year-old boys; of the fourteen-year-old boys.

NOTE. The student is expected merely to glance at the tables to see at what scale interval the greatest number of items are found.

3. From the table of Ex. 4, Art. 285, find the mode for the 113 leaves.

4. From the first table of Art. 285 find the mode for the 220 ears of corn.

5. From the table in Art. 282 find the mode for the Fourth of July accidents.

289. Advantages and disadvantages of the mode. The advantages of the mode may be summarized as follows: (a) the mode eliminates the extremes. In the results of an examination the mode is not affected by the occasional hundred or zero marks. The salary of the superintendent of a division of a shop does not affect the mode; (b) to the ordinary mind the mode means more than does an average. It means more to say that the modal size of classes in a high school is 15 than to say that the average size is 17.24, first, because there is not a single class that actually has the latter number; and, second, because a few large freshman classes in city high schools may tend to increase considerably the average number. In making laws we shall do the greatest good to the greatest number if we keep the mode in mind and not the average. Unfortunately street cars are built for the average number carried,

not for the modal number; hence the "strap hanger."
The manufacturer of ready-made clothing fits the modal
man, not the average man. The spirit of a community's
charity fund is far more evident in the mode than in the
average.

A disadvantage of the mode is that there are a large
number of frequency tables to which it cannot be easily
applied. In such cases we have an irregular group with no
particular type standing out, and the mode is difficult to
find, as will be illustrated presently.

290. Central tendency; the median. If a number of objects are measured with reference to some trait, or attribute,
and then ranked accordingly, they are said to be *arrayed*.
Suppose that your instructor gives an examination which
really tests mathematical ability, and that after the results
are announced the students stand in line, taking the
position corresponding to their marks on the examination;
that is, the student with least mathematical ability at the
foot of the class, the one next in ability next to the foot,
etc. The class is then *arrayed*. If any group of objects is
arrayed, the middle one is known as the *median* item. If
your class had twenty-three pupils standing in the order
of their ability, the twelfth pupil from the foot or the head
of the class is the student whose mark is the median mark.
There are just as many below as above him in ability. The
median is another measure of the central tendency of a
group. If there is an even number of items, the median
is said to exist halfway between the two middle items.
Thus, if your class had twenty-two pupils, the mark halfway between that of the eleventh and that of the twelfth
student from either end would be called the median mark.
The meaning is further illustrated by the exercises given
on pages 251 and 252.

1. Find the median wage in the following table of the weekly wage of the workers in a retail millinery shop.[1]

WEEKLY WAGE	NUMBER OF WORKERS	WEEKLY WAGE	NUMBER OF WORKERS
$4-5	3	$11-12	0
5-6	15	12-13	5
6-7	16	13-14	0
7-8	12	14-15	6
8-9	7	15-16	18
9-10	8	16-17	5
10-11	5		

The table above shows the wages of one hundred girls. We are asked to find a weekly wage so that we shall be able to say that one half the girls in this shop receive less than this sum and one half receive more than this sum; that is, we want a measure of the group.

In the first place, the student should notice that the arithmetic average $10.05 seems too high to be representative, for there are too many girls working for smaller sums. In the second place, the mode is unsatisfactory. The wage $15 to $16 seems to be a mode, but there are more girls working for about $5, $6, or $7; hence neither the arithmetic average nor the mode has very much meaning, so we proceed to locate the median.

There are one hundred girls in the shop; hence we must find a wage halfway between that of the fiftieth and that of the fifty-first girl from the lowest wage. Adding the number of the first four groups of girls (3+15+16+12) gives us forty-six girls and takes us to the 8-dollar wage. We need to count four more of the next seven, who are

[1] For actual facts see "Dressmaking and Millinery," in "The Cleveland Survey," page 68. The table was adapted to meet the purposes of the exercise.

getting between \$8 and \$9. The table assumes that the series is continuous (piecework?); hence the next seven are distributed at equal distances between \$8 and \$9. We may think of the seven girls as being distributed graphically, as shown in Fig. 195.

The graph makes clear the assumption that the first girl (the forty-seventh) earns a sum which is between \$8 and \$8$\frac{1}{7}$; we assume that the wage is at the mid-point of this interval, or \$8$\frac{1}{14}$. Similarly, the second girl (the forty-eighth) earns a sum between \$8$\frac{1}{7}$ and \$8$\frac{2}{7}$, and we assume the wage to be at the mid-point of this interval, or \$8$\frac{3}{14}$. In like manner the wage of the forty-ninth girl is \$8$\frac{5}{14}$, the fiftieth

\$8.00   \$8.50   \$9.00

Girls

FIG. 195

girl \$8$\frac{7}{14}$, and the fifty-first girl \$8$\frac{9}{14}$. Midway between the mid-points of the fiftieth and the fifty-first wage is halfway between \$8$\frac{7}{14}$ and \$8$\frac{9}{14}$, or \$8$\frac{4}{7}$. Hence the median is \$8 plus \$$\frac{4}{7}$, or \$8$\frac{4}{7}$, for this wage is halfway between the wage of the fiftieth girl and that of the fifty-first. The student should study this graph until this point is clear. He should note that the average is found by calculating, the mode by inspection, and the median by counting. Merely count along the imagined scale until a point is found that divides the item into two equal groups. Since a wage problem usually involves a discrete series (why?), a more practical illustration of the principle is given below.

2. Find the median for the attempts of the one hundred and fifteen students in the simple-equation test in Ex. 7, Art. 285.

Solution. We must find the number of equations attempted by the fifty-eighth student from either end, for he will be the middle student of the one hundred and fifteen. Counting from the top of the table (p. 243), we get fifty-five pupils who have finished 19 equations. We need to count 3 more to get the fifty-eighth pupil. There are twenty-two more who were somewhere in the twentieth equation when time was called. If we assume, as we did in finding modes, that the twenty-two students are at equal spaces throughout the twentieth equation, then the median is 19 equations plus $\frac{3}{22}$ of an equation, or just over 19.1 equations.

EXERCISES

1. State the rule for finding the median, as developed in the two preceding exercises.

2. In Ex. 5, Art. 285, find the median weight for 1000 twelve-year-old boys; 1000 thirteen-year-old boys; 1000 fourteen-year-old boys.

3. In Ex. 4, Art. 285, find the median leaf and its measure in the array of 113 leaves.

4. Find the median for the 220 ears of corn (Art. 285).

291. Limitations of statistics. There is a common saying among nonscientific people that anything can be proved by means of statistics. Experience lends conviction to the homely saying "Figures do not lie, but liars will figure." This belief is due to the fact that figures have deceived the public either by being dishonestly manipulated or by being handled unscientifically. A table dishonestly manipulated or based on unreliable data appears at first glance as convincing as the work of a trained scientist. The public does not find it possible to submit every piece of evidence to a critical study and resents such deceptions as those referred to above.

As a beginning the student should determine (1) the reliability and training of those who gathered the facts; (2) how and when they were gathered; (3) to what extent

the statistical studies have been exposed to the critical
judgment of trained experts; (4) to what extent similar
studies show similar results.

292. Law of statistical regularity. In calculating the
value of the farm lands in Indiana it is by no means
necessary to evaluate and tabulate every acre in the state.
To find out the average size of a twenty-five-year-old man
in New York it is not necessary to measure and tabulate
every man in the city. The "Statistical Abstract of the
United States" (published by the Bureau of Foreign and
Domestic Commerce) states the value in dollars of hogs,
sheep, and cattle produced in 1918, but this does not mean
that this total is obtained by tabulating every individual
animal. To find out how fast on an average a twelve-
year-old Chicago boy can run 100 yards we would not need
to hold a stop watch on every boy. In fact, a few chosen
in each class in each school building would probably give
us an average that would be identical with an average
obtained from the whole group. This is due to a mathematical law of nature which states that *if a reasonable number of individual cases are chosen " at random " from among
a very large group, they are almost sure, on the average, to possess the same characteristics as the larger groups.* The phrases
" at random " and " reasonable number " make the law appear
somewhat vague. King, in "Elements of Statistical Method,"
illustrates the law as follows : "If two persons, blindfolded,
were to pick, here and there, three hundred walnuts from
a bin containing a million nuts, the average weight of the
nuts picked out by each person would be almost identical, even though the nuts varied considerably in size."
Gamblers use the principle just illustrated when they have
determined how many times a given event happens out of
a given number of possibilities. They are thus able to ply

their craft continuously and profitably on a small margin in their favor. This principle is the basis of all insurance; thus it is possible to predict with a great degree of accuracy how many men of a given age out of a given one thousand will, under ordinary conditions, die during the next year. The law of statistical regularity is very extensively employed in the Census Bureau. ·The totals are usually estimates based on careful study of sufficient representative cases.

However, the student should be critical of the phrase "at random." It is not asserted that any small group will give the same results as a measurement of the whole group. Thus, if we measured the height of the first four hundred men that passed us as we stood at the corner of Randolph and State Streets, Chicago, we could not be sure of getting an average that would accurately represent the city. Any number of events might vitiate the results; for example, the Minnesota football team might be passing by, or a group of unusually small men might be returning from some political or social meeting limited to one nationality. The sampling should be representative; that is, sufficiently large and at random (here and there). The larger the number of items, the greater the chances of getting a fair sample of the larger group of objects studied.

*293. The law of inertia of large numbers. This law follows from the law of statistical regularity. It asserts that *when a part of a large group differs so as to show a tendency in one direction, the probability is that an equal part of the same group has a tendency to vary in the opposite direction; hence the total change is slight.*

294. Compensating and cumulative errors. The preceding laws are also involved in a discussion of errors. If the pupils in your school were to measure carefully the length of your instructor's desk, the chances would be that as many would give results too large as too short.

The estimates of a thousand observers of crop conditions which are summarized or graphed in a volume such as the "Statistical Atlas" (published by the Department of Commerce) tend to approximate actual conditions. These are illustrations of compensating errors. "In the long run they tend to make the result lower as much as higher." This type of error need not concern us greatly, provided we have a sufficient number of cases.

However, we need to be on our guard against a constant or cumulative error. If we use a meter stick that is too short, we cannot eliminate the error by measuring a very long line. A watch too fast could not eventually be a correct guide. A wholesaler who lost a little on each article sold could not possibly square accounts by selling large quantities.

The value of a mass of facts involving a constant error is seriously vitiated. Hence the student should be constantly critical in his effort to detect this type.

EXERCISE

*Draw as accurately as possible on the blackboard a line segment a certain number of inches in length. Ask as many as from forty to fifty schoolmates, if possible, to stand on a certain spot and estimate the length of the line. Find how many estimated the line too long; how many estimated it too short.

HINT. The work must be done carefully. Have each student estimate four times; that is, estimate, look away, estimate, etc. Reject estimates of all students who do not comply seriously with your request. How many estimated the line too long? How many estimated it too short? Report the results to your class.

*295. Normal distribution. The student has observed the regular rise and fall of the numbers of the frequency tables and the regular rise and fall of the graphs which express these relations. It appears that the large *majority of the items are usually grouped, and as the distance from this point of grouping becomes greater, the items become rapidly fewer in number.* If we measure ability to solve a set of 24 simple equations, we shall discover that the large majority of any representative class can attempt a little more than 19 in 15 minutes. Only a few, possibly none, will try all 24 problems; and only a few, probably none, will have attempted less than 6. If we measure any single human trait, we shall discover the same tendency in the graph of the results toward a *bell-shaped curve.*

FIG. 196. FREQUENCY CHART OF SCALLOP SHELLS PILED ACCORDING TO THE NUMBER OF RIBS. (AFTER BRINTON)

Whether we measure ability to spell, ability to add a column of figures, ability to throw a baseball, the distance boys can broad-jump, always there are a few very good at it and a few very poor at it, with the tendency of the great majority to possess but mediocre ability in a particular trait.

Nature shows the same tendency. The length of leaves, the height of cornstalks, the length of ears of corn, etc. give curves similar to the preceding. Note the piles of scallop shells in Fig. 196. The shells are sorted into separate piles according to the number of ribs. The piles (from left to right) have respectively 15, 16, 17, 18, 19, and 20 ribs. How do you think these piles would have looked if a greater number of shells (say several hundred) had been used?

The same tendency is observed in economic affairs. Thus, if we measured the income of the ordinary agricultural community, we should find out of a thousand persons only a few whose income is less than $300 per year, only a few, if any, with an income over $2500, and the rest grouped and tapering between these limits.

When the rise and fall is regular (that is, the curve falls regularly on both sides from the mode), the distribution is likely to approximate what we call a *normal distribution*, and the curve is called a *normal* distribution curve.

A normal distribution is illustrated by the table and diagram

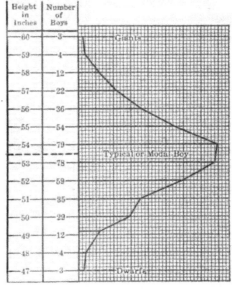

Height in Inches	Number of Boys
60	3
59	4
58	12
57	22
56	36
55	54
54	79
53	78
52	59
51	35
50	29
49	12
48	4
47	3

FIG. 197. PHYSICAL PHENOMENA ILLUSTRATE NORMAL DISTRIBUTION

(Fig. 197) given here, which represents the heights from actual measurement of four hundred and thirty English public-school boys from eleven to twelve years of age.[1]

It will be seen that the numbers conform to a very uniform rule: the most numerous groups are in the middle, at 53 in. and 54 in., while the groups at 51 in. and 56 in.

[1] From Roberts's "Manual of Anthropometry," p. 18.

are less in number, those at 50 in. and 57 in. are still fewer, and so on until the extremely small numbers of the very short and very tall boys of 47 in. and 60 in. are reached. It is shown that the modal, or typical, boy of the class and age given is 53.5 in., and since he represents the most numerous group, he forms the standard.

The curve would probably be smoother if more boys were measured or grouped into half-inch groups. As it is, it approximates very nearly a normal distribution.

Of course it is not asserted that every distribution is of this type. There is merely a tendency in chance and in nature to produce it. There are many causes which make distribution irregular, as we shall presently see.

*296. Symmetry of a curve. The graph in Fig. 198 shows the height of 25,878 American adult men in inches.

This curve, like the one of Art. 295, is more regular than most curves which we have studied. It would probably be much smoother if the class interval were one-fourth inch. If we draw a perpendicular AK from

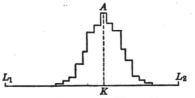

FIG. 198. HEIGHT OF MEN. (AFTER THORNDIKE, "MENTAL AND SOCIAL MEASUREMENTS," p. 98)

the highest point of the curve, we may think of this as an axis around which the rectangles are built. The curve to the right of this axis looks very much like the part to the left. In this respect we say the curve is almost *symmetrical.*

Symmetry of figures may be illustrated by the human head, which is symmetrical with respect to a plane midway between the eyes and perpendicular to the face; thus the left eye and the left ear have corresponding parts to the right of this *axis of symmetry*. Note that the parts are arrayed in reverse order.

Other familiar illustrations of symmetry are (1) the hand and the image obtained by holding the hand in front of a plane mirror; (2) words written in ink and the imprint of those words on the blotting paper with which they are blotted; (3) our clothes, which are largely built on the principle of symmetry; (4) the normal distribution curve.

In architecture, in art, and in higher mathematics the principle of symmetry is very important.

*297. Skewness of a curve. The term "skewness" denotes the opposite of symmetry and means that the items are not symmetrically distributed. The curve is not of the bell-shaped form. It is higher either above or below the mode than a sense of symmetry would have us expect. To illustrate: Suppose that the incomes of all the people living in a certain community were tabulated as follows:

Income in Dollars	Number of Persons	Income in Dollars	Number of Persons
0–500 . . .	20	3500–4000 . . .	4
500–1000 . . .	36	4000–4500 . . .	3
1000–1500 . . .	20	4500–5000 . . .	3
1500–2000 . . .	12	5000–5500 . . .	2
2000–2500 . . .	6	5500–6000 . . .	1
2500–3000 . . .	5	6000–6500 . . .	1
3000–3500 . . .	4		

The graph (Fig. 199) of this table is not symmetrical, but is skewed toward the lower side. The meaning of skewness is clearly shown by the graph. The graph no longer presents the normal, symmetrical, bell-shaped form; the base is drawn out to a greater extent on the one side than on the other.

Distribution is often affected by laws which are disturbing factors in the situation. Thus, in investigating the wages of carpenters we should expect a few to get high wages, say 90 ¢ per hour, and a few very low, say 40 ¢ per hour, and the rest to be grouped, according to ability, between these limits. However, by agreement between unions and contractors, carpenters' wages are fixed in most

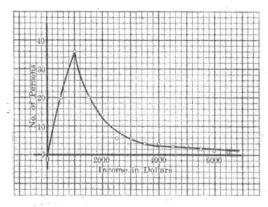

Fig. 199. Graph showing Skewness of a Curve

cities at a price somewhere'between 60 ¢ and 85 ¢. Hence we should have but one interval in a distribution table, for a particular city, say Minneapolis, showing that all carpenters get 75 ¢ per hour.

298. The graph of constant cost relations.[1] Graphs may be constructed and used as "ready reckoners" for determining

[1] Teachers may find it desirable to take up the graphing of formulas from science at this point; for example, the graph of the centigrade-Fahrenheit formula. However, the authors prefer to use a simpler introductory exercise here for the sake of method and to take up more purposeful formulæ in the next chapter.

costs of different quantities of goods without computation. This is shown by the following example:

If oranges sell at 30¢ a dozen, the relation between the number of dozens and the cost may be expressed by the equation $c = 30\,d$, where d is the number of dozens and c the cost per dozen. If values are given to d, corresponding values may be found for c, as given in the following table:

d	0	1	2	3	4	5	10	11
c	0	30	60	90	120	150	300	330

On squared paper draw two axes, OX and OY, at right angles. On OY let a small unit represent 1 doz., and on OX let a small unit represent 10¢. Then, on the 30¢ line

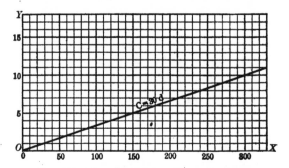

FIG. 200. THE GRAPH OF A COST FORMULA

mark a point representing 1 doz. On the 20¢ line mark a point representing 3 doz. Draw a line through the points thus marked. It is seen that this line, or graph (Fig. 200), is a straight line.

By looking at this price curve we can get the cost of any number of dozens, even of a fractional number. For example, to find the cost of 6 doz. observe the point where the horizontal line six small units up meets the price curve; observe the point directly beneath this on the axis OX; this is eighteen small units from O and hence represents $1.80. Similarly, the cost of $8\frac{1}{2}$ doz. is seen to be $2.55.

EXERCISES

1. By means of the graph in Fig. 200 determine the cost of the following: 9 doz.; 11 doz.; $2\frac{1}{2}$ doz.; $3\frac{1}{2}$ doz.; $10\frac{1}{4}$ doz.; $5\frac{1}{4}$ doz.; $3\frac{1}{4}$ doz.

2. If eggs sell at 45¢ a dozen, draw the price graph.

3. On the price graph drawn for Ex. 2 find the cost of 4 doz.; 3 doz.; 10 doz.; $3\frac{1}{2}$ doz.; $5\frac{1}{3}$ doz.; $4\frac{1}{4}$ doz.

4. Draw a price graph for sugar costing $10\frac{1}{2}$¢ a pound.

5. On the graph drawn for Ex. 4 find the cost of 11 lb.; 31 lb.; $6\frac{1}{2}$ lb.; 10 lb.

6. Construct a graph which may be used in calculating the price of potatoes at $2.10 per bushel.

7. Use the graph of Ex. 6 to find the cost of 3 bu.; $4\frac{1}{2}$ bu.; 2 bu. 3 pk.; $5\frac{1}{4}$ bu.; 5 bu. 3 pk.

8. Since the graphs in Exs. 1–7 are straight lines, how many of the points would have to be located in each case in order to draw the line? Should these be taken close together or far apart, in order to get the position of the price graph more nearly accurate? Why?

299. Graphs of linear equations; locus; coördinates. As shown in the preceding sections the relation between two quantities may be expressed in three ways: (1) by an ordinary English sentence, (2) by an equation, or (3) by a graph. The graph is said to be the graph of the equation. A graph may be constructed for each equation that we have studied to date. The process of drawing the graph of an equation will be given in this article.

Let the equation be $y = 2x + 3$, which we shall suppose is the translation of some sentence which states some definite practical rule; for example, the cost of sending a package by parcel post into a certain zone equals two cents per ounce plus three cents. We want to draw a graph for the equation $y = 2x + 3$.

1. What is the value of y in the equation $y = 2x + 3$ when x equals 0? when x equals 1? when x equals 2? when x equals 3? when x equals -2? when x equals -3?

2. Fill in the following table of values of x and y for the equation $y = 2x + 3$.

x	0	1	2	3	4	5	6	7	-1	-2	-3	-4
y	3	5	7	9								

We are now ready to transfer the data of Ex. 2 to squared paper. The process does not differ very much from our work in frequency tables except that usually in graphing equations we need to consider both positive and negative numbers. For the sake of method we shall extend the discussion to cover this point. Two axes, XX' and YY' (Fig. 201), are drawn at right angles and meet at O. Corresponding to each set of values of x and y a point is located, the values of x being measured along or parallel to XX', and the values of y along or parallel to YY'. Positive values of x are measured to the right of YY' and negative values to the left; positive values of y are measured above XX' and negative values below XX'.

For example, the point A corresponding to $x = 1$ and $y = 5$ is obtained by measuring one space to the right and five spaces upward. The point B corresponding to $x = -1$ and $y = 1$ is obtained by measuring one space to the left and one space upward. The

point C corresponding to $x = -3$ and $y = -3$ is obtained by measuring three spaces to the left and three spaces downward. The x and y values of each point are called the *coördinates* of that point.

Continue finding points which represent corresponding parts of numbers in the table. It soon becomes ap-

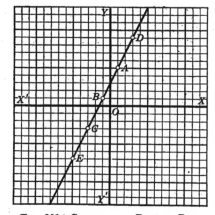

Fig. 201. Graph of a Parcel Post Formula

parent that all the points seem to lie on a straight line. Hence we need to plot only two points to be able to draw the line. However, we are more certain to discover possible errors if we plot three points. Why?

EXERCISES

1. Find the values of x and y at the points D and E (Fig. 201) by inspection. Determine whether they satisfy the equation of the graph.

2. Select any point in the line and determine whether the values of x and y at this point satisfy the equation.

3. Select any point not on the graph, find the values of x and y at this point, and determine whether they satisfy the equation of the graph.

4. Select any point of the graph and determine whether the values of x and y satisfy the equation.

5. How many points could one find on the line?

The preceding exercises illustrate the following facts:

(a) *The coördinates of every point on the line satisfy the equation.*

(b) *The coördinates of every point not on the line do not satisfy the equation.*

These two facts can be proved rigidly in advanced mathematics, and they enable us to say that the straight line found is the *locus* (the place) of all points whose coördinates satisfy the given equation. It is important to observe that the idea of a locus involves two things, specified under (a) and (b) above.

Since it appears that the graph of an equation of the first degree having two unknowns is a straight line, equations of the first degree are called *linear equations.*

A line may be extended indefinitely in either direction, and there are an indefinitely large (infinite) number of points upon a straight line. Since the coördinates of each point on the line satisfy the equation of the line, there are an infinite number of solutions of a linear equation with two unknowns. This fact is evident, also, because for every value of one of the unknowns we can find a corresponding value for the other unknown.

ORAL EXERCISES

1. What is the location (locus) of all points in a plane which are at a distance of 5 ft. from a given point P in the plane? at a distance of $7\frac{1}{2}$ ft. from P? at a distance of x feet?

2. What is the locus of all points in space at a distance of 10 ft. from a given point? 1 cm. from a given point? x yards from a given point?

3. What is the locus of all points in a plane 3 in. distant from a given straight line in the plane? $5\frac{1}{2}$ in. distant? y inches distant?

4. What is the locus of all points in space at a distance of 4 in. from a given straight line? 6 cm.? y feet?

5. What is the locus of all points in a plane equally distant from two given parallel lines in the plane?

*6. What is the locus of all points in space equally distant from two given parallel lines?

7. What is the locus of all points in a plane 6 in. distant from each of two given points in the plane which are 10 in. apart?

8. What is the locus of all points 3 ft. from the ceiling of your classroom?

*9. What is the locus of all points in a plane 5 in. distant from a line segment 7 in. long in the plane?

*10. What is the locus of all points in space 5 in. distant from a line segment 10 ft. long?

300. Terms used in graphing a linear equation. Certain terms used in mathematics in connection with graphical representation will now be given and illustrated by Fig. 202. The lines XX' and YY', drawn at right angles, are called *axes* (XX' the *horizontal* axis and YY' the *vertical* axis). The point O is called the *origin*. From P, any point on the squared paper, perpendiculars are drawn to the axes: the distance PM is called the ordinate of P, and the distance PN is called the *abscissa* of P;

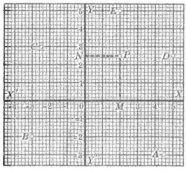

FIG. 202. ILLUSTRATING THE TERMS USED IN PLOTTING A POINT

together they are called the *coördinates* of *P*. The axes are called *coördinate axes*. The scale used is indicated on the axes. The distances on *OX* and *OY* are positive; those on *OX'* and on *OY'* negative. The abscissa of *P* is 2 and the ordinate is $2\frac{1}{2}$; the point *P* is called the *point* $(2, 2\frac{1}{2})$. Notice that the abscissa is written first and the ordinate second. Finding a point on a graphic sheet which corresponds to a given pair of coördinates is called *plotting the point*.

1. What is the abscissa of point *A*? *B*? *C*? *D*? *E*? (Fig. 202).

2. What is the ordinate of the point *A*? *B*? *C*? *D*? *E*? (Fig. 202.)

3. Give the coördinates of points *A*, *B*, *C*, *D*, *E* (Fig. 202).

4. On a sheet of graphic paper draw a set of coördinate axes intersecting near the center of the paper, and plot the following points : (2, 4), (5, 2), (4, − 2), (− 3, 4), (− 3, − 2), (− $2\frac{1}{3}$, $3\frac{1}{4}$).

5. Compare the process of plotting points with the numbering of houses in a city.

6. On a sheet of graphic paper locate the points *A* (2, 2), *B* (5, 3), *C* (2, 7), and *D* (5, 8). What kind of figure do you think is formed when the points *A*, *B*, *C*, and *D* are connected? Draw the diagonals of the figure, and find the coördinates of the point where the diagonals intersect.

301. Summary of the method for the process of graphing a linear equation. With Art. 300 in mind we shall now illustrate and summarize the process of graphing a linear equation.

Draw the graph of $4x - 3y = 6$.

(a) *Solve the equation for either unknown in terms of the other;* thus,

$$x = \frac{6 + 3y}{4}.$$

This throws the equation into a form from which the corresponding pairs of values are more easily obtained.

(b) Let $\qquad\qquad y = 0.$

Then $\qquad\qquad x = 1\frac{1}{2}.$

And let $\qquad\qquad y = 2.$

Then $\qquad\qquad x = 3$, etc.

That is, *build a table of corresponding values* as follows: (Try to get at least two pairs of integral numbers. Why?)

$$x = \frac{6 + 3y}{4}.$$

x	y
$1\frac{1}{2}$	0
3	2
$4\frac{1}{2}$	4
6	6

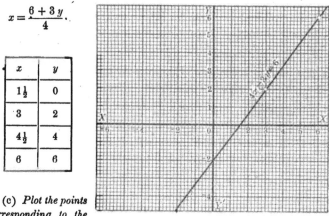

(c) *Plot the points corresponding to the pairs of numbers of the table* (see Fig. 203).

FIG. 203. GRAPH OF THE LINEAR EQUATION
$$4x - 3y = 6$$

(d) To check, choose a point on the line drawn and determine whether its coördinates satisfy the given equation or plot a third pair of numbers in the table. This third point also should fall on the line drawn.

(e) *The two points plotted should not be too near each other. Why?*

Draw the graphs of the following equations, each on a separate sheet of squared paper:

1. $x + y = 7$.
2. $2x - y = 8$.
3. $3x - 2y = 12$.
4. $3x + 2y = 6$.

5. $5x - 4y = 20$.
6. $3x + 5y = 15$.
7. $5x - 2y = 10$.
8. $6x - 4y = 3$.

9. $5x - 2y = -3$.
10. $x + 5y = -12$.
11. $2x = 3 - 4y$.
12. $3y = 4 - 8x$.

HISTORICAL NOTE. Statistics has attained the dignity of a science during the last fifty years. Its growth goes hand in hand with national organization. Even in a crude tribal organization the ruler must needs know something of its wealth to determine the taxes or tribute which may be levied. Our earliest statistical compilations (some time before 3000 B.C.) presented the population and wealth of Egypt in order to arrange for the construction of the pyramids. Many centuries later (about 1400 B.C.) Rameses II took a census of all the lands of Egypt to reapportion his subjects.

In the Bible we read how Moses numbered the tribes of Israel and of the census of the Roman emperor, Augustus Cæsar, in the year which marked the birth of Christ.

The Greeks and Romans and the feudal barons of the Middle Ages made many enumerations for the purposes of apportioning land, levying taxes, classifying the inhabitants, and determining the military strength. In all cases except that of the Romans some special reason existed for collecting the data. The Romans collected such data at regular intervals.

During the Mercantile Age of western Europe the feeling grew that it was the function of a government to encourage the measures aimed to secure a balance of trade. In order to decide correctly concerning the needs of commercial legislation, more detailed information was necessary than had hitherto been gathered. The growth in a centralized monarchy further stimulated statistical study. That monarch was most successful who could in advance most accurately compare his resources with his rivals'.

In 1575 Philip II of Spain made extensive inquiries from the prelates concerning their districts. In 1696 Louis XIV required reports on the conditions of the country from each of the general intendants.

Prussia began in modern times the policy of making periodic collections of statistical data. In 1719 Frederick William I began requiring semiannual reports as to population, occupations, real-estate holdings, taxes, city finance, etc. Later these data were collected every three years. Frederick the Great also was a vigorous exponent of the value of statistics. He enlarged the scope of statistics in general by including nationality, age, deaths and their causes, conditions of agriculture, trade, manufactures, shipping, in fact, anything that might possibly contribute to national efficiency.

A provision in our constitution of 1790 initiated the decennial census. One country after another has adopted some form of regular enumeration, until, in 1911, China took her first official census.

In recent times the censuses have grown extremely elaborate. In 1900 the United States established a permanent Census Bureau whose function it is to study special problems in the light of the data collected and to publish the results of this study. Most leading nations also have special bureaus which attempt to keep the statistics of a nation up to date by means of scientific estimates. An example of such a bureau is our National Bureau of Statistics. Many states have established bureaus to meet the needs of the state. Recently a movement has gained momentum to establish municipal bureaus to collect and study the data of the community and to instruct the public as to the significant results obtained by means of elaborate reports. An example of this idea is illustrated by the Survey Committee of the Cleveland Foundation.

SUMMARY

302. Chapter X has taught the meaning of the following words and phrases: pictogram, cartogram, bar diagrams, graphic curve, frequency table, class interval, central tendency, arithmetic average, mode, median, normal distribution, random sampling, compensating errors, constant or accumulating errors, symmetry, symmetry of a curve, skewness of a curve, price graph, linear equation, locus, axes, horizontal axis, vertical axis, ordinate, abscissa, coördinates, coördinate axes, plotting a point.

303. The graphic curve may be used to show the relation between two quantities. Specific directions were given showing how a graphic curve is drawn.

304. Continuous and discrete series were illustrated and explained.

305. Statistical studies are necessary to solve our social, governmental, and economic problems. The intelligent reader will profit by a knowledge of the elements of statistical methods.

306. Tabulating the facts bearing on a problem in the form of a frequency table enables one to get a grasp on the problem.

307. The word "average" as generally used may mean *arithmetic average, mode,* or *median.* All are measures of the central tendency of a mass of statistical data. The arithmetic average is found by *figuring,* the mode is found by *inspection,* and the median by *counting.*

308. The law of statistical regularity was illustrated.

309. The law of inertia of large numbers was stated.

310. The graph of goods purchased at a constant cost may be used as a "ready reckoner."

311. The chapter has taught how to plot points on squared paper.

312. The graph of a linear equation is a straight line. The coördinates of every point on the line satisfy the equation, and the coördinates of every point not on the line do not satisfy the equation. This illustrates the locus idea.

313. The chapter has taught the method of graphing a linear equation.

CHAPTER XI

GAINING CONTROL OF THE FORMULA; GRAPHICAL INTERPRETATION OF FORMULAS

314. The formula. The formula has been defined as an equation which is an abbreviated translation of some practical rule of procedure. Thus, $I = Prt$ is a formula because it is an equation which is an abbreviated form of the following practical rule for finding interest: *To find the interest* (expressed in dollars) *multiply the principal* (expressed in dollars) *by the product of the rate* (expressed in hundredths) *and the time* (expressed in years).

The formula is applied extensively in shop work, engineering, science, and, in fact, in every field of business and industry where the literature is at all technical. The symbolic form of the rule of procedure is not only more easily understood than the sentence form but is more easily applied to a particular problem.

315. Applying the interest formula. A formula is applied to a problem when the known facts of the problem are substituted in place of the letters of the formula. A formula may be used when all the letters except one appear as known facts in the problem. The pupil should study the following illustration:

What is the interest on $200 at 5% for two years?

Solution. Substituting the known facts in the formula,

$$I = 200 \cdot \tfrac{5}{100} \cdot 2.$$

Simplifying the right member,

$$I = \$20.$$

1. Find the interest on $425 at 4% for $2\frac{1}{2}$ yr.

2. Find the interest on $640 at $4\frac{1}{2}$% for 3 yr.

HINT. Substitute $\frac{4.5}{100}$, or $\frac{9}{200}$, for r. Why?

3. Find the interest on $820 at 4% for 2 yr. 3 mo. 5 da.

HINT. Reduce 2 yr. 3 mo. 5 da. to days, divide this result by 360, and substitute for t. Why?

316. Other types of interest problems conveniently solved by special forms of $I = Prt$. The method of solving other types of interest problems is illustrated by the following problem:

How much money must be invested at 5% for 2 yr. so as to yield $180 interest?

NOTE. This problem differs from Ex. 3, Art. 315, in that rate, time, and interest are given and the problem is to find P (the principal). It may be solved by substituting the three numbers given for the corresponding three letters of the formula. Why? However, it will be found on trial to be far more convenient if we first solve for P in $I = Prt$.

Solution. Dividing both members of the equation by rt, $\frac{I}{rt} = P$.

This may be translated into the following rule of arithmetic: To find the principal divide the interest by the product of the principal and the rate. $P = \frac{I}{rt}$ is only a special form of $I = Prt$, but constitutes complete directions for finding the principal when the other three factors are given.

In the proposed problem we obtain, by substituting,

$$P = \frac{180}{\frac{5}{100} \cdot 2} = \frac{180}{\frac{10}{100}} = \frac{180}{\frac{1}{10}} = 1800.$$

Thus the principal is $1800.

1. What principal must be invested at $4\frac{1}{2}\%$ for 2 yr. to yield $81?

2. What is the principal if the rate is 6%, the time 4 yr. 3 da., and the interest $120?

3. What is the rate if the principal is $500, the time 3 yr., and the interest $90?

Here P, t, and I are given; r is the unknown. Hence we solve $I = Prt$ for r.

Dividing both members by P and then by t or by (Pt),

$$\frac{I}{Pt} = r.$$

Substituting the known facts in $r = \dfrac{I}{Pt}$,

$$r = \frac{90}{500 \cdot 3} = \frac{6}{100} = 6\%.$$

4. Translate $r = \dfrac{I}{Pt}$ into a rule of procedure for finding the rate.

5. What is the rate if the interest is $85.50, the time $1\frac{1}{8}$ yr., and the principal $950?

6. What is a fourth type of interest problem? Find a formula most convenient for the solution of such type problems.

7. Show how to obtain this formula from the form $I = Prt$.

8. Translate into a rule of arithmetic.

9. Into what two parts can 1500 be divided so that the income of one at 6% shall equal the income of the other at 4%?

10. How can a man divide $1800 so that the income of part at 4% shall be the same as that of the rest at 5%?

11. A certain sum invested at $4\frac{1}{2}\%$ gave the same interest in 2 yr. as $4000 gave in $1\frac{1}{2}$ yr. at 4%. How large was the sum?

317. Solving a formula. The process of deriving $t = \dfrac{I}{Pt}$ from $I = Prt$ is called *solving the formula* for t. Similarly, deriving the form $P = \dfrac{I}{rt}$ is called solving the formula for P. The special form obtained is not only the most convenient form for the particular problem, but it may be used to solve the *whole class of problems* to which it belongs. The solving of the formulas of this chapter are of the practical kind and will involve little more than the applications of the axioms of Chapter I.

318. Graphical illustration of interest problems. The relation between any two of the factors that appear in an interest formula may be represented graphically.

How does the yearly interest vary on principals invested at 5%?

Substituting $\tfrac{5}{100}$ for r, and 1 for t, then $I = \tfrac{5}{100} P$.

Note that this is a linear equation involving I and P which may be plotted by the method of Art. 301. The table below was used to make the graph in Fig. 204.

I	P
$2.50	$50.00
$5.00	$100.00
$10.00	$200.00

Let one small unit on the horizontal lines represent $1 of interest, and one large unit on the vertical lines represent $50 of principal invested.

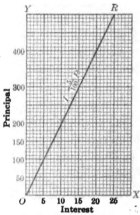

FIG. 204. GRAPH TO BE USED IN CALCULATING INTEREST ON PRINCIPALS INVESTED AT 5%

Use OX as the line for plotting interests and OY for plotting principals. Then the point corresponding to ($2.50, $50) means $2\frac{1}{2}$ small spaces to the right and 1 large space up. Since we know that the graph will be a straight line, the line OR may be safely drawn as soon as two points are plotted.

EXERCISES

1. Look at the graph in Fig. 204 and tell offhand what interest you would expect to collect at 5% for 1 yr. on $300; on $350; on $400; on $60; on $80.

2. Determine by looking at the graph in Fig. 204 how much money you would need to invest at 5% to collect $18 interest in 1 yr.; $20 interest; $27.50 interest; $14 interest.

3. How would you go about finding the interest on $12.50 by means of a graph? on $2000?

4. Check some of the answers given by calculating the interest by the usual method.

5. Graph the equation $I = \frac{8}{100} P$ and use the graph to calculate interest on sums lent at 6%.

6. Let $P = \$100$ and $r = \frac{8}{100}$ in the formula $I = Prt$, thus obtaining $I = 6t$. Graph $I = 6t$ and use the graph to determine the interest on $100 at 6% for 2 yr.; for $2\frac{1}{2}$ yr.; for 3 yr.; for 4 yr.; for 5 yr.; for 2 mo.

7. If possible, report in detail the methods used by your family banker to calculate interest. On what principles do the various "short cuts" rest?

*319. Formulas involving the amount. In the exercises that follow we shall study some formulas a little more difficult to solve, but they can be understood if the fundamental laws in solving equations are carefully applied.

1. If $400 is invested at 4%, what is the amount at the end of 1 yr.? of 2 yr.? of 3 yr.?

2. If $1200 is invested at 3%, what is the amount at the end of 2 yr.?

3. What is the rule for finding the amount when principal, rate, and time are given?

4. Using A for the amount and Prt for the interest, translate the preceding rule into a formula.

5. The formula for the amount may also be written in the form $A = P(1 + rt)$. Prove.

6. Solve $A = P(1 + rt)$ for P.

HINT. Dividing both members of the equation by the coefficient of P, namely, $(1 + rt)$, we obtain $P = \dfrac{A}{1 + rt}$.

7. Translate into a rule of arithmetic the formula obtained in Ex. 6.

8. Find the principal if the rate is 6%, the time 3 yr., and the amount $472.

Solution. $P = \dfrac{A}{1 + rt} = \dfrac{\$472}{1 + 0.18} = \dfrac{\$472}{1.18} = \$400.$

9. Find the principal if the rate is 5%, the time 3 yr., and the amount $1150.

10. Solve the equation $A = P + Prt$ for t. Translate the resulting formula into words.

11. Find the time if the principal is $2500, the amount $2725, and the rate 3%.

12. Solve the equation $A = P + Prt$ for r and translate the resulting formula into words.

13. Find the rate if the principal is $1500, the amount $1740, and the time 4 yr.

14. Summarize the advantages of solving interest problems by formulas.

320. Evaluating a formula. The process of finding the arithmetical value of the literal number called for in a formula is called *evaluating the formula*. The foregoing exercises show that the process consists of

1. *Substituting the known numbers in the formula.*
2. *Reducing the arithmetical number obtained to the simplest form.*

Note. A drill list involving these processes is given in Art. 329.

321. Summary of the discussion of a formula. Cultivating and gaining control of a formula means

1. *Analyzing an arithmetical situation so as to see the rule of procedure.*
2. *Translating the rule into a formula.*
3. *Solving the formula for any letter in terms of all the others.*
4. *Evaluating the formula.*

These steps will now be illustrated in the solution of motion problems. We shall then proceed to solve short lists of exercises which should develop power in these steps.

322. The formula applied to motion problems. In solving the following problems try to observe the steps summarized in Art. 321.

ORAL EXERCISES

1. If a 220-yard-dash man runs the last 50 yd. in 5 sec., at what rate is he finishing?

2. If an automobile makes 75 mi. in $2\frac{1}{2}$ hr., how fast is it being driven?

3. Express the distance covered by a train in 8 hr. at an average rate of 20 mi. per hour; of $12\frac{1}{2}$ mi. per hour; of x miles per hour; of $x + 3$ mi. per hour.

4. Express the distance covered by a train in t hours at the rate of r miles per hour.

5. Express the time it takes an automobile to go 150 mi. at the rate of 10 mi. per hour; of 15 mi. per hour; of 20 mi. per hour; of m miles per hour; of $2\,m$ miles per day; of $2\,m + 4$ mi. per day.

6. How long does it take to make a trip of d miles at the rate of r miles per hour?

7. The rate of a train is 30 mi. an hour. If it leaves the station at 1 A.M., how far away is it at 2 A.M.; at 3 A.M.; at 4 A.M.; at 5 A.M.; etc.? How far away is it at 3.15 A.M.; at 4.30 A.M.; at 6.45 A.M.?

8. Denoting the distance traveled by d, find d when the rate is 45 mi. an hour and the number of hours is six.

323. Distance, rate, time. The preceding exercises show that a problem involving motion is concerned with *distance, rate,* and *time.* The number of linear units passed over by a moving body is called the distance, and the number of units of distance traversed may be represented by d. The rate of uniform motion, that is, the number of units traversed in each unit of time, is called the rate (or speed) and is represented by r. The time, t, is expressed in minutes, hours, days, etc.

1. Illustrate by familiar experiences that *distance equals the rate multiplied by the time*; that is, that $d = rt$.

2. Show how to obtain $t = \dfrac{d}{r}$ from $d = rt$.

3. Translate $t = \dfrac{d}{r}$ into a rule for finding the time.

4. Show how to obtain $r = \dfrac{d}{t}$ from $d = rt$.

5. Translate $r = \dfrac{d}{t}$ into a rule for finding the rate.

6. A motor cycle goes 110 mi. in 5 hr. and 30 min. Assuming the rate to be uniform, what is the rate? Which of the formulas did you use?

7. Sound travels about 1080 ft. per second. If the sound of a stroke of lightning is heard 2.5 sec. after the flash, how far away is the stroke? Which form of the formula is used?

8. How many seconds would it take the sound to reach the ear if a tree 2376 ft. distant were struck by lightning? Which form of the formula is used?

WRITTEN EXERCISES

1. A motor boat starts 10 mi. behind a sailboat and runs 14 mi. per hour, while the sailboat makes 6 mi. per hour. How long will it require the motor boat to overtake the sailboat?

Let x be the number of hours it takes the motor boat to overtake the sailboat.

Then, according to the data of the problem:

for the motor boat,	for the sailboat,
$t = x.$	$t = x.$
$r = 14.$	$r = 6.$
Hence $d = 14\,x.$	Hence $d = 6\,x.$

Since the motor boat must go 10 mi. more than the sailboat, the following equation expresses the conditions of the problem:

$$14\,x = 6\,x + 10.$$

Solve the equation to find the value of x, which turns out to be $1\frac{1}{4}$ hr.

2. A and B live $22\frac{1}{2}$ mi. from each other. In order to meet A, B leaves home an hour earlier than A. If A travels at the rate of 4 mi. an hour and B at the rate of $3\frac{1}{2}$ mi. an hour, when and where will they meet?

3. A northbound and a southbound train leave Chicago at the same time, the former running 4 mi. an hour faster than the latter. If at the end of $1\frac{1}{2}$ hr. the trains are 126 mi. apart, find the rate of each.

4. In running 280 mi. a freight train whose rate is $\frac{2}{5}$ that of an express train takes $3\frac{1}{2}$ hr. longer than the express train. Find the rate of each.

5. An automobile runs 10 mi. an hour faster than a motor cycle, and it takes the automobile 2 hr. longer to run 150 mi. than it takes the motor cycle to run 60 mi. Find the rate of each.

6. A man rows downstream at the rate of 8 mi. an hour and returns at the rate of 5 mi. an hour. How far downstream can he go and return if he has $5\frac{1}{6}$ hr. at his disposal ? At what rate does the stream flow ?

7. Chicago and Cincinnati are about 250 mi. apart. Suppose that a train starts from each city toward the other, one at the rate of 30 mi. per hour and the other at the rate of 35 mi. per hour. How soon will they meet ?

8. A train is traveling at the rate of 30 mi. an hour. In how many hours will a second train overtake the first if the second starts 3 hr. later than the first and travels at the rate of 35 mi. an hour ?

*9. A and B run a mile race. A runs 20 ft. per second, and B $19\frac{1}{2}$ ft. per second. B has a start of 32 yd. In how many seconds will A overtake B ? Which will win the race ?

*10. A bullet going 1500 ft. per second is heard to strike the target 3 sec. after it is fired. How far away is the target ? (Sound travels at the rate of about 1080 ft. per second.)

11. A motor cyclist rode 85 mi. in 5 hr. Part of the distance was on a country road at a speed of 20 mi. an hour and the rest within the city limits at 10 mi. an hour. Find how many hours of his ride were in the country.

12. Two boats 149 mi. apart approach each other, leaving at the same time. One goes 10 mi. per hour faster than the other, and they meet in 2 hr. What is the rate of each ?

324. Graphical illustration of a motion problem. Many motion problems can be conveniently illustrated graphically, as the student will discover if he solves the following exercises.

EXERCISES

1. In the Indianapolis races De Palma drove his car at a rate varying but little from 90 mi. per hour. Draw a graph showing the relation between the distance and time of De Palma's performance.

Substituting 90 in $d = tr$,
$$d = 90\, t.$$

Note that $d = 90\, t$ is a linear equation which may be graphed (see table and Fig. 205). Ten small units on the vertical axis represent 30 mi.; ten small units on the horizontal axis represent $\frac{1}{3}$ hr.

d	t
30	$\frac{1}{3}$
45	$\frac{1}{2}$
60	$\frac{2}{3}$

2. Determine from the graph in Fig. 205 how many miles De Palma drove in 2 hr.; in $1\frac{1}{2}$ hr.; in 1 hr. 24 min.; in 40 min.; in 4 min.; in 2 hr. 12 min.

3. Determine by the graph in Fig. 205 how long it took De Palma to go 50 mi.; 40 mi.; 60 mi.; 75 mi.; 140 mi.; 160 mi.; 10 mi.

Obviously the preceding results could be calculated either by arithmetic or by the formula. However, the graph has the advantage of revealing *all* the results in vivid fashion.

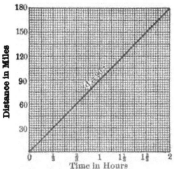

FIG. 205. THE GRAPH OF A MOTION-PROBLEM FORMULA

4. Draw a graph showing the distances traversed by a passenger train running uniformly at the rate of 40 mi. per hour for the first ten hours of its trip.

*5. Find out, if possible, what use railroad officials make of graphs in arranging schedules.

325. Circular motion. Circular motion is of frequent occurrence in mechanics. A familiar illustration is found in the movement of the hands of a clock.

1. At what time between 3 and 4 o'clock are the hands of a clock together?

Solution. Let x (Fig. 206) equal the number of minutes after 3 o'clock when the hands are together; that is, x equals the number of minute spaces over which the minute hand passes from 3 o'clock until it overtakes the hour hand.

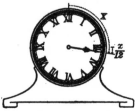

Then $\dfrac{x}{12}$ equals the number of minute spaces passed over by the hour hand. Why?

FIG. 206. CLOCK PROBLEMS ILLUSTRATE A TYPE OF CIRCULAR MOTION

Since the number of minute spaces from 12 to 3 is 15, and since the whole is equal to the sum of its parts, it follows that

$$x = 15 + \frac{x}{12}.$$

Whence $\qquad\qquad x = 16\tfrac{4}{11}$ min.

Therefore the hands are together at $16\tfrac{4}{11}$ min. after 3 o'clock.

2. At what time between 4 and 5 o'clock are the hands of a clock together?

HINT. Draw a figure similar to the one for Ex. 1.

Notice that the formula for a clock problem is $x = \dfrac{x}{12} + m$, where m equals the number of minute spaces the minute hand must gain in order to reach the desired position.

3. At what time between 2 and 3 o'clock are the hands of a clock 15 min. apart?

HINT. Draw a figure, think the problem through, and then try to see how the formula in Ex. 2 applies.

4. At what time between 2 and 3 o'clock are the hands of a clock 30 minute spaces apart?

5. What angle is formed by the hands of a clock at 2.30?

*6. At what time between 5 and 6 o'clock are the hands of a clock 20 min. apart? How many answers? How may these results be obtained from the formula of Ex. 2?

326. Work problems. The work problem is another type of problem easily solved by formula.

EXERCISES

1. One pipe will fill a tank in 3 hr. and a second pipe can fill it in 4 hr. How long will it take to fill the tank if both pipes are left running?

Let $n =$ the number of hours it will take both pipes to fill the tank.

Then $\dfrac{1}{n} =$ the part of the tank filled in 1 hr.,

$\quad\quad \frac{1}{3} =$ the part of the tank filled by the first pipe in 1 hr.,

and $\quad \frac{1}{4} =$ the part of the tank filled by the second pipe.

Hence $\qquad\qquad \dfrac{1}{3} + \dfrac{1}{4} = \dfrac{1}{n}.$ Why?

Multiplying by $12\,n$, $\quad 4\,n + 3\,n = 12,$

or $\qquad\qquad\qquad 7\,n = 12.$

Whence $\qquad\qquad\qquad n = 1\frac{5}{7}$ hr.

2. A can lay a drain in 5 da. and B can do it in 7 da. How long will it take both working together?

3. One boy can drive his car over a trip in 8 hr. and a second boy can make the trip in 5 hr. How long would it take them to meet if each started at an end?

NOTE. It is clear from the foregoing problems that any numbers would be used just as 3 and 4 are used in Ex. 1. Hence a formula may be obtained, as is shown by Ex. 4.

4. A can do a piece of work in a days and B can do it in b days. How long will it take them to do it together?

Let $\qquad n =$ the number of days it will take them together.

Then $\qquad \dfrac{1}{n} =$ the amount of work they can do in 1 da.,

$\dfrac{1}{a} =$ the amount A can do in 1 da.,

and $\qquad \dfrac{1}{b} =$ the amount B can do in 1 da.

Hence $\qquad \dfrac{1}{a} + \dfrac{1}{b} = \dfrac{1}{n}.$

Multiplying by abn, $\quad bn + an = ab,$

$(b + a)n = ab,$

$$n = \frac{ab}{a+b}.$$

NOTE. Any problem of the type of Ex. 1 on page 285 may be solved by using the equation $n = \dfrac{ab}{a+b}$ as a formula. Thus, to solve Ex. 1 let $a = 3$, $b = 4$. Then $n = \dfrac{3 \times 4}{3 + 4} = \dfrac{12}{7} = 1\frac{5}{7}$ hr.

5. One boy can make a paper route in 2 hr. and his friend can make the route in $1\frac{1}{2}$ hr. How long will it take the two together? (Solve by formula.)

*6. Suppose that in Ex. 1 on page 285 the second pipe is an emptying pipe, how long will it take to fill the tank if both pipes are running? What form does the formula take?

*7. A can sweep a walk in 7 min., B in 8 min., and C in 10 min. How long will it take them working together? What form does the formula for a work problem take?

*8. A could lay a sidewalk in 3 da., B in 4 da., and C in 4.5 da. How long does it take them when working together? Solve by substituting in the formula for Ex. 7.

327. Translating rules of procedure into formulas. Write each of the following in the form of a formula:

1. The area of a triangle equals the product of half the base times the altitude.

2. The area of a rectangle equals the product of its base and altitude.

3. The area of a parallelogram equals the product of its base and altitude.

4. The area of a trapezoid equals one half the sum of the parallel bases multiplied by the altitude.

5. The volume of a pyramid equals one third the base times the altitude.

6. The length of a circle is approximately equal to twenty-two sevenths of the diameter.

7. The circumference of a circle is equal to π times the diameter.

8. The area of a circle is π times the square of the radius.

9. The product equals the multiplicand times the multiplier.

10. The product obtained by multiplying a fraction by a whole number is the product of the whole number and the numerator divided by the denominator.

11. The quotient of two fractions equals the dividend multiplied by the inverted divisor.

12. The square root of a fraction equals the square root of the numerator divided by the square root of the denominator.

13. The square of a fraction is the square of the numerator divided by the square of the denominator.

14. The rule for calculating the cost of one article when you know that a certain number of them cost so much; write the cost of m articles.

15. The rule for expressing years, months, and days as years.

16. The rule for calculating the area of three adjacent rooms of different lengths but the same width.

17. The rule for calculating the area of the floor of a square room.

18. The rule for finding the cost of a telegram.

19. The rule for finding the area of a figure cut from cardboard, given its weight and the weight of a square unit of cardboard.

20. The rule for finding the amount of available air for each person in a classroom, given the dimensions of the room and the number in the class.

21. The rule for finding the weight of a single lead shot, given the weight of a beaker with a given number of shot in it and the weight of the empty beaker.

22. The rule for predicting the population of a town after a certain number of months, given the present population, the average number of births, and the average number of deaths.

23. The rule for finding the distance apart, after a given time, of two cars which start from the same point and travel in opposite directions at different speeds.

24. The same as in Ex. 23 except that the cars are m miles apart at starting.

25. The same as in Ex. 23 except that the cars go in the same direction with different speeds.

26. The reading on a Fahrenheit thermometer is always 32° greater than $\frac{9}{5}$ of the reading on a centigrade thermometer.

27. The reading of a centigrade thermometer may be calculated by noting the reading on the Fahrenheit, subtracting 32, and taking $\frac{5}{9}$ of this result.

328. Graphic representation of the relation between the readings on centigrade and Fahrenheit thermometers. The last two exercises deal with two types of thermometers that are used to measure temperature. Fig. 207 shows that the only fundamental difference is the different graduations of the scale. In the Fahrenheit thermometer the place where the mercury stands if immersed in freezing water is 32°; on the centigrade it is zero. This defines the freezing point on each. The boiling point is marked 212° on the Fahrenheit and only 100° on the centigrade. Hence the Fahrenheit thermometer has 180 divisions of the scale in the interval from freezing to boiling, while the centigrade has but 100. This means that a unit on the centigrade is longer, or for any space on the centigrade there are $\frac{180}{100}$ times, or $\frac{9}{5}$ times, as many Fahrenheit units. Hence the number of units in a Fahrenheit reading equals $\frac{9}{5}$ times as many centigrade units plus 32° (which are below the freezing point). Stated as a formula, $F = \frac{9}{5}C + 32$.

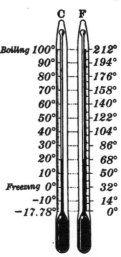

FIG. 207. THE RELATION BETWEEN THE CENTIGRADE AND FAHRENHEIT THERMOMETERS

We could, of course, always translate the reading on one thermometer to the corresponding reading on the other by means of this formula. It is far easier, however, to graph the linear equation $F = \frac{9}{5}C + 32$, which will reveal possible relations, as is shown in Fig. 208.

NOTE. The pupil should construct the graph independently of the text, using a table similar to the following:

C.	F.
0	32
25	77
15	59

Let C. = 0, then F. = 32.

Let C. = 25, then F. = 77.

Let C. = 15, then F. = 59.

EXERCISES

1. Determine by the graph the corresponding Fahrenheit readings for the following centigrade readings : 5°, 10°, 20°, 30°, − 5°, − 10°, − 15°, − 25°.

2. Determine by the graph the centigrade readings corresponding to the following Fahrenheit readings : 80°, 70°, 60°, 30°, 20°, 10°, − 5°, − 10°.

3. In the formula $F = \frac{9}{5} C + 32°$ substitute in each case the two numbers you think are corresponding readings. The error should be very small.

4. Normal room temperature is 68° F. What is it centigrade ?

5. The normal temperature of the human body is 98.4° F. What is it centigrade ?

6. What temperature centigrade corresponds to 0° F. ?

7. Could you go skating at 15° C. ?

8. In your general-science course you are told that mercury freezes at − 40° F. What is this centigrade ?

9. Would your classroom be comfortable at 25° C. ?

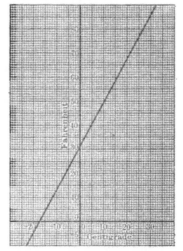

FIG. 208. A GRAPH TO BE USED IN CHANGING CENTIGRADE READINGS TO FAHRENHEIT AND VICE VERSA

329. Evaluating a formula. Find the value of the letter called for in each of the exercises given on page 291. When no explanation is given, it is assumed that the student recognizes the formula.

EXERCISES

1. Given $C = \frac{5}{9}$ (F − 32). Find C. if F. = 0°; 32°; 212°; 100°.

2. Given $F = \frac{9}{5}C + 32$. Find F. if C. = 0°; 100°; − 20°; 60°.

3. Given $d = rt$. Find d if $r = 87.5$ mi. per hour and $t = 12$ hr.; if $r = 10\frac{1}{5}$ ft. per second and $t = 10$ sec.

4. Given $r = \frac{d}{t}$. Find r if $d = 1$ mi. and $t = 4$ min. 16 sec.; if $d = \frac{1}{2}$ mi. and $t = 2.07$ sec.

5. Given $A = P + Prt$. Find A if $P = \$240$, $r = 4\frac{1}{2}\%$, and $t = 1$ yr. 2 mo. 3 da.; if $P = \$128$, $r = 5\%$, and $t = 2$ yr. 3 da.; if $P = \$511$, $r = 6\%$, and $t = 20$ yr.

6. Given $V = lwh$. Find V (see Fig. 209) if $l = 12.2$ ft., $w = 8.3$ ft., and $h = 6.4$ ft.; if $l = 9.3$ in., $w = 5.6$ in., and $h = 1$ in.

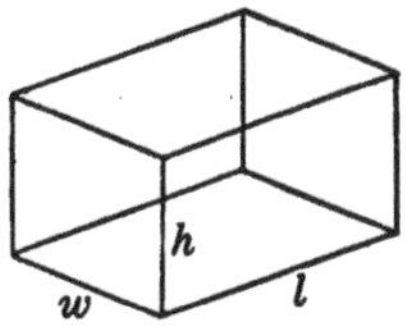

FIG. 209. RECTAN- GULAR PARALLELE- PIPED

7. Given $V = \frac{lwh}{3}$. Find V if $l = 63$ ft., $w = 2.4$ ft., and $h = 1.6$ ft.; if $l = 3$ cm., $w = 2.1$ cm., and $h = 1.4$ cm.

8. Given $c = \frac{22}{7}d$. Find c if $d = 1$ ft.; 1 in.; 4 in.; 10 in.; $5\frac{1}{2}$ in.

9. Given $A = \pi r^2$ $(\pi = \frac{22}{7})$. Find A if $r = 1$ in.; 5 ft.; 10 yd.; 7 m.; 8.5 cm.

10. The volume V of any prism (Fig. 210) is equal to the product of its base B and its altitude h. Find V if $B = 246.12$ sq. in. and $h = 12$ in.; if $B = 212.44$ sq. in. and $h = 2\frac{1}{2}$ ft.

FIG. 210. PRISM

11. The lateral surface L of a right prism equals the perimeter of the base P times the altitude h. Find L if $P = 126$ in. and $h = 11$ in.; if $P = 21.6$ in. and $h = 0.35$ in.

12. The volume of a right cylinder (Fig. 211) is equal to the product of its base and height. The formula is $V = \pi r^2 h$, where r is the radius of the circular base. Find V if $r = 10.2$ cm. and $h = 9$ cm.; if $r = 6$ in. and $h = 12$ in.

13. The lateral surface of a right cylinder equals the product of the altitude and the circumference of the base. The formula usually given is $S = Ch$. Find S if $C = 2\frac{2}{7}$ in. and $h = 10$ in.

14. The entire surface T of a right cylinder equals the circumference of the circular base times the sum of the altitude and the radius of the base; that is, $T = 2\pi r(r + h)$. Find T if $h = 10$ in. and $r = 5$ in.; if $h = 2$ ft. and $r = 1$ ft.

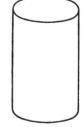

Fig. 211. Right Cylinder

15. The volume V of any pyramid (Fig. 212) is equal to one third the product of its base B and its altitude h; that is, $V = \dfrac{Bh}{3}$. Find V if $B = 200$ sq. in. and $h = 12$ in.; if $B = 24.6$ sq. in. and $h = 2$ ft.

Fig. 212. Pyramid

16. The lateral area S of a regular pyramid is equal to one half the product of the perimeter P of its base and its slant height l; that is, $S = \dfrac{Pl}{2}$. Find A if $P = 10.6$ in. and $l = 8.2$ in.; if $P = 4.3$ cm. and $l = 15$ cm.

17. The lateral area S of a right circular cone (Fig. 213) is equal to one half the product of its slant height l and the circumference C of its base. Write the formula for S, and find S if $l = 14.6$ in. and $C = 10$ in.; if $l = 3.6$ ft. and $C = 31.416$ ft.

Fig. 213. Right Circular Cone

18. The lateral area S of a right circular cone is πrh, where r is the radius of the base and h is the slant height. Find S if $r = 10$ in. and $h = 10$ in.; if $r = 10$ in. and $h = 26.2$ in.

19. The entire surface T of a right circular cone equals the lateral area l plus the area of the base; that is, $T = \pi r l + \pi r^2$, or $\pi r (l + r)$. Find T if $l = 10$ in. and $r = 5$ in.; if $l = 12.6$ in. and $r = 6$ in.

20. An object falling from rest falls in a given time a distance equal to the product of 16 and the square of the number of seconds it has fallen; that is, $d = 16 t^2$. Find d if $t = 1$ sec.; 2 sec.; 3 sec.; 4 sec.

21. An object thrown downward travels in a given time a distance equal to the product of 16 and the square of the number of seconds it has fallen, plus the product of the velocity with which it is thrown and the number of seconds it is falling. The formula is $S = 16 t^2 + Vt$. Find S if $t = 3$ sec. and $V = 13$ ft. per second; if $t = 5$ sec. and $V = 100$ ft. per second.

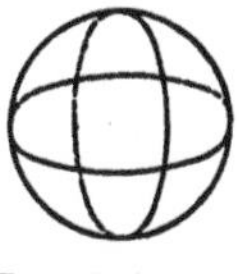

22. The volume of a sphere (Fig. 214) equals the cube of the radius multiplied by $\frac{4}{3} \pi$. Find V if $r = 1$ in.; 10 in.; 5 in.; 10 ft.; 12 ft.

23. The surface S of a sphere is equal to $4 \pi r^2$. Find S if $r = 10$ in.; 12 ft.; $6\frac{1}{2}$ ft.

FIG. 214. THE SPHERE

*24. The force of pressure P of the wind, in pounds per square foot, is given by the equation $P = 0.005 V^2$, where V is the velocity of the wind in miles per hour. What would be the total pressure of this wind against the side of a wall 25 ft. high and 80 ft. long of a wind blowing 30 mi. per hour?

*25. Show that the formula for the length l of a belt passing around two pulleys of the same size whose radii are each r feet, and the distance between whose centers is d feet, is $l = 2 \pi r + 2 d$. Find l when $r = 1\frac{1}{2}$ and $d = 4\frac{1}{2}$.

26. In a price list the cost of sewer pipe per foot of length is given by the formula $C = 0.4 d^2 + 14$, where d is the diameter of the pipe in inches and C the cost in cents. What will be the cost of 20 ft. of pipe 2 in. in diameter?

330. Practice in solving for any letter. It is often desirable to solve a formula for some particular letter in that formula. Too often the student will recognize a formula provided it stands in the form in which it is commonly written, but will not appreciate its meaning if it is written in a different way. For example, how many students would recognize the formula $c = \dfrac{V}{ab}$ as the well-known formula $V = abc$? It is the same formula except that it is in a different form. If the student realizes this, it helps him to gain control of the formula. The following exercises will furnish practice in solving for particular letters.

Solve each of the following formulas for the letter or letters indicated:

1. $A = \dfrac{ab}{2}$ for a; for b.

2. $V = abc$ for c; for a; for b.

3. $d = rt$ for r; for t.

4. $\dfrac{D}{d} = q$ for d; for D.

5. $W_1 l_1 = W_2 l_2$ for l_1; for W_1.

6. $V = \dfrac{lwh}{3}$ for w; for h.

7. $C = \tfrac{2 \cdot 2}{7} d$ for d.

8. $C = \tfrac{4 \cdot 4}{7} r$ for r.

9. $V = Bh$ for B.

10. $V = \tfrac{2 \cdot 2}{7} r^2 h$ for h.

11. $V = \dfrac{Bh}{3}$ for h.

12. $A = \dfrac{Pl}{2}$ for l.

13. $A = P + Prt$ for t.

14. $C = \tfrac{5}{9}(F - 32)$ for F.

15. $S = \dfrac{gt^2}{2}$ for t^2; for g.

16. $S = 2\pi rh + 2\pi r^2$ for h.

17. $A = \dfrac{(b_1 + b_2)h}{2}$ for h; for b_1; for b_2.

18. $C = \dfrac{E}{R + r}$ for E; for R; for r.

SUMMARY

331. This chapter has taught the meaning of the following words and phrases: formula, solving a formula, evaluating a formula, applying a formula, centigrade, Fahrenheit.

332. A formula is a conveniently abbreviated form of some practical rule of procedure.

333. A clear understanding of a formula implies:

1. An analysis of some arithmetical situation so as to arrive at some rule of procedure.

2. Translating the rule into a formula.

3. The ability to solve for any letter in terms of the other letters in the formula.

4. The ability to apply the formula to a particular problem and to evaluate the formula.

334. The preceding steps were illustrated in detail by applications to interest problems, to problems involving motion, to work problems, to thermometer problems, and to geometric problems.

335. The graphical interpretations suggested economical methods of manipulating a formula. For example:

1. Simple-interest problems were solved by the formulas $I = Prt$ and $A = P + Prt$.

2. A problem involving uniform motion in a straight line was solved by the formula $d = rt$.

3. The relation between centigrade and Fahrenheit readings was expressed by the formula $C = \frac{5}{9}(F - 32)$.

336. While the important thing in this chapter is the power of manipulating and evaluating a formula, the student was given the meaning of most of the formulas in order to have him realize from the very outset that both the formulas and their manipulation refer to actual situations.

HISTORICAL NOTE. The development of the formula belongs to a very late stage in the development of mathematics. It requires a much higher form of thinking to see that the area of any triangle can be expressed by $A = \dfrac{ab}{2}$ than to find the area of a particular lot whose base is two hundred feet and whose altitude is fifty feet. Hence, it was very late in the race's development that letters were used in expressing rules.

The early mathematicians represented the unknown by some word like *res* (meaning "the thing"). Later, calculators used a single letter for the unknown, but the problems still dealt with particular cases. Diophantus, representing Greek mathematics, stated some problems in general terms, but usually solved the problems by taking special cases.. Vieta used capital letters (consonants and vowels) to represent known and unknown numbers respectively. Newton is said to be the first to let a letter stand for negative as well as positive numbers, which greatly decreases the number of formulas necessary.

While the race has had a difficult time discovering and understanding formulas, it takes comparatively little intelligence to use a formula. Many men in the industrial world do their work efficiently by the means of a formula whose derivation and meaning they do not understand. It is said that even among college-trained engineers only a few out of every hundred do more than follow formulas or other directions blindly. Thus, it appears that for the great majority only the immediately practical is valuable. However, we can be reasonably sure that no one can rise to be a leader in any field by his own ability without understanding the theoretical as well as the practical.

The formula is very important in the present complex industrial age. A considerable portion of the necessary calculation is done by following the directions of some formula. Therefore to meet this need the study of the formula should be emphasized. In discussing the kind of mathematics that should be required Professor A. R. Crathorne (*School and Society*, July 7, 1917, p. 14) says: "Great emphasis would be placed on the formula, and all sorts of formulas could be brought in. The popular science magazines, the trade journals and catalogues, are mines of information about which the modern boy or girl understands. The pupil should think of the formula as an algebraic declarative sentence that can be translated

ARCHIMEDES (287–212 B.C.)

(Bust in Naples Museum)

into English. The evaluation leads up to the tabular presentation of the formula. Mechanical ability in the manipulation of symbols should be encouraged through inversion of the formula, or what the Englishman calls 'changing the subject of the formula.' We have here also the beginning of the equation when our declarative sentence is changed to the interrogative."

Archimedes (287–212 B.C.), a great mathematician who studied in the university at Alexandria and lived in Sicily, loved science so much that he held it undesirable to apply his information to practical use. But so great was his mechanical ability that when a difficulty had to be overcome the government often called on him. He introduced many inventions into the everyday lives of the people.

His life is exceedingly interesting. Read the stories of his detection of the dishonest goldsmith; of the use of burning-glasses to destroy the ships of the attacking Roman squadron; of his clever use of a lever device for helping out Hiero, who had built a ship so large that he could not launch it off the slips; of his screw for pumping water out of ships and for irrigating the Nile valley. He devised the catapults which held the Roman attack for three years. These were so constructed that the range was either long or short and so that they could be discharged through a small loophole without exposing the men to the fire of the enemy.

When the Romans finally captured the city Archimedes was killed, though contrary to the orders of Marcellus, the general in charge of the siege. It is said that soldiers entered Archimedes' study while he was studying a geometrical figure which he had drawn in sand on the floor. Archimedes told a soldier to get off the diagram and not to spoil it. The soldier, being insulted at having orders given to him and not knowing the old man, killed him.

The Romans erected a splendid tomb with the figure of a sphere engraved on it. Archimedes had requested this to commemorate his discovery of the two formulas: the volume of a sphere equals two-thirds that of the circumscribing right cylinder, and the surface of a sphere equals four times the area of a great circle. You may also read an interesting account by Cicero of his successful efforts to find Archimedes' tomb. It will be profitable if the student will read Ball's "A Short History of Mathematics," pp. 65–77.

CHAPTER XII

FUNCTION; LINEAR FUNCTIONS; THE RELATED IDEAS OF FUNCTION, EQUATION, AND FORMULA INTERPRETED GRAPHICALLY; VARIATION

337. Function the dependence of one quantity upon another. One of the most common notions in our lives is the notion of the dependence of one thing upon another. We shall here study the mathematics of such dependence by considering several concrete examples.

EXERCISES

1. Upon what does the cost of 10 yd. of cloth depend?

2. If Resta drives his car at an average rate of 98.3 mi. per hour, upon what does the length (distance) of the race depend?

3. A boy rides a motor cycle for two hours. Upon what does the length of his trip depend?

4. How much interest would you expect to collect in a year on $200?

5. Upon what does the length of a circular running track depend?

6. A man wishes to buy wire fencing to inclose a square lot. How much fencing must he buy?

7. State upon what quantities each of the following depends:

(a) The amount of sirloin steak that can be bought for a dollar.

(b) The number of theater tickets that can be bought for a dollar.

(c) The height of a maple tree that averages a growth of 4 ft. per year.

(d) The time it takes you to get your mathematics lesson if you solve one problem every three minutes.

(e) The value of a submarine as a merchant vessel.

(f) The rate of interest charged by your local bank.

(g) The perimeter $4x - 4$ of the rectangle in Fig. 215.

The preceding exercises illustrate the *dependence* of one quantity upon another. We have had numerous other examples of dependence in the chapters on statistics and the formula. In fact, every practical formula implies that the value of some quantity depends upon one or more others. Thus the circumference of a circular running track depends upon the diameter. When a quantity depends upon another quantity for its value, it is said to be a *function* of the latter. Thus the area of a circle is a function of the diameter because it depends upon the diameter for its value; the amount of sirloin steak that can be bought for a dollar is a function of the price per pound; and the expression $4x - 4$ is a function of x because its value changes with every change in the value of x.

See if you can illustrate the idea of function by ten familiar examples not given above.

338. Variable. A number that may change, assuming a series of values throughout a discussion, is called a *variable.* It is not obliged to vary—it is "able to vary." Thus the price of wheat and the number s in the equation $A = s^2$ are variables.

339. Dependent and independent variables. In the formula $C = \pi d$ the number d is said to be the *independent variable.* In a discussion or in the construction of circles we may take its value equal to any number we please. On the other hand, the value of C is automatically fixed once the value of d is determined. Because of this fact C is called the *dependent variable.*

EXERCISES

1. What is the value of C in the equation $C = \pi d$ if $d = 2$? if $d = 5$? if $d = 10$?

2. Illustrate the ideas of dependent and independent variables with examples chosen from the text or from your own experience.

340. Constant. The number π in the formula $C = \pi d$ differs from C and d inasmuch as it never changes at any time in the discussion of circles. This number is approximately $2\frac{2}{7}$, or 3.1416, whether we are dealing with small or large circles. We therefore call a number like this, which has a fixed value, a *constant*. Obviously any arithmetical number appearing in a formula is a constant; thus the 2 in $A = \dfrac{ab}{2}$ and the $\frac{9}{5}$ and the 32 in $F = \frac{9}{5}C + 32$ are constants.

EXERCISE

Turn to Chapter XI, on the formula, and find five formulas that illustrate the idea of a constant.

341. Graph of a function. A graph may be constructed showing how a function changes as the value of the independent variable changes. The rectangle in Fig. 215 is a picture (either enlarged or reduced) of every rectangle whose length exceeds its width by two units. We shall now proceed to show graphically that the perimeter varies with every change in the value of x. The table on the following page gives the corresponding values for the length x and for $4x - 4$, the perimeter.

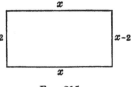

Fig. 215

x	3	4	5	6	7	8	9	10
$4x-4$	8	12	16	20	24			

If we plot the points corresponding to (3, 8). (4, 12), (5, 16), etc., using the horizontal axis to plot the values of x and the vertical axis to plot the values of $4x-4$, we obtain the points as shown on the straight line AB in Fig. 216. The line shows that as x increases, the value of $4x-4$ increases accordingly.

EXERCISES

1. Tell in your own words how the graph in Fig. 216 shows that the function $4x-4$ increases as x increases.

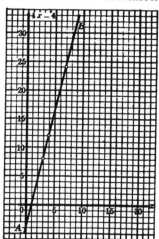

2. Determine from the graph the perimeters of rectangles whose lengths are as follows: 8 in.; 9 in.; 10.5 in.; 11 in.

3. Determine from the graph the length of the rectangles whose perimeters are as follows: 30 in.; 25 in.; 20 in.; 18 in.; 10 in.; 3 in.; 0 in.

4. Suppose you chose to make a particular rectangle 10 in. long. How long would the perimeter be? How does the graph show this?

5. How long would you make a rectangle of the same shape as the one in Fig. 215 so as to have its perimeter 16 in.? How does the graph show this?

FIG. 216. GRAPH SHOWING THAT THE PERIMETER OF THE RECTANGLE IN FIG. 215 IS A FUNCTION OF THE LENGTH

6. Relying on your past experience, tell how many rectangles you could construct in the shop or construct in your notebook " whose length shall exceed their width by two units ".

342. Linear function. Since the graph of the expression $4x - 4$ is a straight line, the function is called a *linear function*. If we let y represent the value of the linear function, we get the corresponding linear equation $y = 4x - 4$.

EXERCISE

Give five examples of linear functions.

343. Solving a family of equations by means of the graph. The graph of the function $4x - 4$ may be used to solve all equations one of whose members is $4x - 4$ and the other some arithmetical number or constant. For example, if in the equation $y = 4x - 4$ we let $y = 16$, then the equation $4x - 4 = 16$ may be interpreted as raising the question, What is the value of x that will make $4x - 4 = 16$? In order to answer this question we find 16 on the y-axis (the vertical axis), pass horizontally to the graph of $4x - 4$, and read the corresponding value of x. The corresponding value of x is seen to be 5. Hence $4x - 4 = 16$ when $x = 5$.

As a verbal problem the equation $4x - 4 = 16$ may be translated into the following interrogative sentence: What shall be the length of the rectangle in order that it may have a perimeter of 16? A glance at the graph is sufficient to determine the answer; namely, 5.

EXERCISES

Solve by graph, and check the following equations:

1. $4x - 4 = 20$.

2. $4x - 4 = 24$.

3. $4x - 4 = 12$.

4. $4x - 4 = 6$.

5. $4x - 8 = 2$.

Hint. Add 4 to both members so as to obtain the equation $4x - 4 = 6$.

6. $4x - 5 = 13$.

7. $4x - 9 = 10.$

8. $4x + 6 = 26.$

HINT. Subtract 10 from both members so as to obtain the result $4x - 4 = 16.$

9. $4x + 2 = 12.$

10. $4x + 5 = 19.$

11. $4x + 15 = 29.$

12. $4x - 4 = 0.$

344. The graphical solution of the function set equal to zero. Problem 12, Art. 343, is an interesting special case for two reasons: (1) It gives us an easy method of finding the value of x in the equation $4x - 4 = 0$. We need only refer to the graph and observe where the line crosses the x-axis. The line is seen to cross where $x = 1$. This value of x checks because $4 \cdot 1 - 4 = 0$. Hence $x = 1$ is a solution of the equation $4x - 4 = 0$. (2) It furnishes us a graphic method for solving all linear equations in one unknown because every equation in one unknown can be thrown into a form similar to $4x - 4 = 0$. Show how this may be done with the equation $3x + 7 = x + 12$.

EXERCISES

1. Solve graphically the equation $3x + 7 = x + 12$.

HINT. The equation may be written in the form $2x - 5 = 0$. Why? Graph the function $2x - 5$ just as we graphed $4x - 4$ (Fig. 216). See where the graph of $2x - 5$ crosses the x-axis. This is the correct value of x.

Check by substituting this value of x in the original equation $3x + 7 = x + 12$.

2. Solve the following linear equations by the graph, and check the results:

(a) $5x + 2 = 2x + 8.$

(b) $6x - 5 = 4x + 2.$

(c) $5x + 8 = 8x - 4.$

(d) $11x - 9 = 14x + 7.$

(e) $2.5x + 9 = 3x + 7.$

(f) $\frac{x}{5} - 7 = x - 5.$

(g) $\frac{x}{3} + 4 = \frac{x}{2} - 7.$

HISTORICAL NOTE. Perhaps the most important idea which a student can learn from an elementary study of mathematics is the idea of a function. This is given far greater prominence in European than in American texts. Indeed, it.is remarkable that though the function idea is generally admitted to be a fundamental notion in mathematics, the teaching of the notion is often neglected.

From the simple illustrations in this text it will appear that many familiar facts and principles of natural phenomena can be expressed as functions. A study of these facts in the form of a mathematical function throws much additional light on them. Thus, a clear understanding of the principles of light, sound, and electricity could not be obtained without a study of the mathematical functions by which these principles are expressed. The dependence of one quantity upon another is one of the fundamental notions of human experience. It is valuable to learn to treat this notion mathematically.

Teachers of mathematics will also remember Professor Felix Klein as one who has improved mathematics teaching by insisting that it be made more meaningful to pupils of high-school age by introducing and emphasizing the notion of a function.

345. Direct variation. If a man walks at the rate of 3 mi. an hour, the distance d which he walks in a given time t is found from the equation $d = 3\,t$. The following table gives the distance passed over in 1 hr., 2 hr., 3 hr., etc. and shows

1. That the greater the time, the greater the distance passed over.

2. That the ratio of any time to the corresponding distance is $\frac{1}{3}$.

Number of hours . .	1	2	3	4	5	6	7	8
Distance passed over	3	6	9	12	15	18	21	24

When two numbers vary so that one depends upon the other for its value, keeping constant the ratio of any value of one to the corresponding value of the other, then one is said to *vary directly* as the other or to be *directly proportional* to the other. Thus the number x is said to vary directly as y if the ratio $\dfrac{x}{y}$ remains constant, as x and y both change or vary. The equation $\dfrac{x}{y} = k$ expresses algebraically, and is equivalent to, the statement that x varies directly as y. The equation $\dfrac{x}{y} = k$ is often written $x = ky$. Show why this is correct.

EXERCISES

Translate the following statements into equations of the form $\dfrac{x}{y} = k$:

1. The cost of 10 yd. of dress goods is directly proportional to the price per yard.

Solution. Using c for the total cost and p for the price per yard,

$$\frac{c}{p} = 10, \text{ or } c = 10\,p.$$

This illustrates direct variation, for the greater the price per yard, the greater the total cost.

2. The railroad fare within a certain state is 3 cents per mile. Write the equation, showing that the distance is directly proportional to the mileage.

3. The weight of a mass of iron varies directly as the volume.

4. If a body moves at a uniform rate, the distance varies directly as the time.

5. The length (circumference) of a circle varies directly as the diameter.

6. The distance d through which a body falls from rest varies directly as the square of the time t in which it falls. A body is observed to fall 400 ft. in 5 sec. What is the constant ratio of d to t^2? How far does a body fall in 2 sec.?

Solution. The equation for d and t is

$$\frac{d}{t^2} = k. \qquad \text{Why?}$$

In this problem $\qquad \frac{400}{25} = k;$

hence $\qquad\qquad k = 16.$

Substituting $k = 16$ and $t^2 = 2^2$ in $\frac{d}{t^2} = k,$

$$\frac{d}{2^2} = 16.$$

Solving, $\qquad\qquad d = 64.$

This solution shows that k may be determined as soon as one value of t and the corresponding value of d is known. Once determined, this value of k may be used in all problems of this type. Thus, in all falling-body problems $k = 16$ (approx.).

7. How far does a body fall from rest in 3 sec.? in 5 sec.?

8. If x varies directly as y, and $x = 40$ when $y = 8$, find the value of x when $y = 15$.

9. If w varies directly as x, and $w = 24$ when $x = 2$, find w when $x = 11$.

10. A stone fell from a building 576 ft. high. In how many seconds did it reach the ground? (Use the method of Ex. 6.)

11. The speed of a falling body varies directly as the time. Write the equation for the speed V and the time t. A body falling from rest moves at the rate of 180 ft. per second five seconds after it begins to fall. What will be the speed attained in nine seconds?

12. The time t (in seconds) of oscillation of a pendulum varies directly as the square root of the length l; that is, $\frac{t}{\sqrt{l}} = k$. A pendulum 39.2 in. long makes one oscillation in one second. Find the length of a pendulum which makes an oscillation in two seconds.

13. The simple interest on an investment varies directly as the time. If the interest for 5 yr. on a sum of money is $150, what will be the interest for 6 yr. 4 mo.?

14. The weight of a sphere of a given material varies directly as the cube of its radius. Two spheres of the same material have radii of 3 in. and 2 in. respectively. If the first sphere weighs 6 lb., what is the weight of the second?

346. Graphing direct variation. Direct variation between two quantities may be represented graphically by means of a straight line. Turn back to Chapter XI, on the formulas, and find three graphs illustrating direct variation.

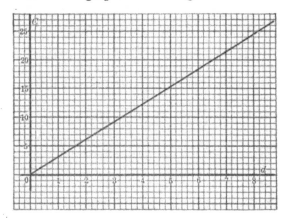

FIG. 217. GRAPH OF $C = \pi d$ SHOWING DIRECT VARIATION

An interesting example is furnished by graphing the equation $\dfrac{C}{d} = \pi$ (where $\pi = 3.14$). This equation says that the circumference of a circle varies directly as its diameter.

Complete the following table, and graph the results so as to obtain the graph in Fig. 217. Interpret the graph.

d	0	1	2	3	4	5	6	7	8
C	0	3.1	6.3	9.4					

Graph the following examples of direct variation:

1. $V = 16\,t$. (Velocity equals 16 times the number of seconds.)

2. $t = 5\,l$. (Turning tendency equals the weight of 5 times the lever arm.)

3. $A = 3\,b$. (The area of a rectangle whose altitude is 3 varies directly as the base.)

347. Inverse variation. We shall now consider a new and interesting kind of variation. Suppose a gardener wishes to seed 64 sq. ft. of his garden in lettuce. If he makes it 16 ft. long, the width must be 4 ft. (Why?) If he makes it 32 ft. long, the width need be only 2 ft. (Why?) How many possible shapes do you think the gardener might choose for his lettuce bed? The following table will help you to answer this question if you remember that it has been decided that the area shall be 64 sq. ft.

Length . . .	40	36	32	25	20	16	8	4	2	1
Width . . .	1.6	1.8	2	2.56						

The table shows that the length must vary so as to leave the area constant, and that because of this fact the greater the length, the smaller the width. The length is thus said to vary *inversely* as the width or to be *inversely proportional* to the width. Algebraically speaking, a number x varies inversely as y if the product xy remains constant as both x and y vary; that is, if $xy = k$. The student may also find this equation written $x = \dfrac{k}{y}$ or $y = \dfrac{k}{x}$.

1. Express each of the following statements by means of equations :

(a) The time needed to go a certain distance varies inversely as the rate of travel.

(b) The heat of a stove varies inversely as the square of the distance from it.

(c) The rate at which a boy goes to the corner drug store varies inversely as the time it takes him.

2. If $z = \dfrac{18}{w}$, show that w varies inversely with z.

3. If y varies inversely as x, and $x = 12$ when $y = 4$, find the value of y when $x = 2$.

Solution. By definition of inverse variation,

$$xy = k.$$

In the first case, $x = 12,$

and $y = 4.$

Therefore $12 \cdot 4 = k,$

or $k = 48.$

In the second case, $x = 2.$

Therefore $2 \cdot y = 48$, since k is constant.

Then $y = 24.$

4. If x varies inversely as y, and $x = 12$ when $y = 13$, find the value of x when $y = 2$.

5. When gas in a cylinder is put under pressure, the volume is reduced as the pressure is increased. The physicist shows us by experiment that the volume varies inversely as the pressure. If the volume of a gas is 14 cc. when the pressure is 9 lb., what is the volume under a pressure of 16 lb.?

6. The number of men doing a piece of work varies inversely as the time. If 10 men can do a piece of work in 33 da., in how many days can 12 men do the same piece of work ?

348. Graphing inverse variation. We shall now proceed to show how inverse variation may be represented graphically. Two cities are 48 mi. apart. Trains running at various rates carry the traffic between the two cities. Suppose we attempt to find out how long it will take a train which moves uniformly at the rate of 24 mi. per hour to make the trip, then 6 mi. per hour, 8 mi. per hour, etc. The following table contains some of the values by means of which the points in Fig. 218 were plotted. The equation representing the situation is $48 = rt$. When the points of the table

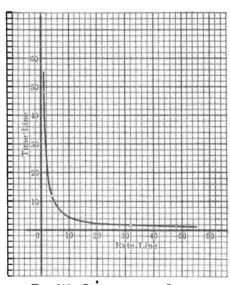

FIG. 218. GRAPH SHOWING INVERSE VARIATION

are plotted, it is clear that they do not lie on a straight line, as was the case in direct variation; but if they are connected, the result is the curved line of Fig. 218. This line is one of two branches of a curve called a *hyperbola*.

r	48	32	30	24	20	16	12	8	6	4	3	2	1
t	1	1.5	1.6	2									

1. Determine from the graph in Fig. 218 the time it takes a train whose rate is 31 mi. per hour; 20 mi. per hour; 25 mi. per hour.

2. Determine from the graph in Fig. 218 how fast a train runs which makes the trip in $1\frac{1}{2}$ hr.; $2\frac{1}{2}$ hr.; $5\frac{1}{2}$ hr.; $8\frac{1}{3}$ hr.

3. Graph the equation $pv = 144$ (see Ex. 5, Art. 347) and interpret the graph.

4. The hyperbola is an interesting mathematical curve. See if you can help your class learn more about it by consulting other books.

349. Joint variation. In the interest formula $I = Prt$, I depends for its value on P, r, and t. A change in any one of these letters causes a corresponding change in the value of I. We express this by saying that the interest varies *jointly* as the principal, rate, and time. The algebraic equation which defines joint variation is $x = kyz$.

1. Turn to Chapter XI, on the formula, and find five illustrations of joint variation.

2. If z varies jointly as x and y, and if $z = 60$ when $x = 3$ and $y = 2$, find z when $x = \frac{1}{3}$ and $y = \frac{1}{2}$.

*3. Write the following law as a formula: The safe load L of a horizontal beam supported at both ends varies jointly as the width w and the square of the depth d and inversely as the length l between the supports.

*4. A beam 12 ft. long, 4 in. wide, and 8 in. deep when supported at both ends can bear safely a maximum load of 1920 lb. What would be the safe load for a beam of the same material 10 ft. long, 3 in. wide, and 6 in. thick?

SUMMARY

350. This chapter has taught the meaning of the following words and phrases: function, linear function, variable, dependent variable, independent variable, constant, direct variation, inverse variation, joint variation.

351. A clear understanding of the dependence of one quantity upon another is very important in the everyday affairs of life.

352. A linear function may be treated algebraically, or geometrically by means of a graph.

353. The equation expressing direct variation is $\dfrac{x}{y} = k$. It is often written $x = ky$. Its graph is a straight line.

354. The equation expressing direct variation is $xy = k$, $x = \dfrac{k}{y}$, or $y = \dfrac{k}{x}$. Its graph is a curved line which is one branch of a hyperbola.

355. The equation expressing joint variation is $x = kzy$.

CHAPTER XIII

SIMILARITY; CONSTRUCTION OF SIMILAR TRIANGLES; PROPORTION

356. Construction of similar triangles; first method; introductory exercises. The following exercises will help to form a basis for the work of this chapter. The student should study them carefully.

EXERCISES

1. On squared paper lay off a line segment AB of any convenient length. At A construct, with the protractor, an angle of 32°. At B construct an angle of 63° and produce the sides of the two angles so as to form a triangle. Call the vertex angle C.

2. Compare the shape of the triangle ABC that you have drawn with the shape of those drawn by your classmates.

3. What was done in Ex. 1 to insure that all members of the class should get triangles of the same shape?

4. With the protractor measure angle C in your figure. How else might you have determined its size?

5. Compare the size of angle C in your figure with angle C in the figures drawn by your classmates.

6. Show that any angle C drawn by any member of the class ought to be equal to any other angle C drawn.

7. Are the triangles drawn by the class of the same size? Are any two necessarily of the same size?

357. Similar triangles. Triangles having the same shape are called *similar triangles.* Similar triangles are not necessarily of the same size. They may be constructed by making two angles of one equal to two angles of the other, as was done in Ex. 1, Art. 356. If two angles of one are equal to two angles of the other, it follows that the third angles are equal. (Why?) The symbol for similarity is $\sim$. Thus $\triangle ABC \sim \triangle A'B'C'$ is read "triangle ABC is similar to triangle $A'B'C'$." The results of Art. 356 may be summed up in the following geometric theorem: *If two angles of one triangle are equal respectively to two angles of another triangle, the triangles are similar.*

358. Second relation of parts in similar triangles. The student should be able to discover a second method of constructing similar triangles if he studies and understands the following exercises.

INTRODUCTORY EXERCISES

1. In the triangle ABC drawn for Ex. 1, Art. 356, letter the side opposite angle C with a small letter c, the side opposite angle B with a small letter b, and the side opposite angle A with a small letter a.

2. Measure the lengths of the sides a, b, and c in Ex. 1 to two decimal places. Find the ratio of a to b, of b to c, of a to c (in each case to two decimal places).

3. Compare your results in Ex. 2 with the results obtained by the other members of your class. What conclusion do you make with reference to the ratios of the sides?

359. Construction of similar triangles; second method. The results of Exs. 1–3, Art. 358, may be summarized as follows: *In similar triangles the ratios of corresponding sides are equal.* The work of Art. 358 suggests a second method for constructing similar triangles.

1. Draw a triangle. Draw a second triangle whose sides are respectively twice as long as the sides of the first triangle.

2. Compare the triangles constructed in Ex. 1 as to shape. Are they similar? Find the ratio of the corresponding sides.

3. Draw a triangle with sides three times as long as the corresponding sides of another triangle. Are they similar? Give reasons for your answer. How do the ratios of the corresponding sides compare? ,

4. Draw a triangle ABC. Bisect the lines AB, AC, and BC. Call the halves x', y', and z'. Construct a second triangle, using the segments x', y', and z' as sides. Compare the two triangles as to shape. Are they similar? What are the ratios of the corresponding sides?

The preceding exercises suggest the following theorem: *Two triangles are similar if the ratios* of *the corresponding sides are equal.* This gives us a second method of constructing similar triangles; namely, by making the ratios of their corresponding sides equal.

360. Construction of similar triangles; third method. We shall study a third method of constructing similar triangles which is suggested by the following exercises:

1. Construct a triangle with two sides 4.6 cm. and 6.2 cm., and with the protractor make the included angle 70°. Construct a second triangle with two sides 9.2 cm. and 12.4 cm. and the included angle 70°. Compare the triangles as to shape. What is the ratio of the corresponding sides? Measure the corresponding angles.

2. If convenient the class should divide itself into sections, the first section constructing a triangle with two sides and the included angle as follows: $a = 12$, $b = 18$, and $C = 40°$; the second section taking $a = 8$, $b = 12$, and $C = 40°$; and the third section taking $a = 4$, $b = 6$, and $C = 40°$. Compare the triangles drawn by the three sections as to shape. What is the ratio of the corresponding sides?

The preceding exercises support the geometric theorem: *Two triangles are similar if the ratio of two sides of one equals the ratio of two corresponding sides of the other, and the angles included between these sides are equal.* This theorem suggests the third method of constructing similar triangles.

361. Summary of constructions for similar triangles. Two triangles are similar

1. *If two angles of one triangle are constructed equal respectively to two angles of the second triangle.*

2. *If the sides of the triangles are constructed so that the ratios of their corresponding sides are equal.*

3. *If the triangles are constructed so that the ratio of two sides of one is equal to the ratio of two sides of the other and the angles included between these sides are equal.*

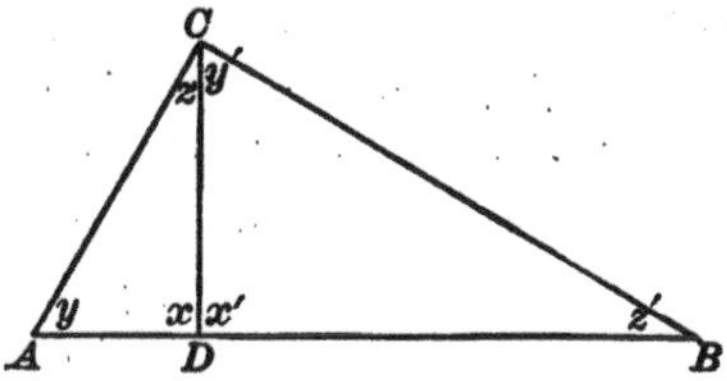

362. Similar right triangles. We shall now prove the following theorem: *The perpendicular to the hypotenuse from the vertex of a right triangle divides the triangle into two triangles that are similar to each other* (see Fig. 219).

FIG. 219

Proof.
$$\angle x = \angle x'. \qquad \text{Why?}$$
$$\angle y = \angle y'. \qquad \text{Why?}$$
$$\therefore \triangle ADC \sim \triangle BDC, \qquad \text{Why?}$$

(Exs. 1-4 refer to Fig. 219)

1. Show that $\triangle ADC \backsim \triangle ABC$.

2. Show also that $\triangle BCD \backsim \triangle ABC$.

3. Translate the results of Exs. 1 and 2 into a geometric theorem.

4. State a theorem expressing the results of this article.

363. Similar polygons. In later work in mathematics we learn that similar polygons also have corresponding angles equal and that the ratios of the corresponding sides are equal. This rests on the fact that two similar polygons may be divided into sets of similar triangles by drawing corresponding diagonals as in Fig. 220.

Similar figures are of frequent occurrence. The plans of construction work, drawings in shop, a sur-

FIG. 220. SIMILAR POLYGONS

veyor's copy of a field triangle, blue prints, a photograph, enlarged and reduced pictures, are all examples. The relation of the different parts in all the foregoing is shown by magnifying or reducing all parts to a definite scale. Thus, you may be able to determine by looking at a photograph of a man that he has large ears, although in the picture the actual measurement of either of his ears may be less than a centimeter. One can tell by looking at the plan of a house whether the windows are large or small, because the relation is brought out by the fact that all parts are reduced to the same scale; that is, *the ratios of the corresponding parts are equal.* See if you can find examples that will illustrate the last statement.

Similar triangles may be regarded as copies of the same triangle magnified or minified to a scale, or both may be regarded as scale drawings of the same triangle to different scales. We shall study the geometric relations more in detail in the next chapter.

364. Algebraic problems on similar figures. The fact that the ratios of the corresponding sides of similar polygons are equal furnishes us with an algebraic method of finding distances.

EXERCISES

1. In the similar triangles of Fig. 221, if $a = 3$ in., $a' = 9$ in., and $b = 3$ in., how long is b'?

2. In the similar triangles of Fig. 222, if $a = 6$ mm., $a' = 8$ mm., and $b = 8$ mm., how long is b'?

3. In the similar triangles of Fig. 223, if $a' = 10.5$ mm., $b = 12$ mm., and $b' = 15$ mm., how long is a?

FIG. 221

4. The sides of a triangle are 16, 20, and 26. The shortest side of a similar triangle is 22. Find the other sides.

5. The sides of a triangle are 2.3 cm., 2.7 cm., and 3 cm. The corresponding sides of a similar triangle are x, y, and 12 cm. Find the values of x and y.

FIG. 222

6. Two rectangular boards are desired. One is to be 4 in. wide and 6 in. long, the other is to be 18 in. long. How wide should the second board be?

FIG. 223

7. At a certain time of day a foot rule casts a shadow 10 in. long. How long is the shadow of a yardstick at the same time? Draw a diagram and prove your work.

8. In Fig. 224 the pole, the length of its shadow, and the sun's rays passing over the top of the pole form a triangle. The shadow of the pole is measured, and is found to be 60 ft. long. At the same time the shadow of a vertical stick $2\frac{1}{2}$ ft. high is measured, and is found to be $7\frac{1}{2}$ ft. long. How may we determine the height of the pole without actually measuring it?

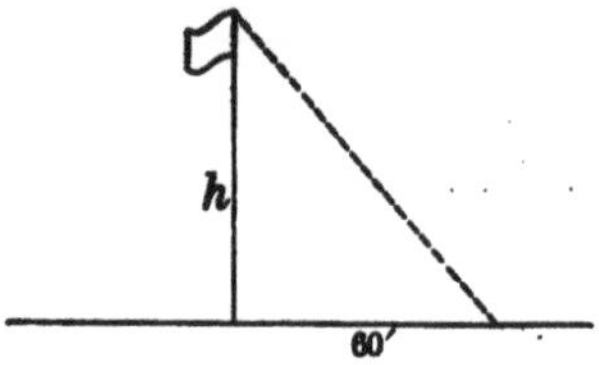

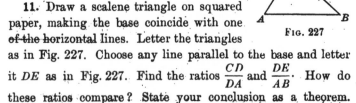

FIG. 224 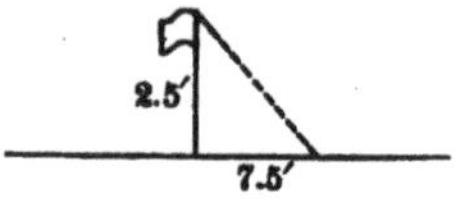   FIG. 225

Solution. The stick, the shadow, and the sun's rays form a triangle similar to the first triangle (see Fig. 225). Why?

If we let h denote the height of the pole, we get

$$\frac{h}{2.5} = \frac{60}{7.5}.$$ Why?

Then $h = 20.$

9. The shadow of a chimney is 85.2 ft. long. At the same time the shadow of a man 6 ft. 2 in. tall is 9 ft. 2 in. How high is the chimney?

10. Draw a triangle ABC on squared paper as in Fig. 226. Through a point D on AC draw line $DE \parallel AB$. Measure the segments CD, DA, CE, and EB to two decimal places. Find the ratios $\frac{CD}{DA}$ and $\frac{CE}{EB}$. How do these ratios compare? What does this show?

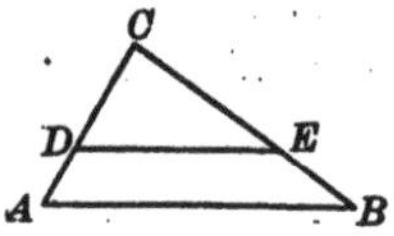

FIG. 226

11. Draw a scalene triangle on squared paper, making the base coincide with one of the horizontal lines. Letter the triangles as in Fig. 227. Choose any line parallel to the base and letter it DE as in Fig. 227. Find the ratios $\frac{CD}{DA}$ and $\frac{DE}{AB}$. How do these ratios compare? State your conclusion as a theorem.

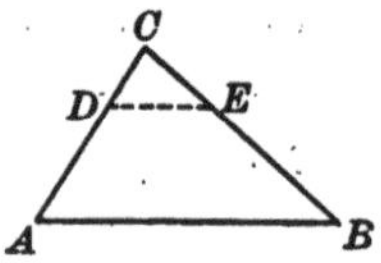

FIG. 227

12. Suppose that in Fig. 227 $DC = 2.5$ mi., $DA = 7.5$ mi., and $CE = 9$ mi., how long is EB?

13. In triangle ABC, Fig. 227, the line DE has been drawn parallel to the base AB. Prove that the small triangle CDE is similar to the large triangle ABC.

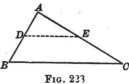

Fig. 227

14. In Fig. 228, if $AD = 3$, $DE = 5$, and $AB = 25.5$, how long is BC?

15. Divide a line segment into two equal parts and show that your construction is correct.

Construction. Let AB, Fig. 229, be the line segment. Draw AC through A, making any convenient angle with AB. On AC lay off AD and DE, each equal to 1 unit. Join E to B. Draw $DF \parallel EB$. Show that $AF = FB$.

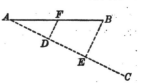

Fig. 229. How to bisect a Line

Hint. Use Ex. 10, p. 320.

16. Divide a line segment into two parts whose ratio is $\frac{2}{3}$.

Construction. Let AB, Fig. 230, be the given segment. Draw AC, making any convenient angle with AB, as shown. On AC lay off $AD = 2$ units and $DE = 3$ units. Join E and B. Through D draw $DF \parallel EB$. Show that $\dfrac{AF}{FB} = \dfrac{2}{3}$.

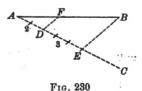

Fig. 230

17. Divide a line segment into parts having the ratios $\dfrac{3}{5}$; $\dfrac{1}{3}$; $\dfrac{2}{7}$; $\dfrac{a}{b}$.

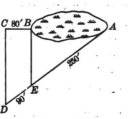

Fig. 231

18. The distance across a swamp (Fig. 231) is to be found. A point C is located in the same line with A and B. At C and B lines CD and BE are drawn

perpendicular to CB, and the line AD is drawn. The lengths
of CB, DE, and EA are found to be 80 ft., 90 ft., and 250 ft.
respectively. Find the distance AB.

19. Show that the distance AB across
the swamp could also be found by measuring the lines shown in Fig. 232.

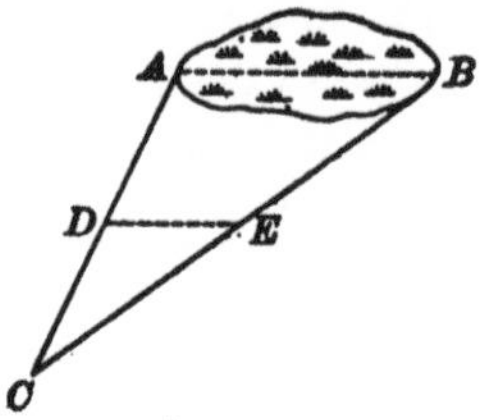

FIG. 232

365. Proportion. The preceding
exercises dealing with similar triangles
were solved by means of a special
type of equation expressing the fact that two ratios in the
geometric figure were equal. Thus in Fig. 233 the line AB
is divided into two parts whose ratio is $\frac{2}{3}$ (see the method
of Ex. 16, Art. 364). In this construction it turns out that

$$\frac{AF}{FB} = \frac{2}{3}, \qquad \text{Why?}$$

$$\frac{AD}{DE} = \frac{2}{3}, \qquad \text{Why?}$$

and $\qquad \frac{AF}{FB} = \frac{AD}{DE}. \qquad \text{Why?}$

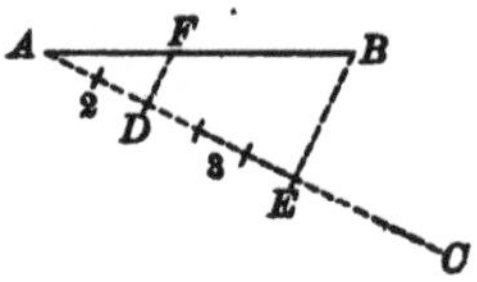

FIG. 233

Such an equation, which expresses equality of two ratios,
is called a *proportion.* The line segments AF, FB, AD, and
DE are said to be proportional, or in proportion. This
means that AF divided by FB will always equal AD
divided by DE.

A proportion may thus be defined as an equation which
expresses the equality of two fractions; as, $\frac{8}{12} = \frac{2}{3}$. Another
example of a proportion is $\frac{a}{b} = \frac{c}{d}$. This may be read
" a divided by b equals c divided by d," or " a is to b as
c is to d," or " a over b equals c over d." Sometimes it is
written $a : b = c : d$, but this form is not desirable.

Is the statement $\frac{2}{3} = \frac{5}{6}$ a proportion? Give reasons for your answer. Is $\frac{3}{7} = \frac{9}{15}$ a proportion? Explain your answer.

366. Means and extremes. The first and last terms in a proportion are called the *extremes* and the second and third terms the *means*. Thus, in the proportion $\frac{a}{b} = \frac{c}{d}$, a and d are the extremes and b and c the means.

1. Compare the product of the means with the product of the extremes in the following proportions:

(a) $\frac{2}{3} = \frac{6}{9}$.   (c) $\frac{10}{2} = \frac{20}{4}$.

(b) $\frac{3}{5} = \frac{6}{10}$.   (d) $\frac{12}{6} = \frac{2}{1}$.

What statement can you make concerning the products?

2. Make up several proportions and compare the product of the means with the product of the extremes.

367. Theorem on the relation between the means and the extremes of a proportion. Exs. 1–2, Art. 366, illustrate a well-known law or theorem; namely, that *in a proportion the product of the means equals the product of the extremes.* If the given proportion is $\frac{a}{b} = \frac{c}{d}$, then the law is algebraically stated thus: $ad = bc$.

The theorem may be proved as follows:

Let $\frac{a}{b} = \frac{c}{d}$ represent any proportion. Multiplying both members by bd we get

$$\frac{abd}{b} = \frac{cbd}{d}.$$

Reducing each fraction to lowest terms,

$$ad = bc.$$

Since a proportion is a special kind of equation, there are special laws which often make a proportion easier to solve than other equations which are not proportions. The law given on page 323, Art. 367, is one of the many principles of proportion convenient to use. Thus, instead of finding the L.C.D. in the equation $\frac{4}{3} = \frac{16}{x}$, and solving in that way, we simply use the preceding law, and say

$$4x = 48.$$
$$x = 16.$$

The law is also a convenient test of proportionality, since it is usually simpler to find the products than to reduce the ratios to lowest terms.

1. Test the following statements to see if they are proportions:

(a) $\frac{3}{7} = \frac{15}{35}$.   (c) $\frac{15}{2.5} = \frac{12}{1.4}$.   (e) $\frac{42\,m}{5\,n} = \frac{21\,m}{2.5\,n}$.

(b) $\frac{5}{7} = \frac{8}{11}$.   (d) $\frac{2\,a}{3\,x} = \frac{5\,a}{7.5\,x}$.   (f) $\frac{11.5}{3.5} = \frac{7.7}{2.2}$.

2. Find the values of the unknowns in the following proportions, and check by substituting in the original equations:

(a) $\frac{x}{28} = \frac{4}{7}$.

(b) $\frac{4}{x} = \frac{52}{3}$.

(c) $\frac{66}{10} = \frac{x}{5}$.

(d) $\frac{y-12}{1-3\,y} = \frac{3}{2}$.

(e) $\frac{3+1}{5} = \frac{3\,z+2}{14}$.

(f) $\frac{y+5}{y+3} = \frac{y-3}{y-4}$.

Solution. $y^2 + y - 20 = y^2 - 9.$

$$y - 20 = -9.$$
$$y = 11.$$

Check. $\frac{11+5}{11+3} = \frac{11-3}{11-4}$.

$$\frac{16}{14} = \frac{8}{7}.$$

(g) $\dfrac{a-4}{a-13}=\dfrac{a-8}{a-14}$.

(h) $\dfrac{a+2}{a+3}=\dfrac{a+3}{a+1}$.

(i) $\dfrac{a-7}{4}=\dfrac{a+3}{3}$.

(j) $\dfrac{x+5}{x^2}=\dfrac{1}{x+5}$.

3. If 5 and 3 are each added to a certain number, and 1 and 2 are each subtracted from it, the four numbers thus obtained are in proportion. Find the number.

4. Show how to divide a board 54 in. long into two parts whose ratio is $\frac{7}{11}$.

5. What are the two parts of a line segment 10 cm. long if it is divided into two parts whose ratio is $\frac{2}{3}$?

6. The acute angles of a right triangle are as 2 is to 5; that is, their ratio is $\frac{2}{5}$. Find the angles.

7. If 10° be subtracted from one of two complementary angles and added to the other, the ratio of the two angles thus formed is $\frac{1}{8}$. Find the angles.

8. If $1\frac{1}{2}$ in. on a railroad map represents 80 mi., what distance is represented by $2\frac{3}{4}$ in.?

9. Two books have the same shape. One is $4\frac{1}{2}$ in. wide and $7\frac{1}{5}$ in. long. The other is 18 in. long; how wide is it?

10. The records of two leading teams in the American League were Boston won 68, lost 32; Chicago won 64, lost 36. If the teams were scheduled to play each other ten more games, how many must Chicago have won to have been tied with Boston?

11. If 1 cu. ft. of lime and 2 cu. ft. of sand are used in making 2.4 cu. ft. of mortar, how much of each is needed to make 96 cu. ft. of mortar?

368. Proportion involved in variation. Many problems in physics, chemistry, general science, domestic science, astronomy, and mathematics may be solved by either variation or proportion. In fact, the whole theory of proportion is involved in our discussion of variation, but this fact is not always so obvious to a beginner. The fact that problems may be stated both in terms of variation and in terms of proportion makes it necessary for the student to recognize clearly the relation between variation and proportion. This relation will be illustrated in the following list of exercises.

EXERCISES

Solve by either variation or proportion:

1. If 11 men can build a cement walk in 82 da., how long will it take 15 men to build it?

(a) **Solution as a variation problem:**

$$mt = k. \quad \text{(The time it takes to build the walk varies inversely as the number of men.)}$$

Then $\qquad 11 \cdot 82 = k.$

Hence $\qquad k = 902.$

Using this value of k in the second case,

$$mt = 902 ;$$

but $\qquad m = 15.$

Whence $\qquad 15\, t = 902,$

and $\qquad t = \frac{902}{15} = 60\frac{2}{15}$ da.

(b) **Solution as a proportion problem.** The number of men is not in the same ratio as the time necessary to build the walk, but in inverse ratio; that is,

$$\frac{m_1}{m_2} = \frac{d_2}{d_1} .$$

This proportion means "the first group of men is to the second group of men as the time it takes the second group is to the time it takes the first group."

Substituting the three known facts,

$$\frac{11}{15} = \frac{d_2}{82} .$$

Whence $\qquad 15\, d_2 = 902,$

and $\qquad d_2 = \frac{902}{15} = 60\frac{2}{15}$ da.

2. If 200 ft. of copper wire weighs 60 lb., what is the weight of 125 ft. of the same kind of wire?

3. The cost of wire fencing of a certain kind varies as the number of yards bought. If 12 rods cost $12.80, how much can be bought for $44.80?

4. Two men are paid in proportion to the work they do. A can do in 24 da. the same work that it takes B 16 da. to do. Compare their wages.

5. A farmer has a team of which one horse weighs 1200 lb. and the other 1500 lb. If they pull in proportion to their weight, where must the farmer place the clevis on a four-foot doubletree so as to distribute the load according to the size of the horses?

369. Different arrangements of a proportion. The student will be interested in seeing in how many different forms a proportion may be arranged. This he may learn by solving the exercises that follow.

EXERCISES

1. Arrange the numbers 3, 6, 7, and 14 in as many proportions as possible. Do the same for the numbers 2, 5, 8, and 20.

2. Can you write two ratios that will not be equal, using the numbers 2, 5, 8, and 20 as terms of these ratios?

3. How do you decide which arrangement constitutes a proportion?

The preceding exercises suggest that a proportion such as $\frac{a}{b} = \frac{c}{d}$ may take four forms, as follows:

(a) The given proportion

$$\frac{a}{b} = \frac{c}{d}.$$

(b) The form obtained by alternating the means in (a):

$$\frac{a}{c} = \frac{b}{d}.$$

(c) The form obtained by alternating the extremes in (a):

$$\frac{d}{b} = \frac{c}{a}.$$

(d) The form obtained by alternating both the means and extremes in (a):

$$\frac{d}{c} = \frac{b}{a}.$$

The last form can be obtained simply by inverting the ratios in (a).

We know that the proportions given above are true, for by applying the test of proportionality we see that the product of the means equals the product of the extremes in each case. Furthermore, any one of them could have been obtained by dividing the members of the equation $ad = bc$ by the proper number. Thus, to get $\frac{d}{b} = \frac{c}{a}$ we must divide both members of the equation $ad = bc$ by ab. Why?

Then $$\frac{ad}{ab} = \frac{bc}{ab};$$

from which $$\frac{d}{b} = \frac{c}{a}, \text{ or form (c)}.$$

370. Theorem. The preceding discussion illustrates the use of the theorem which says that *if the product of two numbers is equal to the product of two other numbers, either pair may be made the means and the other pair the extremes of a proportion.*

1. Start with the equation $ad = bc$ and obtain the forms $\frac{a}{b} = \frac{c}{d}$, $\frac{a}{c} = \frac{b}{d}$, and $\frac{d}{c} = \frac{b}{a}$. This completes the proof of the theorem just stated. Why?

2. Write the four possible forms that can be obtained from the following products:

(a) $5 \cdot 21 = 7 \cdot 15$.

(b) $3 \cdot 28 = 12 \cdot 7$.

(c) $3\,a \cdot 4\,b = a \cdot 12\,b$.

(d) $15 \cdot 7\,t = 105\,t$.

3. In Fig. 234, $\frac{CD}{CE} = \frac{CA}{CB}$. Show that $\frac{CD}{CA} = \frac{CE}{CB}$.

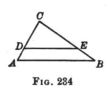

F i g. 234   F i g. 235

4. If two equilateral polygons have the same number of sides, the corresponding sides are proportional (see Fig. 235).

Proof.	$\dfrac{AB}{BC} = 1,$	Why?
and	$\dfrac{A'B'}{B'C'} = 1.$	Why?
Therefore	$\dfrac{AB}{BC} = \dfrac{A'B'}{B'C'}.$	Why?

By alternating the means,

$$\frac{AB}{A'B'} = \frac{BC}{B'C'},$$

and so on for the other corresponding sides.

371. Mean proportional. In the proportion $\frac{a}{b} = \frac{b}{c}$, b is called the *mean proportional* between a and c (note that b appears twice in the proportion).

EXERCISES

1. What is a mean proportional between 4 and 9?

Hint. Let $x =$ the number.

Then $\dfrac{4}{x} = \dfrac{x}{9}.$

From which $x^2 = 36.$

Then $x = \pm 6.$

2. Show that the value of b in the proportion $\dfrac{a}{b} = \dfrac{b}{c}$ is given by the equation $b = \pm \sqrt{ac}$ (read "b equals $+$ or $-$ the square root of ac").

3. What is a mean proportional between 2 and 18? between 10 and 40? between 2 and 800?

4. Find a mean proportional between a^2 and b^2; between x^2 and y^2.

372. How to pick out corresponding sides of similar triangles. The similar triangles of Fig. 236 are placed so that in certain cases a line is a side in each of two similar triangles. Thus, AC is a side of $\triangle ADC$ and also of the similar triangle ABC. This suggests that the line may occur twice in the proportion of the corresponding sides. In this way it is seen that the line becomes a mean proportional between the other two.

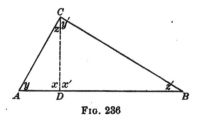

Fig. 236

This analysis can be checked only by actually writing the proportion of pairs of corresponding sides of similar triangles. In order to do this correctly the student must remember that the *corresponding sides of similar triangles are the sides which lie opposite equal angles.* Hence, from the fact that $\triangle ADC \backsim \triangle ABC$ we may write the following proportion:

$$\frac{AD\,(\text{opposite } \angle z \text{ in } \triangle ADC)}{AC\,(\text{opposite } \angle z' \text{ in } \triangle ABC)} = \frac{AC\,(\text{opposite } \angle x \text{ in } \triangle ADC)}{AB\,(\text{opposite } \angle C \text{ in } \triangle ACB)}.$$

That is, $\qquad\qquad \dfrac{AD}{AC} = \dfrac{AC}{AB}.$

AC is thus seen to be the mean proportional between AD and AB.

Show in a similar way that BC is a mean proportional between the hypotenuse AB and the adjacent segment BD; that is, show that $\dfrac{BD}{BC} = \dfrac{BC}{AB}.$

We may summarize the preceding exercises and discussion by the theorem: *In a right triangle either side including the right angle is a·mean proportional between the hypotenuse and the adjacent segment of the hypotenuse made by a perpendicular from the vertex of the right angle to the hypotenuse.*

373. Theorem. *If in a right triangle a perpendicular is drawn from the vertex of the right angle on the hypotenuse, the perpendicular is a mean proportional between the segments of the hypotenuse.*
The truth of the preceding theorem will be seen from the following:

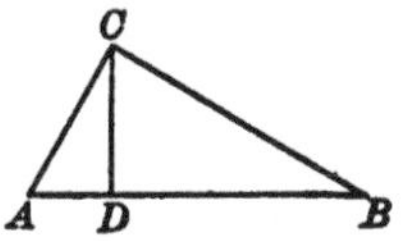

FIG. 237

In $\triangle ABC$ (Fig. 237) $\angle C$ is a right angle, and $CD \perp AB$. $\dfrac{AD}{CD} = \dfrac{CD}{DB}$ because $\triangle ADC \backsim \triangle CDB$, and the corresponding sides are therefore in proportion.

1. Write out the complete proof for the preceding theorem.

2. Find the altitude drawn to the hypotenuse of a right triangle if it divides the hypotenuse into two segments whose lengths are 4 in. and 16 in. respectively. Find also each leg of the right triangle.

*3. In a right triangle ABC (right-angled at C) a perpendicular is drawn from C to AB. If $CD = 8$, then $AD = 4$. Find the length of AB.

374. Construction of a mean proportional. The theorem of Art. 373 on page 331 furnishes us with a method of constructing a mean proportional between any two line segments, as will now be shown.

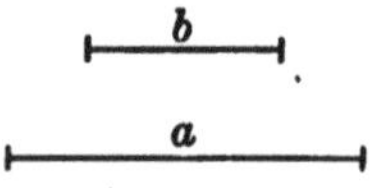

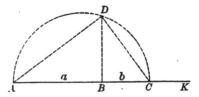

In Fig. 238 we are given two line segments a and b. The problem is to construct a mean proportional (say x units long) between a and b.

Fig. 238

We know that the equation $\dfrac{a}{x} = \dfrac{x}{b}$ will represent the situation.

Construction. On a working line, as AK in Fig. 239, we lay off a from A to B and b from B to C. With AC as a diameter we construct a semicircle. At B we erect a perpendicular intersecting the circle at D. Then BD is the required mean proportional.

Proof. Connect A with D and C with D. Then BD is the required mean proportional between a and b provided we can show that $\angle D$

Fig. 239. Mean Proportional Construction

is a right angle. (Why?) We shall proceed to show that $\angle D$ is a right angle by proving that *if any point on a circle is connected with the ends of a diameter, the angle formed at that point is a right angle.*

In Fig. 240 we have a given circle constructed on the diameter AC and a point D connected with the ends of AC. We must show that $\angle D$ is a right angle.

Connect D and O.

Then $\angle x = \angle s + \angle s'$,   (1)

because an exterior angle of a triangle is equal to the sum of the
two nonadjacent interior angles;

and $\angle y = \angle t + \angle t'$ (2)

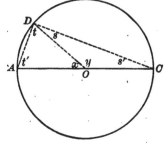

for the same reason.

FIG. 240

By adding (1) and (2),

$$\angle x + \angle y = \angle s + \angle s' + \angle t + \angle t'.$$

Since	$\angle x + \angle y = 180°,$	Why?
	$\angle s + \angle s' + \angle t + \angle t' = 180°.$	Why?
But	$\angle s = \angle s',$	
and	$\angle t = \angle t'.$	Why?
Therefore	$2\angle s + 2\angle t = 180°.$	Why?
	$\angle s + \angle t = 90°.$	Why?
Then	$\angle D = 90°.$	Why?

Then, if in Fig. 239 $\angle D = 90°$, the proportion $\dfrac{a}{BD} = \dfrac{BD}{b}$ is true, and BD is a mean proportional between a and b. Give reasons.

EXERCISES

1. Explain how a mean proportional between two given line segments may be constructed.

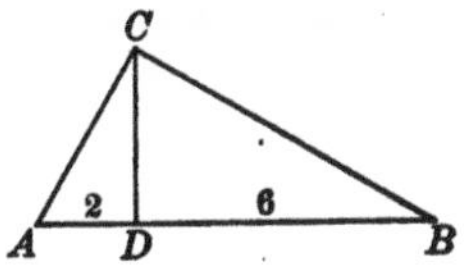

2. Construct a mean proportional between 9 and 16, 4 and 16, 4 and 9, 16
and 25, 25 and 36.

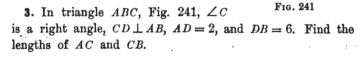

FIG. 241

3. In triangle ABC, Fig. 241, $\angle C$ is a right angle, $CD \perp AB$, $AD = 2$, and $DB = 6$. Find the lengths of AC and CB.

4. Find the mean proportional between the line segments m and n in Fig. 242.

5. Measure m and n in Fig. 242 and the mean proportional constructed in Ex. 4. Square the value of the mean proportional and see how the value compares with the product of m and n.

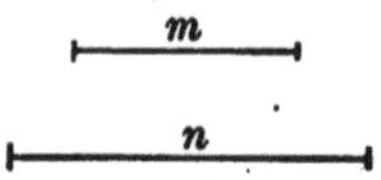

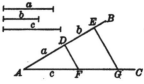

Fig. 242

*6. Construct a square equal in area to a given rectangle; to a given parallelogram; to a given triangle.

375. Fourth proportional. In the proportion $\dfrac{a}{b} = \dfrac{c}{d}$, d is called the *fourth proportional* to a, b, and c. There are two methods of finding the fourth proportional to three given numbers a, b, and c.

Algebraic method. Let x represent the value of the fourth proportional.

Then $\qquad \dfrac{a}{b} = \dfrac{c}{x}$

(by definition of a fourth proportional).

Solving for x, $ax = bc$.

$$x = \frac{bc}{a}.$$

FIG. 243. How to construct a Fourth Proportional

Geometric method. Take three given lines, as a, b, and c in Fig. 243, and draw any convenient angle, as $\angle BAC$. On AB lay off $AD = a$, $DE = b$. On the other line AC lay off $AF = c$. Draw DF. Then draw $EG \parallel DF$ as shown. Then FG is the required fourth proportional.

See if you can show why the construction is correct.

EXERCISES

1. Check the construction above by measuring the four segments to see if $\dfrac{a}{b} = \dfrac{c}{x}$.

2. Construct a fourth proportional to three given line segments 2 cm., 3 cm., and 5 cm. long respectively.

3. Show algebraically that the segment obtained in Ex. 2 should be $7\frac{1}{2}$ cm. long.

4. Construct a fourth proportional to three segments 5 cm., 6 cm., and 9 cm. long respectively.

5. Check your work in Ex. 4 by an algebraic method.

*376. To find the quotient of two arithmetical numbers by a special method. To find $\frac{22}{70}$ in per cent we need to solve the equation $\dfrac{22}{70} = \dfrac{x}{100}$. (Why?) This proportion suggests similar triangles. If we take a horizontal line OM (Fig. 244) as a *dividend* line on squared paper, and ON perpendicular to OM as a *divisor* line, then lay off OA on OM equal to 22 units, and at A erect a perpendicular and mark off AB equal to 70 units, we can solve our problem provided

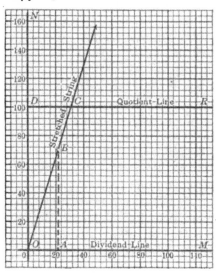

Fig. 244

we draw another line DR 100 units above OM and parallel to it. Call DR the quotient line.

Stretch a string fastened at O so that it passes through B, meeting the quotient line at C.

Then $\qquad \dfrac{DC}{100} = \dfrac{22}{70}$, or $DC = 0.31 +$.

NOTE. The proof is left to the student.

Therefore 22 is approximately 31% of 70.

*1. Point out the similar triangles in the device for expressing quotients used in Fig. 244. Read the sides which are
proportional.

*2. A gardener planted 12 A. of potatoes, 8 A. of beans,
13 A. of onions, 3 A. of celery, and 5 A. of cabbage. By means
of the device used in Fig. 244 show the distribution of his
garden in per cents.

377. Verbal problems solved by proportion. We have
said that many problems of science, the shop, and engineering can be solved by proportion. We shall proceed to
study how to solve some of these problems by using our
knowledge of proportion.

In the study of turning tendency, Art. 233, we recognized
the following familiar principle of the balanced beam: *The
left weight times the left lever arm equals the right weight times
the right lever arm. As a formula
this may be written* $w_1 l_1 = w_2 l_2$.

This principle is already familiar
to all who have played with a
seesaw. They discovered long ago
that a teeter board will balance

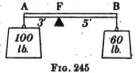

Fig. 245

when equal products are obtained by multiplying the
weight of each person by his distance from the point of
support (fulcrum).

If, in Fig. 245, B weighs 60 lb. and is 5 ft. from the fulcrum F, then A, who weighs 100 lb., must be 3 ft. from
the fulcrum. Thus, $60 \cdot 5 = 100 \cdot 3$ is a special case of
general law $w_1 l_1 = w_2 l_2$.

If we divide both members of the equation $w_1 l_1 = w_2 l_2$ by
$w_1 l_2$, we get $\dfrac{l_1}{l_2} = \dfrac{w_2}{w_1}$, which is in the form of a proportion.

The student will learn that in shop work many problems dealing with the lever or balanced beam may be solved by some form of the preceding proportion.

BEAM PROBLEMS

1. A lever (Fig. 246) 10 ft. long carries weights of 40 lb. and 50 lb. at its ends. Where should the fulcrum be placed so as to make the lever balance?

Solution. Let $x =$ the number of feet from F to A,
and $10 - x =$ the number of feet from F to B.

Then $50 x = 40 (10 - x)$. Why?
$$50 x = 400 - 40 x.$$
$$90 x = 400.$$
$$x = 4\tfrac{4}{9}.$$

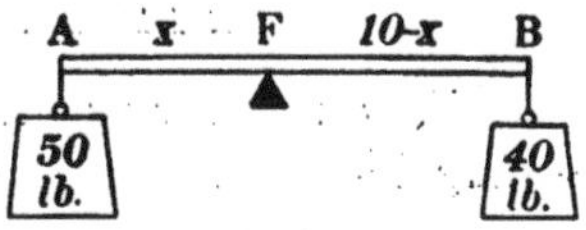

Fig. 246

2. A, who weighs 80 lb., sits 6 ft. from the fulcrum. If B weighs 100 lb., at what distance from the fulcrum should A sit in order to balance B?

3. A and B together weigh 220 lb. They balance when A is 5 ft. and B 6 ft. from the fulcrum. Find the weight of each.

4. A and B are 4 ft. and 6 ft. respectively from the fulcrum. If B weighs 60 lb., how much does A weigh?

5. How could you weigh yourself without a scale?

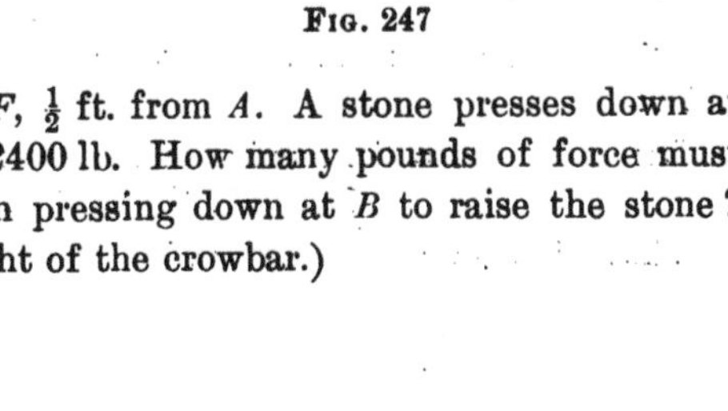

6. AB in Fig. 247 is a crowbar $8\tfrac{1}{2}$ ft.

Fig. 247

long supported at F, $\tfrac{1}{2}$ ft. from A. A stone presses down at A with a force of 2400 lb. How many pounds of force must be exerted by a man pressing down at B to raise the stone? (Disregard the weight of the crowbar.)

7. In attempting to raise an automobile (Fig. 248) a man lifts with a force of 150 lb. at the end of a lever 10 ft. long. The distance from the axle to F is $2\frac{1}{2}$ ft. What force is exerted upward on the axle as a result of the man's lifting?

8. Find l_1 if $l_2 = 18$ ft., $w_2 = 62$ lb., and $w_1 = 51$ lb.

9. Find l_2 if $l_1 = 40$ in., $w_2 = 26$ lb., and $w_1 = 38$ lb.

FIG. 248

MIXTURE AND ALLOY PROBLEMS

1. How much water must be added to 10 gal. of milk, testing $5\frac{1}{2}\%$ butter fat, to make it test 4% butter fat?

Solution. Let $x =$ the number of gallons of water added.

Then $x + 10 =$ the number of gallons of diluted milk,

and $\dfrac{5\frac{1}{2}}{100} \cdot 10 =$ the amount of butter fat in the undiluted milk.

$\tfrac{4}{100}(x + 10) =$ the amount of butter fat in the diluted milk.

Since the amount of butter fat remains constant,

$$\frac{5\frac{1}{2}}{100} \cdot 10 = \tfrac{4}{100}(x + 10), \qquad \text{Why?}$$

$$\frac{110}{200} = \frac{x + 10}{25}. \qquad \text{Why?}$$

$$4x + 40 = 55.$$

$x = 3\frac{3}{4}$, the number of gallons of water to be added.

2. A physician has a 25% mixture of listerine in water. How much water must he add to it to make it a 15% mixture?

Solution. Consider an arbitrary quantity of the mixture, say 100 oz.

Let $x =$ the number of ounces of water added to every 100 oz. of the mixture.

Then $100 + x =$ the number of ounces in the new mixture.

Since 25% of the original mixture is listerine,

$$\frac{25}{100 + x} = \text{the per cent of listerine in the new mixture.}$$

And since 15% of the new mixture is to be listerine,

$$\frac{25}{100 + x} = \frac{15}{100}.$$

$$1500 + 15 x = 2500.$$

$$15 x = 1000.$$

$$x = 66\tfrac{2}{3}.$$

Hence $66\tfrac{2}{3}$ oz. of water must be added to every 100 oz. of the original mixture.

3. How much water should be added to a bottle containing 4 oz. of the original mixture in Ex. 2 to make it a 15% mixture?

4. If a patent medicine contains 30% alcohol, how much of other ingredients must be added to 12 qt. of it so that the mixture shall contain only 20% alcohol?

5. How many quarts of water must be mixed with 30 qt. of alcohol 82% pure to make a mixture 70% pure?

6. What per cent of evaporation must take place from a 5% solution of salt and water (of which 5% by weight is salt) to make the remaining portion of the mixture a 7% solution?

7. Two grades of coffee costing a dealer 25¢ and 30¢ per pound are to be mixed so that 50 lb. of the mixture will be worth 28¢ per pound. How many pounds of each kind of coffee must be used in the mixture?

8. In a mass of alloy for watch cases which contains 80 oz. there are 30 oz. of gold. How much copper must be added in order that in a case weighing 2 oz. there shall be $\tfrac{1}{2}$ oz. of gold?

Solution. Let $x =$ the number of ounces of copper to be added.

Then $\qquad$ $80 + x =$ the number of ounces in the new alloy.

$\dfrac{80 + x}{30} =$ the ratio between the whole mass of alloy and the gold.

$\dfrac{2}{\frac{1}{2}} =$ the ratio of a sample of the new alloy to the gold in the sample.

Then $\qquad$ $\dfrac{80 + x}{30} = \dfrac{4}{1}.$ $\qquad\qquad\qquad$ Why?

$80 + x = 120.$ $\qquad\qquad\qquad$ Why?

$x = 40.$

Hence 40 oz. of copper should be added.

9. In an alloy of gold and silver weighing 80 oz. there are 10 oz. of gold. How much silver should be added in order that 10 oz. of the new alloy shall contain only $\frac{2}{5}$ oz. of gold?

10. Gun metal is composed of tin and copper. An alloy of 2050 lb. of gun metal of a certain grade contains 1722 lb. of copper. How much tin must be added so that 1050 lb. of the gun metal may contain 861 lb. of copper?

*378. Specific-gravity problems. A cubic foot of glass weighs 2.89 times as much as a cubic foot of water (a cubic foot of water weighs 62.4 lb.). The number 2.89 is called the *specific gravity* of glass. In general, the specific gravity of a substance is defined as *the ratio of the weight of a given volume of the substance to the weight of an equal volume of water at 4° centigrade*. What would it mean, therefore, to say that the specific gravity of 14-karat gold is 14.88? A cubic centimeter of distilled water at 4° centigrade weighs just 1 gm. Since the specific gravity of 14-karat gold is 14.88, one cubic centimeter of gold weighs 14.88 gm., 2 cc. weighs 29.76 gm., etc. In short, *the weight of an object in grams equals the product of its volume in centimeters times its specific gravity.*

1. How many cubic centimeters of distilled water (specific gravity equal to 1) must be mixed with 400 cc. of alcohol (specific gravity equal to 0.79) so that the specific gravity of the mixture shall be 0.9?

HINT. Find the weight of the two parts and set the sum equal to the weight of the mixture.

2. Would you accept half a cubic foot of gold on the condition that you carry it to the bank? Explain your answer.

3. Brass is made of copper and zinc. Its specific gravity is 8.5. How many cubic centimeters of copper (specific gravity 8.9) must be used with 100 cc. of zinc (specific gravity 7.15) to make brass?

4. What is the specific gravity of a steel sphere of radius 1 cm. and weight 32.7 gm.?

379. Proportionality of areas. The geometric exercises to be given in this article are important. The student should study them carefully, prove them, and try to illustrate each.

EXERCISES

1. Prove that the areas of two rectangles are to each other as the products of their corresponding dimensions.

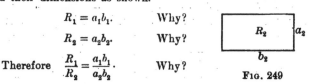

Proof. Denote the areas of the rectangles by R_1 and R_2, as in Fig. 249, and their dimensions as shown.

$$R_1 = a_1 b_1.$$ Why?

$$R_2 = a_2 b_2.$$ Why?

Therefore $\dfrac{R_1}{R_2} = \dfrac{a_1 b_1}{a_2 b_2}.$ Why?

Fig. 249

It is important to note that the last proportion is obtained by dividing the members of the first equation by those of the second.

2. If two rectangles (Fig. 250) have equal bases, they are to each other as their altitudes. (Follow the method of Ex. 1.)

3. If two rectangles have equal altitudes, they are to each other as their bases.

4. The area of a rectangle is 48 sq. ft. and the base is 11 yd. What is the area of a rectangle having the same altitude and a base equal to 27.5 yd. ?

5. Prove that the areas of two parallelograms are to each other as the products of their bases and altitudes.

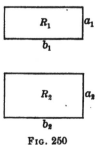

Fig. 250

6. The areas of two triangles are to each other as the products of their bases and altitudes.

7. The areas of two parallelograms having equal bases are to each other as their altitudes; the areas of two parallelograms having equal altitudes are to each other as their bases.

8. The areas of two triangles having equal bases are to each other as their altitudes; the areas of two triangles having equal altitudes are to each other as their bases.

9. Prove that triangles having equal bases and equal altitudes are equal.

*10. Construct the following by means of Ex. 9: a right triangle, an isosceles triangle, an obtuse-angled triangle, each equal to a given triangle.

SUMMARY

380. This chapter has taught the meaning of the following words and phrases: similar triangles, similar polygons, proportion, means, extremes, fulcrum, mean proportional, fourth proportional, alloy, specific gravity.

381. Polygons that have the same shape are similar.

382. In similar triangles the corresponding angles are equal and the corresponding sides are in proportion.

383. Two similar triangles may be constructed by

1. Making two angles of one equal to two angles of the other.

2. Making the ratios of corresponding sides equal.

3. Making the ratio of two sides of one equal to the ratio of two sides of the other, and the angles included between these sides equal.

384. A proportion expresses the equality of two ratios.

385. A convenient test of proportionality is the theorem that says the product of the means equals the product of the extremes.

386. If $ad = bc$, we may write the following four proportions:

(a) $\dfrac{a}{b} = \dfrac{c}{d}$.   (b) $\dfrac{a}{c} = \dfrac{b}{d}$.   (c) $\dfrac{d}{b} = \dfrac{c}{a}$.   (d) $\dfrac{d}{c} = \dfrac{b}{a}$.

387. The fact that the ratios of corresponding sides of similar polygons are equal furnishes us with an algebraic method of finding distances.

388. Inaccessible distances out of doors may often be determined by means of a proportion.

389. Beam problems and mixture, alloy, and specific-gravity problems may be solved by equations which take the form of proportions.

390. If a line is drawn parallel to the base of a triangle, the triangle cut off is similar to the given triangle, and the corresponding sides are in proportion.

391. The following important theorems about the area of two parallelograms have been proved:

1. The areas of two parallelograms are to each other as the product of their bases and altitudes.

2. The areas of two parallelograms having equal bases are to each other as their altitudes, and the areas of two parallelograms having equal altitudes are to each other as their bases.

392. Three theorems similar to those in Art. 391 were proved for the areas of rectangles and triangles.

393. If in a right triangle a line is drawn from the vertex of the right angle perpendicular to the hypotenuse,

1. The triangle is divided into two similar triangles which are each also similar to the given triangle.

2. The perpendicular is a mean proportional between the two segments of the hypotenuse.

3. Either side about the right angle is a mean proportional between the whole hypotenuse and the adjacent segment.

394. The following constructions have been taught:

1. How to construct a mean proportional.

2. How to construct a square equal to a given rectangle, parallelogram, or triangle.

3. How to construct a right triangle or an isosceles triangle equal to a given scalene triangle.

4. How to construct a fourth proportional.

5. How to divide a line segment into two parts which have a given ratio.

CHAPTER XIV

INDIRECT MEASUREMENT; SCALE DRAWINGS; TRIGONOMETRY

395. Scale drawings. Up to this point we have made several uses of *scale drawings*. In Chapter X the relation of

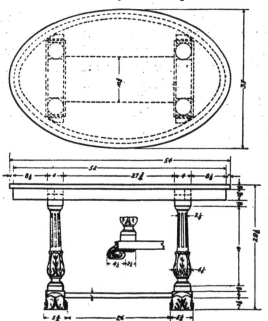

Fig. 251. Scale Drawing of a Library Table

(Courtesy of *Industrial Arts Magazine*)

quantities was shown by line segments whose proportional lengths represented the relative size of the quantities.

345

In another form of graphic work, scale drawings have
helped us to understand the meaning of functions, equations, and formulas. In addition to the foregoing, scale
drawings are probably familiar to the student in the form
of shop drawings, geography maps, blue prints, maps in
railroad guides, and architects' plans.

The shop drawing in Fig. 251 illustrates a use of a scale
drawing, which we shall now study in some detail.

The figure shows that a scale drawing gives us an accurate picture of the real object by presenting all the parts
in the same order of arrangement and showing the relative
sizes graphically by means of proportional line segments.
Obviously this fact rests on the principle of similarity, and
the ratio between any two line segments in the plan equals
the ratio between the lengths of the two corresponding
parts of the library table (Fig. 252).

By means of the scale drawing we are able to determine the dimensions of parts of the table even though
they are not given on the plan. In fact, in the case of
architects' and surveyors' scale drawings we are able to
measure lines which in the real object are inaccessible.

This last procedure illustrates precisely the use which
we want to make of scale drawings in this chapter. In
many cases we shall want to measure distances that cannot be measured directly with steel tape or other surveying
devices; for example, (1) the heights of towers, buildings,
or trees; (2) the width of ponds, lakes, or rivers; (3) the
length of boundary lines passing through houses, barns, or
other obstructions.

We can usually determine such distances by following
the method set forth in the following outline:

1. Measure enough actual lines and angles in the real
object so that a scale drawing of the object can be made.

2. Draw the figure to scale, preferably on squared paper.

3. Measure carefully with the compasses and squared paper the lines in the figure which represent the inaccessible lines of the actual object that is being considered.

FIG. 252. THE FINISHED LIBRARY TABLE
(Courtesy of *Industrial Arts Magazine*)

4. Translate the measurements obtained in (3) into the units used in measuring the lines of the actual figure.

EXERCISES

1. A man walks from his home around a swamp (Fig. 253). He starts from his home at A, walks 0.95 mi. north, then 1.2 mi. east, then 0.35 mi. south. How far from home is he?

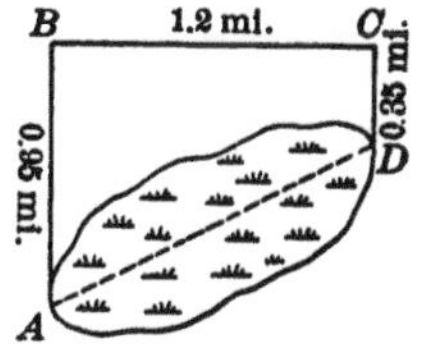

Solution. Let 2 cm. represent 1 mi. Make a drawing on squared paper of the distances as shown in Fig. 253. Then on the squared paper a side of every small square represents 0.1 mi. (Why?) The required distance is the number of miles represented by the segment AD, which is 13.9 small units long. Hence AD represents 1.39 mi. Why?

FIG. 253

2. Show how the four steps given in the outline of Art. 395 are followed in the solution of the preceding problem.

3. A man starting at a point S walks 48 yd. north and then 56 yd. east. Find the direct distance from the stopping-point to the starting-point. (Let 1 cm. = 10 yd.)

4. A man walks 92 yd. south, then 154 yd. east, and then 132 yd. north. How far is he from the starting-point? (Use 1 cm. for every 12 yd.)

5. Two men start from the same point. One walks 15 mi. west, then 9 mi. north; the other walks 12 mi. south, then 16 mi. east. How far apart are they?

6. Draw to scale a plan of your desk top and find the distance diagonally across. (Use the scale 1 cm. = 1 ft.)

7. A baseball diamond is a square whose side is 90 ft. By means of a scale drawing, find the length of a throw from " home plate " to " second base."

8. The broken line ABC (Fig. 254) represents a country road. Find out how much nearer it would be to walk diagonally across country from A to C than it is to follow the road.

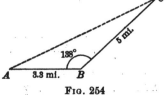

FIG. 254

9. A roadbed is said to have a 6% grade when the level of the road rises 6 ft. in 100 ft. measured horizontally. Draw to scale a roadbed 520 yd. long which has a 6% grade.

10. The sides of a triangular chicken lot are 20 ft., 16 ft., and 18 ft. respectively. Make a scale drawing of this lot on squared paper and estimate the area by counting the small squares and approximating the remaining area.

11. In a map drawn to the scale of 1 to 200,000 what lengths will represent the boundaries of a rectangular-shaped county 40 mi. long and 20 mi. wide? Give the answer to the nearest hundredth of an inch.

12. A railroad surveyor wishes to measure across the swamp at *AB* represented in Fig. 255. He measures the distance from a tree *A* to a stone *C* and finds it to be 110 yd. Find the distance across the swamp if the angle at *C* is 70° and if *BC* = 100 yd.

FIG. 255

NOTE. The lines *BC* and *AC* are measured by means of a *steel tape* (Fig. 256) or a *surveyor's chain* (Fig. 257). The angle at *C* is measured by means of a transit (Fig. 43). *Chaining pins* (Fig. 258) are used by surveyors to mark the end-points of the chain or tape.

FIG. 256. STEEL
TAPE

FIG. 257. SURVEYOR'S
CHAIN

FIG. 258. CHAIN-
ING PINS

*13. If available examine a steel tape, chain, and the pins used by surveyors and report to class on the length, graduations, etc.

14. In Fig. 259, *S* represents a water-pumping station in Lake Michigan. *A* and *B* represent two Chicago buildings on

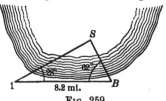

FIG. 259

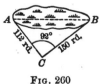

FIG. 260

the lake shore. Reproduce the measurements to scale and determine the distance of *S* from each of the two buildings.

15. In Fig. 260 a swimming course *AB* across a small lake is represented. Find *AB* by means of a scale drawing.

16. A triangular lot has these dimensions: $AB = 20$ yd.; $BC = 40$ yd.; $AC = 30$ yd. Make a scale drawing of the lot on squared paper and determine its area. (Since the formula for the area of a triangle $A = \dfrac{ab}{2}$ calls for an altitude, the student will draw one from A to BC and then apply the formula.)

*17. In order to measure the distance between two pumping stations A and B in Lake Michigan a base line $CD = 18.8$ chains long (1 chain $= 66$ ft.) was measured along the shore. The following angles were then measured: $\angle ACD = 132°$; $\angle BCD = 50°$; $\angle CDA = 46°$; $\angle CDB = 125°$. Draw the figure to scale and find the distance from A to B in feet.

*18. Two streets intersect at an angle of 80°. The corner lot has frontages of 200 ft. and 230 ft. on the two streets, and the remaining two boundary lines of the lot are perpendicular to the two streets. What is the length of these two boundary lines? What is the area of the lot?

HINT. Construct the two perpendiculars with compasses. Then draw a diagonal so as to form two triangles and construct their two altitudes as in Ex. 16, above.

*19. A class in surveying wishes to determine the height of a smokestack as shown in Fig. 261. The transit is placed at B, and the angle y is found to be 62°; then at A, and the angle x is found to be 32°.

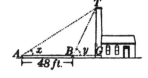

Fig. 261

Line AB is 48 ft. long and is measured along level ground. The transit rests on a tripod $3\frac{1}{2}$ ft. high. Find the height of the chimney.

396. Angle of elevation. The angles x and y which were measured in Ex. 19 are called *angles of elevation.* The angle KAH in Fig. 262 shows what is meant by an *angle of elevation.* To find the angle of elevation the transit is placed at *A* as in Fig. 262. The telescope of the transit is first pointed horizontally toward the smokestack. The farther end is then raised until the top of the chimney *K* is in the line of sight. The angle *KAH*, through which the telescope turns, is the *angle of elevation* of *K* from *A*, the point of observation.

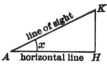

FIG. 262. ANGLE OF ELEVATION

EXERCISES

By means of scale drawings, compasses, and protractor solve the following exercises:

1. When the angle of elevation of the sun is 20° a building casts a shadow 82 ft. long on level ground. Find the height of the building.

2. Find the angle of elevation of the sun when a church spire 80 ft. high casts a shadow 120 ft. long.

3. A roof slopes 1 in. per horizontal foot. What angle does the roof make with the horizontal?

4. A light on a certain steamer is known to be 30 ft. above the water. An observer on the shore whose instrument is 4 ft. above the water finds the angle of elevation of this light to be 6°. What is the distance from the observer to the steamer?

5. What angle does a mountain slope make with a horizontal plane if it rises 150 ft. in a horizontal distance of one tenth of a mile?

6. The cable of a captive balloon is 620 ft. long. Assuming the cable to be straight, how high is the balloon when all the cable is out if, owing to the wind, the cable makes an angle of 20° with the level ground (that is, the angle of elevation is 20°)?

7. On the top of a building is a flagpole. At a point A on level ground 70 ft. from the building the angle of elevation of the top of the flagpole is 42°. At the same point, A, the angle of elevation of the top of the building is 32°. Find the height of the flagpole. How high is the building?

397. Angle of depression. A telescope at M in the top of a lighthouse (Fig. 263) is pointed horizontally (zero reading), and then the farther end is lowered (depressed) until the telescope points to a boat at B. The angle HMB, through which the telescope turns, is the *angle of depression* of the boat from the point M. In Fig. 263, $\angle HMB = \angle MBC$. Why is this true?

EXERCISES

1. If the height of the lighthouse (Fig. 263) is 220 ft. above water, and the angle of depression of the boat, as seen from M, is 40°, what is the distance of the boat from R if RC is known to be 40 ft.?

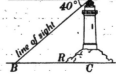

2. A boat passes a tower on which is a searchlight 220 ft. above sea level. Find the angle through which the beam of light must be depressed from the horizontal so that it may shine

FIG. 263. ANGLE OF DEPRESSION

directly on the boat when it is 300 ft. from the base of the tower.

3. How far is the boat from the base of the tower if the angle of depression is 51°? 30°? Note that the height of the lighthouse is known, and that the distance of a boat out at sea depends on the size of the angle; that is, the distance is a function of the angle. In other words, the lighthouse keeper needs only to know the angle of depression to determine the distance of a boat at sea.

4. From the top of a mountain 2500 ft. above the floor of the valley the angles of depression of two barns in the level valley beneath, both of which were due east of the observer, were found to be 27° and 56°. What is the horizontal distance between the two barns?

5. From the top of a hill the angles of depression of two consecutive milestones on a straight level road, running due south from the observer, were found to be 23° and 47°. How high is the hill?

398. Reading angles in the horizontal plane; bearing of a line. The special terms used in stating problems in surveying and navigation make the problems seem unfamiliar, although the mathematics is frequently not more difficult

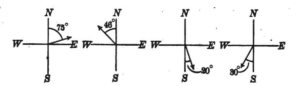

FIG. 264. ILLUSTRATING THE BEARING OF A LINE

than in the exercises given in Art. 397. Thus the acute angle which a line makes with the north-south line is the *bearing of the line.*

The bearings of the lines indicated by the arrows in Fig. 264 are read as follows: 75° east of north, 46° west of north, 20° east of south, and 30° west of south. These are written more briefly as follows: N. 75° E., N. 46° W., S. 20° E., and S. 30° W.

EXERCISES

1. Read the bearings of the arrow lines in Fig. 265.

2. With a ruler and protractor draw lines having the following bearings :

    (a) 26° east of south.   (d) $37\frac{1}{2}°$ west of south.

    (b) 39° east of north.   (e) 33° west of north.

    (c) 40° west of north.   (f) 3° east of south.

3. Write in abbreviated form the bearings of the lines in Ex. 2.

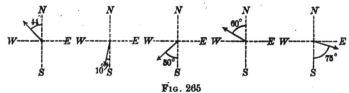

Fɪɢ. 265

399. Bearing of a point. The *bearing of a point B* (Fig. 266) from a point *O* is the bearing of the line *OB* with reference to the north-south line through *O*.

EXERCISES

1. In Fig. 266 read the bearing of

    (a) *A* from *O*.   (d) *O* from *B*.

    (b) *O* from *A*.   (e) *C* from *O*.

    (c) *B* from *O*.   (f) *O* from *C*.

2. Point *A* is 6.4 mi. east and 9.8 mi. north of *B*. Find the distance from *A* to *B*. What angle does *AB* make with the north-south line through *B*? What is the bearing of *B* from *A*? of *A* from *B*?

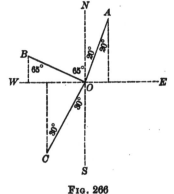

Fɪɢ. 266

3. Sketch the figure for Ex. 2 and show why the angles appearing as results for Ex. 2 are equal.

4. The bearing of a fort B from A, both on the seacoast, is N. 55° W. An enemy's vessel at anchor off the coast is observed from A to bear northwest; from B, northeast. The forts are known to be 8 mi. apart. Find the distance from each fort to the vessel.

400. The limitations of scale drawings. By this time the student probably appreciates the fact that a scale drawing has its limitations. He would probably not agree to buy a triangular down-town lot whose altitude and area had been determined by a scale drawing. If a millimeter on the squared paper represents 0.1 of a mile, a slight slip of the pencil or compasses means disaster to accuracy.

Scale drawing is used extensively by the surveyor and engineer in the following ways: (1) as a method of *estimating* probable results; (2) as a help to clear thinking about the relations of lines and angles involved in a geometric drawing; (3) as a valuable check on results obtained by more powerful methods. But as a matter of fact we need a more refined method to determine lines and angles where a high degree of accuracy is desirable. We shall now proceed to consider a far more efficient method of determining such lines and angles. Most students will find the method fascinating, because the solution is simple and the results obtained are as accurate as the lines and angles which are directly measured.

TRIGONOMETRY

401. Similar right triangles. A few exercises on similar right triangles will help the student to understand the new and more accurate method of determining lines and angles. This method may be used independent of scale drawings, is shorter in most cases, and lays the foundation for future mathematical work.

1. With the protractor construct a right-angled triangle having an angle of 37°. Letter the figure as suggested in Fig. 267. Measure the lines a, b, and c. Let 2 cm. represent 1 unit. Find the value of the ratios $\frac{a}{c}$, $\frac{b}{c}$, and $\frac{a}{b}$ to two decimal places.

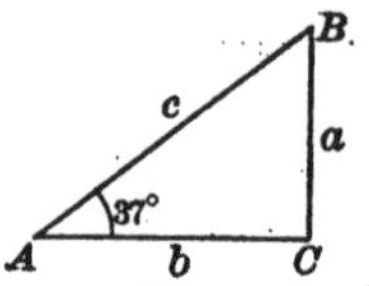

FIG. 267

2. Compare your result with other members of the class. Did all members of the class use the same length for the bases? Are any two of the triangles drawn necessarily of the same size? Show why the result obtained for $\frac{a}{c}$ should be the same number as the results of your classmates.

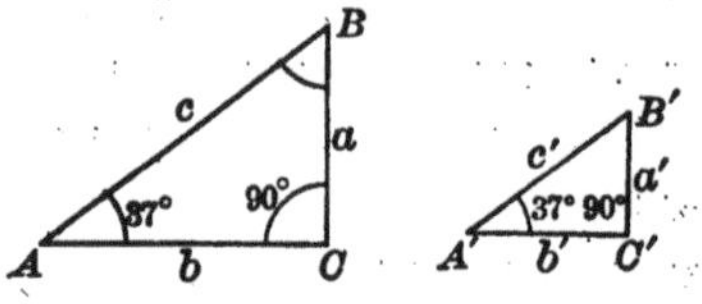

FIG. 268

3. Prove that *if two right triangles have an acute angle of one equal to an acute angle of the other, the ratios of their corresponding sides are equal.* Write two proportions. (Use Fig. 268.)

4. Could you draw a right triangle with angle $A = 37°$ in which $\frac{a}{c}$ does not equal approximately 0.60, or $\frac{3}{5}$? Prove.

HINT. The fact that $\frac{a}{c} = \frac{3}{5}$ means that in every right triangle the side opposite a 37° angle is approximately $\frac{3}{5}$ as long as the hypotenuse.

5. A balloon B (Fig. 269) is fastened by a cable 200 ft. long. Owing to the wind the cable is held practically straight and makes a 37° angle with the horizontal. How high is the balloon?

Solution. This triangle is similar to every triangle drawn by the class in Ex. 1. Prove.

Therefore $\frac{a}{200} = 0.60.$ Why?

Solving, $a = 120$ ft.

FIG. 269

Note that the solution is exceedingly simple (only two equations) and that the accuracy of the result does not now depend upon the accuracy of Fig. 269.

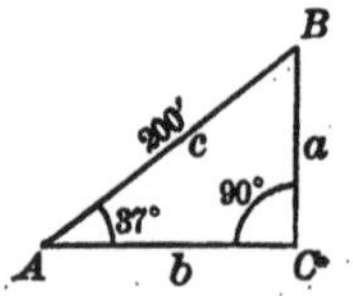

402. Sine of an angle. The ratio $\frac{a}{c}$ (Fig. 270) is called the *sine* of the angle A. The abbreviation for "sine" is "sin." This definition may be written $\sin A = \frac{a}{c}$. Thus, $\sin 37° = \frac{3}{5} = 0.60$ (approx.). Do you think we would have obtained the same value for $\frac{a}{c}$ if in Ex. 1 we had made the angle 47°?

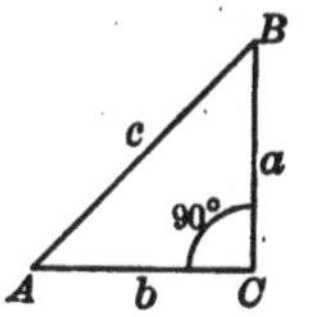

Fig. 270

EXERCISES

1. Find the sine of 20°, using the definition given in Art. 402.

HINT. As in Ex. 1, Art. 401, construct the triangle, measure a and c, and find the value of $\frac{a}{c}$ to two decimal places.

2. Find the sine of each of the following angles: 10°, 15°, 25°, 32°, 47°, 68°, 87°. Compare each result with the results of your classmates.

403. Table of sines. The preceding exercises show that the sine of the angle changes with the angle; that is, sin 68° is not equal to sin 37°. By taking a large sheet of graphic paper and a very large unit we could get a fairly good table, but it would be too much trouble to do this for every problem. Such a table has been very carefully calculated for you in the first column of the table in Art. 410.

EXERCISE

Turn to the table in Art. 410 and see how efficient you have been by comparing your results for Ex. 2, Art. 402, with the table.

404. Cosine of an angle. The exercises given in this article will introduce another trigonometric ratio.

1. Construct a right-angled triangle with angle A (see Fig. 270) equal to 43°. Measure b and c. Find the quotient $\frac{b}{c}$ to two decimal places. Compare the results with those of the other members of the class.

2. Show that all results ought to agree to two decimal places. The ratio $\frac{b}{c}$ (Fig. 270) is called the *cosine* of the angle A. The abbreviation for "cosine" is "cos." Thus, cos 43° = 0.73 (approx.). This means that in any right-angled triangle the *side adjacent* to the angle 43° is about $\frac{73}{100}$ as long as the hypotenuse.

3. Find the cosine of 5°, 18°, 25°, 35°, 47°, 65°, 87°.

4. Compare the results for Ex. 3 with the table of cosines in Art. 410.

405. Tangent of an angle. We shall now introduce a third important ratio connected with similar right triangles. Historically the tangent ratio came first. We shall have occasion to learn more about it.

1. In Fig. 270, what is the value of $\frac{a}{b}$? Compare your result with the results obtained by other members of the class.

2. Show that all the results obtained for $\frac{a}{b}$ in Ex. 1 should agree.

The ratio $\frac{a}{b}$ is called the *tangent* of angle A. In speaking of the tangent of 43° we mean that the side opposite angle A is $\frac{93}{100}$ (approx.) of the length of the side adjacent. The abbreviation for "tangent" is "tan." Thus, tan 45° = 1.

· **1.** Find the tangent of 11°, 36°, 45°, 57°, 82°.

2. Compare the results of Ex. 1 with the table of tangents in Art. 410.

406. Trigonometric ratios. Solving a triangle. The ratios $\dfrac{a}{c}$, $\dfrac{b}{c}$, and $\dfrac{a}{b}$ are called *trigonometric ratios*. We shall now proceed to show that the use of these ratios greatly simplifies the solution of many problems involving indirect measurements. By their use any part of a right triangle can be found if any two parts (not both angles) besides the right angle are given. This process is called *solving the triangle.*

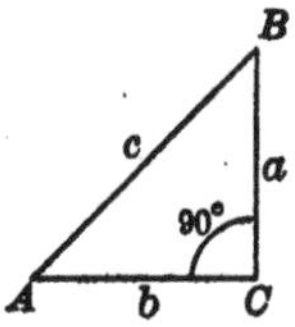

Fig. 271

407. Summary of definitions. The following outline will be found convenient to the student in helping him to remember the definitions (see Fig. 271):

$$1.\ \sin A = \frac{a}{c} = \frac{side\ opposite}{hypotenuse}\ .$$

$$2.\ \cos A = \frac{b}{c} = \frac{side\ adjacent}{hypotenuse}\ .$$

$$3.\ \tan A = \frac{a}{b} = \frac{side\ opposite}{side\ adjacent}\ .$$

408. Trigonometric ratios clear examples of the function idea. Either by your own crude efforts at building a table or by a study of the table of ratios given, it is easy to see that the value of the ratio changes as the angle changes; that is, a trigonometric ratio depends for its value upon the size of the angle. Hence the ratios furnish us with one more clear example of the function idea. We may therefore refer to them as *trigonometric functions.*

HISTORICAL NOTE. Trigonometric ratios are suggested even in the Ahmes Papyrus (c. 1700 B.C. ?), which, as has been stated, may itself be a copy of some other collection written before the time of Moses. In dealing with pyramids Ahmes makes use of one ratio that may possibly correspond roughly to our cosine and tangent.

The first to make any noteworthy progress in the development of trigonometry was Hipparchus, a Greek, who lived about 150 B.C. He studied at Alexandria, and later retired to the island of Rhodes, where he did his principal work. He was able to calculate the length of a year to within six minutes.

The Hindus contributed to the early development of the science, from about A.D. 500, and the Arabs added materially to their work from about A.D. 800 to A.D. 1000

Regiomontanus (or Johann Müller, 1436–1476), a German, freed the subject from its direct astronomical connection and made it an independent science.

In the sixteenth century the subject developed slowly, but in the seventeenth century it made a very decided advance, due to the invention of logarithms, mentioned later, and to the great improvement of algebraic symbolism which made it possible to write trigonometric formulas in a simple manner. Trigonometry in the form that we know it may be said to have been fully developed, except for slight changes in symbols, in the seventeenth century.

409. Table of trigonometric ratios of angles from 1° to 89°. The student should now become familiar with the table on the following page. The ratios are in most cases only approximate, but are accurate enough for all ordinary work.

410. The use of a trigonometry table. The problems beginning on page 362 are intended to furnish the student practice in the use of the table.

Angle	Sine $\left(\dfrac{opp.}{hyp.}\right)$	Cosine $\left(\dfrac{adj.}{hyp.}\right)$	Tangent $\left(\dfrac{opp.}{adj.}\right)$	Angle	Sine $\left(\dfrac{opp.}{hyp.}\right)$	Cosine $\left(\dfrac{adj.}{hyp.}\right)$	Tangent $\left(\dfrac{opp.}{adj.}\right)$
0°	.000	1.000	.000	45°	.707	.707	1.000
1°	.017	1.000	.017	46°	.719	.695	1.036
2°	.035	.999	.035	47°	.731	.682	1.072
3°	.052	.999	.052	48°	.743	.669	1.111
4°	.070	.998	.070	49°	.755	.656	1.150
5°	.087	.996	.087	50°	.766	.643	1.192
6°	.105	.995	.105	51°	.777	.629	1.235
7°	.122	.993	.123	52°	.788	.616	1.280
8°	.139	.990	.141	53°	.799	.602	1.327
9°	.156	.988	.158	54°	.809	.588	1.376
10°	.174	.985	.176	55°	.819	.574	1.428
11°	.191	.982	.194	56°	.829	.559	1.483
12°	.208	.978	.213	57°	.839	.545	1.540
13°	.225	.974	.231	58°	.848	.530	1.600
14°	.242	.970	.249	59°	.857	.515	1.664
15°	.259	.966	.268	60°	.866	.500	1.732
16°	.276	.961	.287	61°	.875	.485	1.804
17°	.292	.956	.306	62°	.883	.469	1.881
18°	.309	.951	.325	63°	.891	.454	1.963
19°	.326	.946	.344	64°	.899	.438	2.050
20°	.342	.940	.364	65°	.906	.423	2.145
21°	.358	.934	.384	66°	.914	.407	2.246
22°	.375	.927	.404	67°	.921	.391	2.356
23°	.391	.921	.424	68°	.927	.375	2.475
24°	.407	.914	.445	69°	.934	.358	2.605
25°	.423	.906	.466	70°	.940	.342	2.747
26°	.438	.899	.488	71°	.946	.326	2.904
27°	.454	.891	.510	72°	.951	.309	3.078
28°	.469	.883	.532	73°	.956	.292	3.271
29°	.485	.875	.554	74°	.961	.276	3.487
30°	.500	.866	.577	75°	.966	.259	3.732
31°	.515	.857	.601	76°	.970	.242	4.011
32°	.530	.848	.625	77°	.974	.225	4.331
33°	.545	.839	.649	78°	.978	.208	4.705
34°	.559	.829	.675	79°	.982	.191	5.145
35°	.574	.819	.700	80°	.985	.174	5.671
36°	.588	.809	.727	81°	.988	.156	6.314
37°	.602	.799	.754	82°	.990	.139	7.115
38°	.616	.788	.781	83°	.993	.122	8.144
39°	.629	.777	.810	84°	.995	.105	9.514
40°	.643	.766	.839	85°	.996	.087	11.430
41°	.656	.755	.869	86°	.998	.070	14.301
42°	.669	.743	.900	87°	.999	.052	19.081
43°	.682	.731	.933	88°	.999	.035	28.636
44°	.695	.719	.966	89°	1.000	.017	57.290
45°	.707	.707	1.000	90°	1.000	.000	

NOTE. The abbreviation *hyp.* means "hypotenuse"; *adj.* means "the side adjacent to the angle"; *opp.* means "the side opposite the angle."

1. A balloon B (Fig. 272) is anchored to the ground at a point A by a rope, making an angle of 57° with the ground. The point C on the ground directly under the balloon is 146 ft. from A. Assuming the rope to be straight, find the height of the balloon.

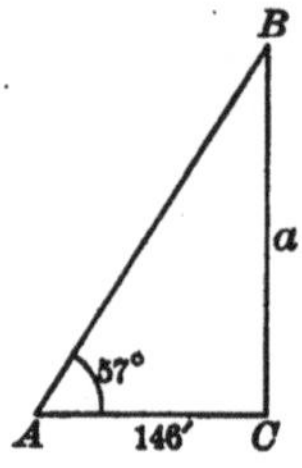

Solution. Let $\quad a = $ height of balloon.

Then $\qquad \dfrac{a}{146} = $ tangent of 57°.

But by the table, Art. 410,

$$\tan 57° = 1.54.$$

Hence $\qquad \dfrac{a}{146} = 1.54.$

Solving for a, $\qquad a = 224.84$ ft.

FIG. 272

NOTE. The figure does not need to be drawn accurately, for our results are obtained independently of it. The solution is brief and depends for its accuracy upon the accuracy of the angle 57°, the accuracy of the length of the line AC, and the accuracy of the tangent table.

2. The angle of elevation of an aëroplane at a point A on level ground is 53°. The point C on the ground directly under the aëroplane is 315 yd. from A. Find the height of the aëroplane.

3. The length of a kite string is 210 yd. and the angle of elevation of the kite is 48°. Find the height of the kite, supposing the line of the kite string to be straight.

4. A pole 20 ft. in length stands vertically in a horizontal area, and the length of its shadow is 16.78 ft. Find the angle of elevation of the sun.

HINT. Find the value of the tangent $\dfrac{a}{b}$. Then look in the table to see what angle has a tangent corresponding to the value of $\dfrac{a}{b}$. It may be necessary for you to approximate, since the table is not calculated for minutes. Ask your instructor to show you a more complete table of trigonometric ratios.

5. A tree is broken by the wind so that its two parts form with the ground a right-angled triangle. The upper part makes an angle of 55° with the ground, and the distance on the ground from the trunk to the top of the tree is 57 ft. Find the length of the tree.

6. A circular pool has a pole standing vertically at its center, and its top is 50 ft. above the surface. At a point in the edge of the pool the angle subtended by the pole is 25°. Find the radius and the area of the pool.

7. A ladder 35 ft. long leans against a house and reaches to a point 19.6 ft. from the ground. Find the angle between the ladder and the house and the distance the foot of the ladder is from the house.

8. Measure two adjacent edges of your desk or of a rectangular table, say your study table. Find the angles that the diagonal makes with the edges (1) by drawing an accurate figure and measuring the angle with a protractor; (2) by use of the trigonometric ratios.

9. The tread of a step on a certain stairway is 11 in. wide; the step rises 8 in. above the next lower step. Find the angle at which the stairway rises (1) by means of a protractor and an accurate figure; (2) by means of a trigonometric ratio.

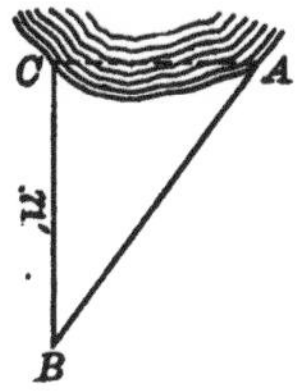

Fig. 273

10. To find the distance across a lake (Fig. 273) between two points A and C, a surveyor measured off 71 ft. on a line BC perpendicular to AC. He then found $\angle CAB = 53°$. Find AC.

11. The Washington Monument is 555 ft. high. How far apart are two observers who from points due west of the monument observe its angles of elevation to be 20° and 38° respectively? (See Fig. 274.)

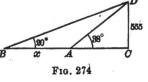

Fig. 274

HINT. Find AC.
Then
$$\frac{555}{x + \text{value of } AC} = \tan 20°.$$

*12. A man standing on the bank of a river observes that the angle of elevation of the top of a tree on the opposite bank is 56°; when he retires 55 ft. from the edge of the river the angle of elevation is 32°. Find the height of the tree and the width of the river.

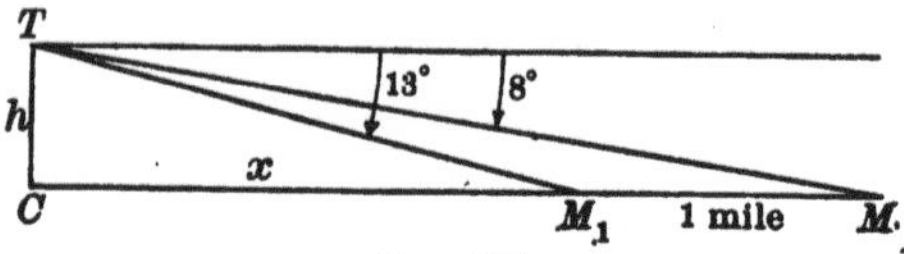

*13. From the summit of a hill (Fig. 275) there are observed two consecutive milestones on a straight horizontal road running from the base of the hill. The angles of depression are found to be 13° and 8° respectively. Find the height of the hill.

Fig. 275

HINT. Construct $TC \perp CM_2$.

Let

$$CM_1 = x.$$

Then

$$\frac{x}{h} = \tan 77°, \quad (Why?) \qquad (1)$$

and

$$\frac{x+1}{h} = \tan 82°. \quad (Why?) \qquad (2)$$

Subtracting (1) from (2), $\frac{1}{h} = \tan 82° - \tan 77°.$

Consult the table on page 36, substitute, and solve for h.

*14. A railroad having a hundred-foot right of way cuts through a farmer's field as shown in Fig. 276. If the field is rectangular and the measurements are made as shown, find the number of square rods occupied by the right of way and the assessed damage if the land is appraised at $200 an acre.

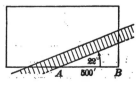

Fig. 276

15. A ship has sailed due southwest a distance of 2.05 mi. How far is the ship south of the starting point? How far is it west of the starting point?

16. From the top of a mountain 4260 ft. above sea level the angle of depression of a distant boat is 41°. How far is the boat from the summit of the mountain ?

*17. Sketch the figure and solve the right-angled triangle *ABC* when

(a) $A = 30°$, $a = 30$ ft.
(b) $B = 42°$, $b = 60$ ft.
(c) $A = 64°$, $b = 22$ ft.
(d) $a = 35°$, $b = 85$ ft.

(e) $b = 92.5°$, $c = 100$ ft.
(f) $a = 15.2°$, $c = 50$ ft.
(g) $A = 40°$, $c = 80$ ft.
(h) $B = 82°$, $c = 100$ ft.

411. A trigonometric formula for the area of a triangle. It can be shown *that the area of a triangle equals half the product of any two sides multiplied by the sine of the included angle ;* that is,

$$T = \frac{ab \sin A}{2}.$$

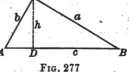

FIG. 277

Solution. In Fig. 277 construct the altitude *CD*.

Then $\qquad T$ (the area) $= \dfrac{ch}{2}$. (Why ?) $\qquad\qquad$ (1)

But $\qquad\qquad \dfrac{h}{b} = \sin A$ (see the definition of "sine"). (2)

Whence $\qquad\qquad h = b \sin A$. (Why ?) $\qquad\qquad$ (3)

Substituting the value of h in (1),

$$T = \frac{bc \sin A}{2}.$$

EXERCISES

1. A boy discovers that his father's drug store completely covers their triangular lot and that it extends 60 ft. and 80 ft. on two sides from a corner. With a field protractor he measures the angle between the streets and finds it to be 58°. He then tries to find the area of the lot. What result should he get ?

*2. Prove that the area of a parallelogram equals the product of two sides and the sine of the angle included between these two sides.

SUMMARY

412. This chapter has taught the meaning of the following words and phrases: scale drawing, surveyor's chain, steel tape, angle of elevation, angle of depression, bearing of a line, bearing of a point, sine of an angle, cosine of an angle, tangent of an angle, trigonometric ratios or trigonometric functions, solving a triangle.

413. Scale drawings were used as a means of indirect measurement.

414. A scale drawing is useful in making estimates of angles, lines, and areas, in getting a clear picture in mind of the relation of the parts that make up the figure, and in checking the accuracy of an algebraic solution. However, it is not as brief and accurate as the algebraic solution.

415. If two right triangles have an acute angle of one equal to an acute angle of the other, the ratios of their corresponding sides are equal.

416. The chapter contains a table of trigonometric ratios of angles from 1° to 89° and correct to three decimal places.

417. Trigonometric ratios furnish us with a powerful method of solving triangles.

418. The area of a triangle may be expressed by the formula $T = \dfrac{bc \sin A}{2}$.

419. The area of a parallelogram equals the product of two sides and the sine of the angle included between these two sides.

CHAPTER XV

THEORY AND APPLICATION OF SIMULTANEOUS LINEAR EQUATIONS; CLASSIFIED LISTS OF VERBAL PROBLEMS

420. Two unknowns; solution by the graphic method. In solving verbal problems it is sometimes desirable to use two unknowns. This chapter aims to teach three methods which the pupil may apply to such problems. The graphic method is shown in the discussion of the following problem:

In a baseball game between the Chicago Cubs and the New York Giants, the Cubs made four more hits than the Giants. How many hits did each team make?

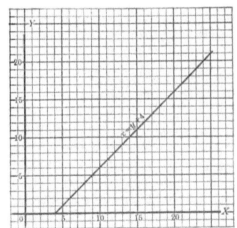

Fig. 278

If we let x represent the number of hits made by the Cubs and y the number made by the Giants, then the equation $x = y + 4$ expresses the condition as set forth in the problem.

Obviously there are any number of possible combinations such that the number of hits made by one team may be four more than the number made by the other team. This is clearly shown in the graph of the equation $x = y + 4$ in Fig. 278.

EXERCISES

1. From the graph in Fig. 278 find the number of hits made by the Giants, assuming that the Cubs made 6; 8; 10; 15; 20.

2. Show that every point (with integral coördinates) on the line will give a possible combination of hits such that $x = y + 4$.

NOTE. By this time the student is no doubt convinced that a definite solution of the problem as stated is impossible, because it involves two unknowns and we have given but one fact. Another fact which should have been included in the problem is that the total number of hits made by both teams was 18.

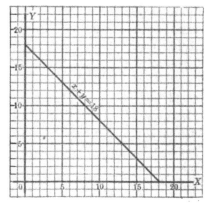

FIG. 279

If we write the equation $x + y = 18$, expressing this second fact, and study it by means of the graph, Fig. 279, we see that there is more than one possible combination such that the total number of hits made is 18.

3. Find from the graph in Fig. 279 the number of hits made by the Giants if the Cubs made 4; 6; 9; 12; 15.

4. Show that every point (with integral coördinates) on the line will give a possible solution for the equation $x + y = 18$.

NOTE. We have not been able to obtain a definite solution, because we have been considering the two facts about the ball game separately. The two equations express different relations between the two unknowns in the ball game. This means that we must find one pair of numbers which will satisfy both equations, and to do this we must graph both equations on the same sheet to the same scale, as shown in Fig. 280.

5. Find a point in the graph of Fig. 280 that lies on both lines. What does this mean ?

6. What are the x-values and y-values of this point ?

7. Show that the pair of values obtained in Ex. 6 will satisfy both equations.

(1)

x	y
4	0
9	5
20	16

(2)

x	y
18	0
12	6
3	15

$x = y + 4,$ (1)

$x + y = 18.$ (2)

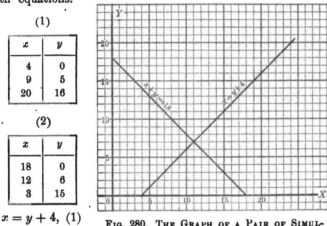

Fig. 280. The Graph of a Pair of Simultaneous Linear Equations

The preceding exercises show that the point of inter-section, namely $x = 11$, $y = 7$, is on both lines, and hence the solution of the problem is $x = 11$, $y = 7$. Thus the number of hits made by the Cubs was 11, and the number made by the Giants was 7.

421. Simultaneous linear equations. A pair of linear equations which are satisfied at the same time (simultaneously) by the same pair of values are called *simultaneous linear equations*. The graph is a pair of intersecting straight lines.

422. System of equations. A pair of equations like those in Art. 420 is often called a *system of two linear equations*. A system of linear equations having a common solution is said to be solved when the correct values of the unknowns are determined. In the graphic method the coördinates of the point of intersection furnish the solution. The following is a summary of the graphic method of solving a pair of simultaneous linear equations:

1. *Graph both equations to the same scale.*
2. *Find the point of intersection of the two lines obtained in* 1.
3. *Estimate as accurately as possible the x-value and the y-value of this point.*
4. *Check by substituting in both equations.*

EXERCISES

1. Solve the following systems by the graphic method and check each:

(a) $\begin{aligned} x + y &= 7, \\ x - y &= 3. \end{aligned}$ (c) $\begin{aligned} 2x + 3y &= 23, \\ 3x + 2y &= 27. \end{aligned}$ (e) $\begin{aligned} 5y - 3x &= 19, \\ 7y + 4x &= 2. \end{aligned}$

(b) $\begin{aligned} 3x + 2y &= 27, \\ 5x - 4y &= 1. \end{aligned}$ (d) $\begin{aligned} 2y + 3x &= 13, \\ 5y - 6x &= -8. \end{aligned}$ (f) $\begin{aligned} 15x + 8y &= 1, \\ 10x - 7y &= -24. \end{aligned}$

2. What difficulties did you have in finding the correct values for the coördinates of the points of intersection in the problems of Ex. 1?

423. Indeterminate equations. A single equation in two unknowns is satisfied by an infinite (unlimited) number of values, but there is no one pair of values which satisfy it to the exclusion of all the others; for example, the equation $x + y = 4$ is satisfied by as many pairs of values as are represented by each distinct point on the graph of the equation $x + y = 4$. Such an equation is called an *indeterminate* equation.

1. Find three solutions for each of the following indeterminate equations:

(a) $x + y = 7$.   (c) $y - z = 6$.   (e) $5x - z = 2$.

(b) $m + 3n = 5$.   (d) $2x - 4y = 3$.   (f) $3x - 4y - 1 = 0$.

424. Contradictory equations. It sometimes happens that even though we have two equations in two unknowns, it is still impossible to obtain a distinct or a unique solution, as is shown by the following example:

Find two numbers such that their difference is 12 and such that twice the first diminished by twice the second is equal to 14.

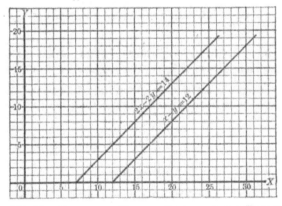

Fig. 281. The Graph of a Pair of Contradictory Equations

If we let x denote one number and y the other, then from the first condition, $$x - y = 12. \tag{1}$$

From the second condition, $2x - 2y = 14.$ (2)

In order to study the problem further we will construct the graphs of (1) and (2) with reference to the same coördinate axes (Fig. 281).

1. What relation seems to exist between the two lines of the graph in Fig. 281 ?

2. Are there, then, any two numbers which will satisfy the conditions of the problem given on the preceding page ?

A system of equations which expresses a contradictory relation between the unknowns is called a system of *contradictory*, or *inconsistent*, equations. The graph consists of two (at least) parallel lines. The definition suggests that in a verbal problem one of the given conditions is not true.

425. Identical equations. A type of problem which has no unique solution but admits of many solutions is illustrated by the following problem:

Divide a pole 10 ft. long into two parts so that 3 times the first part increased by 3 times the second part is equal to 30.

If we let x and y denote the length of the two parts, the conditions of the problem are represented by the equations

$$x + y = 10, \tag{1}$$
and
$$3x + 3y = 30. \tag{2}$$

EXERCISES

1. Graph the equations $x + y = 10$ and $3x + 3y = 30$ to the same scale. Interpret the graph.

2. Divide the equation $3x + 3y = 30$ by 3 and compare the result with the equation $x + y = 10$.

Equations like (1) and (2), above, which express the same relation between the unknowns, are called *identical, dependent,* or *equivalent* equations. Like an indeterminate equation, they have an infinite number of solutions but no distinct solution. Their graphs coincide. If a verbal problem leads to two identical equations, one condition has been expressed in two different ways.

426. Outline of systems of equations and their number of solutions. We have seen that a linear system of equations in two unknowns may be

1. *Determinant and have a distinct solution. (The lines intersect.)*

2. *Contradictory and have no distinct solution. (The lines are parallel.)*

3. *Identical and have an infinite number of solutions. (The lines are coincident.)*

EXERCISES

1. Classify the following systems according to the preceding outline by drawing graphs of each system :

(a) $\begin{aligned} 2x - y &= 3, \\ 3x + y &= 7. \end{aligned}$

(c) $\begin{aligned} x - 2y &= 5, \\ 3x - 6y &= 15. \end{aligned}$

(b) $\begin{aligned} 3x + 4y &= 2, \\ 6x + 8y &= 10. \end{aligned}$

(d) $\begin{aligned} 4x + 2y - 2 &= 0, \\ 2x + 3y &= 3. \end{aligned}$

2. Could you have classified the four systems in Ex. 1 without graphing them ? Explain.

427. Algebraic methods of solving systems of equations in two unknowns. It is often difficult (sometimes impossible) to judge the exact values in a graphic solution. The graphic method helps us to see what is meant by a solution, but it is not, in general, as exact and concise a method as the algebraic methods which we shall now illustrate.

428. Elimination. To solve a system without the use of graphs it will be necessary to reduce the two equations in two unknowns to one equation in one unknown. This process is called *elimination*.

429. Elimination by addition or subtraction. The two problems which follow illustrate the method of elimination by addition or subtraction.

Solve
$$x + y = 6, \qquad (1)$$
$$2x - 3y = 2. \qquad (2)$$

Solution. Multiplying (1) by 3 so as to make the coefficients of y numerically the same in both equations,

$$3x + 3y = 18 \qquad (3)$$
$$2x - 3y = 2 \qquad (4)$$

Adding,
$$5x \qquad = 20$$
$$x = 4.$$

Substituting 4 for x in (1), $\quad 4 + y = 6.$

Solving for y, $\qquad y = 2.$

$$4 + 2 = 6,$$

Check. $\qquad 8 - 6 = 2.$

This method is called *elimination by addition.* Why?

Solve
$$3x - 4y = 1, \qquad (1)$$
$$2x + 5y = -7. \qquad (2)$$

Solution. Multiplying (1) by 2 and (2) by 3 so as to make the coefficients of x numerically equal,

$$6x - 8y = 2 \qquad (3)$$
$$6x + 15y = -21 \qquad (4)$$

Subtracting,
$$-23y = 23$$
$$y = -1.$$

Substituting -1 for y in (1), $3x + 4 = 1.$

$$3x = -3.$$
$$x = -1.$$

Hence $\qquad y = -1,$

and $\qquad x = -1.$

This method is called *elimination by subtraction.* Why?

430. Outline of elimination by addition or subtraction. . To solve two simultaneous linear equations involving two unknowns by the method of addition or subtraction, proceed as follows:

1. *Multiply, if necessary, the members of the first and second equations by such numbers as will make the coefficients of one of the unknowns numerically the same in both equations.*

2. *If the coefficients have the same signs, subtract one equation from the other; if they have opposite signs, add the equations. This eliminates one unknown.*

3. *Solve the equation resulting from step 2 for the unknown which it contains.*

4. *Substitute the value of the unknown found in step 3 in either equation containing both unknowns and solve for the second unknown.*

5. *Check the solution by substituting in both of the given equations the values found.*

EXERCISES

Solve and check the following systems by the method of addition or subtraction:

1. $3x + 2y = 7,$
$2x + 3y = 8.$

2. $4x - 3y = -1,$
$5x + 2y = 16.$

3. $5x - 3y = -14,$
$2x + 4y = 10.$

4. $7x + 9y = -15,$
$5x - 9y = -21.$

5. $3x - 5y = 23,$
$7x + y = -35.$

6. $2x + 3y = 0,$
$3x + 2y = 5.$

7. $11x - 7y = -6,$
$5x + 8y = 42.$

8. $2x = 3y + 1,$
$x + y = 8.$

9. $2x + 3y = 2,$
$7x - 8y = \frac{5}{6}.$

10. $7a + 4b = -5,$
$9a + 7b = -28.$

11. $3x - 2y = 54,$
$\dfrac{x}{2} = \dfrac{y}{3} + 9.$

12. $\dfrac{m}{7} + \dfrac{n}{8} = -2,$
$\dfrac{m}{3} - \dfrac{n}{10} = 11.$

Geometric Exercises for Algebraic Solution

13. The combined height of a tower and flagpole is 110 ft.; the height of the tower is 70 ft. more than the length of the flagpole. Find the height of the tower and the length of the flagpole.

14. A rectangular field is 25 rd. longer than it is wide. The perimeter of the field is 130 rd. Find the dimensions of the field.

15. The perimeter of a football field is 320 yd. and the length is 10 yd. more than twice the width. What are its dimensions?

16. The circumference of a circle exceeds the diameter by 75 ft. Find the circumference and the diameter. (Use the formula $C = \frac{22}{7} d$.)

$4(x+y)^\circ$

60°

$(5x-4y)^\circ$

Fig. 282

17. Two parallel lines are cut by a transversal forming eight angles, as shown in Fig. 282. Find x and y, and all of the angles.

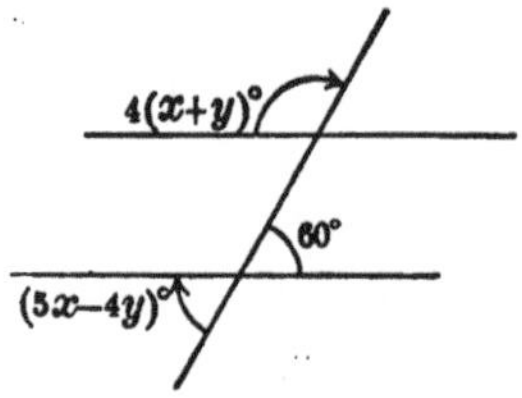

18. The interior angles on the same side of a transversal cutting two parallel lines are $(5x - 3y)^\circ$ and $(x + y)^\circ$. Their difference is 70°. Find x and y.

19. Two adjacent angles of a parallelogram are represented by $3(2m - n)^\circ$ and $\left(\dfrac{3m}{5} + 4n\right)^\circ$, and their difference is 30°. Find m, n, and the angles of the parallelogram.

20. The difference between the acute angles of a right triangle is 43°. Find the acute angles.

Fig. 283

21. A picture frame 1 in. wide (Fig. 283) has an area of 44 sq. in. The picture inside the frame is 4 in. longer than it is wide. Find the dimensions of the picture.

431. Elimination by the method of substitution. The following problem illustrates the method of elimination by substitution:

Solve $\qquad\qquad m + n = 5,$ $\qquad\qquad$ (1)

$\qquad\qquad 2\,m - 5\,n = -11.$ $\qquad$ (2)

Solution. Solving for m in terms of n in the first equation,

$$m = 5 - n. \qquad (3)$$

Substituting this value of m in (2),

$$2\,(5 - n) - 5\,n = -11. \qquad (4)$$
$$10 - 2\,n - 5\,n = -11.$$
$$-7\,n = -21.$$
$$n = 3.$$

Substituting 3 for n in (1), $\quad m + 3 = 5,$

$$m = 2.$$

Hence $\qquad\qquad\qquad m = 22,$ and $n = 3.$

Check. $\qquad\qquad\quad 2 + 3 = 5,$

$$4 - 15 = -11.$$

The preceding method is called the *method of substitution.*

432. Outline of steps in the solution of a system by the substitution method of elimination. To solve a system of linear equations containing two unknowns by the method of substitution, proceed as follows:

1. *Solve one equation for one unknown in terms of the other.*

2. *Substitute for the unknown in the other equation the value found for it in step 1.*

3. *Solve the equation resulting in step 2 for the unknown which it contains.*

4. *Substitute the value of the unknown obtained in step 3 in any equation containing both unknowns and solve for the second unknown.*

5. *Check the solution by substituting in the given equations.*

Solve the following problems by the method of substitution:

1. $3a + 4b = 11,$
   $5a - b = 3.$

4. $-2x - 5w = 17,$
   $3x + 2w = 2.$

7. $3m + 2n = 130,$
   $5m - 6n = 30.$

2. $7x + 3y = 1,$
   $11x - 5y = 21.$

5. $2x + 3y = 8,$
   $3x - 5y = 42.$

8. $\dfrac{x}{5} + \dfrac{y}{2} = 4,$
   $\dfrac{x}{3} - \dfrac{y}{2} = -12.$

3. $9t + 7r = -12,$
   $15t - 2r = 21$

6. $7x - 3y = 8,$
   $8x + 2y = 134.$

NUMBER-RELATION PROBLEMS

Solve the following problems by the method of substitution, and check by one of the other methods:

9. Find two numbers whose sum is 150 and whose difference is 10.

10. Find two numbers whose difference is 15 such that when one is added to twice the other the sum is 295.

11. Find two numbers such that 8 times the first plus 4 times the second equals 100, and 3 times the first plus 7 times the second equals 87.

12. The quotient of two numbers is 2 and their sum is 54. Find the numbers.

13. The value of a certain fraction is $\frac{4}{5}$. If 2 is added to the numerator and 7 to the denominator, the value of the resulting fraction is $\frac{1}{2}$. Find the fraction.

14. The sum of the two digits in a two-place number is 8. If 18 be subtracted from the number, the resulting number will be expressed by the original digits in reverse order. Find the number.

Solution. Let u represent the digit in units' place and t the digit in tens' place.

Then $10t + u$ represents the original number.

From the first condition, $t + u = 8.$

From the second condition,
$$10\,t + u - 18 = 10\,u + t. \tag{2}$$
Simplifying (2), $t - u = 2.$ $\qquad$ (3)

Solving (1) and (3), $2\,t = 10.$

$$t = 5.$$
Substituting 5 for t in (1), $u = 3.$

Therefore the number is 53.

15. The tens' digit of a two-place number is three times the units' digit. If 54 be subtracted from the number, the difference is a number expressed by the digits in the reverse order. Find the number.

16. If a two-digit number be decreased by 13, and this difference divided by the sum of the digits, the quotient is 5. If the number be divided by one fourth of the units' digit, the quotient is 49. Find the number.

433. Summary of methods of elimination. This chapter has taught the following three methods of solving a system of simultaneous linear equations:

1. The graphic method.
2. Elimination by addition or subtraction.
3. Elimination by substitution.

EXERCISES

Some of your classmates may be interested to learn a fourth method called *elimination by comparison.* Turn to a standard algebra and report to your classmates on this method.

MIXTURE PROBLEMS

Solve the following problems by any method:

1. A grocer has two kinds of coffee, one worth 30¢ per pound and another worth 20¢ per pound. How many pounds of the 30-cent coffee must be mixed with 12 lb. of the 20-cent coffee to make a mixture worth 24¢ per pound?

2. A grocer makes a mixture of 20-cent nuts and 32-cent nuts to sell at 28¢ a pound. What quantities of each grade of nuts must he take to make 60 lb. of the mixture?

3. How much milk testing 5% butter fat and cream testing 25% butter fat must be mixed to make 30 gal. that test 22% butter fat?

4. How much milk testing 3.7% butter fat and cream testing 25.5% butter fat must be mixed to make 15 gal. that test 20% butter fat?

5. What number of ounces of gold 75% pure and 85% pure must be mixed to give 10 oz. of gold 80% pure?

6. An alloy of copper and silver weighing 50 oz. contains 5 oz. of copper. How much silver must be added so that 10 oz. of the new alloy may contain $\frac{1}{4}$ oz. of copper?

7. The standard daily diet for an adult requires about 75 g. of protein and 100 g. of fat. Mutton (leg) contains 19.8% protein and 12.4% fat. Bread (average) contains 9.2% protein and 1.3% fat. Find how many grams each of bread and mutton are required to furnish the required amount of protein and fat in a standard ration for one day.

HINT. Let x and y represent the number of grams required of mutton and bread respectively.

Then $$0.198\,x + 0.092\,y = 75, \tag{1}$$

and $$0.124\,x + 0.013\,y = 100. \tag{2}$$

Solve the equations (1) and (2) simultaneously.

If x or y turns out negative, we know that it is not possible to make up a standard diet out of the two foods mentioned.

8. The table on the following page gives the amounts of protein and fats in the various foods often used in the daily diet.

FOOD	PER CENT OF PROTEIN	PER CENT OF FAT
Mutton (leg)	19.8	12.4
Beef (roast)	22.3	28.6
Pork (chops)	16.6	30.1
Eggs	13.4	10.5
Bread (average)	9.2	1.3
Beans (dried) . . . . :	22.5	1.8
Cabbage	1.6	0.3
Rice	8.0	0.3

Find three pairs of food combinations that will make a standard diet and determine the number of grams required of each in the following list:

(a) Mutton and rice.
(b) Eggs and rice.
(c) Bread and eggs.
(d) Pork and bread.
(e) Pork and beans.

(f) Bread and cabbage.
(g) Beans and cabbage.
(h) Bread and beans.
(i) Beef and bread.
(j) Beef and rice.

434. Systems of equations containing fractions. The following list of problems offers no new difficulties. The student merely needs to remember to remove the fractions in each equation by multiplying through by the L.C.M. of the denominators in each, thus reducing each equation to the standard form $ax + by = c$, where a represents the coefficient of x, b the coefficient of y, and c the constant term.

$$\frac{x+y}{3} + \frac{x+y}{2} = \frac{5}{6}, \qquad (1)$$

$$\frac{x-y}{4} + \frac{x-y}{3} = \frac{7}{12}. \qquad (2)$$

The first equation may be written

$$2x + 2y + 3x + 3y = 5. \qquad (3)$$

or $\qquad\qquad\qquad x + y = 1.$ Why?

Similarly, (2) reduces to $x - y = 1$.

EXERCISES

Reduce to the standard form, and solve:

1.
$$\frac{x+y}{3} + \frac{x-3y}{3} = 6,$$
$$\frac{2x+y}{3} + \frac{3y+x}{4} = \frac{5}{4}.$$

2.
$$\frac{7-5y}{5} - \frac{3x+7}{3} = \frac{1}{5},$$
$$\frac{x-y}{2} + \frac{x+y}{3} = \frac{2}{3}.$$

3.
$$\frac{2x+y}{3} + \frac{x-2y}{7} = 3,$$
$$x + 5y = 7.$$

4.
$$\frac{m+1}{n+1} = \frac{1}{2},$$
$$\frac{m-1}{n-1} = \frac{1}{4}.$$

5.
$$\frac{t+3}{5} + \frac{s+4}{10} = \frac{5}{2},$$
$$\frac{2t-5}{7} - \frac{s}{3} = 0.$$

6.
$$0.3x + 0.7y = 5.7,$$
$$2x - 4y = -4.$$

435. Linear systems of the type $\frac{a}{x} + \frac{b}{y} = c$; work problems. In the problems of Art. 434 we have seen the advisability of reducing each of the equations in a system to the standard form by eliminating the fractions and collecting similar terms. There are some problems, however, in which it is advisable to solve without eliminating the fractions. An example will illustrate what is meant.

Two pipes can fill $\frac{9}{10}$ of a cistern if the first runs 2 hr. and the second runs 3 hr., but if the first runs 3 hr. and the second runs 2 hr., they can fill $\frac{14}{15}$ of the cistern.

Solution. Let $x =$ the number of hours it will take the first pipe alone to fill the cistern,

and $y =$ the number of hours it will take the second pipe alone to fill the cistern.

Then $\frac{1}{x} =$ the part of the cistern the first pipe can fill in 1 hr.

and $\frac{1}{y} =$ the part of the cistern the second pipe can fill in 1 hr.

From the first condition,

$$\frac{2}{x} + \frac{3}{y} = \frac{9}{10}.$$ (1)

From the second condition,

$$\frac{3}{x} + \frac{2}{y} = \frac{14}{15}.$$ (2)

Multiplying (1) by 3 and (2) by 2,

$$\frac{6}{x} + \frac{9}{y} = \frac{27}{10},$$ (3)

and

$$\frac{6}{x} + \frac{4}{y} = \frac{28}{15}.$$ (4)

Subtracting,

$$\frac{5}{y} = \frac{27}{10} - \frac{28}{15}.$$ (5)

(Note that this is a linear equation in one unknown.)

Solving, $y = 6$,

$x = 5$.

Problems like the preceding are called *work problems*.

WORK PROBLEMS

1. A and B can build a fence in 4 da. If A works 6 da. and quits, B can finish the work in 3 da. In how many days can each do the work alone?

2. A tank can be filled by two pipes one of which runs 3 hr. and the other 7 hr., or by the same two pipes if one runs 5 hr. and the other 6 hr. How long will it take each pipe alone to fill the tank?

3. A mechanic and an apprentice receive $4.40 for a job of work. The mechanic works 5 hr. and the apprentice 8 hr. Working at another time, and at the same rate per hour, the mechanic works 10 hr. and the apprentice 11 hr., and they receive $7.30. What are the wages per hour for each?

4. Solve the following problems without getting rid of the fractions, and check :

1.
$$\frac{1}{x} + \frac{1}{y} = \frac{5}{6},$$
$$\frac{1}{x} - \frac{1}{y} = \frac{1}{6}.$$

3.
$$\frac{4}{x} - \frac{7}{y} = \frac{15}{4},$$
$$\frac{2}{x} + \frac{8}{y} = 1.$$

2.
$$\frac{2}{m} + \frac{3}{n} = \frac{19}{15},$$
$$\frac{3}{m} + \frac{2}{n} = \frac{7}{5}.$$

4.
$$\frac{11}{s} - \frac{9}{t} = \frac{26}{5},$$
$$\frac{13}{s} - \frac{3}{t} = \frac{8}{5}.$$

436. Review list of verbal problems. The following problems review types studied in earlier chapters. In actual practice many problems may be solved by using either one or two unknowns. In general it is advisable to use one unknown, but sometimes it is easier to translate the problem into algebraic language if two unknowns are used. It will be helpful if some member of the class will show the two methods in contrast.

MOTION PROBLEMS

1. A crew can row 8 mi. downstream in 40 min. and 12 mi. upstream in 1 hr. and 30 min. Find the rate in miles per hour of the current and the rate of the crew in still water.

Solution. Let $x =$ the rate of the crew in still water,
and $y =$ the rate of the current.

Then, if we express the rates in miles per hour,

$$x + y = \frac{8}{\frac{40}{60}} = 12. \tag{1}$$

$$x - y = \frac{12}{\frac{90}{60}} = 8. \tag{2}$$

Adding, $2x = 20.$
Hence $x = 10,$ the rate of the crew in still water,
and $y = 2,$ the rate of the current.

2. A boatman rowed 10 mi. upstream and 4 mi. back in 3 hr. If the velocity of the current was 2 mi. per hour, what was his rate of rowing?

3. The report of a gun traveled 367 yd. per sec. with the wind and 353 yd. per sec. against the wind. Find the velocity of sound and the rate at which the wind was blowing.

4. An aëroplane flying with a wind blowing at the rate of 2 mi. an hour consumes 2 hr. 30 min. in going a certain distance and 2 hr. 42 min. 30 sec. in returning. Find the distance and the rate of the aëroplane in still air.

BEAM PROBLEMS

NOTE. Beam, or lever, problems which involve two unknowns are readily solved by means of the laws of leverages and forces discussed in Art. 233.

5. Two boys carry a bag of coal weighing 25 lb. by hanging it on a pole 8 ft. long at a point 2 ft. from the middle of the pole. How much of the load does each boy carry?

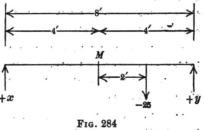

FIG. 284

Solution. Let x and y represent the number of pounds carried by each boy.

Then, using M, Fig. 284 (the middle of the pole), as the turning point,

$$4y - 50 - 4x = 0. \quad \text{(Why?)}$$

From which $\quad\quad\quad y - x = 12.5. \quad\quad\quad\quad\quad$ (1)

$$x + y = 25. \quad \text{(Why?)} \quad\quad (2)$$

Adding (1) and (2), $\quad\quad 2y = 37.5.$

$$y = 18\tfrac{3}{4}.$$

Substituting for y in (2), $18\tfrac{3}{4}x = 6\tfrac{1}{4}.$

6. Two weights balance when one is 14 in. and the other 10 in. from the fulcrum. If the first weight is increased by 2 lb. and placed 10 in. from the fulcrum, the balance is maintained. Find the number of pounds in each weight.

7. Two weights balance when one is 12 in. and the other is 10 in. from the fulcrum. The balance is maintained if the first weight is moved 3 in. nearer the fulcrum and if 3 lb. is subtracted from the second. Find the weights.

8. An iron bar 6 ft. long weighing 20 lb. is used by two boys, one at each end, to carry a load of 150 lb. How many pounds must each boy carry if the load hangs 2 ft. from the right end? (Consider the weight of the entire bar as hanging at the middle of the bar.)

9. A wagon bed 12 ft. long is loaded with 20 cakes of ice weighing 250 lb. The bed extends 2 ft. over the front axle of the running gears and 3 ft. behind the rear axle. Find the load supported by each axle.

10. The material in a 30-foot bridge weighs 3600 lb. The bridge supports two loads: 700 lb. at 3 ft. from one end, and 1500 lb. at 5 ft. from the other end. Find the loads borne by the two supports.

11. Three men have to carry an oak beam 15 ft. long weighing 250 lb. Two of the men lift at the ends of an iron bar placed crosswise beneath the beam, and the third man lifts at the rear end of the beam. Where must the iron bar be placed in order that each man will carry one third of the load?

*RECREATION PROBLEMS

12. A man upon being asked the age of his two sons, answered, "If to the sum of their ages 18 be added, the result will be double the age of the elder; but if 6 be taken from the difference of their ages, the remainder will be equal to the age of the younger." Find the age of each.

13. In a guessing game the leader says, "If you will add 10 years to your age, divide the sum by your age, add 6 to the quotient, and tell me the result, I will tell you your age." How did he find it ?

14. A baseball team has played 40 games, of which it has won 28. How many games must it win in succession in order to bring its average of games won up to 0.750 ?

15. A girl has worked 12 problems. If she should work 13 more problems and get 8 of them right, her average would be 72%. How many problems has she worked correctly thus far ?

16. Two bicycle riders ride together around a circular track, one along the outside edge, where the radius of the circle is R, and the other along the inside edge, where the radius is r. One revolution of the pedals carries the former's bicycle 20 ft. and the latter's 25 ft. Write a formula expressing the difference between the number of pedal revolutions made by the two cyclists in going around the track once; five times; n times.

17. If 10 marbles of one size are dropped into a bucket of water, and the water rises a inches, and 15 equal marbles of another size are dropped into the same bucket, and the water rises b inches, write a formula showing how many times larger one of the first size is than one of the second size.

18. An automobile tire when fully inflated has a radius of 18 in. Owing to a leakage of air, this is reduced to 17 in. Indicate how many more revolutions per mile are necessary because of the leakage. If the original radius is R and the reduced radius r, what is the formula which could be used to calculate the difference of revolutions per mile ?

19. Divide $183 into two parts, so that $\frac{4}{5}$ of the first part shall be equal to $\frac{3}{10}$ of the second part.

20. Each of two brothers wanted to buy a lot valued at $240. The elder brother said to the younger, "You lend me $\frac{3}{4}$ of your money, and I can purchase the lot." "But," said the younger brother, "you lend me $\frac{2}{3}$ of your money, and I can purchase the lot." How much money did each have?

21. A group of boys bought a touring car. After paying for it they discovered that if there had been one boy more, they would have paid $30 apiece less, but if there had been one boy less, they would have paid $60 apiece more. How many boys were there, and what did they pay for the car?

22. The Champion American League team one year (1914) won 46 more games than it lost. The team standing second played 153 games, winning 8 less than the first and losing 9 more than the first. Find the number of games won and lost by each team.

23. It is said that the following problem was assigned by Euclid to his pupils about three centuries B.C.: "A mule and a donkey were going to market laden with wheat. The mule said to the donkey, 'If you were to give me one measure, I would carry twice as much as you; if I were to give you one measure, our burdens would be equal.' What was the burden of each?"

*MISCELLANEOUS PROBLEMS

24. A bar 30 in. long is balanced by a 40-pound weight at one end and a 32-pound weight at the other end. Find the position of the support.

25. A man has a $2000 exemption from income tax, but pays at the rate of 6% on the rest of his income. He finds that after paying income tax his actual income is $3410. On what amount does he pay the 6% tax?

26. A chemist has the same acid in two strengths. If 16 l. of the second are mixed with 24 l. of the first, the mixture is 42% pure, and if 6 l. of the first are mixed with 4 l. of the second, the mixture is 43% pure. Find the per cent of purity of each acid. Problems like this are often given as practical problems. Find out from some chemist why it is not practical.

27. After a strike a corporation decided to raise the wages of each laborer from x to y by the formula $y = mx + b$, where m and b are to be determined by the facts that a man who made \$2 is to receive \$2.30, and one who made \$2.20 is to receive \$2.41. Find m and b, also the new wage of a man who formerly received \$3, \$4, \$4.20.

28. At what market price must one-year 5% bonds be offered for sale in order that the buyer, by holding them until maturity, may make 6% on his investment?

HINT. The profit made must come from two sources: the interest on the par value, which is \$5, and the excess of the maturity value over the price paid for the bonds. If x is the price paid, then $100 - x + 5 = 0.06\,x$.

SUMMARY

437. This chapter has taught the meaning of the following words and phrases: simultaneous equations, linear systems of equations, indeterminate equations, contradictory equations, identical equations, elimination.

438. This chapter has taught the following methods of solving a system of equations in two unknowns:

1. Solution by graph.
2. Solution by addition or subtraction.
3. Solution by substitution.

439. The student has been taught how to solve systems involving fractions, and systems of the type $\dfrac{a}{x} + \dfrac{b}{y} = c$.

440. The following types of verbal problems have been introduced: geometric problems, number-relation problems, mixture problems, work problems, motion problems, beam problems, and recreation problems.

CHAPTER XVI

GEOMETRIC AND ALGEBRAIC INTERPRETATION OF ROOTS AND POWERS

441. Introductory work; square root. The following exercises are introductory to the work of the chapter.

EXERCISES

1. What number multiplied by itself equals 9? 16? 121? 169? x^2? y^2?

2. How many answers are there to each part of Ex. 1? (Why?)

3. One of the two equal factors of a number is called the *square root* of the number. What is the square root of 49? of 64? of 625? of x^2? of $4x^2$? of $\dfrac{4}{9}$? of $\dfrac{4x^2}{9y^2}$?

4. The positive square root of a number is indicated by a sign ($\sqrt{\ \ }$) called the *radical sign,* and either the radical sign alone ($\sqrt{\ \ }$) or the radical sign preceded by the plus sign ($+\sqrt{\ \ }$) means the positive square root of the number underneath the sign. The number underneath the radical sign is called the *radicand.* The negative square root is indicated by the radical sign preceded by the minus sign ($-\sqrt{\ \ }$). With the preceding definitions in mind give the value of the following: $\sqrt{25}$; $\sqrt{16}$; $\sqrt{100}$; $-\sqrt{121}$; $\sqrt{0.25}$; $-\sqrt{144}$; $\sqrt{\tfrac{1}{4}}$; $\sqrt{x^2}$; $\sqrt{\dfrac{4x^2}{9}}$; $\sqrt{\dfrac{16x^2}{25y^2}}$.

5. Express the following statement by means of a formula: *A number y equals the square of another number x.*

6. If $x = 1$ in the formula $y = x^2$, what is the value of y? If $x = 2$, what is the value of y?

7. Calculate the corresponding values of y in the formula $y = x^2$ for each of the following values of x: -1; -2; $+3$; -3; $+\frac{1}{2}$; $+\frac{2}{3}$; $-\frac{2}{3}$.

8. Fill in the proper values in the following table of squares and square roots for use in the next article.

x	1	-1	2	-2	± 3	± 4	± 5	± 6	± 7	$\pm \frac{1}{2}$	$\pm \frac{1}{3}$
y	1	1	4	4						$\frac{1}{4}$	

x	$\pm \frac{1}{4}$	$\pm \frac{3}{4}$	$\pm \frac{2}{3}$	$\pm \frac{3}{2}$	$\pm \frac{5}{2}$	$\pm \frac{7}{2}$	$\pm \frac{9}{2}$	$\pm \frac{11}{2}$	$\pm \frac{13}{2}$	$\pm \frac{15}{2}$
y			$\frac{2}{4}$							

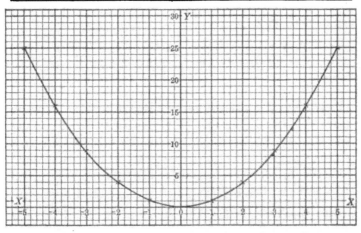

FIG. 285. DEVICE FOR FINDING SQUARES AND SQUARE ROOTS

442. Graph of $y = x^2$; a device for finding squares and square roots. The values of the preceding table have been plotted in Fig. 285. Values for x were laid off horizontally on the x-axis, and the corresponding values for y vertically on the y-axis. The points were then connected by a smooth curve, as shown. This curve serves as a device for determining squares and square roots, as we shall now see.

EXERCISES

1. Determine by the graph in Fig. 285 the square root of 16; 9; 20; 22; 3; 2. How many answers do you obtain for the square root of 9? 4? 25? for the square root of each number shown?

2. By means of the graph in Fig. 285 find the square of 2; 1.4; 2.2; 2.4; 3.3; 5.6; 3.9; 1.7.

3. Check your results for Ex. 2 by squaring the numbers given. The squares should be approximately those you found by means of the graph.

4. How would you make a graph that would give you squares and square roots more accurately than the graph in Fig. 285?

443. A positive number has two square roots. The graph shows that the square root of 4 equals either $+2$ or -2; that is, there are two answers for the square root of a positive number. Thus, $(-3)(-3) = 9$, as also does $(+3)(+3)$. Note the symmetry of the curve in Fig. 285 and see if you can explain it.

444. Quadratic surd. The indicated square root of a number which is not a perfect square is called a *quadratic surd*; for example, $\sqrt{3}, \sqrt{20}, \sqrt{x}$.

445. Quadratic trinomial. Trinomials like $a^2 + 2\,ab + b^2$ and $x^2 - 2\,xy + y^2$ are of the second degree, and are called *quadratic trinomials*. The word "quadratic" comes from the old word "quadrature," which means a geometric square; hence quadratic means that $a^2 + 2ab + b^2$ and $x^2 - 2xy + y^2$ are of the second degree. They are the

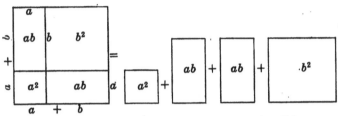

FIG. 286. GEOMETRIC REPRESENTATION OF $(a + b)^2$.

squares of $a + b$ and $x - y$ respectively, as we have already seen earlier in this book. In Fig. 286 the geometric square of $a + b$ is shown.

EXERCISES

1. See if you can point out where we have worked with problems dealing with the square of binomials like $a + b$ and $x - y$.

2. Where, earlier in the book, have we learned how to take the square root of trinomial squares by factoring?

3. Find the value of the following:

$$\sqrt{m^2 + 2mn + n^2}; \quad \sqrt{4x^2 + 12xy + 9y^2}; \quad \sqrt{9a^2 - 12ab + 4b^2}.$$

*446. Square roots of algebraic polynomials and arithmetical numbers. We have already seen in Chapter IX how the square root of a trinomial is found by reversing the process of squaring a binomial; that is, by finding one of the two equal factors of the trinomial. The same process may be explained geometrically if the exercises given on page 394 are carefully solved.

ILLUSTRATIVE EXERCISES

1. Find the square root of $16 x^2 + 40 xy + 25 y^2$

Solution. If this trinomial is a perfect square of some binomial, it may be illustrated by Fig. 287, in which the side of the largest square obtained by inspection and corresponding to a^2 is $4 x$. Therefore the side of each rectangle corresponding to each ab is $4 x$, and the area corresponding to $2 ab + b^2$ must be $40 xy + 25 y^2$. The problem therefore consists in determining the width of the strip which we are adding on two sides and which corresponds to the b of the formula. In this case b is $5 y$. Now $5 y$ may be obtained by dividing $40 xy$ by the sum of $4 x$ and $4 x$, or $8 x$. Hence doubling the term already found ($4 x$) the result $8 x$ serves as a divisor for determin-

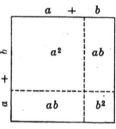

FIG. 287

ing the next term. Fig. 287 shows that we double $4 x$ because $8 x$ is approximately the combined length of the strip to which we are adding. This is illustrated more clearly in the next problem.

2. Two boys were asked to stake out a square plot of ground with an area of 4225 sq. ft. What is the length of a side?

Solution. The boys' thinking about the problem might take some such form as follows:

(a) It is obvious that we can make it at least 60 by 60. We shall suppose that this is constructed. See the square with unbroken lines (Fig. 288). This uses up 3600 sq. ft., leaving 625 sq. ft. We can add

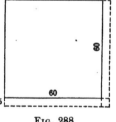

FIG. 288

to the square already constructed by adding to two sides and still keep it a square.

(b) The combined length of the edges to which we are adding is 120 ft. Hence the approximate length of the strip added is 120 ft. Why approximate?

(c) 120 is contained five times in 625 (with a remainder).

(d) If we make the strip 5 ft. wide, the total length will be 125 (for one strip will be 60 ft. and the other 65 ft.).

. (e) 125 is contained exactly five times in 625.

(f) Hence the square must be constructed so as to be 65' by 65'; that is, the square root of 4225 is 65.

3. Find the square root of the polynomial $a^2 + 2\,ab + b^2 + 2\,ac + 2\,bc + c^2$ (see Fig. 289).

Solution. The side of the largest square is a, therefore the trial divisor is $2\,a$. The width of the first strip is b, therefore the divisor is $2\,a + b$. Multiplying by b and subtracting the remainder gives $2\,ac + 2\,bc + c^2$. The length of the square now constructed is $a + b$. The edge to which we are adding is $2\,a + 2\,b$ units long (trial divisor). '$2\,a + 2\,b$ is contained c times in $2\,ac + 2\,bc$. If we make the strip c units wide, the total length of the strip to which we add is $2\,a + 2\,b + c$ (complete divisor). (Why?) Multiplying and subtracting, the remainder is zero. The side of the total square is $a + b + c$, or

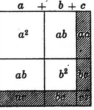

FIG. 289

$$\sqrt{a^2 + 2\,ab + b^2 + 2\,ac + 2\,bc + c^2} = a + b + c.$$

The work may be arranged as follows:

Largest square, a^2 $\underline{a^2 + 2\,ab + b^2 + 2\,ac + 2\,bc + c^2}\,\lfloor\,a + b + c$

    a^2

First trial divisor, $2\,a$ $\overline{2\,ab + b^2}$

First complete divisor, $2\,a + b$ $\underline{2\,ab + b^2}$

Second trial divisor, $2\,a + 2\,b$ $\overline{2\,ac + 2\,bc + c^2}$

Second complete divisor, $2\,a + 2\,b + c$ $2\,ac + 2\,bc + c^2$

4. Find the first digit in the square root of 177,241.

Solution. To determine this first digit we must remember (a) that the square of a number of one digit consists of one or two digits, the square of a number of two digits consists of three or four digits, the square of a number of three digits consists of five or six digits, and so on; (b) that the number of digits in the integral part of the square of a number is twice as large or one less than twice as large as the number of digits in the integral part of the given number. This suggests the following device for determining the number of digits in the integral part of the square root of a number. Beginning at the decimal point, mark off toward the left groups of two digits each. Then the number of digits in the square root will be the same as the number of groups. Thus, since 177,241 is made up of three groups of two digits (17'72'41'), the square root of 177,241 contains three digits in its integral part. We are thus able to estimate the largest square as 400 (that is, the first digit is 4) and then proceed as in Ex. 3. The work may be arranged as follows:

$$17'72'41 | 400 + 20 + 1$$
$$16\ 00\ 00$$

First trial divisor, 800 — $1\ 72\ 41$
First complete divisor, 820 — $1\ 64\ 00$
Second trial divisor, 840 — $8\ 41$
Second complete divisor, 841 — $8\ 41$
Therefore $\sqrt{177241} = 421$.

*447. Steps involved in finding square roots. The following steps were used in Exs. 1–4, above; the student should study them carefully.

1. *Estimate the largest square in the number.*

2. *Double the root already found for a trial divisor.*

3. *Divide the first term of the remainder by the trial divisor, placing the quotient as the next term of the root.*

4. *Annex the term just found to the trial divisor to form a complete divisor and continue the process until the other terms of the root are found.*

EXERCISES

Find the square roots of the following polynomials:

1. $a^2 + 2\,ab + b^2$.

2. $16\,x^2 + 24\,xy + 9\,y^2$.

3. $49\,y^2 - 14\,yz + z^2$.

4. $x^4 + 2\,x^3 + 3\,x^2 + 2\,x + 1$.

5. $4\,a^4 + 4\,a^3 + 9\,a^2 + 4\,a + 4$.

6. $x^4 - 2\,x^3 + 3\,x^2 - 2\,x + 1$.

7. $1 - 4\,a + 6\,a^2 - 4\,a^3 + a^4$.

8. $16\,a^4 - 16\,a^3 + 9 - 12\,a + 32\,a^2$.

9. $x^6 + 4\,ax^4 - 2\,a^3x^3 + 4\,a^2x^2 - 4\,a^4x + a^6$.

10. $9 + 12\,y^2 + 6\,y^3 + 4\,y^4 + 4\,y^5 + y^6$.

11. $x^2 + 8x + 12 - \dfrac{16}{x} + \dfrac{4}{42}$.

12. $\dfrac{9}{4} + 6a - \dfrac{6a^2}{ab^2} + 4a^2 - \dfrac{8a^3}{b^2}$.

13. 576.

14. 9025.

15. 51,529.

16. 61,504.

17. 57,121.

18. 2.

NOTE. Write 2.00′00′00 and proceed as in Ex. 4, Art. 446.

19. 3.

20. 3.1416.

448. Table of roots and powers. In practical situations it is convenient to use a table of roots and powers. There are a number of very useful tables in textbook or leaflet form, and the student is now in a position where he can easily learn how to use them. A very simple table of roots and powers is submitted on page 398. It will frequently prove a great convenience to the student in his work on the following pages.

449. The theorem of Pythagoras. If we study the following exercise carefully we shall discover a well-known geometric theorem which will be useful in later work.

EXERCISE

Construct a right triangle, making the sides including the right angle 3 and 4 units long respectively (see $\triangle ABC$, Fig. 290). Using the same unit, find the length of AB. On each side draw a square and divide each square into unit squares. Counting these squares, find how the square on the hypotenuse compares with the sum of the squares on the other two sides.

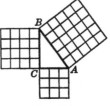

FIG. 290

The preceding exercise illustrates the familiar theorem of Pythagoras:

In a right triangle the sum of the squares on the sides including the right angle is equal to the square on the hypotenuse.

TABLE OF ROOTS AND POWERS

No.	Squares	Cubes	Square Roots	Cube Roots	No.	Squares	Cubes	Square Roots	Cube Roots
1	1	1	1.000	1.000	51	2,601	132,651	7.141	3.708
2	4	8	1.414	1.259	52	2,704	140,608	7.211	3.732
3	9	27	1.732	1.442	53	2,809	148,877	7.280	3.756
4	16	64	2.000	1.587	54	2,916	157,464	7.348	3.779
5	25	125	2.236	1.709	55	3,025	166,375	7.416	3.802
6	36	216	2.449	1.817	56	3,136	175,616	7.483	3.825
7	49	343	2.645	1.912	57	3,249	185,193	7.549	3.848
8	64	512	2.828	2.000	58	3,364	195,112	7.615	3.870
9	81	729	3.000	2.080	59	3,481	205,379	7.681	3.892
10	100	1,000	3.162	2.154	60	3,600	216,000	7.745	3.914
11	121	1,331	3.316	2.223	61	3,721	226,981	7.810	3.936
12	144	1,728	3.464	2.289	62	3,844	238,328	7.874	3.957
13	169	2,197	3.605	2.351	63	3,969	250,047	7.937	3.979
14	196	2,744	3.741	2.410	64	4,096	262,144	8.000	4.000
15	225	3,375	3.872	2.466	65	4,225	274,625	8.062	4.020
16	256	4,096	4.000	2.519	66	4,356	287,496	8.124	4.041
17	289	4,913	4.123	2.571	67	4,489	300,763	8.185	4.061
18	324	5,832	4.242	2.620	68	4,624	314,432	8.246	4.081
19	361	6,859	4.358	2.668	69	4,761	328,509	8.306	4.101
20	400	8,000	4.472	2.714	70	4,900	343,000	8.366	4.121
21	441	9,261	4.582	2.758	71	5,041	357,911	8.426	4.140
22	484	10,648	4.690	2.802	72	5,184	373,248	8.485	4.160
23	529	12,167	4.795	2.843	73	5,329	389,017	8.544	4.179
24	576	13,824	4.898	2.884	74	5,476	405,224	8.602	4.198
25	625	15,625	5.000	2.924	75	5,625	421,875	8.660	4.217
26	676	17,576	5.099	2.962	76	5,776	438,976	8.717	4.235
27	729	19,683	5.196	3.000	77	5,929	456,533	8.774	4.254
28	784	21,952	5.291	3.036	78	6,084	474,552	8.831	4.272
29	841	24,389	5.385	3.072	79	6,241	493,039	8.888	4.290
30	900	27,000	5.477	3.107	80	6,400	512,000	8.944	4.308
31	961	29,791	5.567	3.141	81	6,561	531,441	9.000	4.326
32	1,024	32,768	5.656	3.174	82	6,724	551,368	9.055	4.344
33	1,089	35,937	5.744	3.207	83	6,889	571,787	9.110	4.362
34	1,156	39,304	5.830	3.239	84	7,056	592,704	9.165	4.379
35	1,225	42,875	5.916	3.271	85	7,225	614,125	9.219	4.396
36	1,296	46,656	6.000	3.301	86	7,396	636,056	9.273	4.414
37	1,369	50,653	6.082	3.332	87	7,569	658,503	9.327	4.431
38	1,444	54,872	6.164	3.361	88	7,744	681,472	9.380	4.447
39	1,521	59,319	6.244	3.391	89	7,921	704,969	9.433	4.464
40	1,600	64,000	6.324	3.419	90	8,100	729,000	9.486	4.481
41	1,681	68,921	6.403	3.448	91	8,281	753,571	9.539	4.497
42	1,764	74,088	6.480	3.476	92	8,464	778,688	9.591	4.514
43	1,849	79,507	6.557	3.503	93	8,649	804,357	9.643	4.530
44	1,936	85,184	6.633	3.530	94	8,836	830,584	9.695	4.546
45	2,025	91,125	6.708	3.556	95	9,025	857,375	9.746	4.562
46	2,116	97,336	6.782	3.583	96	9,216	884,736	9.797	4.578
47	2,209	103,823	6.855	3.608	97	9,409	912,673	9.848	4.594
48	2,304	110,592	6.928	3.634	98	9,604	941,192	9.899	4.610
49	2,401	117,649	7.000	3.659	99	9,801	970,299	9.949	4.626
50	2,500	125,000	7.071	3.684	100	10,000	1,000,000	10.000	4.641

This theorem is one of the most famous theorems of geometry. Centuries before Christ the Egyptians used a rope divided by knots so that its three lengths were in the ratio $3:4:5$. This rope was used in land surveying and also in the orientation of their temples. In fact, we read of professional "rope fasteners" (surveyors?). Furthermore, the proof of the theorem itself has always appealed to the interest of mathematicians. When we shall have advanced in our study of mathematics it will be possible for the student to find many proofs of this theorem that he can understand. The earliest general proof is credited to Pythagoras, who lived about 500 B.C.

The student has probably found this theorem to be the basis for one of the most useful rules of arithmetic. The proof given in arithmetic classes is usually that given in the exercise above. However, a general proof demands that we prove the theorem independent of the accuracy of the figure (that is, independent of the measurements and constructions involved). We shall presently give such a proof. The exercises which follow are intended to review the material necessary to establish this proof.

EXERCISES

1. In Fig. 291 $\triangle ABC$ is a right triangle, right-angled at C, with $CD \perp AB$. Review the proof which shows that $\triangle ADC \backsim \triangle ABC$.

2. Prove that in Fig. 291 $\dfrac{c}{b} = \dfrac{b}{m}$ and that $b^2 = cm$.

3. Review the proof which shows that $\triangle BDC \backsim \triangle ABC$.

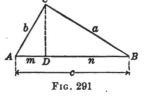

Fig. 291

4. Prove that in Fig. 291 $\dfrac{c}{a} = \dfrac{a}{n}$ and that $a^2 = nc$.

5. Show by using Exs. 2 and 4 that $a^2 + b^2 = c^2$.

450. Theorem of Pythagoras proved. No doubt the student now sees that the theorem of Pythagoras is proved by Exs. 1–5, above. We shall, however, set up the proof for reference.

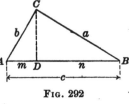

Fig. 292

Given the right triangle ABC, right-angled at C, to prove that the square on the hypotenuse is equal to the sum of the squares on the sides including the right angle. In terms of Fig. 292 this means to prove that $c^2 = a^2 + b^2$.

Proof

STATEMENTS	REASONS
In Fig. 292 draw $CD \perp AB$ and letter the figure as shown.	
Then $\dfrac{m}{b} = \dfrac{b}{c}$, (1)	Because if in a right triangle a line is drawn from the vertex of a right angle perpendicular to the hypotenuse, either side about the right angle is a mean proportional between the whole hypotenuse and the segment of the hypotenuse adjacent to it.
and $\dfrac{n}{a} = \dfrac{a}{c}$. (2)	
In (1) and (2) $b^2 = mc$ and $a^2 = nc$. (3)	Because when four quantities are in proportion the product of the means equals the product of the extremes.
By adding the two equations in (3),	
$a^2 + b^2 = mc + nc$. (4)	Addition axiom.
$a^2 + b^2 = c(m + n)$. (5)	By factoring out c.
But $m + n = c$. (6)	The whole is equal to the sum of all its parts.
$\therefore a^2 + b^2 = c^2$. (7)	By substitution.

PYTHAGORAS

HISTORICAL NOTE. Pythagoras (c. 569 B.C.–c. 500 B.C.), the second of the great philosophers of Greece, is said to have "changed the study of geometry into the form of a liberal education." After some wanderings, he founded the famous Pythagorean School at Croton, a Dorian colony in the south of Italy. Here enthusiastic audiences composed of citizens of all ranks, especially the upper classes, crowded to hear him. It is said that the women went to hear him in direct violation of a law against their public appearance.

Pythagoras divided his audiences into two classes: the Probationers (or listeners) and the Pythagoreans (or mathematicians). After three years in the first class a listener could be initiated into the second class, to whom were confided the main discoveries of the school.

The Pythagoreans formed a brotherhood in which each member was bound by oath not to reveal the teachings or secrets of the school. Their food was simple, their discipline severe, and their mode of life arranged to encourage self-command, temperance, purity, and obedience.

The triple interwoven triangle, or pentagram (star-shaped regular pentagon), was used as a sign of recognition, and was to them a symbol of health. It is related that a Pythagorean while traveling fell ill and, although carefully nursed by a kind-hearted innkeeper, was unable to survive. Before dying, however, he inscribed the pentagram star on a board and begged his host to hang it up outside. This the host did; and after a considerable length of time another Pythagorean, passing by, noticed the sign and, after hearing the innkeeper's story, rewarded him handsomely. One motto of the brotherhood was: "A figure and a step forwards; not a figure to gain three oboli."

The views of society advocated by the brotherhood were opposite to those of the democratic party of Pythagoras's time, and hence most of the brotherhood were aristocrats. For a short time the Pythagoreans succeeded in dominating affairs, but a popular revolt in 501 B.C led to the murder of many prominent members of the school, and Pythagoras himself was killed shortly afterwards.

Though the brotherhood no longer existed as a political party, the Pythagoreans continued to exist a long time as a philosophical and mathematical society, but to the end remained a secret organization, publishing nothing, and thus leaving us little information as to the details of their history. See Ball's "A History of Mathematics," p. 19.

1. The base and altitude of a right triangle (Fig. 293) are 6 and 8 respectively. What is the length of the hypotenuse? (Use the theorem of Pythagoras.)

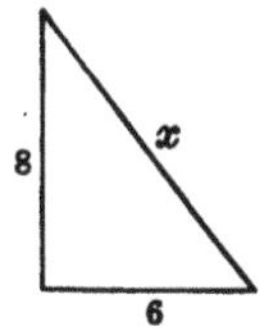

2. How long must a rope be run from the top of a 16-foot tent pole to a point 20 ft. from the foot of the pole?

3. A baseball diamond is a square a side of which is 90 ft. What is the length of a throw from "home" to "second"?

FIG. 293

4. Find the formula for the diagonal of a square whose side is s. Use this formula to determine the diagonal when $s = 10$; when $s = 15$.

5. Prove from the Pythagorean theorem that $a = \sqrt{c^2 - b^2}$ and translate the equation into words.

6. Prove also that $b = \sqrt{c^2 - a^2}$ and translate the equation into words.

7. A ladder 20 ft. long just reaches a window 15 ft. above the ground. How far is the foot of the ladder from the foot of the wall if the ground is level?

8. The hypotenuse of a right triangle is 35 ft. and the altitude is 21 ft. Find the base.

9. Using the formula of Ex. 6, find the value of a when $c = 22$ and $b = 20$.

10. A tree standing on level ground was broken 24 ft. from the ground, and the top struck the ground 18 ft. from the stump, the broken end remaining on the stump. How tall was the tree before breaking?

11. Construct on squared paper a right triangle, using the following pairs of numbers for the base and altitude respectively: 1 and 1; 1 and $\sqrt{2}$; 2 and 2; 2 and 3; 4 and 4; 4 and 5; 1 and 5; 2 and 5; 3 and 5; 12 and 1.

HINT. Use the line segment you obtained for the first part.

12. Calculate for each part of Ex. 11 the length of the hypotenuse.

451. The theorem of Pythagoras furnishes a method of constructing with ruler and compasses the square root of a number. Exercises 11 and 12, Art. 450, suggest a method of finding the square root of a number by means of ruler and compasses. The method is illustrated by the following exercise:

Construct the square root of 42.

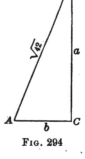

The following study (analysis) of the exercise will help us to understand the problem.

Suppose that we have the figure constructed; that is, let us imagine that Fig. 294 is the required figure and that AB is the required length $\sqrt{42}$.

Now a and b can be of various lengths provided $a^2 + b^2 = 42$. (Why?) Let us suppose that $CB = 6$; then how long is b? We know that $36 + b^2 = 42$ would be the equation from which the value of b can be found. It is clear that b would have to equal $\sqrt{6}$.

FIG. 294

Then the problem merely becomes one of learning how to construct $\sqrt{6}$. Some members of the class may already know how to do this, but we shall proceed with our analysis.

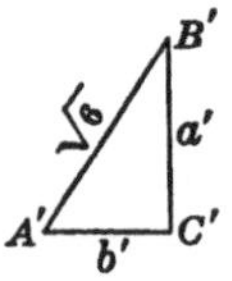

Imagine another triangle, $A'B'C'$ (Fig. 295), so constructed that the hypotenuse turns out to be $\sqrt{6}$ and so that $B'C'$ is 2 units long; then $A'C'$ must equal $\sqrt{2}$. Why?

Our problem finally reduces, then, to a problem of constructing $\sqrt{2}$. If we can find this geometrically we can solve the original exercise, as our analysis has shown.

FIG. 295

We already know how to construct $\sqrt{2}$ by constructing a right triangle with the two legs about the right angle equal to 1. Then the hypotenuse equals $\sqrt{2}$. Why?

We then reverse our analysis as follows:

(a) Construct $\sqrt{2}$ as indicated above.

(b) Construct a second right triangle with a base of $\sqrt{2}$ units long and an altitude 2 units long. Its hypotenuse will equal $\sqrt{6}$. Why?

(c) Construct a third right triangle whose base is $\sqrt{6}$ units long and whose altitude is 6 units long. Its hypotenuse will be $\sqrt{42}$ units. Why?

EXERCISE

Construct with compasses a line segment equivalent to each of the following: $\sqrt{6}$; $\sqrt{11}$; $\sqrt{27}$; $\sqrt{143}$; $\sqrt{214}$; $3\sqrt{3}$; $2\sqrt{2}$.

452. Mean proportional construction a method for finding square roots. We shall now see that our mean proportional construction (Art. 374) furnishes us with an easy method of constructing square roots.

EXERCISES

1. Review the construction (Art. 374) for finding a mean proportional between two line segments a and b (Fig. 296).

2. Construct the mean proportional between 4 and 9; 4 and 16.

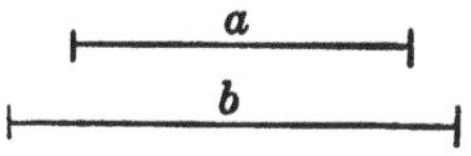

3. Review the proof for the statement that a mean proportional between two line segments a and b equals the square root of the product of a and b.

FIG. 296

The preceding exercises suggest that the mean proportional construction furnishes a method for finding the square root of a number. For example,

Find the square root of 12.

On squared paper find the mean proportional of two factors of 12, for example, 2 and 6. The mean proportional x (Fig. 297) is the square root of 12, for

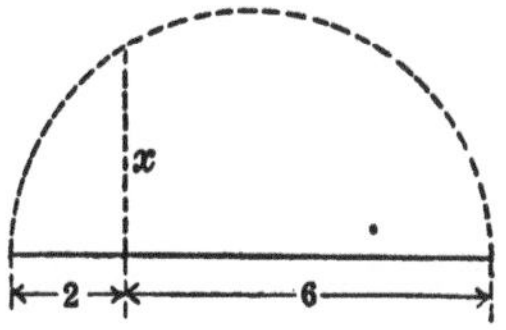

$$\frac{2}{x} = \frac{x}{6}.$$ Why?

$$x^2 = 12.$$ Why?

Whence $x = \sqrt{12}.$ Why?

FIG. 297. MEAN PROPORTIONAL METHOD OF FINDING THE SQUARE ROOT OF A NUMBER

Construct the square root of 21; 6; 5; 18; 42; 84; 66; 76. Compare the results with the table of Art. 449. Your results ought to approximate the second decimal place.

453. Large numbers under the radical signs. When the number under the radical sign is large, the various geometric constructions for finding square roots are neither convenient nor, in general, sufficiently accurate. In this case it is of advantage to reduce the given *quadratic surd* to an equivalent expression which has a smaller number under the radical sign. Suppose we wish to find the value of $\sqrt{5056}$. The square root is at once evident if we resolve the number into two equal groups of factors; thus:

$$\sqrt{5056} = \sqrt{(2^2 \cdot 3 \cdot 7)(2^2 \cdot 3 \cdot 7)} = \sqrt{84 \cdot 84} = 84.$$

Even when the number is not a perfect square, factoring will often enable the student to find its square root much more easily, as will be shown later.

EXERCISES

Find the following indicated square roots:

1. $\sqrt{576}$. 3. $\sqrt{484}$. 5. $\sqrt{3600}$. 7. $\sqrt{289}$.

2. $\sqrt{1296}$. 4. $\sqrt{1089}$. 6. $\sqrt{1936}$. 8. $\sqrt{324}$.

454. The square root of a product. The preceding exercises show that the square root of the product of several factors, each of which is a square, may be found by taking the square root of each factor separately, as in the following examples:

1. $\sqrt{9 \cdot 25} = \sqrt{9}\sqrt{25} = 3 \cdot 5 = 15.$

This is true because $9 \cdot 25$ can be written as the product of two groups of equal factors $(3 \cdot 5)(3 \cdot 5)$. Hence, by the definition of a square root, $(3 \cdot 5)$ is the square root of $9 \cdot 25$.

2. $\sqrt{16\,x^4 y^6} = \sqrt{16}\,\sqrt{x^4}\,\sqrt{y^6} = 4\,x^2 y^3$.

This is true because $16\,x^4 y^6$ may be written as the product of two groups of equal factors $(4\,x^2 y^3)(4\,x^2 y^3)$. Hence $4\,x^2 y^3$ is the square root of $16\,x^4 y^6$.

The preceding exercises show that *the square root of a product is obtained by finding the square root of each factor separately and then taking the product of these roots.* That is, in general,

$$\sqrt{a \cdot b} = \sqrt{a} \cdot \sqrt{b}.$$

This principle may be used to simplify radical surds in the following manner. Suppose we wish to find the value of $\sqrt{11858}$. Then

$$\sqrt{11858} = \sqrt{2 \cdot 11 \cdot 11 \cdot 7 \cdot 7}$$
$$= \sqrt{11 \cdot 11}\,\sqrt{7 \cdot 7}\,\sqrt{2}$$
$$= 11 \cdot 7\,\sqrt{2}$$
$$= 77\,\sqrt{2}.$$

By the table of roots, $\sqrt{2} = 1.414$.

Then $77\,(1.414) = 108.878$.

Hence $\sqrt{11858} = 108.878$.

It will be helpful to observe the following:

(1) The principle enables us to simplify the radicand to a point where we can easily find the root by the table or by several geometric constructions.

(2) A quadratic surd is in its simplest form when the number under the radical sign does not contain a perfect square factor.

In general, if the expression under the radical sign contains a factor which is a square, this factor may be removed by writing its square root before the radical sign.

Change the following so as to leave no factor which is a square under the radical sign:

1. $\sqrt{12}$.	6. $\sqrt{28}$.	11. $\sqrt{x^5}$.	16. $\sqrt{8\,a^2b^2}$.
2. $\sqrt{40}$.	7. $\sqrt{75}$.	12. $\sqrt{x^3y}$.	17. $\sqrt{72\,x^3y}$.
3. $\sqrt{18}$.	8. $\sqrt{125}$.	13. $\sqrt{x^4y}$.	18. $\sqrt{128\,x^3y^2}$.
4. $\sqrt{50}$.	9. $\sqrt{108}$.	14. $\sqrt{a^2b^5}$.	19. $\sqrt{8\,a^8b^8}$.
5. $\sqrt{72}$.	10. $\sqrt{a^3}$.	15. $\sqrt{a^2b^4x}$.	20. $\sqrt{x^{21}}$.

455. Value of memorizing square roots of certain numbers. Exercises 1–9, Art. 454, suggest the manner in which the square roots of a few small numbers, like 2, 3, 5, are made to do service in finding the roots of many large numbers. In fact, many students in other fields find that memorizing these numbers, which occur again and again in their problems, increases their efficiency.

From the table of roots we know that $\sqrt{2}=1.414$, $\sqrt{3}=1.732$, and $\sqrt{5}=2.236$. Using these facts, compute each of the following correct to two decimal places:

1. $\sqrt{75}$.	4. $\sqrt{72}$.	7. $\sqrt{50} + \sqrt{75} - \sqrt{6}$.
2. $\sqrt{80}$.	5. $\sqrt{98}$.	8. $2\sqrt{32} + \sqrt{72} - \sqrt{18}$.
3. $\sqrt{48}$.	6. $\sqrt{363}$.	9. $\sqrt{45} - \sqrt{\frac{1}{5}}$.

456. The square root of a fraction. A fraction is squared by squaring its numerator and its denominator separately and indicating the product thus: $\dfrac{a}{b} \times \dfrac{a}{b} = \dfrac{a^2}{b^2}$. Hence, to extract the square root of a fraction, we find the square root of its numerator and denominator separately.

For example, $\sqrt{\frac{9}{16}} = \frac{3}{4}$, since $\frac{3}{4} \cdot \frac{3}{4} = \frac{9}{16}$.

Find the square roots of the following accurate to two places (use the table for square roots):

1. $\frac{3}{4}$. 2. $\frac{2}{3}$. 3. $\frac{7}{16}$. 4. $\frac{3}{5}$. 5. $\frac{9}{8}$. 6. $\frac{16}{5}$. 7. $\frac{3}{10}$. 8. $\frac{2}{27}$.

457. Rationalizing the denominator of a fraction. It probably has been noticed that the calculation of those problems of the preceding lists in which the denominator is a square is far easier than when this is not the case. This may be illustrated as follows:

$$\sqrt{\frac{2}{3}} = \frac{\sqrt{2}}{\sqrt{3}} = \frac{1.414}{1.732}.$$

Dividing 1.414 by 1.732 is not an easy division. In fact, most people would find it impossible to do mentally. On the other hand, $\sqrt{\frac{6}{9}} = \frac{\sqrt{6}}{\sqrt{9}} = \frac{2.449}{3} = 0.816$ involves an easy mental division.

It is of interest to note that the denominator of a fraction can always be made a square merely by multiplying numerator and denominator by the proper factor; thus, $\sqrt{\frac{2}{3}} = \sqrt{\frac{6}{9}} = \frac{\sqrt{6}}{3} = \frac{2.449}{3} = 0.816$. Note that the division $\frac{2.449}{3}$ is an easy mental division compared with the division $\frac{1.414}{1.732}$, which we had above.

We may summarize this method of taking the square root of a fraction as follows:

1. *To find the square root of a fraction, change the fraction into an equivalent fraction whose denominator is a perfect square.*

2. *The square root of the new fraction equals the square root of its numerator divided by the square root of its denominator.*

3. *If desired, express the result in simplest decimal form.*

The process of changing a radical expression so as to leave no denominator under a radical sign is called *rationalizing* the denominator. Thus, $\sqrt{\dfrac{1}{3}} = \dfrac{1}{3}\sqrt{3}$; $\sqrt{\dfrac{1}{a}} = \dfrac{1}{a}\sqrt{a}$.

EXERCISES

1. Find the value of the following square roots (find values approximately accurate to the second decimal place):

(a) $\frac{7}{5}$.　(b) $\frac{3}{7}$.　(c) $\frac{1}{2}$.　(d) $\frac{1}{8}$.　(e) $\frac{2}{3}$.　(f) $\frac{1}{7}$.　(g) $\frac{1}{10}$.

2. Rationalize denominators of the following, and simplify:

(a) $\sqrt{\dfrac{13}{5}}$.　(c) $\sqrt{\dfrac{1}{2}}$.　(e) $\sqrt{\dfrac{1}{a^3}}$.　(g) $\sqrt{\dfrac{5}{7a}}$.　(i) $\dfrac{1}{\sqrt{ab}}$.

(b) $\sqrt{\dfrac{5}{3}}$.　(d) $\sqrt{\dfrac{1}{3}}$.　(f) $\sqrt{\dfrac{4a^3}{b}}$.　(h) $\sqrt{\dfrac{1}{ab}}$.　(j) $\sqrt{\dfrac{2b}{3a^3}}$.

3. What is the value of the expressions in Ex. 2 from (e) to (j), inclusive, if $a = 3$ and $b = 2$?

458. Addition and subtraction of surds. Sometimes the arithmetic in a problem may be simplified if the surds are combined into one term. Thus,

$$\sqrt{20} + \sqrt{45} = 2\sqrt{5} + 3\sqrt{5}$$
$$= 5\sqrt{5}, \text{ or } 5(2.236)$$
$$= 11.180.$$

By adding $2\sqrt{5} + 3\sqrt{5}$ just as we add $2 \cdot 4$ plus $3 \cdot 4$, we need only to look up the $\sqrt{5}$, whereas $\sqrt{20} + \sqrt{45}$ calls for two square roots.

In the following list simplify each expression as far as possible without using approximate roots; that is, leave your result in indicated form. Practically this is often better than finding an approximation, for in this manner you submit results that are absolutely accurate. It leaves the approximation to the next person, who may find as many decimal places as the needs of his particular problem demand.

EXERCISES

1. $\sqrt{108} + \sqrt{75} + \sqrt{12}$.

2. $2\sqrt{98} - \sqrt{18}$.

3. $6\sqrt{288} - 4\sqrt{18} + \sqrt{128}$.

4. $5\sqrt{432} - 4\sqrt{3} + \sqrt{147}$.

5. $2\sqrt{27} + 3\sqrt{48} - 3\sqrt{75}$.

6. $3\sqrt{20} + 2\sqrt{125} - \sqrt{180}$.

7. $\sqrt{\frac{2}{5}} + \sqrt{\frac{1}{10}} + \sqrt{\frac{18}{5}}$.

8. $\frac{3}{5} + \sqrt{\frac{2}{25}}$.

9. $\sqrt{\frac{2}{3}} + \sqrt{\frac{1}{27}}$.

10. $\sqrt{\frac{3}{8}} - 2\sqrt{24}$.

11. $\frac{2}{3} + \sqrt{\frac{4}{3}}$.

12. $-\frac{5}{6} + \sqrt{\frac{1}{6}}$.

13. $\sqrt{\frac{1}{2}} - 2\sqrt{2} + \sqrt{\frac{9}{2}}$.

14. $4\sqrt{28} + 3\sqrt{63} - \sqrt{112}$.

459. Multiplication and division of quadratic surds. These two processes will be treated briefly. In elementary mathematics there are few verbal problems which involve this process. Further, the principles involved do not offer anything new for us.

Thus, to divide $\sqrt{2}$ by $\sqrt{5}$, we may write this in the form of a fraction $\dfrac{\sqrt{2}}{\sqrt{5}}$ and proceed as we ordinarily do when finding the value of a fraction which involves quadratic surds.

The rule in multiplication is equally familiar. The equation $\sqrt{ab} = \sqrt{a}\sqrt{b}$ may be read just as well from right to left, and we have $\sqrt{a}\sqrt{b} = \sqrt{ab}$. Thus, $\sqrt{2}\sqrt{5}$ is precisely the same as $\sqrt{10}$.

1. Find the product of the following:

(a) $\sqrt{3}\sqrt{27}$.

(d) $\sqrt{6x}\sqrt{12x^3}$.

(b) $\sqrt{x}\sqrt{x^3}$.

(e) $\sqrt{\frac{7}{8}}\sqrt{1\frac{2}{5}}$.

(c) $\sqrt{3}\sqrt{5}$.

(f) $\sqrt{\frac{1}{2}}\sqrt{\frac{2}{3}}\sqrt{\frac{3}{4}}\sqrt{\frac{4}{5}}$.

(g) $(\sqrt{2}+\sqrt{3}-\sqrt{5})(\sqrt{2}-\sqrt{3}+\sqrt{5})$.

Solution. We multiply each term of one polynomial by each term of the other and simplify the result as follows:

$$\begin{array}{r} \sqrt{2}+\sqrt{3}-\sqrt{5} \\ \sqrt{2}-\sqrt{3}+\sqrt{5} \\ \hline 2+\sqrt{6}-\sqrt{10} \\ -\sqrt{6} \qquad -3+\sqrt{15} \\ +\sqrt{10} \qquad +\sqrt{15}-5 \\ \hline 2\sqrt{15}-6 \end{array}$$

(h) $(2\sqrt{7}+\sqrt{3}-\sqrt{5})(\sqrt{5})$.

(i) $(4\sqrt{2}-2\sqrt{3}+\sqrt{5})(2\sqrt{3})$.

(j) $(\sqrt{5}-3\sqrt{2}+\sqrt{10})(\sqrt{5})$.

(k) $(3\sqrt{2}+4\sqrt{3})(2\sqrt{2}-5\sqrt{3})$.

(l) $(\sqrt{3}-\sqrt{4}+\sqrt{5})(\sqrt{3}+\sqrt{4}-\sqrt{5})$.

2. Divide, and express the result in simplest form:

(a) 1 by $\sqrt{5}$.

(c) $\sqrt{6}$ by $\sqrt{3}$.

(b) 24 by $\sqrt{3}$.

(d) $2\sqrt{12}-5\sqrt{15}$ by $\sqrt{3}$.

460. Fractional exponents another means of indicating roots and powers. Thus far we have not used a fraction as an exponent, and evidently it could not be so used without extending the meaning of the word "exponent."

Thus, x^3 means $x \cdot x \cdot x$, but $x^{\frac{1}{2}}$ evidently cannot mean that x is to be used as a factor one half of a time.

It is very important that all exponents should be governed by the same laws; therefore, instead of giving a formal definition of fractional exponents, we shall lay down the one condition that the laws for integral exponents shall be generally true, and we shall permit the fractional exponent to assume a meaning necessary in order that the exponent laws shall hold.

Since we agree that $x^{\frac{1}{2}} \cdot x^{\frac{1}{2}} = x$, we see that $x^{\frac{1}{2}}$ is one of the two equal factors of x; that is, $x^{\frac{1}{2}}$ is the square root of x, or we may write $x^{\frac{1}{2}} = \sqrt{x}$.

Similarly, since $x^{\frac{1}{3}} \cdot x^{\frac{1}{3}} \cdot x^{\frac{1}{3}} = x$, $x^{\frac{1}{3}}$ is the cube root of x; that is, $x^{\frac{1}{3}} = \sqrt[3]{x}$.

Again, $x^{\frac{2}{3}} \cdot x^{\frac{2}{3}} \cdot x^{\frac{2}{3}} = x^{\frac{6}{3}} = x^2$. This means that $x^{\frac{2}{3}}$ is the cube root of x^2; that is, $x^{\frac{2}{3}} = \sqrt[3]{x^2}$.

This discussion is sufficient to show that the fractional exponent under the laws which govern integral exponents takes on a meaning which makes a fractional exponent just another way of indicating roots and powers; that is, *the denominator indicates the root, and the numerator indicates the power.*

Thus, $8^{\frac{2}{3}}$ means to take the cube root of 8 and square the result, or square 8 and take the cube root of the result. In either case the final result is 4. Again, $10^{\frac{2}{3}}$ (or $10^{0.6666}$) means to take the cube root of 100, which, by the table of Art. 449, is 4.641. Note that a common-fraction exponent may appear as a decimal fraction.

From this it will be obvious that the student needs only to become familiar with the new method of writing roots and powers. The following brief list of problems presents precisely the same ideas as those in the preceding list dealing with surds; only the form is different.

1. Write in simplest form:

(a) $4^{\frac{1}{2}} + 9^{\frac{1}{2}} + 16^{\frac{1}{2}} + 25^{\frac{1}{2}} + 36^{\frac{1}{2}}$.

(b) $1^{\frac{1}{3}} + 8^{\frac{1}{3}} + 64^{\frac{1}{3}} + 0^{\frac{1}{3}}$.

(c) $64^{\frac{1}{6}} + 9^{\frac{1}{2}} + 16^{\frac{1}{4}} + (-32)^{\frac{1}{5}} - (-27)^{\frac{1}{3}}$.

(d) $24^{\frac{1}{2}} + 54^{\frac{1}{2}} - 6^{\frac{1}{2}}$.

(e) $18^{\frac{1}{2}} + 32^{\frac{1}{2}} - \sqrt{128} + \sqrt{2}$.

(f) $(\frac{1}{2})^{\frac{1}{2}} + 8^{\frac{1}{2}} - (\frac{9}{2})^{\frac{1}{2}} + (50)^{\frac{1}{2}}$.

(g) $(81)^{\frac{1}{2}} - 2(24)^{\frac{1}{3}} + \sqrt{28} + 2(63)^{\frac{1}{2}}$.

(h) $\left(\dfrac{m}{3}\right)^{\frac{1}{2}} + (3\,m)^{\frac{1}{2}} + (27)^{\frac{1}{2}}\sqrt{m} - \sqrt{\dfrac{100\,m}{3}}$.

2. Multiply:

(a) $x^{\frac{1}{2}}x^{\frac{1}{4}}$.

(c) $10^{2.5} \cdot 10^{0.125} \cdot 10^{1.25}$.

(b) $10^{\frac{3}{2}} \cdot 10^{\frac{1}{4}} \cdot 10^{\frac{3}{4}}$.

(d) $10^{2.6250} \cdot 10^{0.3750} \cdot 10^{0.0625}$.

3. Translate (c) and (d), Ex. 2, into expressions with common fractions as exponents and estimate how large the numbers would be if we had a way of finding the result.

NOTE. $10^{0.375}$ means $10^{\frac{3}{8}}$, or the eighth root of 1000. Another way to look at it is that 10 is to be raised to the 375th power and the thousandth root taken. These ideas are of very great importance in getting a clear understanding of the chapters on logarithms and the slide rule. In these chapters we shall learn how to find a root (say the *15th*) just as easily as the square root.

461. Zero exponents. Under the laws which govern integral exponents $a^0 = 1$, as is shown by the following:

$a^5 \div a^5 = a^0$. (By the Division Law.)

$a^5 \div a^5 = 1$. (The quotient of any number divided by itself is 1.)

Hence $a^0 = 1$. (By the equality axiom.)

Thus the zero power of any number (except zero) is 1.

Thus, $15^0 = 1$; $(560)^0 = 1$; $(-6\,x)^0 = 1$; $10^0 = 1$.

462. Negative exponents. If x^{-3} obeys the same law as integral exponents, then

$$\frac{x^{-3}}{1} \times \frac{x^3}{x^3} = \frac{x^0}{x^3}, \quad \text{or} \quad \frac{1}{x^3};$$

that is,
$$x^{-3} = \frac{1}{x^3}.$$

Similarly, if we multiply the numerator and denominator of $\frac{x^{-a}}{1}$ by x^a, we obtain $x^{-a} = \frac{1}{x^a}$.

Thus, $\dfrac{1}{10^{-2}} = \dfrac{10^2}{1}$, or 100; $10^{-2} = \dfrac{1}{100}$; $10^{-3} = \dfrac{1}{1000}$; $\dfrac{1}{10^{-4}} = 10,000$.

See if you can state in simple language the meaning of a negative exponent.

EXERCISES

Simplify:

1. $10^{-2} \times 10^{3.125} \times 10^{0.0625} \times 10^{-1.03875}$.

2. $10^{\frac{3}{4}} \times 10^0 \times (56)^0 \times 10^{\frac{1}{4}}$.

3. $(39)(169)^{-\frac{1}{2}}$.

4. $1000 \cdot (100)^{-\frac{3}{2}}$.

5. $2^x \times 2^{-x} \times 2$.

6. $16 \cdot 2^{-4}$.

7. $1000 \cdot 10^{-3}$.

8. $144^{-\frac{1}{2}} \cdot 24$.

9. $x^m \cdot x^n$.

10. $x^{\frac{a}{b}} \cdot x^{\frac{a}{c}}$.

11. $x^m \div x^n$.

12. $(+625)^{\frac{1}{4}}$; $(-125)^{-\frac{1}{3}}$.

13. $(x^2)^3$; $(x^3)^4$; $(x^5)^2$.

   HINT. $(x^2)^3 = x^2 \cdot x^2 \cdot x^2$.

14. $(10^2)^2$; $(10^2)^3$; $(10^2)^4$.

15. $(10^{0.125})^2$; $(10^{0.0625})^4$; $(10^{0.125})^8$.

16. $(x^m)^n$; translate the formula $(x^m)^n = x^{mn}$ into an algebraic rule.

17. $\sqrt[3]{x^6}$; $\sqrt[2]{x^8}$; $\sqrt[3]{x^{12}}$.

   NOTE. The 3 in $\sqrt[3]{x^6}$ means "find the cube root."

18. $\sqrt[3]{10^3}$; $\sqrt[2]{10^4}$.

19. Since $(x^m)^n = x^{mn}$, what is $\sqrt[n]{x^{mn}}$? $\sqrt[n]{x^m}$?

Translate the formula $\sqrt[n]{x^m} = x^{\frac{m}{n}}$ into an algebraic rule.

20. Find the value of:

(a) $\sqrt{10^{2.125}}$.   (b) $\sqrt[3]{10^{3.375}}$.   (c) $\sqrt[4]{10^{3.6250}}$.   (d) $\sqrt[5]{10^{5.8750}}$.

463. Cube of a binomial. We shall now see how certain other short cuts in finding powers may be illustrated and explained.

INTRODUCTORY EXERCISES

1. Find the cube of $x + y$ by first finding the square of $x + y$ and multiplying the result by $x + y$.

2. By multiplication find $(a + b)^3$.

3. Find the cube of $(x - y)$; of $(a - b)$. Compare these cubes with the results of Exs. 1 and 2.

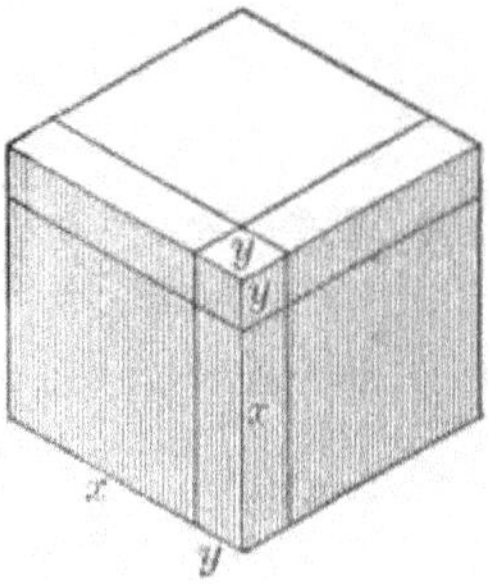

4. It will be helpful to your classmates if you will make a set of blocks, as shown in Fig. 298, in order to show that

$$(x + y)^3 = x^3 + 3 x^2 y + 3 x y^2 + y^3.$$

How many blocks are needed?

5. Find the following cubes, doing as many as you can mentally:

FIG. 298

(a) $(c + d)^3$.   (c) $(c - d)^3$.   (e) $(x + 2 y)^3$.   (g) $(2 x + 3 y)^3$.

(b) $(m + n)^3$.   (d) $(m - n)^3$.   (f) $(2 x - y)^3$.   (h) $(2 x - 3 y)^3$.

Exercises 1–5 show that *the cube of a binomial is equal to the cube of the first term, plus three times the square of the first term multiplied by the second, plus three times the first term multiplied by the square of the second, plus the cube of the second term.*

SIR ISAAC NEWTON

HISTORICAL NOTE. The first use of positive and negative fractions as exponents is found in a book written by the great English mathematician and physicist, Sir Isaac Newton (1642-1727). He discovered the binomial theorem and numerous laws of physics; for example, the law of gravitation, the law about lenses and prisms, and the explanation of the rainbow: Among his numerous books are " Universal Arithmetic " (really an algebra) and " Principia " (one of the greatest books of all times).

The biography of Newton (see Ball's " A Short History of Mathematics," pp. 328-362, and Cajori's "A History of Elementary Mathematics," pp. 238-240) is very interesting and inspiring. As a boy he was expected to be learning how to take care of his father's farm, but he spent much of his time studying and trying mechanical experiments. Thus, we read of his constructing a clock run by water which kept very fair time. His mother noticing this sensibly resolved to send him to Cambridge. Here followed a brilliant career of thirty-five years as student and teacher. As a professor it was his practice to lecture publicly once a week, and then only from half an hour to an hour at a time. In the week following he gave four hours of consultation to students who wished to discuss the results of the previous lecture. It is said that he never repeated a course and that one course began at the point where the preceding course had ended. The result of his second study during this period has dazed master minds who have attempted to understand all that Newton accomplished. Perhaps you will later agree with some of the following tributes to him:

> Nature and Nature's laws lay hid in night :
> God said, " Let Newton be ! " and all was light. — POPE

> There, Priest of Nature ! dost thou shine,
> Newton ! a king among the kings divine. — SOUTHEY

Taking mathematics from the beginning of the world to the time when Newton lived, what he had done was much the better half. — LEIBNITZ

I don't know what I may seem to the world, but as to myself, I seem to have been only as a boy playing on the sea-shore, and diverting myself in now and then finding a smoother pebble or a prettier shell than ordinary, whilst the great ocean of truth lay all undiscovered before me. — NEWTON

464. Cube roots. The equation $y = x^3$ asserts that y is the cube of x, or, inversely, x is the cube root of y.

If the equation is graphed we shall obtain a curve analogous to the curve for squares and square roots which may be used to find cube roots and cubes. We proceed to find corresponding values for y and x in order that we may plot sufficient points for the curve.

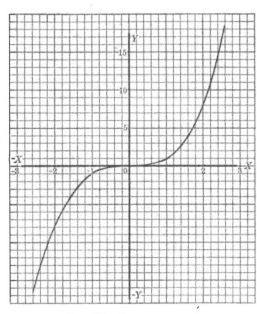

Fig. 299. Graph of $y = x^3$

EXERCISES

1. What is the value of y in the equation $y = x^3$ when x equals 0? when $x = +1$? when $x = -1$? when $x = +2$? when $x = -2$?

2. Calculate values as in Ex. 1 and fill the blank spaces of the following table. If the curve is not obvious, expand the table until you have enough points to draw the curve.

x	0	+1	+2	-2	±3	±4	±5	±6	±7	±$\frac{1}{2}$	±$\frac{1}{3}$	±$\frac{2}{3}$	±$\frac{3}{4}$	±$\frac{3}{2}$	±$\frac{5}{2}$	±$\frac{7}{2}$
y	0	+1	+8	-8	±27											

From this table we may obtain the curve in Fig. 299. One small square vertically represents 1 unit, and 5 small squares horizontally represent 1 unit.

From this curve we can read off, approximately, the cube or the cube root of any number; thus the cube of 2.2 is seen to be about 10.5 (by the table actually 10.64); the cube root of 13 is seen to be a little over 2.4 (see the table for values accurate to two decimal places). More accurate results can be obtained by drawing the curve to a large scale.

465. Cube roots of arithmetical numbers. An arithmetical method for finding cube roots based on an algebraic formula for $(a + b)^3$ could be devised. But this method is seldom used, because cube roots as well as higher roots are more quickly found by means of logarithms. This method will be taught in the next chapter. In the meantime the student may for all practical purposes use the table in Art. 449.

Furthermore, we could devise analogous rules and curves for fourth roots, fifth roots, fourth powers, and so on, but these too are more readily found by logarithms.

466. Indicating higher roots. By means of an *index figure* the radical sign is made to indicate other roots than square roots.

Thus the cube root of 8 or one of its three equal factors is written $\sqrt[3]{8} = 2$. The fourth root of 16 is written $\sqrt[4]{16} = 2$. The 3 in $\sqrt[3]{8}$ is the *index* of the root.

Any expression which contains an indicated root is called a *radical expression*.

The principles of reducing surds to simpler forms, discussed in detail for quadratic surds, may be applied to higher indicated roots.

1. Simplify the following (remove any factor which is a perfect power of the degree indicated by the index):

$\sqrt[3]{32}$; $\sqrt[5]{64}$; $\sqrt[5]{64\,x^6 y^6}$; $\sqrt[4]{48\,a^4}$; $\sqrt[4]{16\,a^4 b^7}$; $\sqrt[6]{64}$; $\sqrt[6]{x^{24} y}$.

2. Add and subtract as indicated:

(a) $\sqrt[3]{16} + \sqrt[3]{54} - \sqrt[3]{250} + \sqrt[3]{128}$.

(b) $\sqrt[3]{54} + \sqrt[3]{128} + \sqrt[3]{1024} + \sqrt[3]{2000}$.

(c) $\sqrt[4]{32} + \sqrt[4]{162} + \sqrt[4]{512} - \sqrt[4]{1250}$.

SUMMARY

467. This chapter has taught the meaning of the following words and phrases: square root of a number, quadratic surd, radical sign, radicand, quadratic trinomial square, index.

468. The graph of the equation $y = x^2$ was used as a device for finding squares and square roots.

469. A positive number has two square roots; thus, $\sqrt{4} = + 2$ or $- 2$.

470. The square of the sum or difference of two numbers may be found by the formula

$$(a \pm b)^2 = a^2 \pm 2\,ab + b^2.$$

This formula was illustrated geometrically.

471. To find the square root of a perfect square trinomial: *Extract the square roots of the two perfect square terms and connect them by the sign of the remaining term.*

472. The square of a trinomial consists of the sum of the squares of its terms plus twice the product of each term by each succeeding term. By remembering this rule the square roots of some polynomials may be found by inspection.

473. The chapter taught a method of finding the square root of algebraic polynomials and arithmetical numbers.

474. The chapter includes a simple table of square roots and cube roots.

475. Quadratic surds may often be simplified by applying the principle $\sqrt{ab} = \sqrt{a}\sqrt{b}$.

476. We find the square root of a fraction by dividing the square root of the numerator by the square root of the denominator; that is, $\sqrt{\dfrac{a}{b}} = \dfrac{\sqrt{a}}{\sqrt{b}}$.

477. Rationalizing the denominator simplifies the calculation; that is, $\sqrt{\dfrac{3}{2}}$ is more difficult than $\dfrac{\sqrt{6}}{2}$.

478. When the same number occurs as the radical in a series of terms, the terms may be combined by the rule for adding similar terms. This usually simplifies the calculation.

479. The theorem of Pythagoras was proved.

480. The theorem of Pythagoras furnishes a method of constructing the square root of a number.

481. The mean proportional construction furnishes another method of finding the square root.

482. A fractional exponent is another method of indicating roots and powers; thus, $x^{\frac{2}{3}}$ means $\sqrt[3]{x^2}$. The numerator indicates the power, and the denominator the root.

483. a^0 is defined as 1.

484. A number with a negative exponent is defined so as to be equal to the reciprocal of the same number with a positive exponent; that is, $a^{-5} = \dfrac{1}{a^5}$.

485. The cube of a binomial may be found by the following formula:

$$(a + b)^3 = a^3 + 3\,a^2b + 3\,ab^2 + b^3.$$

486. Cube roots may be found by the table, graph, or more easily by logarithms and the slide-rule (the last two methods will be shown in the next two chapters).

CHAPTER XVII

*LOGARITHMS APPLIED TO MULTIPLICATION, DIVISION, ROOTS AND POWERS, AND VERBAL PROBLEMS INVOLVING EXPONENTIAL EQUATIONS

LOGARITHMS

487. Labor-saving devices. In Chapter IV we showed how extensive calculations even with only four or five place numbers are apt to become laborious and, in some cases, inaccurate and involving unnecessary steps. We showed how to minimize the inaccuracy and how some of the unnecessary steps may be eliminated, especially with regard to the processes of multiplication and division by the so-called "abbreviated method." But in many cases the work remains long and tedious, even with the use of these abbreviated methods.

In Art. 449 will be found a table of powers and roots which are given for the purpose of saving time and labor. Scientific books include similar tables which help to save time and conserve our energy. Other labor-saving devices commonly used are adding machines, cash registers, graphs, etc.

One of the greatest labor-saving devices by which difficult problems may be readily solved is the method of calculation by logarithms. This chapter will be devoted to a simple explanation of this method. If the student will study the chapter carefully and solve the problems correctly, he will get a foundation in logarithmic work that will be very helpful in subsequent work.

488. Two methods of multiplying. We are already familiar with the two methods of multiplying illustrated by the following examples:

$$100 \times 1000 = 100{,}000.$$
$$10^2 \times 10^3 = 10^5$$
$$= 100{,}000.$$

The student will observe that the product is the same in both examples, but that the method used in the second has reduced the operation of actually multiplying the two numbers to a simple problem in the addition of exponents.

Although the numbers multiplied here are in each case powers of 10, the method will hold for other bases as well. However, we shall consider only the base 10 in our subsequent discussion since it is the one commonly used.

Find the product of the following pairs of numbers by the two methods given above:

10 and 100.	10,000 and 100,000.
1000 and 1000.	1000 and 1,000,000.

489. Powers of 10. From the preceding exercises it is clear that we can multiply together numbers which are integral powers of 10 merely by adding the exponents of these powers. Since every positive number may be expressed exactly or approximately as a power of 10, we may obtain the product of any two numbers in a similar manner by adding the exponents of the powers of 10 which equal the respective numbers. For example, we may multiply 17.782 and 3.162 by adding the exponents of the powers of 10, which equal 17.782 and 3.162 respectively.

This raises two important questions: (1) What powers of 10 equal 17.782 and 3.162? (2) What is the value of 10 when raised to the sum of these two powers? It is possible for us to work out a table which will give us the powers of 10 which equal 17.782 and 3.162. The table below shows how the different values are obtained. The table is not complete, as will be shown later, but it contains the approximate values of several integral and fractional powers of 10 which we need at this point.

We know that $10^0 = 1$, $10^1 = 10$, $10^2 = 100$, $10^3 = 1000$, and so on. We can find the value of $10^{0.5}$ as follows:

$$10^{0.5} = 10^{\frac{1}{2}} = \sqrt{10} = 3.162 \text{ (approx.)}.$$

From these values the other values in the table are easily found, as the student can verify.

TABLE OF POWERS OF 10

10^0			$= 1.0000$
$10^{0.25}$	$= (10^{0.5})^{\frac{1}{2}}$	$= \sqrt{3.162}$	$= 1.7782$
$10^{0.5}$	$= 10^{\frac{1}{2}}$	$= \sqrt{10}$	$= 3.1623$
$10^{0.75}$	$= (10^{1.5})^{\frac{1}{2}}$	$= \sqrt{31.62}$	$= 5.6234$
10^1			$= 10.0000$
$10^{1.25}$	$= 10^1 \cdot 10^{0.25}$		$= 17.782$
$10^{1.5}$	$= 10^1 \cdot 10^{0.5}$		$= 31.623$
$10^{1.75}$	$= 10^1 \cdot 10^{0.75}$		$= 56.234$
10^2			$= 100.000$
$10^{2.25}$	$= 10^1 \cdot 10^{1.25}$		$= 177.82$
$10^{2.5}$	$= 10^1 \cdot 10^{1.5}$		$= 316.23$
$10^{2.75}$	$= 10^1 \cdot 10^{1.75}$		$= 562.34$
10^3			$= 1000.00$

We may now resume the solution of the problem proposed above, namely, multiplying 17.782 by 3.162. We can see by referring to the table that $17.782 = 10^{1.25}$ and that $3.162 = 10^{0.5}$. Hence, $17.782 \times 3.162 = 10^{1.25} \times 10^{0.5} = 10^{1.75}$, which, by referring to the table, we see is equal to 56.234 (this product is accurate to the second decimal place).

Check the preceding result by actually multiplying 17.782 by 3.162, and account for the difference in results. Is there a significant difference? Is the result obtained by actual multiplication accurate to more than two decimal places?

490. Logarithms; notation for logarithms. In the equation $17.782 = 10^{1.25}$ the exponent 1.25 (which indicates the power to which 10 must.be raised to give 17.782) is called the *logarithm* of 17.782 to the, *base* 10.

Thus *the logarithm of a number to the base 10 is the exponent of the power to which 10 must be raised to equal that number.* From now on we shall assume that the base is 10 when we speak of the logarithm of a number. The symbol for logarithm is *log*. Thus, $\log 1000 = 3$ is read ": the logarithm of 1000 equals 3," the base 10 being understood.

By means of the table of powers of 10 in Art. 489 find $\log 1$; $\log 10$; $\log 100$; $\log 1.78$; $\log 316.23$.

491. A logarithm is an exponent. The student will do well to remember the two ways of thinking of an exponent; for example, in the equation $10^2 = 100$ the 2 can be thought of (a) as the exponent of the power to which 10 must be raised to equal 100; that is, $10^2 = 100$; (b) as the logarithm of 100 to the base 10; that is, $2 = \log_{10} 100$.

Read the following in two ways:

1. $10^1 = 10$. 2. $10^2 = 100$. 3. $10^3 = 1000$. 4. $10^4 = 10,000$.

492. Characteristic; mantissa. A glance at the table of Art. 489 will show that each exponent of 10 (each logarithm of the corresponding numbers to the right) may contain an integral part and a fractional part. For example, in the equation $10^{1.25} = 17.782$ the 1.25 (that is, log 17.782) has 1 for its integral part and 0.25 for its decimal (fractional) part. In $10^2 = 100$ the entire logarithm is integral. (Why?) The integral part of a logarithm is called the *characteristic* of the logarithm, and the decimal part is called the *mantissa* of the logarithm.

The characteristic of a logarithm of any number can always be determined at sight. For example:

$$\log 10 = 1, \text{ because } 10^1 = 10;$$
$$\log 100 = 2, \text{ because } 10^2 = 100;$$
$$\log 1000 = 3, \text{ because } 10^3 = 1000;$$

and so on. But these numbers are all integral powers of 10. However, the characteristic of the logarithm of any other number may be obtained as well by observing what powers of 10 inclose it. For example, the characteristic of log 525 is 2 because 525 lies between the second and the third powers of 10; that is, between $10^2 = 100$ and $10^3 = 1000$ (see the table, Art. 489).

It is not so easy to determine the mantissas (the decimal part) of the logarithms of numbers. We have worked out a few of these in the table of Art. 489, but to compute the mantissas for all other numbers in this way would be a tedious task. Moreover, the methods necessary to compute them would be beyond us in difficulty. However, these mantissas have been computed for all the various powers of 10 (by more advanced methods), and they appear in the table of mantissas which follows. So that now when we want to know what the logarithm of any number is, we decide (by inspection) what the characteristic is and then look in the table for the mantissa.

1. Look in the table (pp. 430–431) for the decimal part of the logarithms of 10; 15; 20; 38; 86; 99.

2. What is the decimal part of the logarithm of 100?

3. What is the power to which 10 must be raised to produce 10,000?

4. What, then, is the logarithm of 10,000 to the base 10?

5. Examine the table carefully and tell what numbers have integers for logarithms; that is, those that have zero mantissas.

6. When will a logarithm have a decimal mantissa?

7. Find the product of 48 and 55.

Solution. By means of the table we see that
$$48 = 10^{1.6812},$$
and that $\qquad 55 = 10^{1.7404}.$

Therefore $\qquad 48 \times 55 = 10^{1.6812} \times 10^{1.7404}$
$$= 10^{3.4216}.$$

The 3 in the exponent 3.4216 tells us that the product of 48×55 is a number between the 3d and 4th powers of 10; that is, the 3 tells us where to put the decimal point. We must find the mantissa 0.4216 in the table of logarithms and see what number corresponds to it.

If we look in the table of mantissas we find that 0.4216 is the mantissa of the logarithm of the number 264. Now since the characteristic of the logarithm is 3, the number must be between the 3d and 4th powers of 10; that is, between 1000 and 10,000. This means that the decimal point comes after the fourth place, so that we must add a cipher to 264. Hence the number is 2640.

TABLE OF MANTISSAS

No.	0	1	2	3	4	5	6	7	8	9
10	0000	0043	0086	0128	0170	0212	0253	0294	0334	0374
11	0414	0453	0492	0531	0569	0607	0645	0682	0719	0755
12	0792	0828	0864	0899	0934	0969	1004	1038	1072	1106
13	1139	1173	1206	1239	1271	1303	1335	1367	1399	1430
14	1461	1492	1523	1553	1584	1614	1644	1673	1703	1732
15	1761	1790	1818	1847	1875	1903	1931	1959	1987	2014
16	2041	2068	2095	2122	2148	2175	2201	2227	2253	2279
17	2304	2330	2355	2380	2405	2430	2455	2480	2504	2529
18	2553	2577	2601	2625	2648	2672	2695	2718	2742	2765
19	2788	2810	2833	2856	2878	2900	2923	2945	2967	2989
20	3010	3032	3054	3075	3096	3118	3139	3160	3181	3201
21	3222	3243	3263	3284	3304	3324	3345	3365	3385	3404
22	3424	3444	3464	3483	3502	3522	3541	3560	3579	3598
23	3617	3636	3655	3674	3692	3711	3729	3747	3766	3784
24	3802	3820	3838	3856	3874	3892	3909	3927	3945	3962
25	3979	3997	4014	4031	4048	4065	4082	4099	4116	4133
26	4150	4166	4183	4200	4216	4232	4249	4265	4281	4298
27	4314	4330	4346	4362	4378	4393	4409	4425	4440	4456
28	4472	4487	4502	4518	4533	4548	4564	4579	4594	4609
29	4624	4639	4654	4669	4683	4698	4713	4728	4742	4757
30	4771	4786	4800	4814	4829	4843	4857	4871	4886	4900
31	4914	4928	4942	4955	4969	4983	4997	5011	5024	5038
32	5051	5065	5079	5092	5105	5119	5132	5145	5159	5172
33	5185	5198	5211	5224	5237	5250	5263	5276	5289	5302
34	5315	5328	5340	5353	5366	5378	5391	5403	5416	5428
35	5441	5453	5465	5478	5490	5502	5514	5527	5539	5551
36	5563	5575	5587	5599	5611	5623	5635	5647	5658	5670
37	5682	5694	5705	5717	5729	5740	5752	5763	5775	5786
38	5798	5809	5821	5832	5843	5855	5866	5877	5888	5899
39	5911	5922	5933	5944	5955	5966	5977	5988	5999	6010
40	6021	6031	6042	6053	6064	6075	6085	6096	6107	6117
41	6128	6138	6149	6160	6170	6180	6191	6201	6212	6222
42	6232	6243	6253	6263	6274	6284	6294	6304	6314	6325
43	6335	6345	6355	6365	6375	6385	6395	6405	6415	6425
44	6435	6444	6454	6464	6474	6484	6493	6503	6513	6522
45	6532	6542	6551	6561	6571	6580	6590	6599	6609	6618
46	6628	6637	6646	6656	6665	6675	6684	6693	6702	6712
47	6721	6730	6739	6749	6758	6767	6776	6785	6794	6803
48	6812	6821	6830	6839	6848	6857	6866	6875	6884	6893
49	6902	6911	6920	6928	6937	6946	6955	6964	6972	6981
50	6990	6998	7007	7016	7024	7033	7042	7050	7059	7067
51	7076	7084	7093	7101	7110	7118	7126	7135	7143	7152
52	7160	7168	7177	7185	7193	7202	7210	7218	7226	7235
53	7243	7251	7259	7267	7275	7284	7292	7300	7308	7316
54	7324	7332	7340	7348	7356	7364	7372	7380	7388	7396
No.	0	1	2	3	4	5	6	7	8	9

TABLE OF MANTISSAS

No.	0	1	2	3	4	5	6	7	8	9
55	7404	7412	7419	7427	7435	7443	7451	7459	7466	7474
56	7482	7490	7497	7505	7513	7520	7528	7536	7543	7551
57	7559	7566	7574	7582	7589	7597	7604	7612	7619	7627
58	7634	7642	7649	7657	7664	7672	7679	7686	7694	7701
59	7709	7716	7723	7731	7738	7745	7752	7760	7767	7774
60	7782	7789	7796	7803	7810	7818	7825	7832	7839	7846
61	7853	7860	7868	7875	7882	7889	7896	7903	7910	7917
62	7924	7931	7938	7945	7952	7959	7966	7973	7980	7987
63	7993	8000	8007	8014	8021	8028	8035	8041	8048	8055
64	8062	8069	8075	8082	8089	8096	8102	8109	8116	8122
65	8129	8136	8142	8149	8156	8162	8169	8176	8182	8189
66	8195	8202	8209	8215	8222	8228	8235	8241	8248	8254
67	8261	8267	8274	8280	8287	8293	8299	8306	8312	8319
68	8325	8331	8338	8344	8351	8357	8363	8370	8376	8382
69	8388	8395	8401	8407	8414	8420	8426	8432	8439	8445
70	8451	8457	8463	8470	8476	8482	8488	8494	8500	8506
71	8513	8519	8525	8531	8537	8543	8549	8555	8561	8567
72	8573	8579	8585	8591	8597	8603	8609	8615	8621	8627
73	8633	8639	8645	8651	8657	8663	8669	8675	8681	8686
74	8692	8698	8704	8710	8716	8722	8727	8733	8739	8745
75	8751	8756	8762	8768	8774	8779	8785	8791	8797	8802
76	8808	8814	8820	8825	8831	8837	8842	8848	8854	8859
77	8865	8871	8876	8882	8887	8893	8899	8904	8910	8915
78	8921	8927	8932	8938	8943	8949	8954	8960	8965	8971
79	8976	8982	8987	8993	8998	9004	9009	9015	9020	9025
80	9031	9036	9042	9047	9053	9058	9063	9069	9074	9079
81	9085	9090	9096	9101	9106	9112	9117	9122	9128	9133
82	9138	9143	9149	9154	9159	9165	9170	9175	9180	9186
83	9191	9196	9201	9206	9212	9217	9222	9227	9232	9238
84	9243	9248	9253	9258	9263	9269	9274	9279	9284	9289
85	9294	9299	9304	9309	9315	9320	9325	9330	9335	9340
86	9345	9350	9355	9360	9365	9370	9375	9380	9385	9390
87	9395	9400	9405	9410	9415	9420	9425	9430	9435	9440
88	9445	9450	9455	9460	9465	9469	9474	9479	9484	9489
89	9494	9499	9504	9509	9513	9518	9523	9528	9533	9538
90	9542	9547	9552	9557	9562	9566	9571	9576	9581	9586
91	9590	9595	9600	9605	9609	9614	9619	9624	9628	9633
92	9638	9643	9647	9652	9657	9661	9666	9671	9675	9680
93	9685	9689	9694	9699	9703	9708	9713	9717	9722	9727
94	9731	9736	9741	9745	9750	9754	9759	9763	9768	9773
95	9777	9782	9786	9791	9795	9800	9805	9809	9814	9818
96	9823	9827	9832	9836	9841	9845	9850	9854	9859	9863
97	9868	9872	9877	9881	9886	9890	9894	9899	9903	9908
98	9912	9917	9921	9926	9930	9934	9939	9943	9948	9952
99	9956	9961	9965	9969	9974	9978	9983	9987	9991	9996
No.	0	1	2	3	4	5	6	7	8	9

The preceding work may be briefly arranged as follows:

Let $N = 48 \times 55$

$$\log 48 = 1.6812$$
$$\log 55 = 1.7404$$

Then $\overline{\log N = 3.4216}$

By the table, $N = 2640.$

493. Logarithm of a product. The discussion and examples in Art. 492 have shown that to the problem of multiplying two powers of 10 there corresponds the problem of adding their logarithms (exponents). This may be stated briefly as the first law thus: *The logarithm of the product of two numbers is the sum of the logarithms of the factors; or, by formula,* $\log (ab) = \log a + \log b.$

It is easily shown that the law also holds for any number of factors in a product; that is, $\log abc = \log a + \log b + \log c,$ and so on.

EXERCISES

1. Check by actual multiplication the logarithmic method of finding the product of 48 and 55.

2. Find by means of logarithms the products of the following numbers:

(a) $10 \times 100 \times 1000.$ (b) $51 \times 40.$ (c) $83 \times 6 \times 2.$

3. Find by using logarithms the area of a triangular garden plot whose base is 38 ft. and whose altitude is 17 ft.

Solution. The formula for the area of any triangle is

$$A = \frac{ab}{2}.$$

Hence, in this case, $A = 19 \cdot 17.$

$$\log 19 = 1.2788$$
$$\log 17 = 1.2304$$

Then $\overline{\log A = 2.5092}$

By the table, $A = 323.$

4. Solve the following problems by means of logarithms:

(a) What is the area of a rectangle whose base is 70 and whose altitude is 32?

(b) What is the area of a parallelogram whose base is 64 and whose altitude is 35?

(c) What is the area of a square, a side of which is 29?

Solution. The formula for the area of a square is

$$A = s \cdot s = s^2.$$

In this case

$$A = 29 \times 29 = 29^2.$$

$$\log 29 = 1.4624$$
$$\log 29 = 1.4624$$

Therefore

$$\overline{\log A = 2.9248}$$

and, by the table,

$$A = 841.$$

494. Logarithm of a power. Obviously the result in Ex. 4, (c), would have been the same if we had multiplied the logarithm of 29 by 2 instead of adding it to itself. In like manner, if we want the logarithm of 50^3, we can obtain it either by using the logarithm of 50 three times as an addend or by taking three times the logarithm of 50. Thus, $\log 50^3 = 3 \log 50 = 3 \times 1.6990 = 5.0970$.

This discussion illustrates a very important law; namely, *that the logarithm of a number raised to a power is the exponent of the power times the logarithm of the number; or, by formula, $\log a^n = n \log a$.*

EXERCISES

1. Find by the preceding method the logarithms of the following numbers: 22^2; 11^3; 15^4.

2. Find by logarithms the volume of a cubical cake of ice one edge of which is 10 in.; 11 in.

3. The area A of a circle is given by the formula $A = \pi r^2$, where r is the radius of the circle. What is the area of a circle whose radius is 6 in.? (Use $\log \pi = 0.4971$.)

495. Logarithm of a quotient. The method of computing by logarithms is as useful in division as in multiplication. In order to make the method clear, let us review our two methods of dividing one number by another.

(a) $\dfrac{100,000}{100} = 1000$, by actual division.

(b) $\dfrac{100,000}{100} = \dfrac{10^5}{10^2} = 10^3 = 1000$, by subtracting the exponents.

Here, as in multiplication, we obtain the same result by either method, but the second method reduces the operation of actual division to a simple problem of subtracting exponents.

EXERCISES

1. Find the following quotients by the two methods just discussed:

(a) $\dfrac{100,000}{1000}.$

(b) $\dfrac{1,000,000}{10,000}.$

2. Divide 100 by 31.623 by using the table of Art. 489.

Solution. $\dfrac{100}{31.623} = \dfrac{10^2}{10^{1.5}} = 10^{0.5} = 3.162.$

NOTE. The student should check this result by actual division.

3. Divide 562.34 by 31.62 by using the table of Art. 489.

We may obtain the quotient of any two numbers in like manner by subtracting the exponent of the power of 10 equal to the divisor from the exponent of the power of 10 equal to the dividend. Keeping in mind the definition of a logarithm it is clear that this fact may be expressed as a law; thus, *the logarithm of the quotient of two numbers is the logarithm of the dividend minus the logarithm of the divisor;* or, as a formula, $log\left(\dfrac{a}{b}\right) = log\ a - log\ b.$

1. Given $\log 2 = 0.3010$, $\log 3 = 0.4771$, find $\log \frac{3}{2}$; $\log \frac{9}{4}$

2. Find the value of the following fractions to three significant figures by using logarithms:

(a) $\dfrac{59 \times 85}{43}$

(c) $\dfrac{381 \times 11^3}{43^2}$.

(b) $\dfrac{752 \times 350}{683}$.

(d) $\dfrac{71 \times 48 \times 253}{47 \times 81}$.

HINT. To find the logarithm of each fraction, add the logarithms of the factors of the numerator and from this sum subtract the sum of the logarithms of the factors of the denominator.

496. Position of the decimal point. Since the multiplication or division of a number by 10 amounts to a moving of the decimal point one place to the right in multiplication and one place to the left in division, and since the multiplication or division of a number by 100 amounts to moving the decimal point two places to the right or left, and so on, *the position of the decimal point in a number whose logarithm we are seeking affects the characteristic only.*

The truth of the foregoing statement can be seen best by means of the table in Art. 489. In this table, for example,

$$10^{0.25} = 1.7782, \text{ or } \log 1.7782 = 0.25.$$

If we multiply both sides of this equation by 10, we get

$$10^{1.25} = 17.782, \text{ or } \log 17.782 = 1.25.$$

Again, multiplying both sides of this last equation by 10,

$$10^{2.25} = 177.82, \text{ or } \log 177.82 = 2.25,$$

and so on. The student will observe that only the integral part of the exponent of 10 (the logarithm of the number) is changing, and that the array of figures remains the

same even though the decimal point moves one place to
the right after each multiplication. In like manner, if we
divide both sides of the equation $10^{0.25} = 1.778$ by 10, and
continue the division, we obtain

$$10^{0.25-1} = 0.1778, \text{ or } \log 0.1778 = 0.25 - 1,$$
$$10^{0.25-2} = 0.01778, \text{ or } \log 0.01778 = 0.25 - 2,$$
$$10^{0.25-3} = 0.001778, \text{ or } \log 0.001778 = 0.25 - 3,$$

and so on.

The logarithms $0.25 - 1$, $0.25 - 2$, $0.25 - 3$, etc. are
negative quantities, but they are not in the form in which
we usually write negative numbers. However, if we adopt
these forms, the mantissas of all our logarithms will not
only be positive but they will be the same for the same
array of figures no matter where the decimal point is found.

Thus the mantissa of $\log 1.778$ is the same as the
mantissa of $\log 0.001778$, as was shown above. These two
logarithms differ, therefore, only in their characteristics.
In some texts $\log 0.1778$ is written $\bar{1}.25$ instead of $0.25 - 1$.
To agree with this statement the dash above the 1 means
that only the 1 is negative. Some books prefer the form
$9.25 - 10$ instead of $0.25 - 1$ or $\bar{1}.25$. The student can
easily see that $9.25 - 10$ has the same value as $0.25 - 1$.
We shall later see another advantage of the form $9.25 - 10$.

The preceding discussion may be summarized in two
statements:

1. *We agree to express the logarithm of any number in a
form such that its mantissa shall be positive.* This can
always be done, whether the number is greater or less than
unity. In either case the positiveness or negativeness of
the number is shown entirely by means of the characteristic.

2. *Two numbers containing the same succession of digits,
that is, differing only in the position of the decimal point,*

will have logarithms that differ only in the value of the characteristics. This explains why we called the table a table of mantissas and why, in looking up the logarithm of a number, we need pay no attention to the decimal point in the number. The same table of mantissas serves both for numbers greater and less than unity.

497. Table of characteristics. The following table is given in order that the student may determine more quickly the characteristic of the logarithm of any number between 10 to the minus 6th power and 10 to the plus 7th power. This is about as much of a range as we shall ever need. The table can be extended upward or downward at will.

TABLE OF CHARACTERISTICS

$$10^{-6} = 0.000001 \qquad 10^1 = 10$$
$$10^{-5} = 0.00001 \qquad 10^2 = 100$$
$$10^{-4} = 0.0001 \qquad 10^3 = 1,000$$
$$10^{-3} = 0.001 \qquad 10^4 = 10,000$$
$$10^{-2} = 0.01 \qquad 10^5 = 100,000$$
$$10^{-1} = 0.1 \qquad 10^6 = 1,000,000$$
$$10^0 = 1 \qquad 10^7 = 10,000,000$$

For example, if we want the logarithm of 2142, we know that its characteristic is 3, because 2142 lies between the 3d and 4th powers of 10. Again, if we want the logarithm of 0.0142, we know that the characteristic of the logarithm is -2, because 0.0142 lies between the minus 2d and the minus 1st power of 10.

498. Interpolation. So far we have shown the student how to find the logarithms of three-digit numbers only. In order to be able to find the logarithms of numbers of more than three digits, and to find the numbers corresponding to various logarithms which we may obtain in calculation, it is necessary for us to learn how to make further use of the table in Art. 492. We shall proceed to consider two typical examples.

1. Find the logarithm of 231.6.

Solution. From the table of Art. 497 it is clear that the characteristic of the logarithm is 2. To find the mantissa, we ignore the decimal point and look in the table of Art. 492 for the mantissa of 2316. Reading down the left-hand column of the table, headed " No.," we find 23. The numbers in the same horizontal row with 23 are the mantissas of the logarithms 230, 231, 232, and so on. We want to find the logarithm of 2316. We can now write

$$\log 232 = 2.3655$$
$$\log 231 = 2.3636$$
$$\text{Tabular difference} = 0.0019$$

Now since 231.6 is $\frac{6}{10}$ of the way from 231 to 232, we add $\frac{6}{10}$ of the tabular difference 0.0019 to the logarithm of 231. Thus,

$$\log 231.6 = 2.3636 + \frac{6}{10} \times 0.0019.$$

Therefore $\log 231.6 = 2.3647.$

The process of obtaining the logarithm of a number in this way is called *interpolation*. The student should practice this method by finding the logarithms of several four-digit numbers.

2. Find the number whose logarithm is $0.3883 - 1$.

Solution. We know at once that the number is a decimal fraction lying between the minus 1st and the 0 power of 10. This tells us that the decimal point comes just before the first significant figure in the number. If we look in the table of Art. 492 we do not find the mantissa 3883, but we find 3892, which is a little greater, and 3874, which is a little less; that is,

$$0.3892 - 1 = \log 0.245.$$
$$0.3874 - 1 = \log 0.244.$$

Since $0.3883 - 1$ is the logarithm of the number we want, the number lies between 0.244 and 0.245. Now $0.3883 - 1$ is $\frac{9}{18}$ of the way from log 0.244 to log 0.245; hence the number corresponding to the logarithm 0.3883 -1 lies $\frac{9}{18}$, or $\frac{1}{2}$, of the way from 0.244 to 0.245. Therefore the number desired is 0.2445.

Here the process of interpolation is used on the inverse problem, that of finding a number when its logarithm is given.

EXERCISES

1. Find the logarithms of the following numbers: 745; 83.2; 91200; 0.567; 0.00741. (No interpolation.)   .

2. Find the logarithms of the following numbers: 6542; 783.4; 91243; 0.4826; 0.002143. (Interpolation.)

3. Find the numbers whose logarithms are 2.6075; 1.4249; 0.3054; 0.0212 $-$ 2; 0.8457 -1. (No interpolation.)

4. Find the numbers whose logarithms are 2.3080; 1.936; 0.8770; 0.0878 $-$ 2. (Interpolation.)

499. Extraction of roots by means of logarithms. In Art. 460 we discussed the meaning of fractional exponents and showed that

$$a^{\frac{1}{2}} = \sqrt{a}; \ a^{\frac{1}{3}} = \sqrt[3]{a}; \ a^{\frac{1}{4}} = \sqrt[4]{a}; \ \text{etc.}$$

If we assume that the theorem of Art. 494, regarding the logarithm of a number raised to a power, holds for fractional exponents, then

$$\log \sqrt{a} = \log a^{\frac{1}{2}} = \tfrac{1}{2} \log a,$$
$$\log \sqrt[3]{a} = \log a^{\frac{1}{3}} = \tfrac{1}{3} \log a,$$

and so on. This illustrates the truth of another theorem, namely, that *the logarithm of any root of a number is equal to the logarithm of the number divided by the index of the root.*

Thus, $\log \sqrt{542} = \tfrac{1}{2} \log 542 = \dfrac{2.7340}{2} = 1.3670.$

Now 1.3670 is the logarithm of 23.28 $-$. Therefore the square root of 542 is approximately 23.28 $-$.

If the logarithm of the number is negative, the root may be found as in the following examples.

Find by logarithms:

(a) $\sqrt{0.472}$. (b) $\sqrt[3]{0.472}$. (c) $\sqrt[4]{0.472}$.

Solution. Log $0.472 = 0.6739 - 1$. Now if we attempt to take $\frac{1}{2}$ of this negative logarithm, we shall obtain a fractional characteristic that would be confusing. Therefore, in order to make it possible to keep the mantissa positive and the characteristic (after the division) an integer, we write

$$\log 0.472 = 19.6739 - 20,$$

a number which the student can readily see is equal to $0.6739 - 1$, and which has the added advantage referred to above. We now get

(a) $\log \sqrt{0.472} = \frac{1}{2}(19.6739 - 20) = 9.8369 - 10.$

In like manner,

(b) $\log \sqrt[3]{0.472} = \frac{1}{3}(29.6739 - 30) = 9.8913 - 10,$

and (c) $\log \sqrt[4]{0.472} = \frac{1}{4}(39.6739 - 40) = 9.9185 - 10.$

In (a), above, $\log \sqrt{0.472} = 9.8369 - 10$. This means that the characteristic is -1 and that the mantissa is 0.8369. By reference to the table, we find that 0.8369 is the mantissa of the logarithm of 687. Since the characteristic is -1, the number lies between the minus 1st and the 0 power of 10; hence the decimal point comes just before the 6, and $\sqrt{0.472} = 0.687$. The student should check this result by actually extracting the square root of 0.472 by the method given in Art. 446.

EXERCISES

1. Find by logarithms:

$$\sqrt{9604}; \ \sqrt{153.76}; \ \sqrt{0.000529}; \ \sqrt[3]{10648};$$
$$\sqrt[3]{42875}; \ \sqrt[3]{3.375}; \ \sqrt[3]{0.001728}.$$

2. Given $a = 4.25$, $b = 22.1$, and $c = 0.05$, find by logarithms the value of $\sqrt{\dfrac{ab^2}{c^3}}$ to three significant figures.

3. Find by logarithms the value of $\sqrt{\dfrac{82.41}{4.832}}$ and $\sqrt[3]{\dfrac{2.42 \times 35.1}{75.2 \times 10^2}}$ to three significant figures.

4. The velocity v of a body that has fallen a distance of s feet is given by the formula $v = \sqrt{2\,gs}$. If $g = 32.16$, what is the velocity acquired by a body in falling 30 ft.?

5. If a bullet is shot upwards with an initial velocity of v, the height s to which it will rise is given by the equation $v = \sqrt{2\,gs}$. What must be the minimum velocity at the start of a bullet fired upwards if it is to strike a Zeppelin 1500 ft. high? (Assume $g = 32.16$.)

6. The time t of oscillation of a pendulum l centimeters long is given by the formula $t = \pi\sqrt{\dfrac{l}{980}}$. Find the time of oscillation of a pendulum 78.22 centimeters long.

*7. If the time of oscillation of a pendulum is 1 sec., what is its length?

*8. The area of any triangle is given by the formula
$$A = \sqrt{s(s-a)(s-b)(s-c)},$$
where a, b, and c are the sides of the triangle, and s equals one half the perimeter, or $\dfrac{a+b+c}{2}$.

Using the preceding formula, find by means of logarithms the number of acres in a triangular field whose sides are 15, 38.2, and 45.3 rods respectively. (1 A. = 160 sq. rd.)

*9. The area A of the cross section of a chimney in square feet required to carry off the smoke is given by the formula
$$A = \frac{0.6\,P}{\sqrt{h}},$$
where P is the number of pounds of coal burned per hour, and h is the height of the chimney in feet. Find out what the area of a cross section of a chimney 80 ft. high should be to carry off the smoke if 560 lb. of coal are burned per hour.

*10. The average velocity v of the piston head in inches per second for a steam engine is given by the formula

$$v = 1.7 \sqrt[3]{s \sqrt{\frac{p}{15}}},$$

where s denotes the distance (in inches) over which the piston head moves, and p is the number of pounds of pressure of steam in the cylinder. Find v if $s = 30.24$ in. and $p = 115$ lb.

*11. In the equation $x = 10^y$ what is the value of x when $y = 0$? when $y = 1$? when $y = 2$? when $y = -1$?

*12. Fill in the following table for the equation $x = 10^y$.

y	0	1	2	-1	-2	-3	$\frac{1}{2}$	$\frac{1}{3}$	$\frac{5}{2}$	4	5
x	1	10	100					•			

Note. For y equaling $\frac{1}{2}$, $\frac{1}{3}$, $2\frac{1}{2}$, etc., use the table of mantissas, Art. 492.

*13. Plot the results in the table of Ex. 12 and draw the curve, thus obtaining the graph for $x = 10^y$ (or $y = \log x$) (Fig. 300).

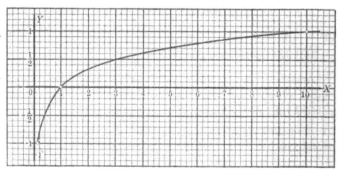

Fig. 300. Graph of $x = 10^y$

*14. Show that the graph for $x = 10^y$ (Fig. 300) makes clear the following principles:

(a) A negative number does not have a real number for its logarithm.

(b) The logarithm of a positive number is positive or negative according as the number is greater or less than 1.

(c) The greater the value of x, the greater its logarithm.

(d) As x gets smaller and smaller, its logarithm decreases and becomes smaller and smaller.

*15. Find by the graph of Ex. 13 the logarithm of 2.25; of 4.5; of 1.1; of 2.8.

*16. Of what number is 0.35 the logarithm? 0.5? 0.42?

*17. Check your results for Exs. 15 and 16 by the results given in the table of Art. 492.

*500. Exponential equations. Instead of finding the logarithm of 1000 to the base 10, we could arrive at the same result by solving the equation $10^x = 1000$, for this equation asks the question, What power of 10 equals 1000? In other words, What is the logarithm of 1000 to the base 10? An equation like this, in which an unknown is involved in the exponent, is called an *exponential equation*.

EXERCISE

Give five examples of exponential equations where 10 is the base.

*501. Method of solving exponential equations. The simplest exponential equations may be solved by inspection just as the logarithms of many numbers can be given by inspection. Where an exponential equation cannot be solved readily by inspection, logarithms may be employed to simplify the process. We will illustrate each case.

Solution I (by inspection).

(a) If $2^x = 4$, then $x = 2$. (e) If $10^y = 100$, then $y = 2$.

(b) If $3^x = 9$, then $x = 2$. (f) If $10^x = 1000$, then $x = 3$.

(c) If $2^y = 8$, then $y = 3$. (g) If $10^y = 10,000$, then $y = 4$.

(d) If $3^x = 81$, then $x = 4$.

Solution II (by using logarithms).

Solve the equation $2^x = 6$ for x.

Taking the logarithms of both sides:

$$\log 2^x = \log 6,$$

or $$x \log 2 = \log 6.$$

$$\therefore x = \frac{\log 6}{\log 2} = \frac{0.7782}{0.3010} = 2.58.$$

The student must remember that $\dfrac{\log 6}{\log 2}$ is not equal to $\log \dfrac{6}{2}$. The first is a fraction obtained by dividing one logarithm by another, and involves *division*; the second indicates that the logarithm of a fraction is to be found, and involves *subtraction*.

EXERCISE

Solve the following equations for x:

(a) $2^x = 7$.   (b) $3^x = 5$.   (c) $4^x = 10$.   (d) $(1.12)^x = 3$.

502. Interest problems solved by logarithms. Some important problems in interest may be solved by means of exponential equations and logarithms. The following simple example will illustrate the principle:

In how many years will a sum of money double itself at 6% if the interest is compounded annually?

Solution. In one year $1 will amount to $1.06; in two years the amount will be 1.06×1.06, or $(1.06)^2$; in three years the amount will be $(1.06)^3$; and so on. Therefore in x years the amount of $1 will be $(1.06)^x$. Then, if the money is to double itself in x years, the conditions of the problem will be represented by the equation $(1.06)^x = 2$. Solving this equation for x, we get $x = 12.3$ (approx.). Therefore a sum of money will double itself at 6% (compounded annually) in about 12.3 yr.

1. Explain the solution of the problem given in Art. 502.

2. If the interest is compounded annually, in how many years will a sum of money double itself at 3%? 3½%? 4%? 5%?

3. In how many years will a sum of money treble itself at 4% interest compounded annually? semiannually?

4. The amount of P dollars for n years at r%, compounded annually, is given by the formula $A = P(1 + r)^n$. Find the amount of $1200 for 10 yr. at 4%.

Solution. In this problem $P = 1200$, $r = 0.04$, $n = 10$.

$$A = 1200(1 + 0.04)^{10}.$$

The computation may be arranged as follows:

$$\begin{aligned} \log 1200 &= 3.0792 \\ 10 \log 1.04 &= \underline{0.1700} \\ \log A &= \overline{3.2492} \end{aligned}$$

Therefore $A = 1775$, number of dollars in the amount.

NOTE. As a matter of fact, this value of A is not exact, because we are using only four-place tables. In practice the value of the problem should determine the kind of tables used. The greater the number of places given in the tables used, the greater the accuracy of the result.

5. What will $5000 amount to in 5 yr. at 3%, interest compounded annually? semiannually? quarterly?

6. Approximately three hundred years ago the Dutch purchased Manhattan Island from the Indians for $24. What would this $24 amount to at the present time if it had been placed on interest at 6% and compounded annually?

7. What would be the amount of 1¢ at the present time if it had been placed on 3% annual compound interest fifty years ago?

8. A boy deposited 30¢ in a savings bank on 3% interest, the interest to be compounded annually. He forgot about his deposit until fifteen years later, when he found the receipt covering the original deposit. What did the 30¢ amount to in the fifteen years ?

9. What sum will amount to $1600 in 10 yr. at 6%, interest being compounded annually ?

10. What sum will amount to $2500 in 5 yr. at 3%, interest being compounded annually ?

11. In how many years will $4000 amount to $8500 at 6%, interest being compounded annually ?

12. What would be the amount to-day of 1 cent which nineteen hundred and twenty years ago was placed on interest at 6%, compounded annually ? Find the radius in miles of a sphere of gold which has this value.

Note. A cubic foot of gold weighs 1206 pounds avoirdupois, one pound being worth approximately $290.

The volume of a sphere is given by the formula $V = \frac{4}{3}\pi r^3$, where V is the volume and r the radius of the sphere.

No doubt the pupil is convinced of the value of logarithms as a labor-saving device in complicated arithmetic computations. Since he will meet numerous opportunities for applications, the lists of problems in the chapter are brief, the aim being to give just enough illustrations to make clear the meaning of the principles involved.

Historical Note. Logarithms were invented by John Napier (1550–1617), baron of Merchiston in Scotland. His greatest purpose in studying mathematics was to simplify and systematize arithmetic, algebra, and trigonometry. The student should read about Napier's "rods," or "bones," which he designed to simplify multiplication and division (Encyclopædia Britannica, 11th ed.).

It was his earnest desire to simplify the processes that led him to invent logarithms; and, strange as it may seem, he did not consider a logarithm as an exponent. In his time the theory of exponents was not known. A Swiss by the name of Jobst Bürgi (1552–1632) may have conceived the idea of logarithms as early or earlier than Napier and quite independently of him, but he neglected to publish his results until after Napier's logarithms were known all over Europe.

Henry Briggs (1561–1630), who, in Napier's time, was professor of geometry in Gresham College, London, became very much interested in Napier's work and paid him a visit. It is related that upon Briggs's arrival he and Napier stood speechless, observing each other for almost a quarter of an hour. At last Briggs spoke as follows: "My lord, I have undertaken this long journey purposely to see your person, and to know by what engine of wit or ingenuity you came first to think of this most excellent help in astronomy, namely, the logarithms, but, my lord, being by you found out, I wonder nobody found it out before, when now known it is so easy."

After this visit Briggs and Napier both seem to have seen the usefulness of a table of logarithms to the base 10, and Briggs devoted himself to the construction of such tables. For this reason logarithms to the base 10 are often called Briggsian logarithms.

Abbott says that when Napoleon had a few moments for diversion, he often spent them over a book of logarithms, which he always found recreational.

Miller in his "Historical Introduction to Mathematical Literature (p. 70) says: "The fact that these logarithms had to be computed only once for all time explains their great value to the intellectual world. It would be difficult to estimate the enormous amount of time saved by astronomers and others through the use of logarithm tables alone." (For further reading see Cajori's "History of Elementary Mathematics," pp. 155–167. Consult also the New International Cyclopedia, which contains a great deal of excellent historical material.)

SUMMARY

503. This chapter has taught the meaning of the following words and phrases: logarithm, characteristic, mantissa, interpolation, and exponential equation.

504. The theory and practical value of logarithms has been discussed in as elementary a way as possible so that the student may be able to appreciate the value of this powerful labor-saving device.

505. This chapter has taught the student four important logarithmic formulas:

(a) $\log ab = \log a + \log b.$ (c) $\log a^n = n \log a.$

(b) $\log \frac{a}{b} = \log a - \log b.$ (d) $\log \sqrt[n]{a} = \frac{\log a}{n}.$

506. The position of the decimal point in any result depends entirely upon the characteristic of the logarithm of the number sought. Thus, two numbers having the same succession of digits will have the same mantissa. The mantissa of the logarithm of a number is always positive; the characteristic may be either $+$ or $-$.

507. This chapter has taught methods of solving logarithmic and exponential equations.

508. The student has been taught how to solve verbal problems by means of logarithms, for example, the interest problem.

CHAPTER XVIII

THE SLIDE RULE AND GEOMETRIC REPRESENTATION OF LOGARITHMS PRACTICALLY APPLIED TO THE SLIDE RULE

509. General description of the slide rule. The theory of the slide rule is based on the elementary ideas and principles of logarithms, and anyone can learn to use the slide rule who has the ability to read a graduated scale.

The slide rule may be used in nearly all forms of calculation and is gradually coming into general use in many different fields: to the practicing engineer and to the student of the mathematical sciences it is invaluable; to the accountant and the statistician it is an instrument of great service. The student will therefore find it advisable to learn all he can about the actual use of this important device.

In Chapter II we discussed the graphical method of adding and subtracting line segments as an interpretation of the addition and subtraction of numbers. Since to a multiplication of two numbers there corresponds an addition of their logarithms, it is possible to obtain the logarithm of a product graphically by adding line segments whose lengths represent the logarithms of the factors. In order to carry out this plan, a method of actually finding a line segment whose length shall represent the logarithm of a given number has been developed.

The slide rule is a mechanical device for determining products, quotients, powers, and roots of numbers by graphical addition and subtraction.

Mantissas of logarithms of numbers from 1 to 10 (which, as we have seen, are the same for numbers from 100 to 1000 or from 1000 to 10,000) are laid off to a certain scale on two pieces of rule (see Fig. 301) which are made to slide by

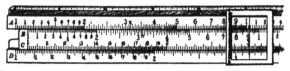

FIG. 301. SLIDE RULE

each other so that the sums or differences of the logarithms can be obtained mechanically.

The scale is numbered from 1 to 10 at the points which mark the logarithms of the several numbers used. The common scale is 5 in. long and the common rule 10 in. long, so that the series of logarithms is put on twice, and the numbering either repeated for the second set or continued from 10

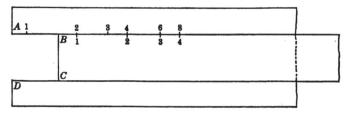

FIG. 302

to 100. The most common form of the rule is the Mannheim Slide Rule. On this rule, which is made essentially as shown in Figs. 302 and 303, there are two scales A and B just alike (A on the rule and B on the slide), and two other scales, C and D, just alike (D on the rule and C on the slide).

The student will note that the distance from 1 to 2 on scales A and B is the same as the distance from 2 to 4 and

from 4 to 8. This means that if we add the distance from
1 to 2 on scale B to the distance from 1 to 2 on scale A by
means of the slide B, we shall obtain the product 2×2,
or 4. In like manner, if we add the distance from 1 to
4 on scale B to the distance from 1 to 2 on scale A, we
shall obtain the product 4×2, or 8.

C and D differ from A and B in being graduated to a
unit twice as large as the unit to which A and B are
graduated, so that the length representing the logarithm of
a given number on C and D is twice as long as the length

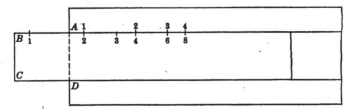

Fig. 303

on A and B representing the logarithm of the same number.
Therefore, any number on the lower rule or slide is opposite its square on the upper rule or slide; and if the upper
rule and slide be regarded as standard logarithmic scales,
the lower rule and slide will be standard logarithmic scales
of the squares of the numbers shown. The student can
easily understand from the preceding statement how the
square roots of numbers are found.

It should be said, however, that the values of the logarithms themselves are not shown on the scales. What we
find is the numbers which correspond to the logarithms.
Each unit length on the scales (graduated lengths) represents equal parts of the logarithmic table. Thus, if the
logarithm of 10 be selected as the unit, then the logarithm

of 3, or 0.477, will be represented by 0.477 of that unit;
4 by 0.602; 5 by 0.699; and so on, as can be seen by
referring to the following table of corresponding values:

Number	1	2	3	4	5	6	7	8	9	10
Logarithm	0	0.301	0.477	0.602	0.699	0.778	0.845	0.903	0.954	1.000

The numbers between 1 and 2, 2 and 3, 3 and 4, and
so on, are represented on the logarithmic scales by inter-
mediate divisions, and the entire scale has been graduated
as closely as is possible for convenience in reading.

The preceding discussion should therefore make it clear
that at the $\frac{301}{1000}$th division along the scale on the slide rule
we should find 2 and not its logarithm, and at the $\frac{699}{1000}$th
division we should find 5 and not 0.699, and so on.

It is clear that this scheme eliminates entirely the
process of finding the numbers corresponding to certain
logarithms, as we had to do when we computed by means
of the table in Art. 492.

The student will observe, further, that the left index of
the scales (that is, the division marked 1) may assume
any value which is a multiple or a decimal part of 1 (for
example, 10, 100, 1000, 0.1, 0.01, 0.001, etc.), but when
these values are assumed, this same ratio must be held
throughout the entire scale. In this case the proper values
for the subsequent divisions of the scale in order would be
20, 30; 200, 300; 2000, 3000; 0.2, 0.3; 0.02, 0.03; 0.002,
0.003. It follows that as the value of the 1 at the beginning of each scale varies any number such as 382 may·
have the value 38200, 3820, 382, 38.2, 3.82, 0.382, 0.0382,
and so on.

If a number which the student has to read does not
come exactly at a graduation he must estimate the values

as closely as possible ; for example, if a certain number were indicated $\frac{1}{3}$ of the way from 152 to 153, he would read 152.3, on the assumption, of course, that the left index of the scale has the value 100. We shall now proceed to show by specific examples how the slide rule is used.

510. Multiplication with the slide rule. All calculations in multiplication, division, and proportion are worked out on scales C and D, as by reason of the greater space allotted to each of the divisions the results obtained are more accurate. To find the product 2×3 set scale C so that its left-hand index (the division marked 1) falls exactly opposite the division marked 2 on scale D (see Fig. 302). Then directly opposite the division marked 3 on scale C we shall find on scale D the division marked 6, which is the required product.

This process is justified by the fact that to log 2 on scale D we add log 3 on scale C, thus obtaining log 6 on scale D.

In general, *to multiply any constant number a by another number b, set 1 of scale C opposite a of scale D and read the product ab on scale D opposite b of scale C.*

EXERCISES

1. Use the slide rule to find the products in the following problems :

(a) 2 and 4; 2 and 5; 2 and 6; 2 and 7; 2 and 8; 2 and 9; 2 and 10.

(b) 3 and 2; 3 and 3; 3 and 4; 3 and 5; 3 and 6; 3 and 7; 3 and 8; 3 and 9; 3 and 10.

2. How would you find the product of 20 and 30 ?

NOTE. The Mannheim Slide Rule will enable us to secure results correct to three significant figures, and in exceptional cases results correct to even four significant figures may be obtained. However, in the work of this chapter we shall be content if we make our computation correct to two, or perhaps three, significant figures, because in actual practice this is sufficient.

511. Division with the slide rule. To divide 6 by 3, set 3 of scale C opposite 6 of scale D (see Fig. 302) and read the quotient 2 on scale D opposite 1 of scale C. This process is justified from the fact that from log 6 we subtract log 3, thus obtaining log 2 on scale D.

In general, *to divide any constant number a by another number b, set b of scale C opposite a of scale D and read the quotient $\frac{a}{b}$ on scale D opposite 1 of scale C.*

EXERCISE

1. Use the slide rule to find the quotients in the following problems:

(a) $\frac{4}{2}$; $\frac{6}{2}$; $\frac{8}{2}$; $\frac{10}{2}$. (b) $\frac{8}{3}$; $\frac{8}{4}$; $\frac{8}{5}$; $\frac{8}{6}$. (c) $\frac{10}{3}$; $\frac{10}{4}$; $\frac{10}{5}$; $\frac{10}{10}$.

512. The runner. Each slide rule is equipped with a *runner* which slides along the rule in a groove and by means of which the student is enabled to find more quickly coincident points on the scales. It is also valuable to mark the result of some part of a problem which contains several computations. Thus, if

$$x = \frac{25.2 \times 3.5 \times 3.68}{22.6},$$

we can compute $25.\overset{.}{2} \times 3.5$ by one setting of the slide and then bring the runner to 88.2, the result. We then bring the index of the slide to 88.2 and multiply by 3.68; this gives 324.6 (approx.). Bring the runner to this result and divide by 22.6; the quotient should be 14.4 (approx.).

The student can easily determine the use of the runner in finding powers and roots after he has read the next two articles.

513. Raising to powers with the slide rule. The student will observe that if the logarithm of any number in the table of Art. 492 be multiplied by 2, the logarithm thus obtained will correspond to the square of that number. Thus, if the logarithm of 2 (0.301) be multiplied by 2, the result (0.602) is the logarithm of 2^2, or 4. This is in accord with the law of Art. 494 regarding the logarithm of a number raised to a power.

In like manner, the logarithm of 2 multiplied by 3 is 0.903, which is the logarithm of 2^3, or 8, and so on. Since this same relation holds for any number to any power, we may raise a number to any power by using the slide rule as follows:

1. *Squares of numbers.*

To find the value of 3^2 look for 3 on scale D and read $3^2 = 9$ directly opposite 3 on scale A.

2. *Cubes of numbers.*

To find the value of 3^3, set 1 of scale B opposite 3 of scale A and find 3^3, or 27, on scale A opposite 3 of scale C.

3. *Fourth power of numbers.*

To find the value of 3^4, set 1 of scale C to 3 on scale D and find 3^4, or 81, on scale A opposite 3 of scale C.

4. *Higher powers.*

Higher powers of numbers may be found by a method similar to the preceding, but we shall not need to discuss these here, as most of our problems will deal with the lower process of numbers.

514. Square roots found by means of the slide rule. To find the square root of any number, bring the runner to the number on scale *A*, and its square root will be found at the runner on scale D exactly opposite the number. This process is seen to be the exact inverse of finding the square of a number.

If the number contains an odd number of digits to the left of the decimal point, its square root will be found on the left half of the rule; if it contains an even number its square root will be found on the right half. If the number is a fraction, and contains an odd number of zeros to the right of the decimal point, the root is on the left half; if it contains an even number (or no zeros) the root is on the right half. If the student prefers he may determine the first figure of the root mentally and then find the proper half of the rule to use by inspection.

EXERCISES

1. Find the square roots of the following numbers by means of the slide rule and compare your results with those of the table in Art. 449: 169; 576; 625; 900; 2.25; 3.24; 1.96; 4.41.

2. What is the side of a square whose area is 784 sq. ft.?

515. Cube roots found by means of the slide rule. To find the cube root of a number by means of the slide rule, move the slide either from left to right or from right to left until the same number appears on scale B opposite the given number on scale A as appears on scale D opposite the left or right index (division 1) on C. The number which appears on both scales B and D is the cube root of the given number. For example, to find the cube root of 125, move the slide to the left till 5 on scale B appears opposite 125 of scale A, and 5 on scale D lies opposite 1 (the right index) on scale C. Thus 5 is the cube root of 125.

A second method of finding the cube root is to invert the slide (see Art. 517) and set 1 on scale C under the given number on scale A and then find the number on scale B which lies opposite the same number on scale D. This number will be the cube root sought. The student should observe that the process of extracting the cube root is the inverse of that of cubing a number.

EXERCISES

1. Find the cube roots of the following numbers by means of the slide rule and compare your results with those of the table in Art. 449: 64; 125; 0.729; 2197; 0.001331.

2. Find one edge of a cube whose volume is 1728 cu. in.

516. Proportion. A great many problems in proportion can be solved very easily by means of the slide rule. The student will observe that if the left-hand indexes of scales C and D coincide, the readings on the slide are in direct proportion 1:1 to the opposite readings on the rule.

In like manner, if the left index of C is made to coincide with 2 on D, the ratio will be 1:2, and so on. Hence, to find the fourth term in the proportion $\dfrac{10}{15} = \dfrac{25}{x}$, we move the slide to the right until 10 on scale C is opposite 15 on scale D, and opposite 25 on C read off $x = 37.5$ on D.

In general, *to find the fourth term in a proportion, set the first term of the proportion on scale C to the second term on scale D and find the fourth term (unknown) on scale D opposite the third term on C.*

517. Inverted slide. The slide may be inverted so that scale C faces scale A. This gives inverted readings on scale C which are the reciprocals of their coincident readings on scale D, and vice versa. Thus, 3 on scale D lies opposite 0.33 on scale C, and vice versa.

The inverted slide is useful, as is shown in finding cube roots and also in problems involving an inverse proportion, as in the following example:

If 10 pipes can empty a cistern in 22 hr., how long will it take 50 pipes to empty the cistern ?

Solution. Invert the slide and set 10 of scale B at 22 on scale D, and opposite 5 on C find 4.4 (the result) on scale D.

518. Position of the decimal point. The student will be able in most practical problems to determine the position of the decimal point. If there is any considerable difficulty in any later work he should consult some standard manual on the use of the slide rule.

MISCELLANEOUS EXERCISES

Solve the following problems by means of the slide rule:

1. Find the product of 58.2×2.55; 33.4×75.6; $22.5 \times 33.3 \times 8.2$; $0.12 \times 0.09 \times 0.003$.

2. Find the following quotients: $\dfrac{82.5}{3.3}$; $\dfrac{3.5}{0.09}$; $\dfrac{0.04}{75.2}$; $\dfrac{35.3 \times 75.5}{22.8}$; $\dfrac{7.2 \times 83.5 \times 0.09}{3.6}$.

3. Perform the indicated operations: 25^2; $3 \cdot 3^8$; $2 \times 2^2 \times 15^8$; 12^4; $1.2^2 \times 7.5^2 \times 0.9^2$.

4. Extract the indicated roots: $\sqrt{2}$; $\sqrt{3}$; $\sqrt{5}$; $\sqrt{7}$; $\sqrt{12}$; $\sqrt{576}$; $\sqrt{10.6}$; $\sqrt{137.2}$; $\sqrt[3]{8}$; $\sqrt[3]{15}$; $\sqrt[3]{14.2}$; $\sqrt[3]{64}$; $\sqrt[3]{1728}$.

5. Find the circumference of a circle whose diameter is 6; 5.5; 2.83. (See a slide-rule manual for a short cut.)

6. If 10 men can do a piece of work in 4 da., how long will it take 5 men to do the work if they work at the same rate?

7. What will be the cost of $13\frac{3}{4}$ ft. of rope at $3\frac{1}{2}$ ¢ per foot?

8. What is the volume of a cubical stone 6.3 ft. long, 4.5 ft. wide, and 3.2 ft. high?

9. What distance will a train travel in 10 hr. and 20 min. at a rate of 30.5 mi. per hour?

10. What is the interest on .$5600 for 1 yr. at $3\frac{1}{2}\%$? at 5%? at 6%?

11. In how many hours will a train travel 756 mi. if it travels at the rate of 41.2 mi. per hour?

12. How many miles in 2783 ft.? in 17,822 ft.?

13. Find the area of a circle whose diameter is 10 in.; 7.5 in.; 0.351 in. (Use $A = 0.7854\, d^2$.)

14. Find the volume of a cube one of whose edges is 3.57 in.; of a cube one of whose edges is 82.1 in.

15. If a man can save $3120 in 26 mo., how many dollars will he save at the same rate in 1 mo.? 6 mo.? 12 mo.?

16. Find the mean proportional between 6 and 27.

17. If goods cost 55¢ a yard, at what price must they be sold to realize 15% profit on the selling price?

18. The formula for the area of the ring in Fig. 304 is $A = \pi R^2 - \pi r^2$. Since $2r = d$, this formula may be written $A = \dfrac{\pi (D^2 - d^2)}{4}$, or $A = \dfrac{(D+d)(D-d)}{1.2732}$. Using the last formula, find the area of the ring when $R = 8.5$ in. and $r = 5.3$ in.

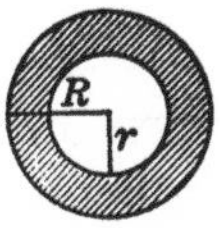

FIG. 304

19. Find the amount of $225 invested for 12 yr. at 6% simple interest. (Use the formula found under logarithms or refer to a slide-rule manual for a short cut.)

20. What force must be applied to a lever 5.2 ft. from the fulcrum to raise a weight of 742 lb. which is $1\frac{1}{2}$ ft. on the opposite side of the fulcrum?

21. A shaft makes 28 revolutions and is to drive another shaft which should make 42 revolutions. The distance between their centers is 60 in. What should be the diameter of the gears ? (See Fig. 305.)

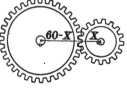

HINT. Refer to a slide-rule manual or, better, develop the formula between the diameter of the gears, the number of revolutions, and the distance between their centers, as follows :

FIG. 305

28 circumferences of the large gear = 42 circumferences of the small gear.   Why ?

Then $28(60 - x) = 42x$ (see Fig. 305).

$$28 \cdot 60 = 70x.$$ Why ?

$$\frac{x}{6} = \frac{28}{7}.$$ Why ?

Then apply the slide rule.

22. Since $F = \frac{9}{5}C + 32$ is the equation representing the relation between the Fahrenheit and centigrade thermometers, we may compare readings of these two thermometers by the following scheme :

C	Set 5	Below degrees centigrade
D	to 9	Read degrees plus 32 equals Fahrenheit

What then is F. when C. = 25° ? 18° ?

***23.** Trigonometric applications are greatly simplified by the slide rule. The solution of a formula like $A = \dfrac{bc \sin A}{2}$ is readily obtained. $\operatorname{Sin} A$ may be used directly as a factor in performing the operation. Find the area of the corner lot in Fig. 306.

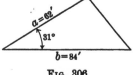

FIG. 306

***24.** Find the value of the lot in Ex. 23 at $871.20 per acre.

NOTE. For numerous applications of the slide rule to practical problems the student should consult a standard slide-rule manual.

SUMMARY

519. This chapter has taught the meaning of the following words and phrases: slide rule, runner, inverted slide.

520. The theory and practical value of the slide rule have been discussed and illustrated so that the student can get at least an elementary working knowledge of this powerful labor-saving device.

521. The student has been taught how to use the slide rule in multiplying, dividing, raising to powers, and extracting roots.

522. The student has been shown how problems in proportion and many other verbal problems may be solved by the slide rule.

523. The student has been referred to the slide-rule manual for methods of solving the more difficult problems.

CHAPTER XIX

QUADRATICS; QUADRATIC FUNCTIONS; QUADRATIC EQUA-TIONS; GRAPHS OF QUADRATIC EQUATIONS; FORMULAS INVOLVING QUADRATIC TERMS

524. Quadratic-equation problem. An engineer increased the speed of his train 2 mi. an hour and made a run of 180 mi. in 1 hr. less than schedule time. What was the speed when running according to schedule?

Solution. Let x = the ordinary rate of the train.

Then $x + 2$ = the rate after the increase.

$$\frac{180}{x} = \text{the schedule time.}$$

$$\frac{180}{x + 2} = \text{the time it takes after the speed is increased.}$$

Then $\dfrac{180}{x} = \dfrac{180}{x + 2} + 1.$ Why?

The L.C.D. is $x(x + 2)$.   Why?

Multiplying through by $x(x + 2)$ we get

$$180(x + 2) = 180 x + x(x + 2).$$
$$180 x + 360 = 180 x + x^2 + 2 x.$$
$$360 = x^2 + 2 x.$$ Why?
$$x^2 + 2 x - 360 = 0.$$ Why?

We are not able to simplify the equation $x^2 + 2x - 360 = 0$ further. The methods of the preceding chapters will not solve it. In fact we appear to have come to the end of the road. It is clear that the problem is solved if we can find a value of x which will make the value of the quadratic trinomial $x^2 + 2x - 360$ equal to zero.

462

An equation in which the highest power of the unknown is the second power is called a *quadratic equation*. Many problems in geometry, science, and mechanics are solved by quadratic equations. It is our purpose in this chapter to develop the power to solve quadratic equations and to apply quadratic methods to verbal problems. This process will be illustrated by the solution of the given equation, $x^2 + 2x - 360 = 0$.

525. Quadratic function. The expression $x^2 + 2x - 360$ is a *quadratic function* of x, or a *function of the second degree*; with every change in the value of x the value of the function $x^2 + 2x - 360$ changes. We shall get some light on the question, What value of x will make the expression $x^2 + 2x - 360$ equal to 0? by studying how the value of the expression $x^2 + 2x - 360$ changes as we give different values to x. This variation is best shown by means of the graph.

526. Graph of a quadratic function. In order to understand more about the graph of a quadratic function we shall consider a few simple exercises.

INTRODUCTORY EXERCISES

1. Find the value of the function $x^2 + 2x - 360$ for each of the following values of x: $0, 10, -10, -15, 15, 20, 18, 19, 21$.

2. Fill in the following table of corresponding values for x and the function $x^2 + 2x - 360$:

x	0	10	-10	$+15$	-15	$+16$	-16	$+17$	-17
$x^2 + 2x - 360$	-360	-240	-280						

x	$+19$	-19	$+21$	-21	$+25$	-25	$+30$	-30
$x^2 + 2x - 360$								

If we transfer the corresponding values of x and the func...on $x^2 + 2x - 360$ from the table to a sheet of cross-section paper

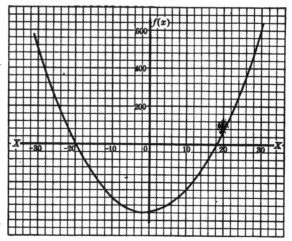

Fig. 307. Showing the Graph of a Quadratic Function

so as to secure the points which correspond to these values, we shall obtain a series of points which, when connected by a smooth curve, will be like the curve in Fig. 307.

EXERCISES

1. From the graph (Fig. 307) determine how the value of $x^2 + 2x - 360$ changes as x changes from 25 to 20; from 0 to 15; from 0 to -15; from -25 to -30; from $+25$ to $+30$.

2. What value of x will make the function $x^2 + 2x - 360$ equal to 300? 200? 150? -250? -300?

The preceding exercises show us that the graph enables us to see what value x must have in order that the expression $x^2 + 2x - 360$ shall have a given value. The pupil will recall that, in the speed problem with which we started, the one question we could not answer was, What value of x will make the expression $x^2 + 2x - 360$ equal to zero? This question is now easily answered. A glance at the graph shows that the expression becomes 0 at two places; namely, when $x = 18$ or when $x = -20$. Thus the equation $x^2 + 2x - 360 = 0$ is satisfied by $x = 18$ or $x = -20$. Check these values by substituting in the equation. Hence the speed of the train running according to schedule was 18 mi. per hour. We reject the -20 as meaningless. (Why?)

527. The two solutions of a quadratic equation. In the preceding article we rejected -20 as a meaningless solution. Though a quadratic equation has two solutions, this does not mean that every verbal problem that leads to a quadratic equation has two solutions. The nature of the conditions of the verbal problem may be such as to make one or even both of the solutions of the quadratic impossible or meaningless. When neither of the two solutions of the quadratic is a solution of the problem it usually means that the conditions of the problem are impossible, or that the problem is erroneously stated. In fact it would be easy to make up an arithmetic problem whose result could not be interpreted; for example, it would be difficult to jump out of the window $2\frac{1}{3}$ times. To decide which solution, if either, meets the conditions stated in a verbal problem, it is necessary to reread the problem, substituting the solutions in the conditions of the problem, and to reject solutions of the equation which do not meet the conditions.

528. How to solve a quadratic equation graphically. We may now summarize the method of solving a quadratic equation revealed in the discussion of Arts. 526–527 as follows: (1) Reduce the equation to the form $ax^2 + bx + c = 0$. (2) Make a table showing the corresponding values of x and the function $ax^2 + bx + c$. (3) Transfer the data of the table to squared paper and construct the curve representing the function $ax^2 + bx + c$. This curve shows the values of $ax^2 + bx + c$ which correspond to the different values of x. (4) By inspection determine the points of the curve where the expression is zero. The values of x for these points are the solutions of the equation.

Solve the following equations graphically, and check :

1. $x^2 - 9x + 14 = 0$.

Plot the function between the limits 0 to 12. This means construct the table by letting x equal the following values: 0, 1, 2, 3, 4, $\cdots$, 12.

2. $x^2 - 6x + 5 = 0$.

Plot from -1 to 7.

3. $x^2 - 3x - 10 = 0$.

Plot from -3 to 6.

4. $x^2 - 11x + 24 = 0$.

Plot from 1 to 10.

5. $x^2 - 11x + 25 = 0$.

Plot from 1 to 10.

6. $4x^2 - 12x + 5 = 0$.

Plot from -2 to 5.

7. $4x^2 + 8x - 5 = 0$.

Plot from -4 to $+2$.

8. $100x^2 - 5x - 495 = 0$.

Plot from -5 to $+5$.

9. $6x^2 - 17x = 20$.

Subtract 20 from both members and plot $6x^2 - 17x - 20$.

10. $2x^2 - 9 = 3x$.

Subtract $3x$ from both members and plot the function $2x^2 - 9 - 3x$.

11. $9x^2 + 3x + 20 = 2x^2 + 2x + 50$.

Subtract $2x^2 + 2x + 50$ from both members of the equation.

529. The graph solves a family of equations. At this point the student should note that a single graph may be used to solve a whole family of equations. Thus, if we turn to Fig. 307 we see that the curve for $x^2 - 2x - 360$ can be used not only to solve the equation $x^2 + 2x - 360 = 0$ but also to solve every equation of the type $x^2 + 2x - 360 = c$ (where c is some arithmetical number). For example, if we ask what value of x will make $x^2 + 2x - 360$ equal to 100, we can tell by looking at the curve that the answer is 20.5 or -22.5, and this is precisely the same as saying that the two roots of the equation $x^2 + 2x - 360 = 100$ are 20.5 and -22.5.

EXERCISES

Solve by the graph:

1. $x^2 + 2x - 360 = 200.$
2. $x^2 + 2x - 360 = 180.$
3. $x^2 + 2x - 360 = 400.$
4. $x^2 + 2x - 360 = -250.$
5. $x^2 + 2x - 360 = -360.$

6. $x^2 + 2x = 400.$

HINT. Subtract 360. Why?

7. $x^2 + 2x - 500 = 0.$

Add 140. Why?

The last two exercises show that the graph solves all equations in which $x^2 + 2x = c$ (some arithmetical number). For we can write the given equation $x^2 + 2x - 500 = 0$ in the form $x^2 + 2x - 360 = 140$. This last form we are able to solve at sight by the graph.

530. The parabola. The curve representing the function $x^2 + 2x - 360$ shown in Fig. 307 is called a *parabola*. Study and discuss the general shape and symmetry of the curve. Compare the curves you and your classmates have drawn in the exercises of this chapter and see if you can find a parabola in an earlier chapter of this text.

The graph of a quadratic function in one unknown is a parabola. It is a symmetrical curve. No three points of the curve lie on a straight line. The parabola is a common notion in physics and mechanics. Thus, the path of a projectile (for example, a bullet) is a parabola. A knowledge of the theory and application of many such curves was of extreme importance in the recent world war. The soldiers who had been trained in some of the more advanced mathematical courses, especially in trigonometry and graphical work, were in demand and were given plenty of opportunity to put into practice what they had learned in school.

In plotting functions like $x^2 + 2x - 360$ we plot the values of x along the x-axis and the corresponding values of the function on the y-axis. This suggests that the curve obtained in Fig. 307 is the graph of the equation $y = x^2 + 2x - 360$.

It follows that whenever y is a quadratic function of x, or when x is a quadratic function of y, the graph of the equation is a parabola.

EXERCISES

Graph each of the following equations :

1. $y = x^2 - 4$.

2. $y = x^2 + 3x + 2$.

3. $x = y^2 + 5y + 4$.

4. $x = y^2 - 7y + 6$.

531. Maxima and minima: The theory of *maxima* (greatest values) and *minima* (least values) of functions has many important applications in geometry, physics, and mechanics.

This article will present one example drawn from each subject. A careful study of the following example will suggest the proper method of attack.

ILLUSTRATIVE EXAMPLE

A rectangular garden is to be inclosed on three sides, the fourth side being bounded by a high wall. What is the largest garden that can be inclosed with 20 rd. of fencing ?

Solution. Let x represent the width.

Then $20 - 2x$ represents the length,

and $20x - 2x^2$ represents the area.

We are now interested in a maximum (greatest possible) value that $20x - 2x^2$ can have. By trial we obtain the corresponding values for x and the function $20x - 2x^2$ shown in the table below.

Common sense, the table, and the curve of Fig. 308 show us that if the garden is made very wide or very narrow the area is very small. The table and the curve of Fig. 308 suggest that 50 is probably the largest area. In this case the dimensions of the garden are 5 and 10. By taking x first a little larger and then a little smaller than 5, we may check our conclusion.

x	$20x - 2x^2$
0	0
1	18
2	32
3	42
4	48
5	50
6	48
7	42
10	0

We can as a matter of fact, save ourselves much of the labor of these computations by an algebraic method, which we shall present in Art. 538. At this

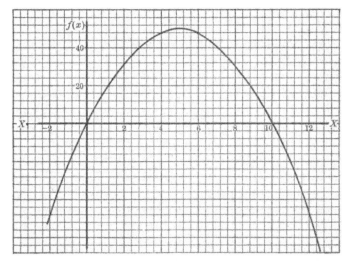

FIG. 308. SHOWING THE MAXIMUM VALUE OF A QUADRATIC FUNCTION

stage, however, we shall be content to plot the curves and find the highest or the lowest point on the curve.

1. If a ball is thrown upward with a velocity v_0, the distance d from the earth to the ball after a given time t is given by the physics formula

$$d = v_0 t - 16\, t^2.$$

How high will a ball rise which is thrown with an initial velocity of 100 ft. per second?

HINT. The formula becomes $d = 100\, t - 16\, t^2$. Plot the function and find by inspection its greatest value.

2. Divide 10 into two parts such that their squares shall be a minimum.

*3. Find the most advantageous length of a lever for lifting a weight of 100 lb. if the distance of the weight from the fulcrum is 2 ft. and the lever weighs 4 lb. to the foot.

532. Limitations of the graphic method of solving quadratic equations. By this time the student is no doubt convinced that the graphic method of solving quadratic equations has its limitations. We may enumerate the following: (1) The results are frequently rough approximations. This is evident the moment we attack problems of some slight difficulty. In fact the earlier problems of the chapter are artificially built so that in all probability the student will accidentally get an accurate result. We must remember that the graphic method depends for its accuracy upon the mechanical (or nonintellectual) conditions, such as the skill of the student at this type of work, the exactness of squared paper, and our ability to estimate fractional parts of the unit. (2) Aside from the fact that the significance of a graph is sometimes obscure, the work is a bit cumbersome and tedious. (3) It is not economical of time, as we shall presently show.

533. More powerful methods of solving quadratic equations. Because of the foregoing limitations of the graphic method we are ready to proceed to the study of more efficient methods. These methods rest purely on an intellectual basis (that is, the accuracy is independent of constructed figures). We shall observe that they get the results quickly and with absolute accuracy.

534. Quadratic equations solved by factoring. The factoring method may be illustrated by the following solution of the speed problem with which we opened the chapter:

Solution. Given $x^2 + 2x - 360 = 0$.

Factoring the left member,

$$(x + 20)(x - 18) = 0.$$

The preceding condition, namely, $(x + 20)(x - 18) = 0$, will be satisfied either if $x + 20 = 0$ or if $x - 18 = 0$, for we learned in Art. 236 that the product of two numbers is zero if either factor is zero. Thus, $5 \times 0 = 0$ or $0 \times 8 = 0$.

Now if $\qquad x + 20 = 0,$

then $\qquad x = -20.$

And if $\qquad x - 18 = 0,$

then $\qquad x = 18.$

Hence $\qquad x = +20,$

or $\qquad x = -18.$

In the next solution we shall omit a considerable part of the discussion and show how the work may be arranged in a few simple statements.

Solve $\qquad x^2 - 9x + 14 = 0.$

Factoring, $\qquad (x - 7)(x - 2) = 0.$ $\qquad$ (1)

This equation is satisfied if $x - 7 = 0,$ $\qquad$ (2)

or if $\qquad x - 2 = 0.$ $\qquad$ (3)

From equation (2) $\qquad x = 7,$

and from equation (3) $\qquad x = 2.$

The numbers satisfy the equation, consequently 2 and 7 are the roots of the equation $x^2 - 9x + 14 = 0.$

Solve the following quadratic equations by the method of factoring and test the results by substituting in the equations :

1. $x^2 - 5x + 6 = 0.$

2. $y^2 - 7y + 12 = 0.$

3. $s^2 - 4s + 3 = 0.$

4. $x^2 - 6x - 27 = 0.$

5. $x^2 - 2x - 35 = 0.$

6. $x^2 + 5x = 6.$

HINT. Subtract 6 from both members before applying the method. Why?

7. $x^2 + x = 56.$

8. $x^2 - 15 = 2x.$

HINT. Subtract $2x$ from both members and rearrange terms before factoring.

9. $y^2 + 4 = 4y.$

10. $x^2 - 85 = 12x.$

11. $z^2 = 10z + 24.$

12. $w^2 - 91 = 6w.$

13. $x^2 + x = 42.$

14. $m^2 + 112 = 23m.$

15. $20x - 51 = x^2.$

16. $77 + 4d = d^2.$

17. $2x^2 + 5x = 3.$

18. $10t^2 + 33t = 7.$

19. $6x^2 = 23x + 4.$

20. $\dfrac{x}{2} + \dfrac{1}{2} = \dfrac{1}{x}.$

21. $15x + 4 = \dfrac{3}{x}.$

22. $5 = \dfrac{4}{m} + \dfrac{33}{m^2}.$

23. $5x - 8 = \dfrac{21}{x}.$

24. $\dfrac{y}{2} + \dfrac{15}{7} = \dfrac{y^2}{14}.$

25. $\dfrac{4y}{y-1} + \dfrac{y-10}{y} = 4.$

26. $\dfrac{a+3}{2} = \dfrac{10}{3} - \dfrac{2}{a+3}.$

27. $\dfrac{x}{x-3} - \dfrac{x-1}{x+3} = 2.$

VERBAL PROBLEMS

Solve the following problems by the factoring method and test the results by substituting the solution in the conditions of the problem :

1. A crew rows across a calm lake (12 mi. long). On the return trip it decreases the rate by 1 mi. per hour and makes the trip in 7 hr. Find the rate of the crew both going and returning.

2. A man drives a car 80 mi. out of town. On the return trip he increases his rate 8 mi. per hour. He makes the trip in $4\frac{1}{2}$ hr. What was his rate while driving out?

3. The base of a rectangle exceeds the altitude by 5 in. The area equals 150 sq. in. Find the base and altitude.

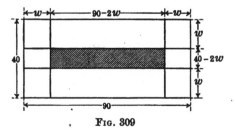

Fig. 309

4. The base of a triangle is 7 in. less than the altitude. The area equals 85 sq. in. Find the base and altitude.

5. A farmer is plowing a field of corn 40 rd. wide and 90 rd. long (Fig. 309). At the end of a certain day he knows that he has plowed five sixths of the field. How wide a strip has he plowed around the field?

6. A piece of tin in the form of a square is taken to make an open box. The box is made by cutting a 1-inch square from each corner of the piece of tin and folding up the sides (Fig. 310). The box thus made contains 36 cu. in.

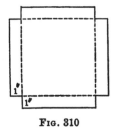

Fig. 310

Find the length of the side of the original piece of tin.

535. Limitations of the factoring method. In some of the preceding exercises the quadratic expressions were very difficult to factor. This is usually the case when the constant terms are large numbers. Indeed, most verbal problems lead to quadratic equations which cannot be solved by the factoring method. The following problem is a simple illustration:

What is the length of a side of a square (Fig. 311) whose diagonal is 2 ft. longer than a side?

Attempted solution by factoring method :

Let $x =$ a side of the square.

Then $x + 2 =$ the length of the diagonal.

By the theorem of Pythagoras

$$x^2 + x^2 = x^2 + 4\,x + 4.$$

Simplifying, $x^2 - 4\,x - 4 = 0.$

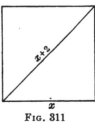

Fig. 311

This appears to be the end of the road; we cannot factor $x^2 - 4\,x - 4$, for we cannot obtain a combination of whole numbers or fractions whose product is -4 and whose sum is -4. And yet we are probably convinced that such a square does exist though we are forced to admit that the solution of the problem by the factoring method is hopeless.

536. Solution of the quadratic equation by the method of completing the square. If we were able to make the left member of the equation $x^2 - 4\,x - 4 = 0$ a perfect square without introducing the unknown (x) into the right member, we could take the square root of each member of the equation and thus obtain a *linear* equation which would be easily solved. This is precisely the method we wish to employ. However, we must first learn to make the left member $x^2 - 4\,x - 4$ a perfect square.

ORAL EXERCISES

1. Find $(x + 2)^2$; $(x + 3)^2$; $(x + 4)^2$; $(x - 2)^2$.

2. When is a trinomial a perfect square ? (See Art. 250.)

3. Make a perfect square trinomial of the following: $x^2 - 6\,x$; $x^2 - 10\,x$; $x^2 - 4\,x$; $x^2 - 8\,x$; $x^2 + 8\,x$; $x^2 + 16\,x$; $x^2 + 5\,x$; $x^2 + 7\,x$; $x^2 + 9\,x$; $x^2 + \dfrac{7\,x}{2}$.

The preceding exercises show that it is easy to complete the square of a binomial of the form $x^2 + ax$, for we need only *to add the square of half the coefficient of x*. Then, too, the constant term of a trinomial can always be made to appear in the right member of the equation, leaving the left member in the form $x^2 + ax$. We now proceed to solve the equation $x^2 - 4x - 4 = 0$. Write the equation thus: $x^2 - 4x = 4$. Add $\left(\dfrac{-4}{2}\right)^2$, or 4, to make the first side a trinomial square, and we obtain

$$x^2 - 4x + 4 = 8.$$

Taking the square root of both sides and remembering that 8 has two square roots, $+\sqrt{8}$ or $-\sqrt{8}$, we get

$$x - 2 = +\sqrt{8}, \tag{1}$$

or
$$x - 2 = -\sqrt{8}. \tag{2}$$

From equation (1) we get $x = 2 + \sqrt{8}$, and from equation (2) we get $x = 2 - \sqrt{8}$.

If we obtain $\sqrt{8}$ either by the arithmetical method taught by Art. 446 or by using the table of Art. 449, the result (accurate to three places) is 2.828. Then $x = 2 + 2.828$, or 4.828. Hence the side of the square whose diagonal is 2 ft. longer than a side is 4.828 ft. We can check this result by applying the theorem of Pythagoras:

We reject $2 - \sqrt{8}$, or -0.828, because it does not satisfy the conditions of the problem. However, the student should realize that -0.828 is just as much a solution of the equation $x^2 - 4x + 4 = 8$ as is 4.828.

The method of completing the square is further illustrated by the following solution of the equation

$$10 x^2 - 9x + 2 = 0.$$

Write the equation $10 x^2 - 9 x = - 2.$ Why?

Dividing by 10, $x^2 - \dfrac{9 x}{10} = -\dfrac{1}{5}.$

Note that the left member is now more easily completed. Why?

Then $x^2 - \dfrac{9 x}{10} + \left(\dfrac{9}{20}\right)^2 = \left(\dfrac{9}{20}\right)^2 - \dfrac{1}{5}.$

$x^2 - \dfrac{9 x}{10} + \dfrac{81}{400} = \dfrac{1}{400}.$ Why?

Taking the square root of each member,

$$x - \tfrac{9}{20} = \pm \tfrac{1}{20}.$$

Whence $x = \tfrac{1}{2} \text{ or } \tfrac{2}{5}.$

537. Summary of the method for solving quadratic equations by the method of completing the square.

1. *Simplify the equation and reduce to the form $ax^2 + bx = c$.*

2. *If the coefficient of x^2 is not 1, divide both members of the equation by the coefficient so that the equation takes the form $x^2 + px = q$.*

3. *Find half the coefficient of x; square the result; add the square to both members of the equation obtained in step 2. This makes the left member a perfect square.*

4. *Express the right member in its simplest form.*

5. *Take the square root of both members, writing the double sign $\pm$ before the square root in the right member.*

6. *Set the left square root equal to the positive root in the right member of the equation in 5. Solve for the unknown. This gives one root.*

7. *Repeat the process, using the negative root in 5. This gives the second root of the equation.*

8. *Express the roots first in simplest form.*

Solve by the method of completing the square, and check :

1. $x^2 - 6x = 91$.

2. $x^2 - 8x = 42$.

3. $x^2 - x - 3 = 0$.

4. $y^2 + 4y + 3 = 0$.

5. $y^2 + 4y - 5 = 0$.

6. $b^2 + 8b - 20 = 0$.

7. $y^2 + 14y - 51 = 0$.

8. $m^2 + 5m - 6 = 0$.

9. $x^2 - 13x + 40 = 0$.

10. $x^2 + 6x + 5 = 0$.

11. $4x^2 + 45x - 36 = 0$.

12. $6x^2 + 7x - 20 = 0$.

13. $z^2 + 6z = 1$.

HINT. Compute roots to the nearest hundredth.

14. $x^2 + 4x = 16$.

15. $x^2 = 24 + 4x$.

16. $7 + 2x = x^2$.

17. $75 - 3x^2 = 75x$.

18. $19 - a = 4a^2$.

VERBAL PROBLEMS

1. If 4 is taken from a certain number the result equals 96 divided by that number. Find the number.

2. Find the two consecutive numbers the sum of whose squares equals 113.

3. In physics we learn that the distance in feet which a stone thrown downward goes in a given time equals 16 multiplied by the square of the number of seconds it has fallen, plus the product of the velocity with which it is thrown and the number of seconds fallen; that is, $s = vt + 16t^2$. Suppose that $v = 20$ ft. per second and $s = 1800$ ft. Find the value of t. Try to state the meaning of this problem in simple (nontechnical) words.

4. How long will it take a baseball to fall from the top of the Washington Monument (555 ft.) if it starts with a velocity of 50 ft. per second ?

HINT. Solve the equation $16t^2 + 50t = 555$.

5. How long will it take a body to fall **800 ft.** if it starts at **20 ft.** per second?

6. How long will it take a bomb to fall from a Zeppelin **1000 ft.** high if it starts with no initial velocity?

7. Two trains are **175** mi. apart on perpendicular roads and are approaching a crossing. One train runs **5** mi. an hour faster than the other. At what rates must they run if they both reach the crossing in **5** hr.?

NOTE. The 175 means the distance along the track.

8. The circumference of the fore wheel of a carriage is less by 3 ft. than the circumference of the hind wheel. In traveling 1800 ft. the fore wheel makes 30 revolutions more than the hind wheel. Find the circumference of each wheel.

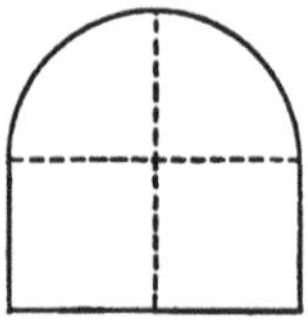

9. A window (Fig. 312) in the form of a rectangle surmounted by a semicircle is found to admit the most light when the width and height are equal. If the area of such a window is 175 sq. ft., what is its width?

FIG. 312

10. A boy has a piece of board 16 in. square. How wide a strip must he cut from each two adjacent sides to leave a square piece whose area is three fourths that of the original piece? In what form would you state your result to meet all practical purposes?

11. A lawn is 30 ft. by 80 ft. Two boys agree to mow it. The first boy is to mow one half of it by cutting a strip of uniform width around it. How wide a strip must he cut?

12. A farmer has a field of wheat 60 rd. wide and 100 rd. long. How wide a strip must he cut around the field in order to have one fifth of the wheat cut?

13. In a circle of radius 10 in. the shortest distance from a given point on the circumference to a given diameter is 8 in. Find the segments into which the perpendicular from the point divides the diameter.

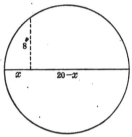

Hint. Study Fig. 313 and try to recall the various theorems we have proved involving mean proportional. If you fail to get a solution, refer to the mean proportional construction (Art. 374).

FIG. 313

14. A broker sells a number of railway shares for $600. A few days later, the price having risen $10 a share, he buys for the same sum three less shares than he sold. Find the number of shares transferred on each day and the price paid.

15. A boy sold a bicycle for $24 and lost as many per cent as the bicycle had cost him in dollars. Find the cost.

16. A line 20 in. long is divided into two parts, AC and CB, so that AC is the mean proportional between CB and AB. Find the length of AC.

*538. Maxima and minima algebraically determined. We have seen in Art. 531 that the graph of a quadratic function may be used to determine the maximum or minimum values of the function. This method is not as exact, however, as the algebraic method of determining maxima and minima, and it is longer. Take, for example, the problem of Art. 531 to find the maximum value for $20\,x - 2\,x^2$. If we represent this maximum value by m, then we may write $20\,x - 2\,x^2 = m$. If we divide both sides of the equation by 2 and complete the square on the left side of the equation,

$$(x - 5)^2 = 25 - \frac{m}{2}.$$

It is evident from this equation that if x is a real number, m cannot be greater than 50. Therefore the maximum value of m, or of $20\,x - 2\,x^2$, is 50.

In like manner by letting m represent the minimum value of a function we can determine when m is a minimum more quickly and more accurately than we can by the graphic method.

EXERCISES

Determine the maximum or minimum values of the following functions:

1. $3\,x^2 - 4\,x - 1.$ 3. $-\,x^2 - x - 1.$ 5. $x^2 - 6\,x + 8.$
2. $2 + 2\,x - 2\,x^2.$ 4. $1 - x^2.$ 6. $6 - x - x^2.$

SUMMARY

539. This chapter has taught the meaning of the following words: parabola, maxima and minima.

540. This chapter has taught three methods of solving a quadratic equation of one unknown: the graphical method, the factoring method, and the method of completing the square.

541. The graphical method proved to be the most concrete. It presented a clear picture of the changes in the value of the function which correspond to changes in the value of the unknown. It also served as a sort of "ready reckoner."

542. The factoring method was more expedient; the results were obtained by this method much more quickly and with greater accuracy.

543. The method of completing the square was used to solve quadratic equations which were not solvable by the method of factoring.

544. Both the graphical and algebraic methods of determining maxima and minima were presented.

INDEX

Lightning Source UK Ltd.
Milton Keynes UK
UKHW010643080321
379980UK00002B/706